Mastering Xamarin UI Development
Second Edition

Build robust and a maintainable cross-platform mobile UI with Xamarin and C# 7

Steven F. Daniel

BIRMINGHAM - MUMBAI

Mastering Xamarin UI Development
Second Edition

Commissioning Editor: Amarabha Banerjee
Acquisition Editor: Shweta Pant
Content Development Editor: Aishwarya Gawankar
Technical Editor: Rutuja Vaze
Copy Editor: Safis Editing
Project Coordinator: Sheejal Shah
Proofreader: Safis Editing
Indexer: Pratik Shirodkar
Graphics: Jason Monteiro
Production Coordinator: Arvindkumar Gupta

First published: January 2017
Second edition: August 2018

Production reference: 1310818

Published by Packt Publishing Ltd.
Livery Place
35 Livery Street
Birmingham
B3 2PB, UK.

ISBN 978-1-78899-551-1

www.packtpub.com

To my favorite uncle, Benjamin Jacob Daniel: thank you for always making me smile and for inspiring me to work hard and achieve my dreams; you are a true inspiration and I couldn't have done this without your love, support, and guidance. Thank you.

As always, to Chan Ban Guan, for the continued patience, encouragement, and support, and most of all for believing in me during the writing of this book. I would like to thank my family for their continued love and support, and for always believing in me throughout the writing of this book.

This book would not have been possible without your love and understanding and I would like to thank you from the bottom of my heart.

`mapt.io`

Mapt is an online digital library that gives you full access to over 5,000 books and videos, as well as industry leading tools to help you plan your personal development and advance your career. For more information, please visit our website.

Why subscribe?

- Spend less time learning and more time coding with practical eBooks and Videos from over 4,000 industry professionals

- Improve your learning with Skill Plans built especially for you

- Get a free eBook or video every month

- Mapt is fully searchable

- Copy and paste, print, and bookmark content

PacktPub.com

Did you know that Packt offers eBook versions of every book published, with PDF and ePub files available? You can upgrade to the eBook version at `www.PacktPub.com` and as a print book customer, you are entitled to a discount on the eBook copy. Get in touch with us at `service@packtpub.com` for more details.

At `www.PacktPub.com`, you can also read a collection of free technical articles, sign up for a range of free newsletters, and receive exclusive discounts and offers on Packt books and eBooks.

Contributors

About the author

Steven F. Daniel is the CEO and founder of GENIESOFT STUDIOS, a software development company based in Melbourne, Victoria, that focuses primarily on developing games and business applications for the iOS, Android, and Mac OS X platforms. He is an experienced software engineer with more than 17 years' experience and is extremely passionate about making people employable by helping them use their existing skills in iOS, Android, and Xamarin to get the job done. He is a member of the SQL Server Special Interest Group (SQLSIG), CocoaHeads, and the Java Community. He was the co-founder and Chief Technology Officer (CTO) at SoftMpire Pty Ltd., a company focused primarily on developing business applications for the iOS and Android platforms.

About the reviewer

Jeremy Clough has been a programmer for 18 years, and just remembers the early days of C# when it was known as "Cool". Since then he has developed a passion for F# and other functional programming languages, enjoying it when some of their features make it back into C#.

Senior Principal Developer at SEEK, and officially part of the furniture, Jeremy has been there long enough to have his most embarrassing code refactored out of existence.

Packt is searching for authors like you

If you're interested in becoming an author for Packt, please visit `authors.packtpub.com` and apply today. We have worked with thousands of developers and tech professionals, just like you, to help them share their insight with the global tech community. You can make a general application, apply for a specific hot topic that we are recruiting an author for, or submit your own idea.

Acknowledgments

No book is the product of just the author; he just happens to be the one with his name on the cover. Several people contributed to the success of this book, and it would take more space than thanking each one individually.

First and foremost, I want to thank Chan Ban Guan for his constant guidance, support, encouragement, and understanding, throughout the whole writing process. My sincere gratitude to my Acquisition Editors, Shweta Pant and Devanshi Doshi, for giving me the opportunity to author the second edition of this book. To my Content Development Editor, Aishwarya Gawankar, for her understanding and support throughout the whole writing process.

I would also like to thank my Technical Editor, Rutuja Vaze, for her support throughout the final stages of this book. It was a pleasure to be able to work with you on this book; thanks goes to each and everyone of you for making the whole writing process such an enjoyable process. I would like to thank my technical reviewer, Jeremy Clough, for doing an awesome job of reviewing the contents and sharing his valuable feedback to make this book what it is; I am truly grateful.

Thank you also to the entire Packt Publishing team who worked on this book so diligently and tirelessly to help bring out such a high-quality final product. Finally, a big shout out to the engineers at Microsoft for creating Visual Studio for Mac and C#, the number one programming language, and the .NET platform, which helps provide developers with a rich set of tools that enables them to create fun, sophisticated applications using Xamarin and the power of Xamarin.Forms.

Finally, I would like to thank all my friends for their continued support, understanding, and encouragement during the book writing process. I am extremely grateful to have each and everyone of you as my friends, and it is a privilege to know each one of you.

Table of Contents

Preface   1

Chapter 1: Setting Up Visual Studio for Mac   11
  Downloading and installing Visual Studio for Mac   12
    Installing Visual Studio for Mac and Xamarin   12
  Exploring the Microsoft Visual Studio for Mac IDE   17
    Configuring and including additional .NET Runtimes   19
    Defining your Android and iOS SDK locations   20
  Understanding the Xamarin mobile platform   22
    Benefits of developing apps using the Xamarin mobile platform 23
    Developing native apps using the Xamarin approach   23
    Developing apps using the Xamarin.Forms approach   24
  Creating a Xamarin project for both iOS and Android   25
    Creating the user interface for our Planetary app using XAML 32
    Displaying a list of planet names using C#   33
    Launching the Planetary app using the iOS simulator   35
  Using and setting Breakpoints in your code   38
    Setting a Breakpoint in your Planetary App solution   38
    Using the Breakpoints Pad to view Breakpoints that have been set 39
    Creating conditional Breakpoints to perform an action   41
  Using the Visual Studio for Mac built-in debugger   43
    Overview of the Visual Studio for Mac debugger   44
    Using the debugger to step through your code   45
    Using the Immediate window to print code variable contents   48
  Summary   50

Chapter 2: Building a PhotoLibrary App Using Android   51
  Creating a native Android app using Visual Studio for Mac   52
    Adding the Xamarin Media Plugin NuGet package to our solution 56
    Creating the user interface for our PhotoLibrary app using XML 59
    Updating the Strings XML file to include our UI control values 62
    Creating the Styles XML file for our Photo Library app   64
  Creating and implementing the PhotoLibrary Activity class   67
    Updating the MainActivity class to call the PhotoLibrary Activity 70
  Implementing Material Design in the PhotoLibrary app   72
    Creating custom themes for the PhotoLibrary application   72
      Creating custom styles for the Photo Library application UI controls 73
      Applying the custom theme to the PhotoLibrary application 75
  Setting up camera and photo album permissions   77
    Interacting with the device camera and photo album   78

Launching the Photo Library app using the Android emulator   83
Summary   85
Chapter 3: Building a SlidingTiles Game Using Xamarin.iOS   87
  Creating a native iOS app using Visual Studio for Mac   88
  Creating the SlidingTiles user interface using Storyboards   93
    Adding a label to our ViewController in the Storyboard   95
    Adding a View to our View Controller in the Storyboard   99
    Adding a reset button to our View Controller in the Storyboard   102
    Adding the Shuffle Button to our View Controller in the Storyboard   106
    Adding the GameTile image to our SlidingTiles game   110
  Implementing the game logic for our SlidingTiles Game   111
    Creating and implementing the GameTile Interface class   111
    Creating and implementing the GameTile class   115
    Updating the ViewController class to implement our class methods   121
    Creating and implementing the CreateGameBoard method   123
    Creating and implementing the ResetGame_Clicked method   126
    Randomly shuffling our Game Tiles on the Game Board   128
    Implementing the StartNewGame Instance method   129
    Handling touch events in the Game Board user interface   130
  Working with and applying animations to your app   132
    Creating and implementing animations for the SlidingTiles game   132
  Launching the SlidingTiles game using the iOS simulator   134
  Summary   136
Chapter 4: Creating the TrackMyWalks Native App   137
  Creating the TrackMyWalks project solution   138
    Updating the NuGet packages within our solution   142
  Creating and implementing our data model   143
  Creating the WalksMainPage interface using XAML   147
  Implementing the WalksMainPage code using C#   150
  Creating the WalkEntryPage interface using XAML   153
  Implementing the WalkEntryPage code using C#   155
  Creating the WalkTrailInfoPage interface using XAML   156
  Implementing the WalkTrailInfoPage code using C#   158
    Integrating and implementing maps within your app   160
  Creating the WalkDistancePage interface using XAML   162
  Implementing the WalkDistancePage code using C#   164
  Updating the TrackMyWalks.iOS AppDelegate   166
  Updating the TrackMyWalks.Android MainActivity   168
  Creating the SplashPage interface using XAML   169
  Implementing the SplashPage code using C#   171
    Updating the App.xaml class to target various platforms   172
  Launching TrackMyWalks using the iOS simulator   174

Summary   177

Chapter 5: MVVM and Data Binding   179
  Understanding the MVVM architectural pattern   180
  Creating and implementing the BaseViewModel   182
  Creating the WalksMainPageViewModel using C#   186
    Updating the WalksMainPage user interface using XAML   190
    Updating the WalksMainPage code-behind using C#   192
  Creating the WalkEntryPageViewModel using C#   195
    Updating the WalkEntryPage user interface using XAML   199
    Updating the WalkEntryPage code-behind using C#   201
  Creating the WalkTrailInfoPageViewModel using C#   203
    Updating the WalkTrailInfoPage user interface using XAML   205
    Updating the WalkTrailInfoPage code-behind using C#   206
  Creating the WalkDistancePageViewModel using C#   208
    Updating the WalkDistancePage user interface using XAML   210
    Updating the WalkDistancePage code-behind using C#   211
  Launching the TrackMyWalks app using the iOS simulator   214
  Summary   218

Chapter 6: Navigating Within the Mvvm Model   219
  Understanding the Xamarin.Forms Navigation API   220
  Differences between the Navigation and ViewModel approaches   222
  Creating and implementing the NavigationService interface   223
  Creating and implementing the NavigationService class   228
  Updating the BaseViewModel to use the navigation service   232
  Updating the WalksMainPageViewModel using C#   234
  Updating the WalksMainPage code-behind using C#   236
  Updating the WalkEntryPageViewModel using C#   239
  Updating the WalkEntryPage code-behind using C#   240
  Updating the WalkTrailInfoPageViewModel using C#   242
  Updating the WalkTrailInfoPage code-behind using C#   244
  Updating the WalkDistancePageViewModel using C#   245
  Updating the WalkDistancePage code-behind using C#   247
  Updating the SplashPage code-behind using C#   249
  Updating the App.xaml class to use the navigation service   251
  Summary   254

Chapter 7: Adding Location-based Features Within Your App   255
  Creating and using platform-specific services within your app   256
    Adding the plugin geolocator NuGet package to our solution   257
  Creating and implementing the ILocationService interface   259
  Creating and implementing the LocationService class   262
  Updating the WalkEntryPageViewModel using C#   267

Updating the WalkDistancePageViewModel using C#   270
Creating the CustomMapOverlay class using C#   272
Updating the WalkDistancePage user interface using XAML   274
Updating the WalkDistancePage code-behind using C#   275
Creating and implementing the CustomMapRenderer (iOS)   280
Creating and implementing the CustomMapRenderer (Android)   284
Enabling background location updates and permissions   286
Launching the TrackMyWalks app using the iOS simulator   291
Summary   296

Chapter 8: Customizing the User Interface   297
Customizing the DataTemplate in the WalksMainPage   298
Applying padding and margins to XAML layouts   300
    Updating the WalksMainPage user interface using XAML   301
    Updating the WalkEntryPage user interface using XAML   303
    Updating the WalkTrailInfoPage user interface using XAML   305
Creating and implementing Styles in your App   307
    Creating and implementing Global Styles using XAML   307
    Updating our WalksMainPage to use the Device Style   309
    Updating our WalkTrailInfoPage to use Explicit and Global Styles   312
    Updating our WalksEntryPage to use our Implicit Style   314
Creating and using PlatformEffects in your app   317
    Creating and Implementing the ButtonShadowEffect (iOS)   317
    Creating and implementing the LabelShadowEffect (iOS)   321
    Creating and implementing the ButtonShadowEffect (Android)   323
    Creating and implementing the LabelShadowEffect (Android)   326
    Implementing the ButtonShadowEffect RoutingEffect class   328
    Implementing the LabelShadowEffect RoutingEffect class   331
    Updating the WalksMainPage to use the LabelShadowEffect   333
    Updating the WalkTrailInfoPage to use the LabelShadowEffect   335
    Updating the WalkTrailInfoPage to use the ButtonShadowEffect   336
Creating and implementing ValueConverters in your app   339
    Updating the BaseViewModel class to include additional properties   342
    Updating the WalksMainPageViewModel to use our property   344
    Updating the WalksMainPage to use our ImageConverter class   347
    Updating the WalkEntryPage to use our ImageConverter class   350
    Updating the WalkTrailInfoPage to use our ImageConverter class   353
Launching the TrackMyWalks app using the iOS simulator   355
Summary   358

Chapter 9: Working with Animations in Xamarin.Forms   359
Creating and using Simple Animations in Xamarin.Forms   360
    Updating the WalkEntryPage to use Simple Animations   362
    Updating the WalkTrailInfoPage to use Simple Animations   365
Creating and using Easing Functions in Xamarin.Forms   368

Updating the WalkTrailInfoPage to use Easing Functions   369
Creating and implementing your own Custom Animations   371
Updating our WalkTrailInfoPage to use Custom Animations   371
Updating our WalksMainPage to use Custom Animations   373
Creating and implementing Entrance Animations   378
Updating the WalkTrailInfoPage to use Entrance Animations   378
Updating our WalksMainPage to use Entrance Animations   381
Updating our WalkEntryPage to use Entrance Animations   383
Launching the TrackMyWalks app using the iOS simulator   385
Summary   388

Chapter 10: Working with the Razor Templating Engine   389
Understanding the Razor templating engine   390
Building a BookLibrary app using the Razor templating engine   392
Adding the SQLite-net NuGet package to our solution   397
Creating and implementing the BookLibrary data model   399
Creating and implementing the BookDatabase interface   403
Creating and implementing the BookDatabase class   408
Creating and implementing the BookLibraryListing page   413
Creating and implementing the BookLibraryAddEdit page   416
Updating the Book Library cascading style sheet (CSS)   420
Updating the WebViewController class using C#   422
Launching the BookLibrary app using the iOS simulator   429
Summary   432

Chapter 11: Incorporating Microsoft Azure App Services   433
Understanding the Microsoft Azure App services platform   434
Setting up and configuring Microsoft Azure App services   435
Adding the Newtonsoft.Json NuGet package to our solution   443
Updating the WalkDataModel for our TrackMyWalks app   445
Creating and implementing the RestWebService interface   446
Creating and implementing the RestWebService class   449
Updating the BaseViewModel class to include our RestWebService   456
Updating the WalksMainPage code-behind using C#   458
Updating the WalksMainPageViewModel using C#   460
Updating the WalkEntryPage user interface using XAML   462
Updating the WalkEntryPageViewModel using C#   466
Launching the TrackMyWalks app using the iOS simulator   469
Summary   472

Chapter 12: Making Our App Social Using the Twitter API   473
**Creating and registering the TrackMyWalks app with the Twitter
Developer Portal**   475
Adding the Xamarin.Auth NuGet Package to our solution   485
Creating and implementing the TwitterAuthDetails class   486

Creating and implementing the TwitterWebService interface   489
Creating and implementing the TwitterWebService class   491
Creating and implementing the TwitterSignInPageViewModel using C#   495
Creating and implementing the user interface for the TwitterSignInPage   496
Creating and implementing the TwitterSignInPageRenderer (iOS)   498
Updating the WalksMainPage code-behind using C#   502
Updating the WalkDistancePage user unterface using XAML   504
Registering the TwitterSignInPage within the App.xaml class   509
Launching the TrackMyWalks app using the iOS simulator   511
Summary   515

Chapter 13: Unit Testing Your Xamarin.Forms Apps   517
Creating the Unit Testing project within the TrackMyWalks solution   518
    Adding the Moq NuGet package to the TrackMyWalks.UnitTests project   523
    Adding the TrackMyWalks project to the TrackMyWalks.UnitTests project   525
    Creating and implementing the WalksMainPageViewModelTest class   526
    Creating and implementing the WalksEntryPageViewModelTest class   529
Running unit tests within the Visual Studio for Mac IDE   532
Creating a UITest project within the TrackMyWalks solution   535
    Understanding the most commonly used Xamarin.UITest testing methods   538
    Creating and implementing the CreateNewTrailDetails class for iOS   540
Updating the WalksMainPage code-behind using C#   547
Adding the Xamarin.Test Cloud.Agent NuGet package   549
Running UITests within the Visual Studio for Mac IDE   553
Summary   557

Other Books You May Enjoy   559

Index   563

Preface

Xamarin is the most powerful cross-platform mobile development framework. If you are interested in creating stunning user interfaces for the iOS and Android mobile platforms using the power of Xamarin and Xamarin.Forms, then this is your ticket.

This book will provide you with the knowledge and practical skills that are required to develop real-world Xamarin and Xamarin.Forms applications. You'll learn how to create native Android app that will interact with the device camera and photo gallery, and then create a native iOS sliding tiles game. Moving on, you will learn how to implement complex user interface layouts and create customisable control elements based on the platform, using **XAML** and C# 7 code to interact with control elements within your XAML ContentPages.

You'll be introduced to the **Model-View-ViewModel** (**MVVM**) architecture pattern, and you'll learn how to implement this within your application by creating a NavigationService class that will be used to navigate between your Views and ViewModels. You will also learn how to implement data binding to connect your XAML pages to your ViewModels.

We will then discuss how you can add location-based features by to your apps by creating a LocationService class and using the Xam.Plugin.Geolocator cross-platform library, which will be used to obtain the current device location, and you will learn how to properly perform location updates, whether the application's state is in the foreground or background, by registering the app as a background-necessary application.

We discuss more advanced topics such as how to integrate Microsoft Azure App Services and use the Twitter APIs to incorporate social networking features to obtain information about a Twitter user, as well as posting walk information to the user's Twitter feed.

Moving on, you will learn how to use third-party libraries, such as the Razor Templating Engine, which allows you to create your own HTML5 templates, within the Visual Studio for Mac environment to build a book library HTML5 solution that will use a SQLite.net library to store, update, retrieve, and delete information within a local SQLite database. You'll also implement key data binding techniques that will make your user interfaces dynamic and create personalised animations and visual effects within your user interfaces using custom renderers and the PlatformEffects API to customise and change the appearance of control elements.

At the end of this book, you'll learn how to create and run unit tests using the xUnit and UITest testing frameworks within the Visual Studio for Mac IDE. You'll learn how to write unit tests for your ViewModels that will essentially test the business logic to validate that everything is working correctly, before moving on to test the user interface portion using automated UI testing.

In this book, I have tried my best to keep the code simple and easy to understand by providing a step-by-step approach, with lots of screenshots at each step to make it easier to follow. You will soon be mastering the technology behind the Xamarin and Xamarin.Forms platforms, as well as obtaining the skills required to create your own applications for the Xamarin and Xamarin.Forms platforms.

Feel free to contact me at `steven.daniel@geniesoftstudios.com` with any queries, or just drop me an email to say a friendly hello.

Who this book is for

This book is intended for readers who have experience of the C# 6.0 programming language and are interested in learning how to create stunning native and cross-platform user interfaces for the iOS and Android platforms using the Xamarin and Xamarin.Forms frameworks with C# 7. It is assumed that you are familiar with object-oriented programming (OOP) techniques and have experience of developing C# applications using Visual Studio.

What this book covers

Chapter 1, *Setting Up Visual Studio for Mac*, focuses on how to download and install Visual Studio Community 2017 for Mac, as well as the Xamarin components for both the iOS and Android platforms. You'll explore some of the features contained within the Visual Studio for Mac IDE, and then gain an understanding of the Xamarin mobile platform. You'll learn how to create your very first `Xamarin.Forms` cross-platform application and create the user interface using XAML and the underlying C# code. We we also cover how to set and define conditional breakpoints within your code, as well as how to use the built-in debugging tools to debug your application.

Chapter 2, *Building a Photo Library App Using Android*, focuses on how to develop native Android app using Visual Studio for Mac, Xamarin.Android and C#. You'll learn how to use and work with the Visual Designer to construct the user interface for our PhotoLibrary app using XML and implement Material Design within your apps, as well as creating your own custom themes and then apply theming to your app. You'll learn how to provide the necessary permissions to the AndroidManifest.xml so that we can interact with the device camera and photo album, before launching the app within the Android emulator.

Chapter 3, *Building a SlidingTiles Game Using Xamarin.iOS*, focuses on how to develop a native iOS app using Visual Studio for Mac, Xamarin.iOS, and C#. You'll learn how to use and work with Storyboards to construct the user interface for our SlidingTiles game by dragging a number of Labels, Views, and Buttons that will make up our game. You'll create a GameTile interface and class that will be used to create each of the tiles for our game, and then implement the remaining logic within the ViewController class to build the game board and create each of our game tiles using the images from an array.

You'll also create an instance method that will randomly shuffle each of our game tiles within our game board using the Random class, and work with the UITouch class to handle touch events to determine when a game tile has been tapped within the game boards UIView, and work with CoreAnimation so that you can apply simple animations to your UIViews by using View Transitions within an animation block, before deploying and launching the app within the iOS Simulator.

Chapter 4, *Creating the TrackMyWalks Native App*, will focus on how to develop a cross-platform app using Xamarin.Forms and C#, by creating each of the Content Pages that will form the user interface for our app using XAML, as well as creating a C# class that will act as the data-model for our application.

Chapter 5, *MVVM and Data Binding*, teaches you the concepts behind the MVVM architectural pattern, as well as how to implement the MVVM architectural pattern within the TrackMyWalks application. You'll learn how to create a BaseViewModel base class that every ViewModel will inherit from, as well as creating the associated C# class files for each of our ViewModels that will data-bind to each of the properties defined within our XAML Pages.

The associated properties that we define within the ViewModel for the ContentPage will be used to represent the information that will be displayed within the user interface for our application. You'll also learn how to add ContextActions to your (XAML) content pages, and how to implement the code action events within your code, so that you can respond to those actions.

Chapter 6, *Navigating Within the MVVM Model*, shows you how you can leverage what you already know about the MVVM architectural design pattern to learn how to navigate between each of the ViewModels within our TrackMyWalks application. You'll learn how to create a `NavigationService` class and update our `BaseViewModel` base class that will include a reference to our `NavigationService` class that each of our ViewModels will utilize. You will then proceed to update each of the ViewModels as well as each of the XAML pages to allow navigation between these pages to happen.

Chapter 7, *Adding Location-Based Features within Your App*, shows how you can incorporate platform-specific features within your application, which is dependent on the mobile platform that is being run. You will then learn how to incorporate the `Xam.Plugin.Geolocator` NuGet package that you will use in order to create a `LocationService` class so that you can obtain current GPS coordinates and handle location updates in the background on the device.

You'll update both the `WalkEntryPageViewModel` and `WalkDistancePageViewModel` to allow location-based features to happen and create a `CustomMapOverlay` class that will be used to display a native Map control, based on the platform. You'll learn how to perform location updates in the background so that you can update the native map control automatically, whenever new location coordinates are obtained.

Chapter 8, *Customizing the User Interface*, shows how you can use and customize `DataTemplates` to lay out your Views beautifully and neatly within your user interfaces by modifying your ContentPages. You'll learn how to create and implement various styles within each of your XAML pages, prior to getting accustomed to working with the `PlatformEffects` API to customize the appearance, as well as applying styling to native control elements for each platform. You'll learn how to set up your margins and apply padding, as well as how to create and implement `ValueConverters` and `ImageConverters`.

Chapter 9, *Working with Animations in Xamarin.Forms*, shows you how to work with the `Animation` class that comes part of the `Xamarin.Forms` platform, so that you can apply really cool animations and transition effects to your user interfaces and control elements, by implementing Simple Animations, Easing Functions, and Entrance Animations using C# code.

Chapter 10, *Working with the Razor Templating Engine*, focuses on how you can use the Razor Templating Engine to create a Book library mobile application using the power of Razor templates. You'll learn how to create a BookItem data-model within your application, as well as how to incorporate the SQLite-net NuGet package within your application, that you will use to create a BookDatabase class, that will include various methods to communicate with a SQLite database to Create, Update, Retrieve, and Delete book items. Finally, you will learn how to create the necessary Razor Template Pages, that will use our BookItem data model to display book information.

Chapter 11, *Incorporating Microsoft Azure App Services*, focuses on showing you how you can use the Microsoft Azure App Services Platform to create your cloud-based databases. You will learn how to set up and configure a Microsoft Azure App Service, as well as configuring the SQL Server database and the WalkEntries table for our app. You'll incorporate the Newtonsoft.Json NuGet package, as well as modify the WalkDataModel data model. You will then create a RestWebservice class, which will include a number of class instance methods that will be used to communicate with our TrackMyWalks SQL Server database, so you can perform CRUD operations to Create, Update, Retrieve, and Delete walk entries.

Chapter 12, *Making Our App Social – Using the Twitter API*, focuses on showing you how to create and register our TrackMyWalks app within the Twitter Portal, by applying for a Twitter developer account. You'll incorporate the Xamarin.Auth NuGet package within our solution and create a TwitterService class that we can use to communicate with the Twitter APIs using RESTful web service calls. You will then create a TwitterSignInPage and the associated TwitterSignInPageViewModel and TwitterSignInPageRenderer class, so users can sign into your app using their Twitter credentials.

Finally, you'll update the WalksMainPage code-behind to call our TwitterSignInPage to check to see if the user has signed in, as well as making changes to our WalkDistancePage XAML and code-behind so that we can utilize our TwitterService class to display profile information, as well as posting information about the trail to the user's Twitter feed.

Chapter 13, *Unit Testing Your Xamarin.Forms Apps*, focuses on showing you how to create and run each of your unit tests using the xUnit and Xamarin.UITest frameworks. You will also learn how to write unit tests for our ViewModels that will essentially test the business logic to validate that everything is working correctly, after which, we will move on to learning how to use the UITest framework to perform testing on the TrackMyWalks user interfaces, using automated testing.

To get the most out of this book

The minimum requirement for this book is an Intel-based Macintosh computer running macOS High Sierra 10.13. We will be using Visual Studio Community 2017, which is the Integrated Development Environment (IDE) used for creating Xamarin and Xamarin.Forms applications using C# 7, as well as Xcode 9.4.1 to compile our iOS app and run it within the simulator.

Almost all the projects that you create with the help of this book will work and run on the iOS simulator. However, some projects will require an actual iOS or Android device to work correctly. You can download the latest versions of Visual Studio Community 2017 and Xcode from here:

- Visual Studio Community 2017 for Mac: `http://xamarin.com/download`
- Xcode 9.4.1: `https://itunes.apple.com/au/app/xcode/id497799835?mt=12`

Downloading the example code

You can download the example code files for this book from your account at `http://www.packtpub.com`. If you purchased this book elsewhere, you can visit `http://www.packtpub.com/support` and register to have the files e-mailed directly to you.

You can download the code files by following these steps:

1. Log in or register to our website using your e-mail address and password.
2. Hover the mouse pointer on the **SUPPORT** tab at the top.
3. Click on **Code Downloads & Errata**.
4. Enter the name of the book in the **Search** box.
5. Select the book for which you're looking to download the code files.
6. Choose from the drop-down menu where you purchased this book from.
7. Click on **Code Download**.

Once the file is downloaded, please make sure that you unzip or extract the folder using the latest version of:

- WinRAR / 7-Zip for Windows
- Zipeg / iZip / UnRarX for Mac
- 7-Zip / PeaZip for Linux

The code bundle for the book is also hosted on GitHub at `https://github.com/ PacktPublishing/Mastering-Xamarin-UI-Development-Second-Edition`. We also have other code bundles from our rich catalog of books and videos available at `https://github. com/PacktPublishing/`. Check them out!

Download the color images

We also provide a PDF file that has color images of the screenshots/diagrams used in this book. You can download it here: `https://www.packtpub.com/sites/default/files/downloads/MasteringXamarinUID evelopmentSecondEdition_ColorImages.pdf`.

Conventions used

In this book, you will find a number of text styles that distinguish between different kinds of information. Here are some examples of these styles and an explanation of their meaning.

Code words in text, database table names, folder names, filenames, file extensions, pathnames, dummy URLs, user input, and Twitter handles are shown as follows: "Before we can proceed, we need to create our `PlanetaryApp` project."

A block of code is set as follows:

```
//
//  GameTile.cs
//  Creates each of our tile images for our Tile Slider Game.
//
//  Created by Steven F. Daniel on 24/04/2018.
//  Copyright © 2018 GENIESOFT STUDIOS. All rights reserved.
//
using UIKit;
using SlidingTiles.Interfaces;
using CoreGraphics;
using System;

namespace SlidingTiles.Classes
{
```

When we wish to draw your attention to a particular part of a code block, the relevant lines or items are set in bold:

```xml
<?xml version="1.0" encoding="UTF-8"?>
<ContentPage xmlns="http://xamarin.com/schemas/2014/forms"
xmlns:x="http://schemas.microsoft.com/winfx/2009/xaml"
             xmlns:maps="clr-
namespace:Xamarin.Forms.Maps;assembly=Xamarin.Forms.Maps"
             x:Class="TrackMyWalks.Views.WalkDistancePage">
    <ContentPage.Content>
        <ScrollView Padding="2,0,2,2">
            <StackLayout Orientation="Vertical"
HorizontalOptions="FillAndExpand"
                VerticalOptions="FillAndExpand">
                <maps:Map x:Name="customMap"
IsShowingUser="true" MapType="Street" />
                <Button x:Name="EndThisTrail" Text="End this
Trail"
                        TextColor="White"
BackgroundColor="#008080"
                        Clicked="EndThisTrailButton_Clicked"
Margin="20" />
            </StackLayout>
        </ScrollView>
    </ContentPage.Content>
</ContentPage>
```

Any command-line input or output is written as follows:

```
Last login: Fri Aug 24 16:40:41 on console
stevens-mbp:~ stevendaniel$ curl
https://trackmywalk.azurewebsites.net/tables/WalkEntries
--header "ZUMO-API-VERSION:2.0.0
```

New terms and **important words** are shown in bold. Words that you see on the screen, for example, in menus or dialog boxes, appear in the text like this: "Alternatively, you can specify it for the Android platform by selecting the **Android** node in the **SDK Locations** section."

Warnings or important notes appear in a box like this.

 Tips and tricks appear like this.

Get in touch

Feedback from our readers is always welcome.

General feedback: Email feedback@packtpub.com and mention the book title in the subject of your message. If you have questions about any aspect of this book, please email us at questions@packtpub.com.

Errata: Although we have taken every care to ensure the accuracy of our content, mistakes do happen. If you have found a mistake in this book, we would be grateful if you would report this to us. Please visit www.packtpub.com/submit-errata, selecting your book, clicking on the Errata Submission Form link, and entering the details.

Piracy: If you come across any illegal copies of our works in any form on the Internet, we would be grateful if you would provide us with the location address or website name. Please contact us at copyright@packtpub.com with a link to the material.

If you are interested in becoming an author: If there is a topic that you have expertise in and you are interested in either writing or contributing to a book, please visit authors.packtpub.com.

Reviews

Please leave a review. Once you have read and used this book, why not leave a review on the site that you purchased it from? Potential readers can then see and use your unbiased opinion to make purchase decisions, we at Packt can understand what you think about our products, and our authors can see your feedback on their book. Thank you!

For more information about Packt, please visit packtpub.com.

Setting Up Visual Studio for Mac

1

Since Xamarin made its appearance several years ago, developers have been delighted with being able to create native mobile applications that can target different OS platforms, as well as having the option of developing apps using either the C# or F# programming languages, enabling developers to distribute their app ideas to either the iOS, Android, or Windows platforms.

As you progress through this book, you'll learn how to apply best practices and design principles when developing cross-platform mobile applications using the **Xamarin.Forms** platform, to allow developers to build cross-platform user interface layouts that can be shared across the Android, iOS, and Windows mobile platforms.

Since each of these apps can be written using a single programming language, it makes sense to write a single codebase that would compile and build into separate apps for each of these different platforms.

This chapter will begin by showing you how to download and install the Visual Studio for Mac IDE, as well as the Xamarin components for both the iOS and Android platforms. You'll explore some of the features contained in the Visual Studio for Mac IDE and then gain an understanding of the Xamarin mobile platform.

You'll learn how to create your very first cross-platform `Xamarin.Forms` application for both the iOS and Android platforms, create the user interface using XAML, and create some C# code that will communicate with the XAML code.

To end this chapter, you'll learn how to set **Breakpoints** and define conditional Breakpoints in your code to pause execution, before moving on to learning how to use the built-in debugging tools to debug your application and launch it in the iOS simulator.

This chapter will cover the following points:

- Downloading and installing the Visual Studio for Mac IDE and the Xamarin Platform SDKs
- Exploring the Visual Studio for Mac IDE
- Understanding the Xamarin mobile platform
- Creating a new `Xamarin.Forms` project for both iOS and Android
- Setting Breakpoints and defining conditional Breakpoints in your code
- Using the Visual Studio for Mac built-in debugger

Downloading and installing Visual Studio for Mac

In this section, we will take a look at how to download and install Microsoft Visual Studio for Mac as well as the Xamarin Platform SDKs for both the iOS and Android platforms.

Installing Visual Studio for Mac and Xamarin

Before we can begin developing applications for the Xamarin platform, we will need to download Visual Studio for Mac. Simply follow these steps:

1. Open your browser and type in `https://www.visualstudio.com/`.
2. Next, hover your mouse cursor over the **Download for Mac** button and click on the **Community 2017 for Mac** menu option to proceed:

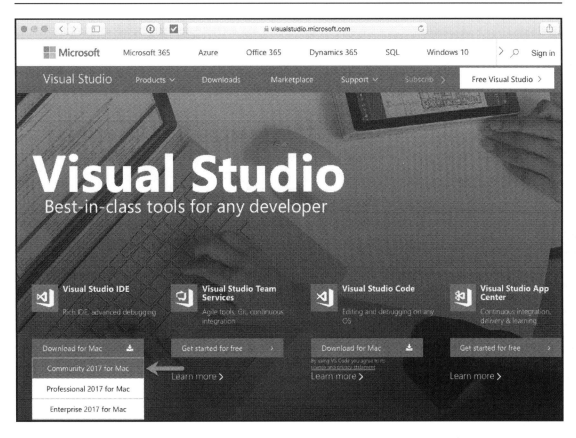

Downloading Visual Studio Community 2017 for Mac

3. Next, once the Visual Studio for Mac installer has been downloaded, double-click on it to display **Visual Studio for Mac – Installation.**

4. Then, click on the **Continue** button to proceed to the next step in the wizard, which can be seen in the following screenshot:

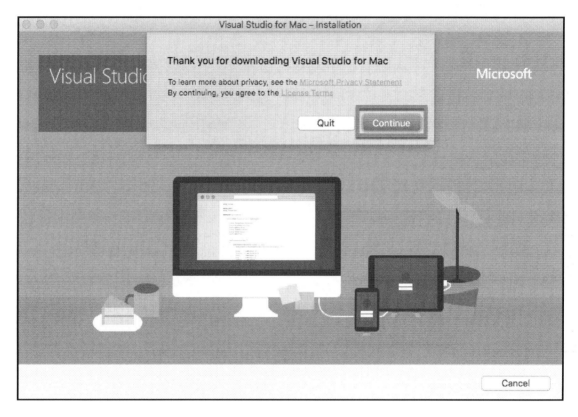

Visual Studio for Mac - Installation

5. Next, ensure that the checkboxes for **Android**, **iOS**, and **macOS**, as well as **.NET Core**, have been selected under the **Platforms** group and ensure that the checkbox for **Xamarin Workbooks & Inspector** has been selected under the **Tools** group, which can be seen in the following screenshot:

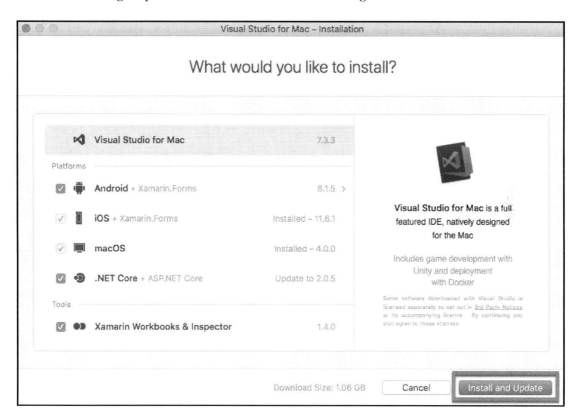

Choosing Visual Studio for Mac Platform Components

6. Next, click on the **Install and Update** button to proceed to the next step in the wizard and begin installing the Visual Studio for Mac IDE along with the Xamarin platform SDK and tools, which can be seen in the following screenshot:

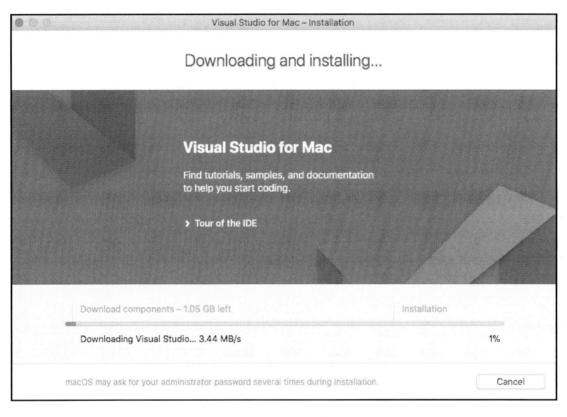

Visual Studio for Mac Downloading Components

7. Finally, **Visual Studio for Mac - installation** will proceed to download and begin installing the Microsoft Visual Studio for Mac IDE, as well as downloading the components for the platforms that you have selected.

Now that you have installed the Microsoft Visual Studio for Mac IDE and the Xamarin Platform SDK, as well as the tools for both the iOS and Android platforms, our next step is to explore some of the features of the Visual Studio for Mac IDE, which we will be covering in the next section.

Exploring the Microsoft Visual Studio for Mac IDE

In this section, we'll take some time and explore the Visual Studio for Mac IDE and learn how to configure its visual appearance, how to set font styles, and how to go about configuring and including additional .NET runtime versions. Lastly, you'll learn how to define the Android and iOS SDK locations.

To begin exploring the Visual Studio for Mac IDE, simply follow these steps:

1. From the **Visual Studio Community** menu, choose the **Preferences...** menu option, or alternatively press the *command + ,* key combination that can be seen in the following screenshot:

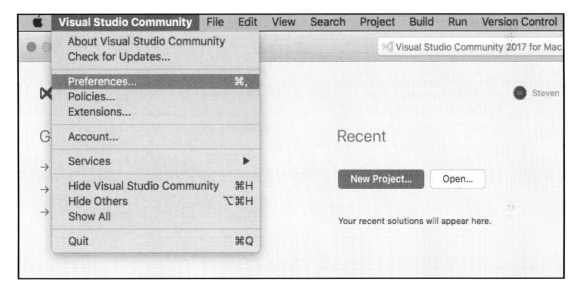

Visual Studio Community for Mac IDE

2. Once you have clicked on the **Preferences...** button, you will be presented with the following screen:

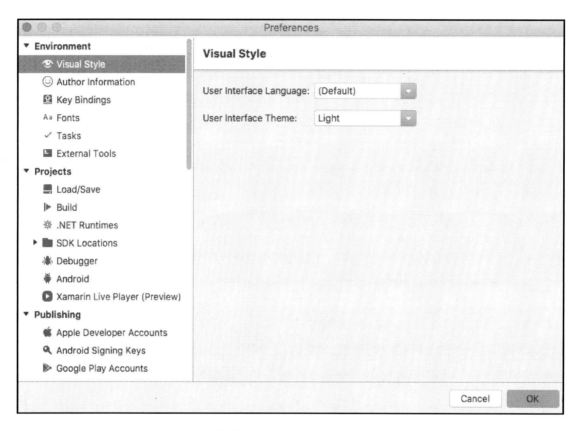

Visual Studio Community for Mac - Preferences

As you can see in the preceding screenshot, you have the ability to configure environment settings, such as **Visual Style**, **Fonts**, **.NET Runtimes**, **SDK Locations**, and **Tasks**, as well as your **Google Play Accounts** and **Apple Developer Accounts**.

Configuring and including additional .NET Runtimes

The Visual Studio for Mac IDE **Preferences** pane provides you with the ability to configure and include additional **.NET Runtimes** that you would like to compile your application against.

The default runtime that has been set will contain the word **(Default)** at the end, which signifies that this is the default **.NET Runtime** that will be used for building and running applications when none has been specified. Refer to the following screenshot:

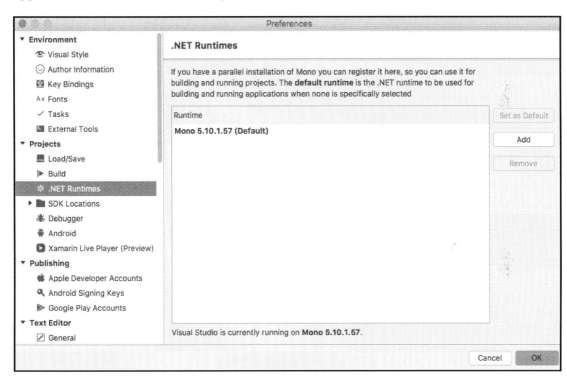

Visual Studio Community for Mac - .NET Runtimes

From this screen, you have the ability to add new or remove existing **.NET Runtimes** that you would like to test your applications with, by using the **Add** or **Remove** buttons. In the next section, we will look at how to define your Android and iOS SDK locations.

Defining your Android and iOS SDK locations

The Visual Studio for Mac IDE **Preferences** pane allows you to define both your Android and iOS SDK locations that you can compile your application against:

1. When configuring the **SDK Locations** for the iOS platform, this will initially default to the current location where the Xcode.app application is located. This is typically found in the Applications folder and will contain the latest iOS platform SDK that has been installed for your version of Xcode:

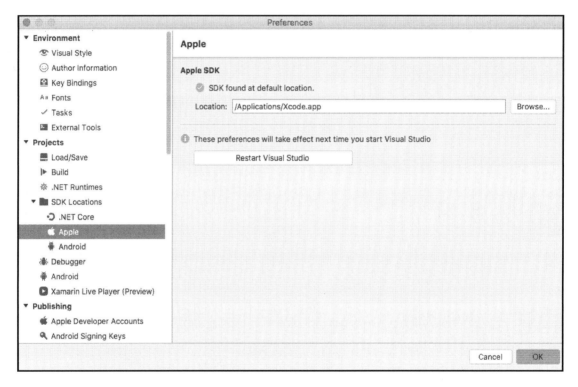

Visual Studio Community for Mac - Apple SDK Location

2. In order to specify a different location for where Xcode.app is located, click on the **Browse...** button, which can be seen in the preceding screenshot. Alternatively, you can specify it for the Android platform by selecting the **Android** node in the **SDK Locations** section.

3. In this section, you can specify the **Android SDK Location** and **Android NDK Location**, as well as the **Java SDK (JDK) Location**:

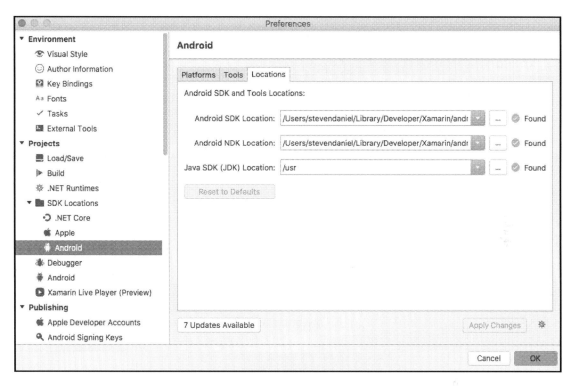

Visual Studio Community for Mac - Android SDK Locations

4. You can also install additional SDK **Platforms** and **Tools** for the Android platform that you would like to build your application against, or remove those platforms and system images that you no longer wish to target; this can be seen in the following screenshot:

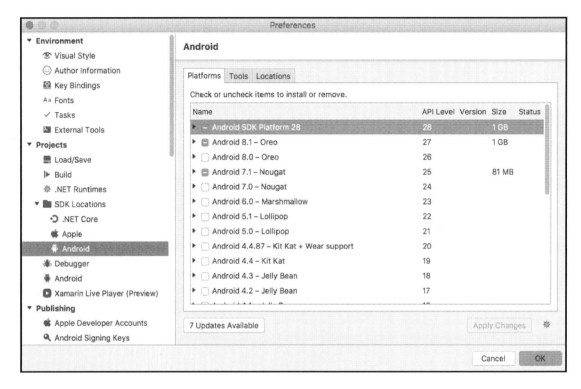

Visual Studio Community for Mac - Choosing Android Platforms

Now that you have explored some of the features contained in the Visual Studio for Mac IDE, our next step is to take a look at, and understand a bit more about, the Xamarin mobile platform, which we will be covering in the next section.

Understanding the Xamarin mobile platform

The Xamarin platform is essentially a framework that enables developers to develop cross-platform mobile applications, using either the C# or F# programming languages, as well as a runtime that runs on the Android, iOS, and Windows platforms, giving you an app that looks, feels, and behaves completely native.

In this section, we will gain an understanding of what the Xamarin mobile platform is and the benefits of using Xamarin to develop your iOS, Android, and Windows apps.

Benefits of developing apps using the Xamarin mobile platform

When you use the Xamarin platform to build your mobile apps, you'll have access to all of the features available in the native SDK and you can even use your existing APIs, so that these can be shared across each of the different mobile platforms for iOS, Android, and Windows.

That said, anything you can do in Objective-C, Swift, or Java can be done in C# or F#, with Xamarin and Visual Studio for Mac.

Developing native apps using the Xamarin approach

When considering developing native iOS, Android, or Windows apps, most developers would either choose to use Objective-C, Swift, or Java. However, there are more ways to build performant and user-friendly mobile apps and Xamarin is one of them. Let's take a look at the benefits of developing native apps using Xamarin.

The Xamarin platform uses a single programming language, C# or F#, which can be used to create apps for the iOS, Android, and Windows platforms, as well as providing you with the flexibility of writing C# code so that you can design your user interfaces specifically for each platform.

The C# programming language is a mature language that is strongly typed to prevent code from producing unexpected behavior. Since C# is one of the .NET framework languages, it can be used with a number of useful .NET features, such as Lambdas, LINQ, and asynchronous programming. The C# source code that you write is then compiled into a native app for each platform.

Technically speaking, Xamarin uses C# and native libraries wrapped in the .NET layer for cross-platform app development. Such applications are often compared to native ones for both iOS and Android mobile development platforms in terms of performance and user experience:

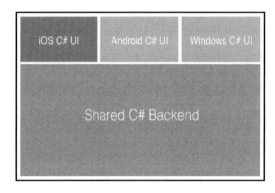

Developing native apps using the Xamarin approach

As you can see from the preceding screenshot, this shows each platform for the Xamarin.iOS, Xamarin.Android, and Windows platforms, each containing their own platform-specific UI code layer and a common **Shared C# Backend** containing the business logic, which can be shared across all platforms.

Developing apps using the Xamarin.Forms approach

Developing iOS, Android, or Windows apps using the Xamarin.Forms approach is very different from developing apps using the native approach. Let's take a look at the benefits of developing apps using the Xamarin.Forms approach.

The Xamarin.Forms approach allows you to build your user interfaces, which can then be shared across each of the different mobile development platforms using 100% percent shared C# or F# code.

Using the `Xamarin.Forms` approach means that your applications will have access to over 40 user interface controls and layouts, which are then mapped to each of the native controls specific to the platform at runtime:

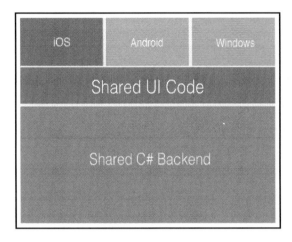

Developing apps using the Xamarin.Forms approach

As you can see from the preceding screenshot, each platform for the Xamarin.iOS, Xamarin.Android, and Windows platforms shares common user interface code, which will be rendered differently on each platform, as well as a common **Shared C# Backend** containing the business logic that can be shared across all platforms.

Now that you have a good understanding of developing Xamarin apps using the native approach versus developing apps using the Xamarin.Forms approach, we can start to build our first app, which we will be covering in the next section.

Creating a Xamarin project for both iOS and Android

In this section, we will take a look at how to create a Xamarin.Forms solution for the first time. We will begin by developing the basic structure for our application, as well as creating and designing the user interface files using XAML, and then creating the C# code to display planetary information.

Before we can proceed, we need to create our `PlanetaryApp` project. It is very simple to create this using Visual Studio for Mac. Simply follow these steps:

1. Firstly, launch the Visual Studio application; depending on your version of Visual Studio installed, you'll be presented with the following screen:

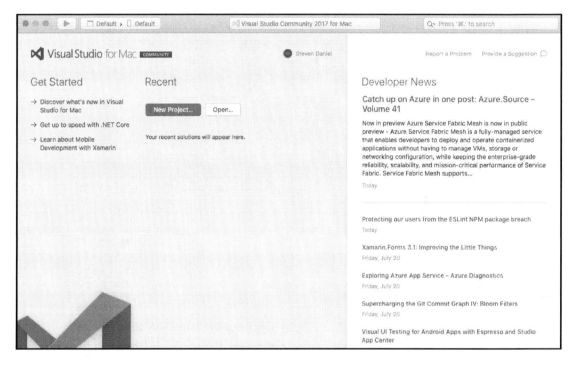

Visual Studio Community IDE

2. Next, choose the **New Project...** option, or alternatively choose **File|New Solution...**, or simply press *Shift + command + N*.

3. Then, choose the **Blank Forms App** option, which is located under the **Multiplatform|App** section, and ensure that you have selected **C#** as the programming language to use.

4. Next, click on the **Next** button to proceed to the next step in the wizard:

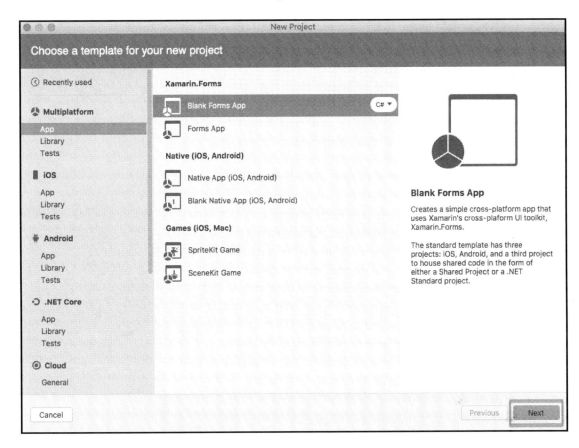

Choosing a template for your new project

5. Next, enter `PlanetaryApp` to use as the name for your app in the **App Name** field and then specify a name for the **Organization Identifier** field.

6. Then, ensure that both the **Android** and **iOS** checkboxes have been selected for the **Target Platforms** field and ensure that the **Use .NET Standard** option has been selected in the **Shared Code** section, as shown in the following screenshot:

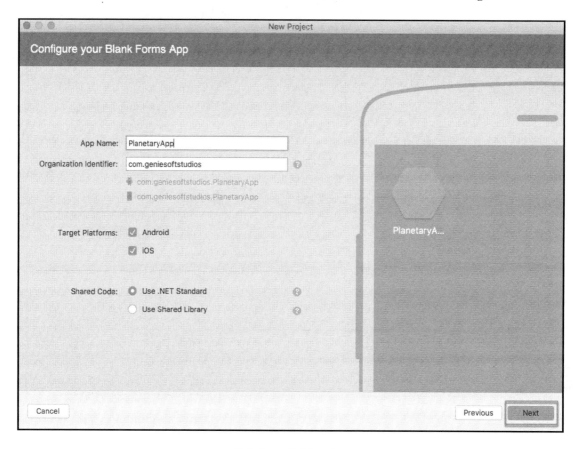

Configuring your Blank Forms App

 The **Organization Identifier** option for your app needs to be unique. Xamarin recommends that you use the reverse domain style (for example, `com.domainName.appName`).

7. Then, click on the **Next** button to proceed to the next step in the wizard:

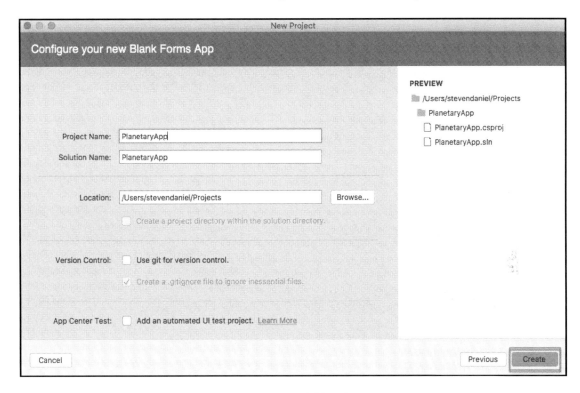

Configuring your new Blank Forms App

8. Finally, click on the **Create** button to save your project at the specified location.

Once your project has been created, you will be presented with the **Visual Studio Community 2017 for Mac** development environment, containing several project files that the template has created, as shown in the following screenshot:

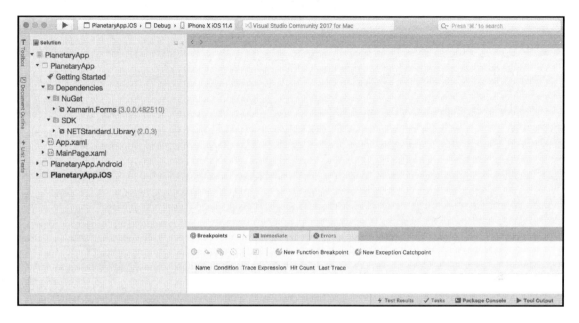

Components of the PlanetaryApp solution

As you can see from the preceding screenshot, the PlanetaryApp solution has been divided into three main areas. The following table provides a brief description of what each area is used for:

Project details	Description
PlanetaryApp	This is the .NET Standard (Shared Library) project that will be responsible for acting as the main architectural layer for the PlanetaryApp solution. This project contains all of the business logic, data objects, Xamarin.Forms ContentPages, Views, and other non-platform-specific code. Any code that you create in this project can be shared across multiple platform-specific projects.
PlanetaryApp.Android	This is an Android-specific project that contains all of the code and assets required to build and deploy the Android app contained in the solution. By default, this project contains a reference to the PlanetaryApp (.NET Standard Shared Library).

PlanetaryApp.iOS	This project is an iOS-specific project that contains all of the code and assets required to build and deploy the iOS app contained in the solution. By default, this project contains a reference to the PlanetaryApp (.NET Standard Shared Library).

One thing you will notice is that our solution contains a file called `App.xaml.cs`, which is part of the .NET Standard (Shared Library). The `App.xaml.cs` file contains a class named `App` that inherits from the `Xamarin.Forms.Application` class hierarchy, as can be seen in the following code snippet:

```
//
//  App.xaml.cs
//  Main class that gets called whenever our PlanetaryApp is started
//
//  Created by Steven F. Daniel on 17/02/2018.
//  Copyright © 2018 GENIESOFT STUDIOS. All rights reserved.
//
using Xamarin.Forms;

namespace PlanetaryApp
{
    public partial class App : Application
    {
        public App()
        {
            InitializeComponent();

            MainPage = new MainPage();
        }

        protected override void OnStart()
        {
            // Handle when your app starts
        }

        protected override void OnSleep()
        {
            // Handle when your app sleeps
        }

        protected override void OnResume()
        {
            // Handle when your app resumes
        }
    }
}
```

The `App` constructor method sets up the `MainPage` property to a new instance of the `ContentPage` that will simply display some default text as created by the project wizard. Throughout this chapter, we will be building the initial user interface using XAML and then populating a list of planet names in the control elements contained in the XAML.

Creating the user interface for our Planetary app using XAML

In this section, we will begin defining the user interface for our `MainPage` using XAML. This page will be used to display a list of planet names, as well as information relating to the distance the planet is from the sun. There are a number of ways you can go about presenting this information, but for the purpose of this app, we will be using a `ListView` to present this information.

Let's start by creating the user interface for our `MainPage` by performing the following steps:

1. Open the `MainPage.xaml` file, which is located as part of the `PlanetaryApp` group, ensure that it is displayed in the code editor, and enter the following code snippet:

```xml
<?xml version="1.0" encoding="utf-8"?>
<ContentPage xmlns="http://xamarin.com/schemas/2014/forms"
             xmlns:x="http://schemsas.microsoft.com/winfx/2009/xaml"
             xmlns:local="clr-namespace:PlanetaryApp"
    x:Class="PlanetaryApp.MainPage">
        <ListView x:Name="planetsListView" RowHeight="80"
HasUnevenRows="True">
            <ListView.ItemTemplate>
                <DataTemplate>
                    <TextCell Text="{Binding Name}" TextColor="Black"
                              Detail="{Binding Distance}"
DetailColor="Red" />
                </DataTemplate>
            </ListView.ItemTemplate>
        </ListView>
    </ContentPage>
```

Let's take a look at what we covered in the preceding code snippet:

1. We started by defining a `ListView` and specified the `RowHeight` to be used for each of the rows that will be allocated and displayed, as well as providing our `ListView` control with a name, `planetsListView`.

2. Next, we defined the `ItemTemplate` property of our `ListView` control, which will be used to display the data items, and then defined a `DataTemplate` that will be used to handle displaying data from a collection of objects in our `ListView`.

3. Finally, we used the `TextCell` control and then set the `Text` property to bind to our `name` property, and we set the `Detail` property to bind our `distance` property, then set the `Textcolor` and `DetailColor` properties of our `TextCell` control.

Displaying a list of planet names using C#

In this section, we will begin by creating the C# code that will be used to communicate with our `PlanetaryApp` user interface XAML for our `MainPage`. We will start by adding code in the `MainPage` code-behind file.

Let's take a look at how we can achieve this:

1. Open the `MainPage.xaml.cs` code-behind file, ensure that it is displayed in the code editor, and enter in the following code snippet:

```
//
// PlanetaryAppPage.xaml.cs
// Displays Planetary Information in a Listview control from an
array
//
// Created by Steven F. Daniel on 17/02/2018.
// Copyright © 2018 GENIESOFT STUDIOS. All rights reserved.
//
using System.Collections.ObjectModel;
using Xamarin.Forms;

namespace PlanetaryApp
{
    public partial class MainPage : ContentPage
    {
        public class Planet
        {
            public string Name { get; set; }
```

```
            public string Distance { get; set; }
        }

    public PlanetaryAppPage()
    {
        InitializeComponent();

        // Create and populate a List of Planetary names
        var planets = new ObservableCollection<Planet>() {
        new Planet
        {
            Name = "Mercury",
            Distance = "Distance from Earth: 77 million
kilometers"
        },
        new Planet
        {
            Name = "Venus",
            Distance = "Distance from Earth: 261 million
kilometers"
        },
        new Planet
        {
            Name = "Earth",
            Distance = "Distance from Sun: 149.6 million
kilometers"
        },
        new Planet
        {
            Name = "Mars",
            Distance = "Distance from Earth: 54.6 million
kilometers"
        },
        new Planet
        {
            Name = "Jupiter",
            Distance = "Distance from Earth: 588 million
kilometers"
        },
        new Planet
        {
            Name = "Saturn",
            Distance = "Distance from Earth: 1.2 billion
kilometers"
        },
        new Planet
        {
            Name = "Uranus",
```

```
                         Distance = "Distance from Earth: 2.6 billion
kilometers"
                     },
                     new Planet
                     {
                         Name = "Neptune",
                         Distance = "Distance from Earth: 4.3 billon
kilometers"
                     }};

                     // Set the PlanetList Item to our ListView to display
the items
                     planetsListView.ItemsSource = planets;
             }
         }
     }
```

Let's take a look at what we covered in the preceding code snippet:

1. We created a subclass called `Planets` in the `MainPage ContentPage`, containing two getters and setters for `Name` and `Distance`
2. Next, we declared an `ObservableCollection` called `planets`, which essentially is a collection that allows any code that has been declared outside the collection to be aware of any changes that occur
3. We then initialized our objects for `Name` and `Distance`, before finally setting the `planets` collection to the `ItemSource` property of the `planetsListView` property that is contained in the `MainPage.xaml` file

Now that you have created the user interface and the necessary C# code to populate the `ListView` contained in our `MainPage` XAML, our next step is to compile, build, and run the `PlanetaryApp` in the iOS simulator.

Launching the Planetary app using the iOS simulator

In this section, we will take a look at how to compile and run our `PlanetaryApp`. You have the option of choosing to run your application using an actual device, or choosing from a list of simulators available for an iOS device.

Let's begin by performing the following steps:

1. Ensure that you have chosen the `PlanetaryApp.iOS` project from the drop-down menu.

2. Next, choose your preferred device from the list of available iOS simulators.

3. Then, select the **Run|Start Without Debugging** menu option, as shown in the following screenshot:

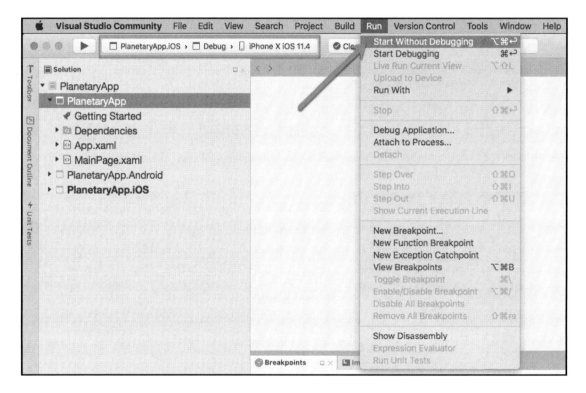

Launching the PlanetaryApp within the iOS Simulator

4. Alternatively, you can also build and run the `PlanetaryApp` by pressing *command + Enter*.

When the compilation is complete, the iOS simulator will appear automatically and the `PlanetaryApp` application will be displayed, as shown in the following screenshot:

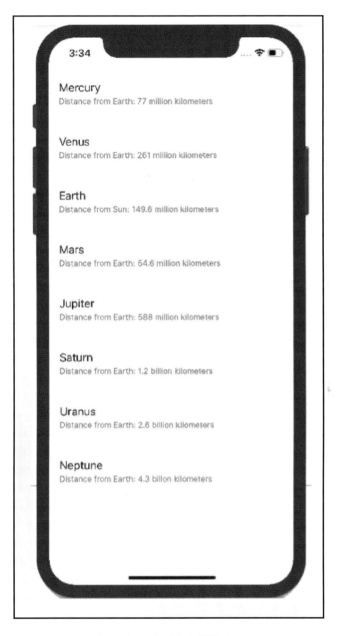

PlanetaryApp running within the iOS Simulator

As you can see from the preceding screenshot, this currently displays a list of static planetary entries that are displayed in our `ListView` control contained in our XAML. Congratulations, you have successfully built your first Xamarin.Forms application, as well as the user interface using XAML for the `PlanetaryApp ContentPage` used by our app!

Using and setting Breakpoints in your code

In this section, we will learn how we can use the Visual Studio for Mac IDE to set Breakpoints in our `PlanetaryApp` solution. We'll learn how to create conditional Breakpoints that can be used to perform a specific action.

Next, we will learn how we can utilize the Breakpoints Pad to view all Breakpoints that have been set in a solution. Finally, we will learn how we can use the Visual Studio for Mac debugger to step through our code and display the contents of variables in the Immediate window.

Setting a Breakpoint in your Planetary App solution

Breakpoints are a good way for you to pause execution at a particular point in the code contained in your project solution, so that you can debug your code or check the contents of a variable.

To set a breakpoint, simply follow the steps outlined here:

1. Locate `MainPage.xaml.cs` in the .NET Standard (Shared Library) and ensure that the `MainPage.xaml.cs` file is displayed in the code editor window
2. To set a Breakpoint, simply click to the left of the line number at the place in your code that you need to troubleshoot, as you can see in the following screenshot:

Setting a Breakpoint within the PlanetaryApp solution

As you can see from the preceding screenshot, whenever you set a breakpoint in your code, you will notice that the line will turn red, but this can be overridden in the Visual Studio for Mac **Preferences** pane.

Using the Breakpoints Pad to view Breakpoints that have been set

Whenever you set Breakpoints in your code, rather than navigating through each of your individual code files in your project solution, you can quickly see all of these in one place by viewing them using the Breakpoints Pad.

To view all of the Breakpoints that have been set in your project, follow the steps outlined here:

1. Ensure that the `MainPage.xaml.cs` file is displayed in the code editor window and choose the **View | Debug Pads | Breakpoints** menu option:

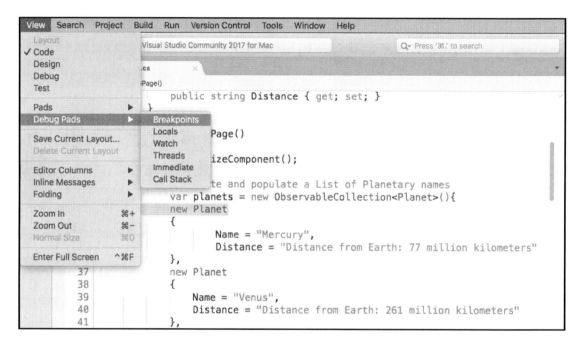

Enable viewing of Breakpoints within your solution

2. You will then see all **Breakpoints** that have been set in your `PlanetaryApp` project solution, including the ones that have been set in your subprojects, as can be seen in the following screenshot:

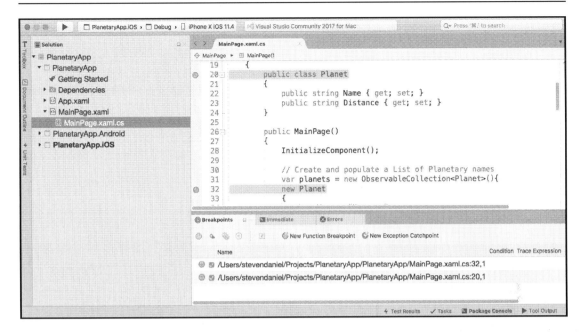

Displays all Breakpoints within your solution

As you can see in the preceding screenshot, you will see all Breakpoints that have been set in your .NET Standard (Shared Library) project, and even the ones that have been set in your **PlanetaryApp.iOS**, **PlanetaryApp.Android** and **PlanetaryApp.UWP** subproject solutions.

Creating conditional Breakpoints to perform an action

In the previous section, we learned about Breakpoints and how you can set these in the code to pause execution whenever your code hits one of them. We also learned how to use the Breakpoints Pad to view all Breakpoints that have been set in your project solution.

Aside from setting Breakpoints, you can also set Conditional Breakpoints that will pause execution based upon whether a condition has been met, which we will covering in this section.

To create a conditional Breakpoint in your project, follow the steps outlined here:

1. Ensure that the `MainPage.xaml.cs` file is displayed in the code editor window.
2. Next, right-click in the sidebar to bring up the pop-up menu and choose the **New Breakpoint...** menu option:

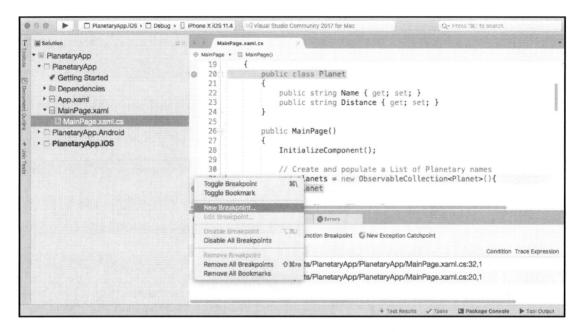

Creating a conditional breakpoint

This will then display the **Create a Breakpoint** dialog where you can specify properties for certain actions, which can be seen in the following screenshot:

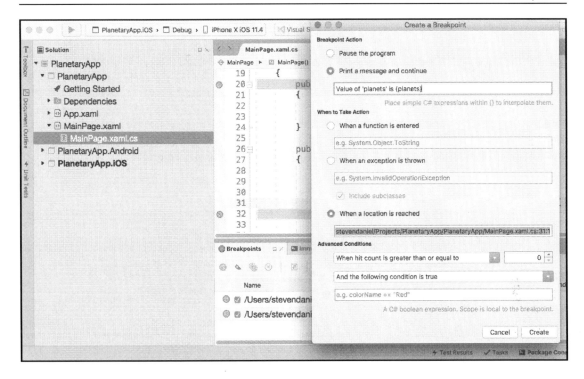

Specifying Breakpoint properties

As you can see in the preceding screenshot, you will see that you can specify either a
Breakpoint Action or **When to Take Action**, as well as setting **Additional Conditions**
whenever a certain condition happens.

Using the Visual Studio for Mac built-in debugger

In this section, we will learn about the Visual Studio for Mac built-in debugger and how we
can use this debugging tool to step through our code and debug our `PlanetaryApp`. You'll
also learn how to work with and use the Immediate window to print out the contents of
your code variables.

Overview of the Visual Studio for Mac debugger

Visual Studio for Mac includes a built-in native debugger that provides debugging support for your iOS, Android, UWP, and Mac applications. The Visual Studio for Mac IDE uses the Mono Soft Debugger, which is a new debugging framework that has been implemented directly into the Mono Framework runtime.

Having this integrated directly into the Mono Framework runtime allows Visual Studio for Mac to debug your managed C# code across each of the different platforms, which can be seen in the following screenshot:

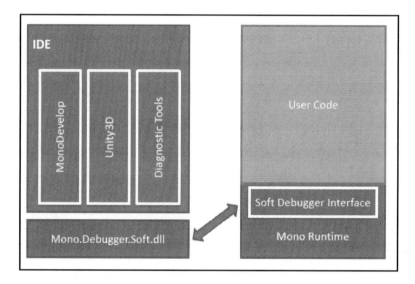

Mono Soft Debugger Interface

For more information on the **Mono Soft Debugger**, refer to `http://www.mono-project.com/docs/advanced/runtime/docs/soft-debugger`.

Using the debugger to step through your code

To start debugging any application, you will need to ensure that your configuration has been set to **Debug**, as can be seen in the following screenshot:

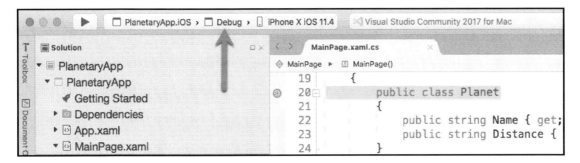

Setting up your application for debugging

Setting this configuration provides you with a set of helpful tools that support debugging, such as Breakpoints, visualizing the contents of your variables, and viewing the call stack.

Once you have set the configuration for your project solution to **Debug**, you will need to ensure that you have set the target device or your iOS simulated device that you would like to use, which can be seen in the preceding screenshot.

To start debugging your application, follow these steps:

1. Ensure that the `MainPage.xaml.cs` file is displayed in the code editor window.

2. Next, deploy your application by pressing the Play button, or alternatively pressing *command + Enter*:

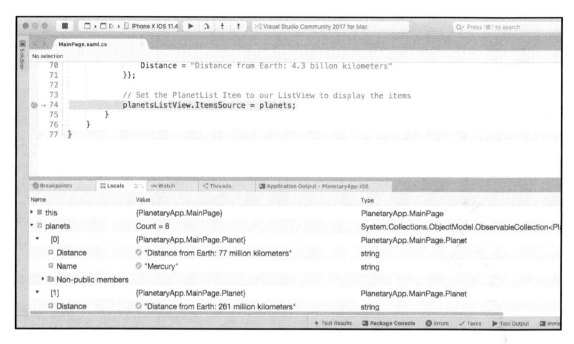

Displays the Breakpoint hit within the Visual Studio Community IDE

Whenever you hit a Breakpoint, your code will pause and the line will be highlighted in yellow, as can be seen in the preceding screenshot:

Visual Studio Community IDE Debugging Buttons

You will notice that the debugging tools will appear in the Visual Studio for Mac IDE and consist of four buttons that allow you to run and step through your code.

The following table provides a list of each of the debugging tool buttons, as well as a brief description:

Debugging button	Description
Play	When this button is pressed, it will begin executing the code until the next breakpoint is reached.
Step Over	When this button is pressed, it will execute the next line of code. If the next line is a function call, the Step Over button will execute the code contained in the function, and will then stop at the next line of code after the function call.
Step Into	When this button is pressed, it will execute the next line of code, and if it is determined that the next line is a function call, the Step Into button will stop at the first line of the function. This will allow you to continue line-by-line debugging of the function. Alternatively, if the next line is not a function, it will behave in the same way as the Step Over button.
Step Out	When this button is pressed, it will return to the line where the current function was called.

Now that you have an overview of the Visual Studio for Mac built-in debugger and how you can use the debugger to step through your code by using each of the four buttons, our next step is to take a look at how we can use the Immediate window to print the contents of your code variables, which we will be covering in the next section.

Using the Immediate window to print code variable contents

You can also use the Visual Studio for Mac built-in debugger to investigate and analyze the content of your code variables whenever a Breakpoint is reached. In this section, we will learn how to use the Immediate window to analyze the content of code variables.

To display the Immediate window, follow the steps outlined here:

1. Ensure that the `MainPage.xaml.cs` file is displayed in the code editor window and choose the **View|Debug Pads|Immediate** menu option:

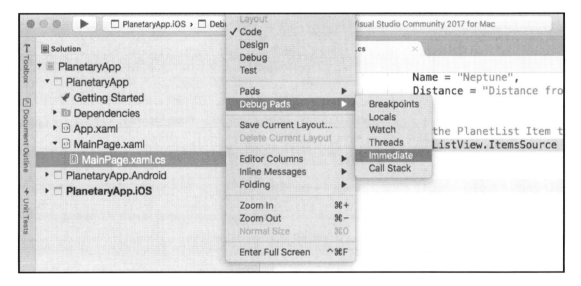

Enable viewing of the Immediate Window

2. You will then see the **Immediate** window displayed, as can be seen in the following screenshot:

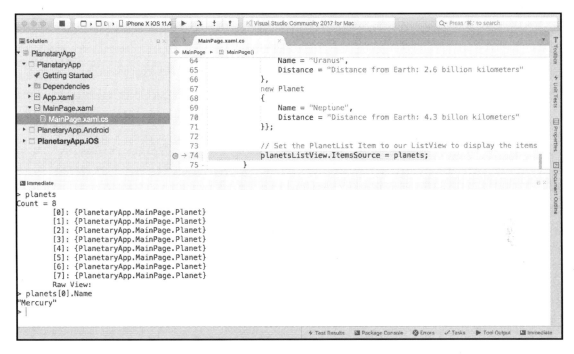

variable contents displayed within the Immediate Window

As you can see in the preceding screenshot, you can see the contents of the `planets` variable by simply typing the name of the variable in the **Immediate** window. Since our `planets` variable is a collection, you can reference properties of the collection. Also, in the **Immediate** window you can change the contents of any item in the collection.

Summary

In this chapter, we learned how to download and install the Visual Studio for Mac IDE, along with the Xamarin Platform SDKs. We then explored the Visual Studio for Mac IDE environment and how we can use the **Preferences** pane to customize the look and feel of the Visual Studio for Mac IDE. Next, we looked at how to configure and include additional .NET Runtimes, as well as how to go about defining your Android and iOS SDK locations. We also learned about the Xamarin mobile platform and the benefits of developing native versus Xamarin.Forms apps using it.

We then learned how to create a cross-platform Xamarin project for both iOS and Android platforms, create the user interface using the XAML syntax, then write the C# code that will be used to communicate with the XAML to populate the `ListView` control with planet names, before launching this in the iOS simulator.

Next, we learned how to set Breakpoints, as well as create conditional Breakpoints in your code; we learned how to use the Breakpoints Pad to view all existing Breakpoints that have been set in your `PlanetaryApp` solution.

Finally, we learned about the built-in debugger in the Visual Studio for Mac IDE, and how you can step through your code and use the Immediate window to print the contents of your variables. In the next chapter, you will learn how to build a Photo Library app using Xamarin.Android and C#.

2
Building a PhotoLibrary App Using Android

In the previous chapter, we learned how to download and install the Visual Studio for Mac IDE as well as the Xamarin Platform SDKs and components for both the **iOS** and **Android** platforms. We also covered some of the features contained in the Visual Studio for Mac IDE and then dived into learning about the Xamarin Mobile platform, as well as the benefits of developing Native versus Xamarin.Forms apps.

We learned how to create a cross-platform Xamarin project for both the iOS and Android platforms, and constructed the user interface by using the XAML syntax and writing the **C#** code that will be used to communicate with the XAML to populate a `ListView` control with planet names.

Finally, we learned how to set breakpoints and create conditional breakpoints, as well as using the built-in debugger in the Visual Studio for Mac IDE, which allows you to step through your code and use the Immediate window to print the content of your variables.

This chapter will focus primarily on how to develop a native Android app using Visual Studio for Mac, Xamarin.Android, and C#. You'll learn how to use and work with the Visual Designer in the Visual Studio for Mac IDE to construct the user interface for our **PhotoLibrary** app using XML and implement Material Design in your apps, as well as create your own custom themes and then apply theming to your app.

To end this chapter, you'll learn how to provide the necessary permissions to `AndroidManifest.xml` so that we can interact with the device camera and photo album, before launching the app in the Android emulator.

This chapter will cover the following points:

- Creating a native app for the Android platform using Visual Studio for Mac
- Constructing the user interface for the Photo Library app using the Android Visual Designer
- Incorporating the Xamarin Media Plugin NuGet package
- Setting up camera and photo album permissions
- Creating custom themes and styles and applying these to the Photo Library app
- Interacting with the device camera and photo album
- Launching the Photo Library app using the Android emulator

Creating a native Android app using Visual Studio for Mac

In this section, we will take a look at how to create a native Android solution for the first time. We will begin by developing the basic structure for our application, as well as adding the Xamarin Media Plugin NuGet package and designing the user interface using XML for our `PhotoLibrary` application.

We will also learn how to update the Strings XML file to include values for our UI control elements that are contained in our XML file. Finally, we will create the `styles` XML file for our Photo Library app that will be used to style our UI control elements.

Before we can proceed, we need to create our `PhotoLibrary` project. It is very simple to create this using Visual Studio for Mac. Simply follow these steps:

1. Firstly, launch the Visual Studio for Mac application.
2. Next, choose the **New Solution...** option, or alternatively choose **File | New | Solution...**, or simply press *Shift + command + N*.
3. Then, choose the **Android App** option, which is located under the **Android | App** section, and ensure that you have selected **C#** as the programming language to use:

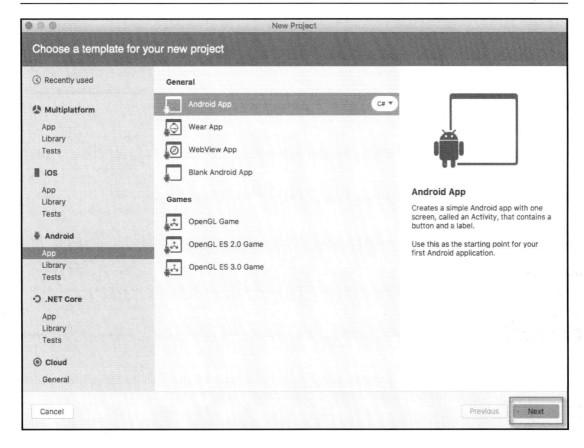

Choose a template for your new project

4. Next, enter PhotoLibrary in the **App Name** field and then specify a name for the **Organisation Identifier** field.
5. Then, ensure that the **Maximum Compatibility** option has been selected for the **Target Platforms** field.

6. Next, ensure that the **Default** option has been selected for the **Theme** section, as shown in the following screenshot:

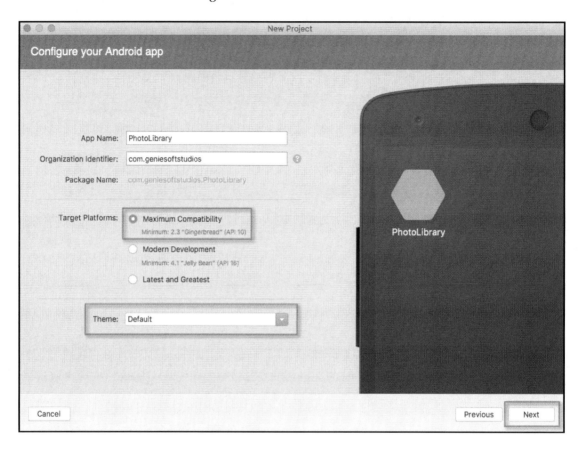

Configuring your Android app

 The **Organization Identifier** for your app needs to be unique. **Xamarin** recommends that you use the reverse domain style (for example, com.domainName.appName).

7. Then, click on the **Next** button to proceed to the next step in the wizard:

Configure your new Android app

8. Next, ensure that the **Create a project directory within the solution directory** checkbox has been selected.
9. Then, click on the **Create** button to save your project at the specified location.

Once your project has been created, you will be presented with the Visual Studio for Mac Community development environment, containing the project files that the template has created for you.

Now that we have created our PhotoLibrary Android application, our next step is to begin adding the Xamarin Media Plugin NuGet package to allow our app to communicate with the device camera and photo gallery, which we will be covering in the next section.

Adding the Xamarin Media Plugin NuGet package to our solution

In this section, we will begin by adding the Xamarin Media Plugin NuGet package to our solution. The Xamarin Media Plugin is essentially a cross-platform library that you can use to gain access to the device camera and photo album by writing a few lines of code.

Let's start by adding the Xamarin Media Plugin Nuget package to our `PhotoLibrary` solution by performing the following steps:

1. Firstly, ensure that you have the `PhotoLibrary` solution currently open in the Visual Studio for Mac IDE.

2. Then, right-click on the `Packages` folder and choose the **Add Packages...** menu option:

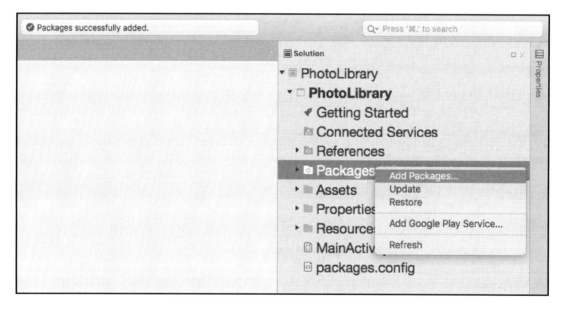

PhotoLibrary Solution Contents

3. Next, select the **Xam.Plugin.Media** package from the list, ensuring that you have chosen the latest version from the **Version** dropdown.

4. Finally, click on the **Add Package** button to add the `NuGet` Package to the **PhotoLibrary** solution:

Adding the Xam.Plugin.Media NuGet Package

Once you've added the Xamarin Media Plugin NuGet package to your `PhotoLibrary` solution, this will add two additional files, `Plugin.CurrentActivity` and `Plugin.Permissions`, as well as `Xam.Plugin.Media`, which can be seen in the following screenshot:

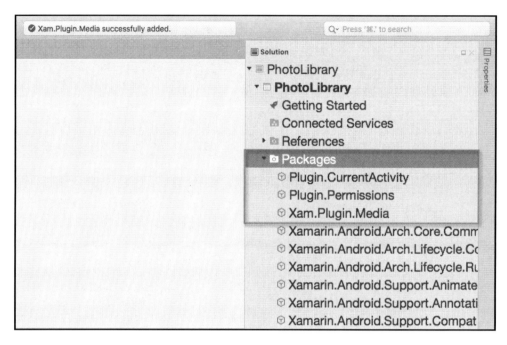

Xam.Plugin.Media added to the Package Folder

The following table provides an explanation of each of the Plugins that have been added to the `Packages` folder, as well as a brief description:

Plugin name	Description
`Plugin.CurrentActivity`	Provides developers with an easy alternative to accessing an Android application's current activity that is being displayed.
`Plugin.Permissions`	This is essentially a cross-platform plugin that is used to request and check for permissions to use the device camera and photo gallery.
`Xam.Plugin.Media`	This is essentially a simple cross-platform plugin to take photos and video using the device camera or pick them from the device gallery.

Now that we have added the Xamarin Media Plugin NuGet package to our `PhotoLibrary` solution, the next step is to create the user interface for our `PhotoLibrary` application using the Android Visual Designer in the Visual Studio for Mac IDE, which we will cover in the next section.

Creating the user interface for our PhotoLibrary app using XML

In this section, we will begin by constructing the user interface for our **PhotoLibrary** application using XML. This will contain two buttons, as well as an **ImageView** control to display images that have been taken using the device camera or chosen from the device photo gallery.

Let's start by creating the user interface for our **PhotoLibrary** app by performing the following steps:

1. Expand the `Resources` folder in the `PhotoLibrary` solution and right-click on the `layout` folder to display the popup, as shown in the following screenshot.

2. Next, choose the **New File...** option, which is located in the **Add** menu:

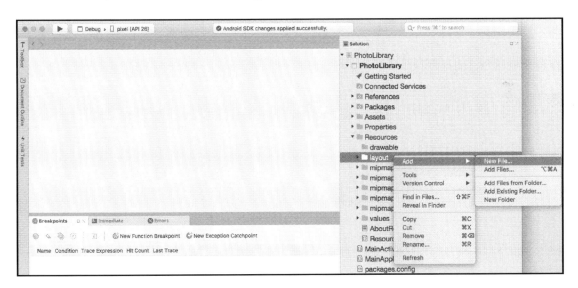

Adding a new file within the layout folder

3. Then, choose the **Layout** option under the **Android** section, and enter **PhotoLibraryUI** for the name of the new layout file to be created, as shown in the following screenshot:

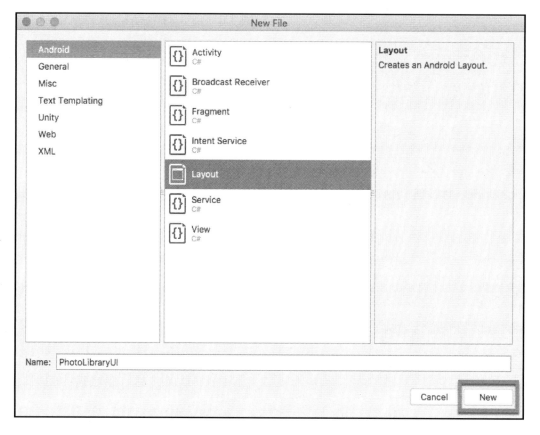

Creating a new Android Layout file

4. Next, click on the **New** button to allow the wizard to proceed and create the new file, as shown in the preceding screenshot.

Congratulations, you have created your very first **layout** file for our **PhotoLibrary** solution. Our next step is to proceed with creating the user interface:

5. Open the `PhotoLibraryUI.axml` file, which is located as part of the **PhotoLibrary|Resources|layout** group. You will notice that it opens a blank canvas that contains a header, `PhotoLibrary`, which is the name for our application.

6. Next, ensure that you have selected the **Source** button, which is located at the bottom of the designer:

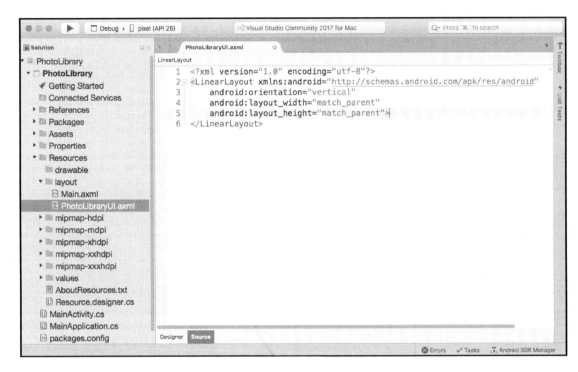

Creating the PhotoLibrary user interface

7. Then, ensure that the `PhotoLibraryUI.axml` layout information file is displayed in the code editor and enter the following code snippet:

```xml
<?xml version="1.0" encoding="utf-8"?>
<LinearLayout
xmlns:android="http://schemas.android.com/apk/res/android"
        android:orientation="vertical"
        android:layout_width="match_parent"
        android:layout_height="match_parent">
    <Button
        android:layout_width="match_parent"
        android:layout_height="wrap_content"
        android:text="@string/takePicture"
        android:id="@+id/takePicture" />
    <Button
        android:layout_width="match_parent"
        android:layout_height="wrap_content"
```

```
        android:text="@string/chooseFromGallery"
        android:id="@+id/chooseFromGallery" />
    <ImageView
        android:layout_width="fill_parent"
        android:layout_height="fill_parent"
        android:scaleType="fitXY"
        android:id="@+id/photoImageView" />
</LinearLayout>
```

Let's now start by taking a look at what we covered in the preceding code snippet:

1. We started by defining a `Button` tag and specified `layout_width` and `layout_height` to match the parent layout information. We also specified the `text` tag and assigned the `takePicture` string value that will be used to display the associated text for the button. Lastly, we used the `id` tag to provide an identifier for the button control that we can use and reference in our code.

2. Next, we declared another `Button` tag and specified `layout_width` and `layout_height` to match the parent layout information. We also specified the `text` tag and assigned the `chooseFromGallery` string value that will be used to display the associated text for the button. Lastly, we used the `id` tag to provide an identifier for the button control that we can use and reference in our code.

3. Finally, we declared an `ImageView` tag, and specified `layout_width` and `layout_height`, to fill the image in the parent. We also specified the `scaleType` tag and assigned the `fitXY` string value that will scale the image so that it fits nicely in our user interface. Lastly, we used the `id` tag to provide an identifier for the `ImageView` control that we can use and reference in our code.

Now that you have created the user interface for our Photo Library Android application, our next step is to update the Android Strings XML file to include text values for each of our buttons.

Updating the Strings XML file to include our UI control values

In this section, we will begin by updating the Android `Strings.xml` file, which will be used by our application. `Strings.xml` is essentially a single file that you can use to declare the various strings your application requires; every string that you define must contain a unique ID, so you can reference the ID in your code to use that string.

Let's start by updating the `Strings.xml` file for our `PhotoLibrary` app by performing the following steps:

1. Expand the **Resources** | **values** folder in the `PhotoLibrary` solution, as shown in the following screenshot:

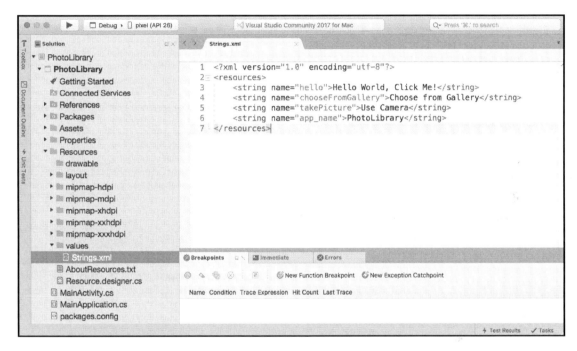

Contents of the Strings.xml file

2. Open the `Strings.xml` file, which is located as part of the **PhotoLibrary|Resources|values** group.

3. Next, ensure that the `Strings.xml` file is displayed in the code editor and enter the following code snippet:

```xml
<?xml version="1.0" encoding="utf-8"?>
<resources>
    <string name="hello">Hello World, Click Me!</string>
    <string name="chooseFromGallery">Choose from Gallery</string>
    <string name="takePicture">Use Camera</string>
    <string name="app_name">PhotoLibrary</string>
</resources>
```

Let's now start by taking a look at what we covered in the preceding code snippet:

1. We started by defining a string value called chooseFromGallery and assigning the associated text of Choose from Gallery. This assigned text value will be associated with our chooseFromGallery button, which we defined in our user interface.

2. Next, we declared another string value called takePicture and assigned the associated text of Use Camera. This assigned text value will be associated with our takePicture button, which we defined in our user interface.

Now that you have created the user interface and updated the Strings.xml file for our PhotoLibrary application, our next step is to create the styles.xml file that will be used to style our UI elements.

Creating the Styles XML file for our Photo Library app

In this section, we will look at how to create a styles.xml file that will be used to apply styling to our user interface. The benefit of using a styles.xml file is that you can apply styling to our application, as well as each of the UI elements, such as by setting font sizes and colors, and customizing the appearance of control elements.

Let's start by creating the Styles file for our PhotoLibrary app by performing the following steps:

1. Expand the Resources folder in the PhotoLibrary solution and right-click on the values folder to display the popup, as shown in the following screenshot.

2. Next, choose the **New File...** option, which is located in the **Add** menu:

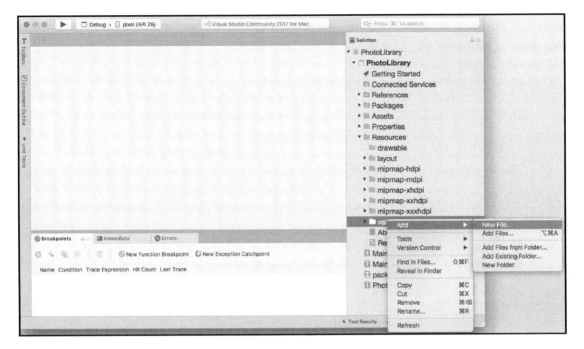

Creating a new Styles.xml file for our PhotoLibrary app

3. Then, choose the **Empty XML File** option under the **XML** section and enter `styles.xml` as the name of the new XML file to be created, as shown in the following screenshot:

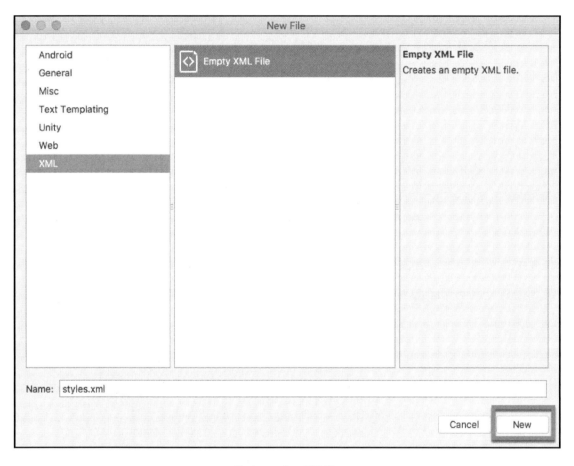

Creating a new Empty XML File

4. Next, click on the **New** button to allow the wizard to proceed and create the new file, as shown in the preceding screenshot.

Now that we have created our `styles.xml` file, we can now proceed with creating the PhotoLibrary `Activity` class that will be used to interact with our user interface control elements.

Creating and implementing the PhotoLibrary Activity class

In this section, we will start by creating the PhotoLibrary `Activity` class that will be used to interact with our `PhotoLibraryUI` user interface, and handle when each of the buttons has been pressed.

Let's start by creating the `PhotoLibraryActivity` class for our PhotoLibrary app in the following steps:

1. Ensure that the `PhotoLibrary` solution is currently open in the Visual Studio for Mac IDE.

2. Next, right-click on the **PhotoLibrary** project and choose **Add | New File...** from the pop-up menu, as shown in the following screenshot:

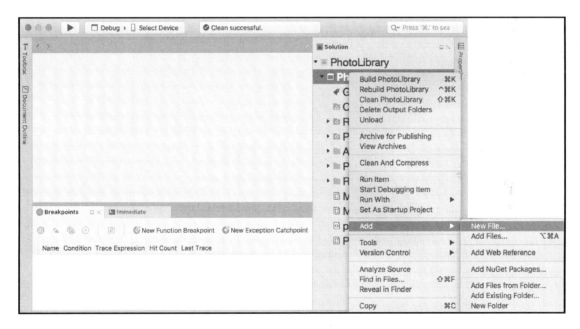

Creating a new Android Activity Class

3. Then, choose the **Activity** option under the **Android** section and enter
   `PhotoLibraryActivity` for the name of the new **Activity** file to be created, as
   shown in the following screenshot:

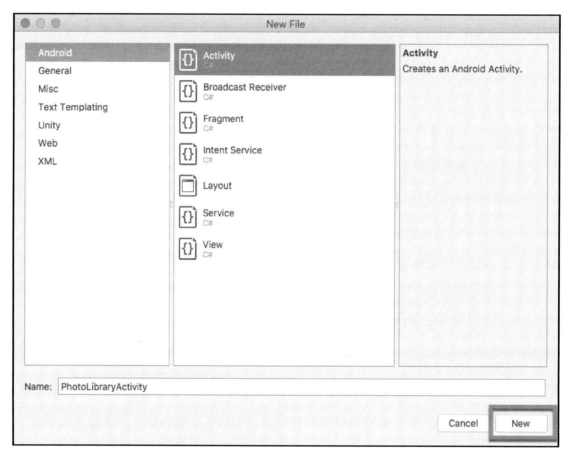

Creating the PhotoLibraryActivity Class

4. Next, click on the **New** button to allow the wizard to proceed and create the new
   file, as shown in the preceding screenshot.

Now that we have created our `PhotoLibraryActivity` file, we can proceed with implementing the required code for our `Activity` file and setting up our button click events, as well as incorporating the **Xamarin Media Plugin** and **Permissions Plugin** namespaces.

5. Open the `PhotoLibraryActivity.cs` file, which is located as part of the `PhotoLibrary` group, ensure that it is displayed in the code editor, and enter the following code snippet:

```
//
//  PhotoLibraryActivity.cs
//  Main Activity for the Photo Library Gallery PhotoLibraryUI XML
//  representing the application user interface elements.
//
//  Created by Steven F. Daniel on 13/03/2018.
//  Copyright © 2018 GENIESOFT STUDIOS. All rights reserved.
//
using System;
using System.Threading.Tasks;
using Android.App;
using Android.OS;
using Android.Widget;

// Xamarin Media Plugin
using Plugin.Media;
using Plugin.Media.Abstractions;

// Xamarin Permissions Plugin
using Plugin.Permissions;
using Plugin.Permissions.Abstractions;

namespace PhotoLibrary
{
    [Activity(Label = "PhotoLibraryActivity", MainLauncher = true,
Icon = "@mipmap/icon")]
    public class PhotoLibraryActivity : Activity
    {
        protected override void OnCreate(Bundle savedInstanceState)
        {
            base.OnCreate(savedInstanceState);

            // Set our view from the "PhotoLibraryUI" layout resource
            SetContentView(Resource.Layout.PhotoLibraryUI);

            // Get our chooseGallery button from the layout resource,
            // and attach an event to it
            Button useCamera =
```

```
FindViewById<Button>(Resource.Id.takePicture);
            useCamera.Click += TakePictureButton_Clicked;
            Button chooseFromGallery =
FindViewById<Button>(Resource.Id.chooseFromGallery);
            chooseFromGallery.Click += ChooseFromGalleryButton_Clicked;
        }
    }
}
```

Let's now start by taking a look at what we covered in the preceding code snippet:

1. We started by including a reference to the `System.Threading.Tasks` namespace, which will be used for asynchronous procedure calls.
2. Next, we included a reference to the `Plugin.Media` and `Plugin.Permissions` namespaces, which will be used to communicate with the device camera and photo gallery.
3. Finally, we set our view from the `PhotoLibraryUI` layout resource, then we created two `Button` variables, `useCamera` and `chooseFromGallery`, using the `id` from the layout resource file, and then we modified their `Click` events so that they point to their respective methods, which we will be creating later as we progress throughout this chapter.

Updating the MainActivity class to call the PhotoLibrary Activity

Now that we have created our `PhotoLibraryActivity` class and have implemented the necessary method calls, our next step is to make some changes to the `MainActivity` class, so that it calls our `PhotoLibraryActivity` class.

The `MainActivity` class is the main class that gets called from any Android application upon launching, so we will need to make some changes so that our `PhotoLibraryActivity` will be displayed when our application launches.

Let's start by updating the `MainActivity` class for our PhotoLibrary app by performing the following steps:

1. Open the `MainActivity.cs` file, which is located as part of the PhotoLibrary group, ensure that it is displayed in the code editor, and then enter the following code snippet:

```
using Android.App;
using Android.Widget;
```

```
using Android.OS;

namespace PhotoLibrary
{
    [Activity(Label = "PhotoLibrary", MainLauncher = true, Icon =
"@mipmap/icon")]
    public class MainActivity : Activity
    {
        int count = 1;
        protected override void OnCreate(Bundle savedInstanceState)
        {
            base.OnCreate(savedInstanceState);

            // Start our Photo Library Activity
            this.StartActivity(typeof(PhotoLibraryActivity));

            // Set our view from the "main" layout resource
            SetContentView(Resource.Layout.Main);

            // Get our button from the layout resource,
            // and attach an event to it
            Button button = FindViewById<Button>(Resource.Id.myButton);
            button.Click += delegate { button.Text = $"{count++}
clicks!"; };
        }
    }
}
```

Let's take a look at what we covered in the preceding code snippet:

1. First, we started by using the StartActivity method of the main activity class
2. Next, we used the typeof keyword to ensure that the PhotoLibraryActivity that we are passing in is definitely a class
3. Then, if the typeof keyword returns True, we begin instantiating our PhotoLibraryActivity and display this when the MainActivity class is launched.

Implementing Material Design in the PhotoLibrary app

In the previous sections, we looked at how to create the user interface for our app, update the `Strings.xml` file, and create the `styles.xml` file. Lastly, we looked at creating `PhotoLibraryActivity` and making some changes to the `MainActivity` class.

In this section, we will learn how to go about creating and implementing custom **Material Design Themes**, and how to implement **Material Design** in the PhotoLibrary application.

Creating custom themes for the PhotoLibrary application

Creating custom themes for your apps is extremely easy. Android themes are similar to using CSS style sheets in your web applications for user interface design. Themes allow you to separate styles from your UI components, which makes maintaining your applications look and feel a lot easier.

Let's take a look at how to create a simple style in our `styles.xml` file for our PhotoLibrary app by following these simple steps:

1. Open the `styles.xml` file, which is located as part of the **PhotoLibrary| Resources|values** group, ensure that it is displayed in the code editor, and then enter the following code snippet:

    ```
    <?xml version="1.0" encoding="UTF-8"?>
    <resources>
        <!-- A custom theme that is a variation on the light theme with
            a different background color. -->
        <style name="MyCustomTheme">
            <item name="android:windowNoTitle">true</item>
            <item name="android:colorPrimary">#3F51B5</item>
            <item name="android:statusBarColor">#ffffff</item>
            <item name="android:colorPrimaryDark">#303F9F</item>
        </style>
    </resources>
    ```

2. Let's now start by taking a look at what we covered in the preceding code snippet. Firstly, we started by using `<style name` to provide a name for our style, which can be anything you want.

3. Next, we specified a number of `<item name` fields, using the `android:` namespace and specifying values for the `windowNoTitle`, `colorPrimary`, `statusBarColor`, and `colorPrimaryDark` colors. `windowNoTitle` will essentially hide the name of the activity and prevent this from being displayed.

Creating custom styles for the Photo Library application UI controls

Now that you have created the custom theme in the `styles.xml` file, we can continue modifying this file and create custom styles for our UI components that we created in our `PhotoLibraryUIlayout` file.

Let's take a look at how to create the required styles for our UI controls in our `styles.xml` file for our PhotoLibrary app by following these simple steps:

1. Open the `styles.xml` file, which is located as part of the **PhotoLibrary|Resources |values** group, ensure that it is displayed in the code editor, and then enter the following code snippet:

```xml
<?xml version="1.0" encoding="UTF-8"?>
<resources>
    <!-- A custom theme that is a variation on the light theme with
        a different background color. -->
    <style name="MyCustomTheme">
        <item name="android:windowNoTitle">true</item>
        <item name="android:colorPrimary">#3F51B5</item>
        <item name="android:statusBarColor">#ffffff</item>
        <item name="android:colorPrimaryDark">#303F9F</item>
    </style>
```

2. Create a new `<style name` tag with the name of `camera_button`, which will be used by our `takePictureButton` that we declared in our `PhotoLibraryUI.axml` layout file. Enter the following code snippet:

```xml
<style name="camera_button">
    <item name="android:layout_width">match_parent</item>
    <item name="android:layout_height">wrap_content</item>
    <item name="android:textColor">#ffffff</item>
    <item name="android:gravity">center</item>
    <item name="android:layout_margin">3dp</item>
    <item name="android:textSize">20dp</item>
    <item name="android:textStyle">bold</item>
    <item name="android:shadowColor">#000000</item>
    <item name="android:shadowDx">1</item>
```

```
        <item name="android:shadowDy">1</item>
        <item name="android:shadowRadius">2</item>
        <item name="android:background">#0433ff</item>
        <item name="android:text">@string/takePicture</item>
    </style>
```

3. Create a new `<style name` tag with the name of `gallery_button`, which will be used by our `chooseFromGallery` that we declared in our `PhotoLibraryUI.axml` layout file, and enter the following code snippet:

```
<style name="gallery_button">
        <item name="android:layout_width">match_parent</item>
        <item name="android:layout_height">wrap_content</item>
        <item name="android:textColor">#ffffff</item>
        <item name="android:gravity">center</item>
        <item name="android:layout_margin">3dp</item>
        <item name="android:textSize">20dp</item>
        <item name="android:textStyle">bold</item>
        <item name="android:shadowColor">#000000</item>
        <item name="android:shadowDx">1</item>
        <item name="android:shadowDy">1</item>
        <item name="android:shadowRadius">2</item>
        <item name="android:background">#ff2600</item>
        <item name="android:text">@string/chooseFromGallery</item>
    </style>
```

4. Finally, create another `<style name` tag with the name of `photoImageView`, which will be used by our `photoImageView` that we declared in our `PhotoLibraryUI.axml` layout file, and enter the following code snippet:

```
<style name="photoImageView">
        <item name="android:layout_width">fill_parent</item>
        <item name="android:layout_height">fill_parent</item>
        <item name="android:scaleType">fitXY</item>
        <item name="android:gravity">center</item>
        <item name="android:layout_margin">3dp</item>
        <item name="android:shadowColor">#000000</item>
        <item name="android:shadowDx">1</item>
        <item name="android:shadowDy">1</item>
        <item name="android:shadowRadius">2</item>
        <item name="android:background">#ff9300</item>
    </style>
</resources>
```

Let's now start by taking a look at what we covered in the preceding code snippet:

1. Firstly, we started by declaring a number of custom styles `<style name>` and provided a name for our style.
2. Next, we specified a number of `<item name>` fields using the `android:` namespace, and specified values for `layout_width` and `layout_height`. We also specified the `textColor`, `textSize`, `textStyle`, and `background` colors, as well as specifying the text to display in our buttons.
3. For the `photoImageView` style, we specified the `scaleType` property, which will fit our chosen image in the `imageView`.

Applying the custom theme to the PhotoLibrary application

We have just created a custom theme and created a number of styles for our `PhotoLibrary` application; our next step is to apply the custom theme to our PhotoLibrary layout file, as well as update our `PhotoLibraryActivity` class to use our custom theme, which will then apply the theming for our application:

1. Open the `PhotoLibraryUI.axml` file, which is located as part of the **PhotoLibrary | Resources | layout** group, and ensure that it is displayed in the code editor. Enter the following code snippet:

```xml
<?xml version="1.0" encoding="utf-8"?>
<LinearLayout
    xmlns:android="http://schemas.android.com/apk/res/android"
        android:orientation="vertical"
        android:layout_width="match_parent"
        android:layout_height="match_parent">
        <Button
            android:id="@+id/takePicture"
            style="@style/camera_button" />
        <Button
            android:id="@+id/chooseFromGallery"
            style="@style/gallery_button" />
        <ImageView
            android:id="@+id/photoImageView"
            style="@style/photoImageView" />
    </LinearLayout>
```

2. Next, we need to open the `PhotoLibraryActivity.cs` file, which is located as part of the `PhotoLibrary` group, and set the `Theme` for our activity.

3. Ensure that the `PhotoLibraryActivity.cs` file is displayed in the code editor and enter the following code snippet:

```
//
// PhotoLibraryActivity.cs
// Main Activity for the Photo Library Gallery PhotoLibraryUI XML
// representing the application user interface elements.
//
// Created by Steven F. Daniel on 13/03/2018.
// Copyright © 2018 GENIESOFT STUDIOS. All rights reserved.
//
using System;
using System.Threading.Tasks;
using Android.App;
using Android.OS;
using Android.Widget;

// Xamarin Media Plugin
using Plugin.Media;
using Plugin.Media.Abstractions;

// Xamarin Permissions Plugin
using Plugin.Permissions;
using Plugin.Permissions.Abstractions;

namespace PhotoLibrary
{
        [Activity(Label = "PhotoLibraryActivity", MainLauncher = true,
                Icon = "@mipmap/icon", Theme =
"@style/MyCustomTheme")]
        ...
        ...
}
```

In the preceding code snippet, we modified the [Activity section to include an additional parameter, called Theme. Here, we specified the name of our custom theme, called MyCustomTheme, which we created in our `styles.xml` file. When using themes in your application, you will need to include the @style parameter. If you don't include this, your application will not compile and will produce application errors.

Setting up camera and photo album permissions

Before we can start accessing the camera and photo album, we will need to assign certain permissions for our `PhotoLibrary` Android app. To do this, we need to make some changes to our Android Manifest file to give access to our camera and photo album.

Let's start by updating the `AndroidManifest.xml` file for our PhotoLibrary app by performing the following steps:

1. Expand the `Properties` folder in the `PhotoLibrary` solution and double-click on the `AndroidManifest.xml` file. Ensure that you have selected the **Source** button, which is located at the bottom of the screen, as shown in the following screenshot:

Setting up Camera and Photo Album Permissions

2. Then, ensure that the `AndroidManifest.xml` file is displayed in the code editor and enter the following code snippet:

```
<?xml version="1.0" encoding="utf-8"?>
<manifest xmlns:android="http://schemas.android.com/apk/res/android"
android:versionCode="1"
```

```
                    android:versionName="1.0"
    package="com.geniesoftstudios.PhotoLibrary">
            <uses-sdk android:minSdkVersion="10" />

            <uses-permission android:name="android.permission.CAMERA"/>
            <uses-permission
    android:name="android.permission.READ_EXTERNAL_STORAGE"/>
            <uses-permission
    android:name="android.permission.WRITE_EXTERNAL_STORAGE"/>
            <application android:allowBackup="true"
    android:icon="@mipmap/icon"
                        android:label="@string/app_name">
            </application>
        </manifest>
```

Now that we have added the necessary permissions for our PhotoLibrary app in
`AndroidManifest.xml`, we need to implement the remaining instance methods in our
`PhotoLibraryActivity` class and use the `Plugin.Permissions` namespace to check to
see whether we can access our **Camera** and **Photo Gallery**.

Interacting with the device camera and photo album

Now that we have made the necessary changes in the `AndroidManifest.xml` file, we can
proceed to implement the remaining instance methods in our `PhotoLibraryActivity`
class, which will complete our PhotoLibrary application.

1. Open the `PhotoLibraryActivity.cs` class, which is located in the
   PhotoLibrary solution, and ensure that it is displayed in the code editor window:

```
namespace PhotoLibrary
{
    [Activity(Label = "PhotoLibraryActivity", MainLauncher = true,
Icon = "@mipmap/icon",
                Theme =
"@android:style/Theme.Material.Light.DarkActionBar")]
    public class PhotoLibraryActivity : Activity
    {
        protected override void OnCreate(Bundle savedInstanceState)
        {
            base.OnCreate(savedInstanceState);

            // Set our view from the "main" layout resource
            SetContentView(Resource.Layout.PhotoLibraryUI);
```

```
        . . .
        . . .
        . . .
    }
```

2. Next, underneath the `OnCreate` method, we need to create a new instance method called `TakePictureButton_Clicked` and enter the following code snippet:

```
#region Take Picture using the Android device camera
public async void TakePictureButton_Clicked(object sender,
System.EventArgs args)
    {
        await CrossMedia.Current.Initialize();
        if (!CrossMedia.Current.IsCameraAvailable ||
!CrossMedia.Current.IsTakePhotoSupported)
        {
            // Display alert dialog - Device has no camera and photo
support is denied
            ShowMessageDialog("Permission Denied", "Unable to gain access
to the camera.");
            return;
        }
        // Check to see if we have the appropriate permissions
        if (!await Task.Run(() => CheckCameraAlbumPermissions()))
        {
            // Display alert dialog - Permission denied to Camera
            ShowMessageDialog("Permission Denied", "Unable to gain access
to the camera.");
            return;
        }
        var imageFilename = await CrossMedia.Current.TakePhotoAsync(new
StoreCameraMediaOptions()
        {
            Name = $"{DateTime.UtcNow}.jpg",
            DefaultCamera = CameraDevice.Rear,
            PhotoSize = PhotoSize.Medium,
            SaveToAlbum = true,
        });
        if (imageFilename == null)
            return;

        // Get our chooseGallery button from the layout resource,
        // and attach an event to it
        ImageView photoImageView =
FindViewById<ImageView>(Resource.Id.photoImageView);
photoImageView.SetImageURI(Android.Net.Uri.Parse(imageFilename.Path));
    }
```

```
#endregion
```

3. Next, underneath the `TakePictureButton_Clicked` instance method, we need to create a new instance method called `ChooseFromGalleryButton_Clicked` to allow the user to choose a picture from the device's gallery. Enter the following code snippet:

```
#region Allow the user to choose a Picture from the phone
async void ChooseFromGalleryButton_Clicked(object sender,
System.EventArgs args)
    {
        if (!CrossMedia.Current.IsPickPhotoSupported)
        {
            // Display our message dialog if choosing a photo is not
supported
            ShowMessageDialog("Not Supported", "Choosing a photo is not
supported.");
            return;
        }
        // Check to see if we have the appropriate permissions
        if (!await Task.Run(() => CheckCameraAlbumPermissions()))
        {
            // Display our message dialog if we are unable to gain access
to the photo album
            ShowMessageDialog("Permission Denied","Unable to gain access to
the Photo Album.");
            return;
        }
        var imageFilename = await CrossMedia.Current.PickPhotoAsync();
        if (imageFilename != null)
        {
            ImageView photoImageView =
FindViewById<ImageView>(Resource.Id.photoImageView);
photoImageView.SetImageURI(Android.Net.Uri.Parse(imageFilename.Path));
        }
    }
    #endregion
```

4. Next, underneath the `ChooseFromGalleryButton_Clicked` instance method, we need to create a new instance method called `CheckCameraAlbumPermissions` that will check to see whether we have the necessary permissions to access the device camera and gallery. Enter the following code snippet:

```
#region Checking for Camera and Photo Album Permissions
public async Task<bool> CheckCameraAlbumPermissions()
{
```

```
        // Determine if we have permission to our Camera and photo album
        var deviceCameraStatus = await
CrossPermissions.Current.CheckPermissionStatusAsync(Permission.Camera);
        var deviceAlbumStatus = await
CrossPermissions.Current.CheckPermissionStatusAsync(Permission.Storage);

        if (deviceCameraStatus != PermissionStatus.Granted ||
            deviceAlbumStatus != PermissionStatus.Granted)
        {
            var results = await
CrossPermissions.Current.RequestPermissionsAsync(new[] {
                               Permission.Camera, Permission.Storage
            });
            deviceCameraStatus = results[Permission.Camera];
            deviceAlbumStatus = results[Permission.Storage];
        }
        // Check to see if we have access to the camera and photo album
        return (deviceCameraStatus == PermissionStatus.Granted &&
                deviceAlbumStatus == PermissionStatus.Granted);
    }
    #endregion
```

5. Next, underneath the `CheckCameraAlbumPermissions` instance method, we need to create a new instance method called `ShowMessageDialog` that will display an alert dialog using `title` and `message` as parameters. Enter the following code snippet:

```
#region Shows a Message Dialog using the parameters specified
public void ShowMessageDialog(string title, string message)
{
    var dialog = new AlertDialog.Builder(this);
    var alert = dialog.Create();
    alert.SetTitle(title);
    alert.SetMessage(message);
    alert.SetButton("OK", (c, ev) =>
CrossPermissions.Current.OpenAppSettings());
    alert.Show();
}
```

Let's now start by taking a look at what we covered in the preceding code snippet:

1. In the `TakePictureButton_Clicked` instance method, we begin by creating a `Task.Run()` and call the `CheckCameraAlbumPermissions` instance method, which, when it completes, will return a `True` or `False` value.

2. Next, if everything is okay, we proceed to display the camera; otherwise, we display an alert dialog informing the user that permissions have been denied using the camera, and then we proceed to launch the device settings app, so the user can manually provide access to the camera.

3. Then, in the `ChooseFromGalleryButton_Clicked` instance method, we again start by creating `Task.Run()` and calling the `CheckCameraAlbumPermissions` instance method, which, when it completes, will return a `True` or `False` value.

4. Next, if everything is okay, we proceed as normal and allow the user to choose a photo from the album; otherwise, we display an alert dialog informing the user that permissions have been denied to the photo album, and then we proceed to launch the settings app so the user can manually provide access to the photo album.

5. Then, in the `CheckCameraAlbumPermissions` instance method, we begin by declaring two variables, `deviceCameraStatus` and `deviceAlbumStatus`, and we use the `CheckPermissionsStatusAsync` method to check for permissions to our Camera and Storage.

6. Next, we check to see whether we have been granted permission to use the camera or photo album, and if we haven't, we use the `RequestPermissionsAsync` method and pass in two parameters to request access to our Camera and Storage. This will then return a `results` array containing the key-value binding, as well as a value of either Granted or Denied for our Camera and Photo Album. We check to see whether we have been granted access to use the Camera or Photo Album and return a `Boolean` result.

7. Finally, we create the `ShowMessageDialog` instance method that will be used to display an alert dialog using the `title` and `message` parameters for our alert dialog that will be displayed to the user.

Now that you have created the Custom Themes and Styles, and have created the necessary C# code and implemented the necessary instance methods, our next step is to compile, build, and run the `PhotoLibrary` app using the Android emulator.

Launching the Photo Library app using the Android emulator

In this section, we will take a look at how to compile and run our `PhotoLibrary`. You have the option of choosing to run your application using an actual device or choosing from a list of emulators available for an Android device.

Let's begin by performing the following steps:

1. Ensure that you have chosen the `PhotoLibrary` project from the drop-down menu.
2. Next, choose your preferred device from the list of available Android emulators.
3. Then, select the **Run | Start Debugging** menu option, as shown in the following screenshot:

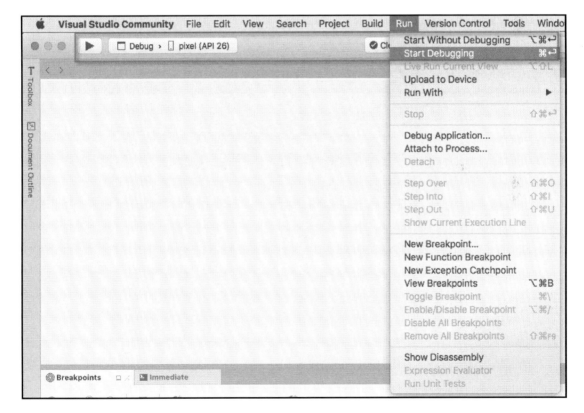

Launching the PhotoLibrary App within the Android Emulator

4. Alternatively, you can also build and run the `PhotoLibrary` application by pressing *Command + Enter*.

When the compilation is complete, the Android emulator will appear automatically and the **PhotoLibrary** application will be displayed, as shown in the following screenshot:

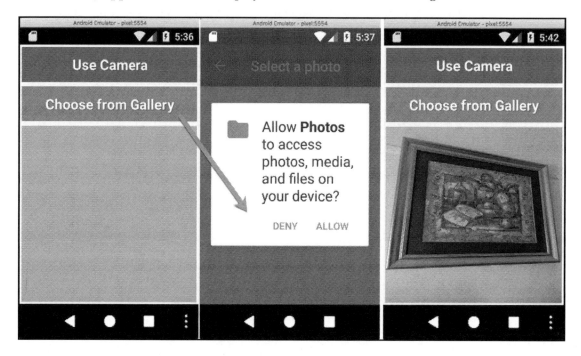

PhotoLibraryApp displayed within the Android Emulator

As you can see from the preceding screenshot, this currently displays our beautifully themed application, and when the **Choose from Gallery** button is clicked, we check to see whether we have previously allowed access to our PhotoLibrary by calling our `CheckCameraAlbumPermissions` instance method. Clicking on the **Allow** button will display the images that you can choose from, which, upon selection, will download and display the image in the `ImageView`. Alternatively, clicking on the **Use Camera** button will not work in the Android emulator, and you will need to run this on a physical device to avoid issues.

Summary

In this chapter, we focused primarily on how to develop a native Android app using Visual Studio for Mac, Xamarin.Android, and C#. You learned how to use and work with the **Visual** Designer in the Visual Studio for Mac IDE to construct the user interface for your PhotoLibrary app using XML and implement Material Design in your apps, as well as create your own custom themes and then apply theming to your app.

Finally, you learned how to provide the necessary permissions to `AndroidManifest.xml` so that we can interact with the device camera and photo album, before launching the app in the Android emulator. In the next chapter, you will learn how to build a tile sliding game using Xamarin.iOS and C#.

3
Building a SlidingTiles Game Using Xamarin.iOS

In the previous chapter, we learned how to develop a native Android app using Visual Studio for Mac, Xamarin.Android, and C#. You learned how to use and work with the Visual Designer in the Visual Studio for Mac IDE to construct the user interface for our **PhotoLibrary** app using XML, and implement Material Design in your apps, as well as create your own custom themes and then apply theming to your app.

Finally, we learned how to provide the necessary permissions to `AndroidManifest.xml` so that we could interact with the device camera and photo album before launching the app in the Android emulator.

This chapter will focus primarily on how to develop a native iOS app using Visual Studio for Mac, Xamarin.iOS, and C#. You'll learn how to use and work with Storyboards in the Visual Studio for Mac IDE to construct the user interface for our **SlidingTiles** game by dragging a number of `Labels`, `Views`, and `Buttons` that will make up our game. You'll work with Interfaces and Classes to create the `GameTile` Interface and Class that will be used to create each of the tiles for our game, and then implement the remaining logic in the `ViewController` class to build the game board and create each of our game tiles using images from an array.

You'll also create an instance method that will randomly shuffle each of our game tiles on our game board using the `Random` class and work with the `UITouch` class to handle touch events to determine when a game tile has been tapped in the game board's `UIView`.

To end this chapter, you'll learn how to work with **CoreAnimation** so that you can apply simple animations to your UIViews by using **View Transitions** in an animation block, before deploying and launching the app in the **iOS Simulator**.

This chapter will cover the following points:

- Creating a native app for the iOS platform using Visual Studio for Mac
- Constructing the user interface for the Sliding Tiles game using Storyboards
- Working with and handling touch events in the `UIView`
- Launching the Sliding Tiles game using the iOS Simulator

Creating a native iOS app using Visual Studio for Mac

In this section, we will take a look at how to create a native iOS solution for the first time. We will begin by developing the basic structure for our application, as well as designing the user interface for our Sliding Tiles game using Storyboards.

We will also learn how to create an Interface and Class for our `GameTile`, as well as implementing the various methods to create the `GameBoard`, and seeing how to shuffle game titles randomly in the `GameBoard`, and how to handle touch events in the `GameBoard` UI. Finally, we will learn how to work with and implement animations in our GameBoard UI for our SlidingTiles game, before launching our game in the iOS Simulator.

Before we can proceed, we need to create our SlidingTiles project. It is very simple to create this using Visual Studio for Mac. Simply follow the steps listed here:

1. Firstly, launch the Visual Studio for Mac application.
2. Next, choose the **New Solution...** option, or alternatively choose the **File | New | Solution...**, or simply press *Shift + command + N*.
3. Then, choose the **Single View App** option, which is located in the **iOS | App** section, and ensure that you have selected **C#** as the programming language to use:

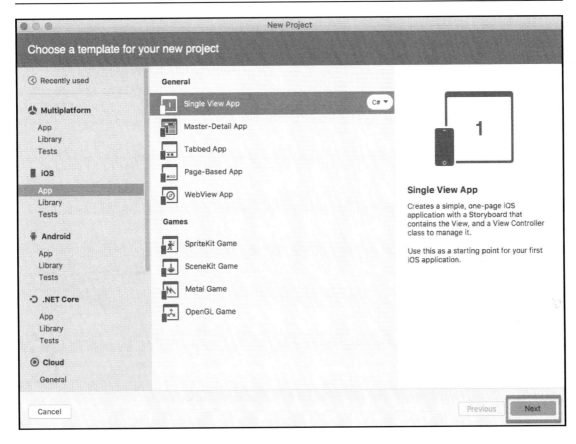

Creating a new Single View App

4. Next, enter **SlidingTiles** to use as the name for your app in the **App Name** field, and then specify a name for the **Organization Identifier** field.

5. Then, ensure that the **iPad** and **iPhone** options have been selected for the **Devices** field.

6. Next, ensure that you have selected **iOS 11.3** as the **minimum iOS version that you want to support** for the **Target** field, as shown in the following screenshot:

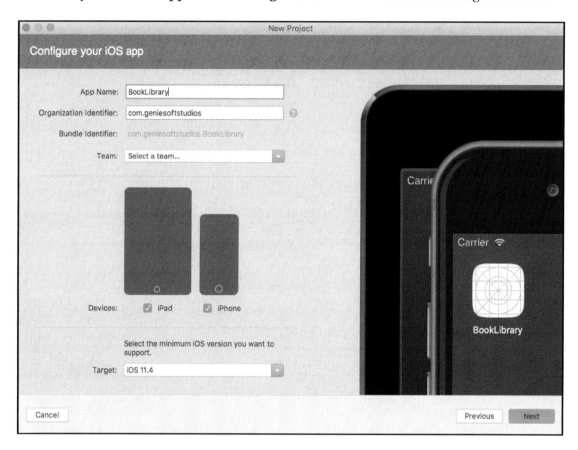

Configuring your iOS app

 The **Organization Identifier** option for your app needs to be unique. Xamarin recommends that you use the reverse domain style (for example, `com.domainName.appName`).

7. Then, click on the **Next** button to proceed to the next step in the wizard:

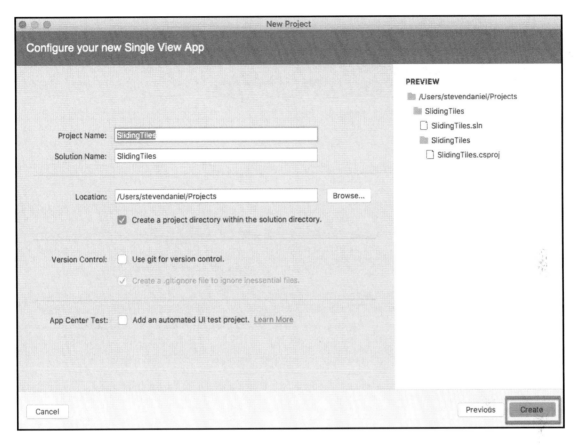

Configuring your new Single View App

8. Next, ensure that the **Create a project directory in the solution directory** checkbox has been selected.
9. Then, click on the **Create** button to save your project to the specified location.

Once your project has been created, you will be presented with the **Visual Studio for Mac Community** development environment containing the project files that the wizard created for you:

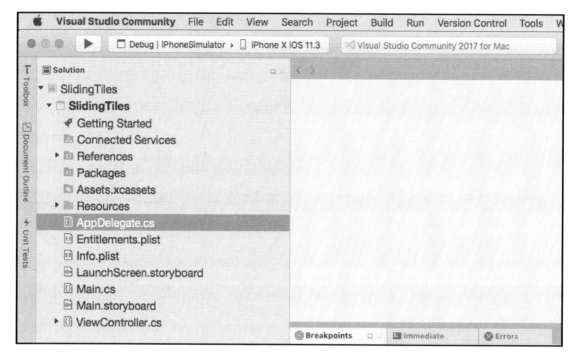

Structure of the SlidingTiles solution

The following table shows a number of important files that are contained in the **SlidingTiles** solution, as well as a brief description of what each file is used for:

Name	Description
Connected Services	This folder allows you to bring the Azure portal workflow into Visual Studio for Mac, so you don't have to leave your project to add services.
References	This folder contains references to .NET assemblies and any other assemblies that you create, which you can reference throughout your solution.
Packages	This folder allows you to add NuGet package libraries to your solution.
Assets.xcassets	This folder allows you to manage and group all versions of your image assets that are required by your application.

AppDelegate.cs	`AppDelegate` is basically an object that receives notifications whenever the `UIApplication` object reaches a certain state and is responsible for handling special `UIApplication` states.
Resources	This folder allows you to add additional images, fonts, PDFs, and so on that will be used by your solution.
Entitlements.plist	iOS apps run in a sandbox, which provides a set of rules that limit access between your application and certain system resources and user data. `Entitlements.plist` allows you to provide additional application capabilities and security permissions so that the system can expand the application sandbox, which will give your application additional capabilities.
Info.plist	The `Info.plist` file is essentially a structured text file that contains configuration information for a bundled executable.
Main.Storyboard	This file contains a visual representation of all the screens that make up your application. It contains a sequence of scenes, with each scene representing View, along with any User Interface Control elements and their associated View Controller.

Now that we have created our **SlidingTiles** iOS application and have a good understanding of the various folders and files that are contained in our solution, our next step is to create the user interface for our **SlidingTiles** application using Storyboards in the iOS Visual Designer in the Visual Studio for Mac IDE, which we will cover in the next section.

Creating the SlidingTiles user interface using Storyboards

In this section, we will begin by constructing the user interface for our **SlidingTiles** application using Storyboards and the Visual Designer for iOS that is included as part of the Visual Studio for Mac IDE.

You will notice that our **Main.storyboard** already contains a View Controller, which we will be adding UI control elements to, such as a Label, a View, and two Buttons that will be used to reset the current game in progress, as well as randomly shuffling each of the tiles on our game board.

Let's start by opening the Storyboard for our **SlidingTiles** application and performing the following steps:

1. Firstly, locate the **Main.storyboard** that is contained in the **SlidingTiles** solution.
2. Next, double-click on the **Main.storyboard** file to display our Storyboard Canvas, as shown in the following screenshot:

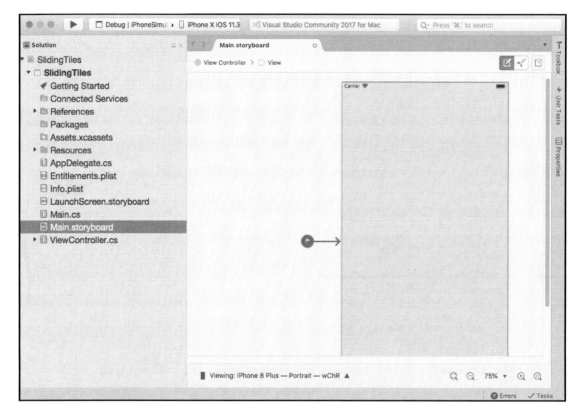

Creating the SlidingTiles User Interface within the Storyboard

As you can see from the screenshot, our **ViewController** is pretty much bare and doesn't contain anything exciting at this stage. As we progress through this section, we will be adding various UI components that will make up our game. Our next step is to add a **Label** control to our **ViewController**, which will act as the title for our game.

Adding a label to our ViewController in the Storyboard

In this section, we will take a look at how we can use labels to display informative text to the user. The **Label** object is one of the ways in which we can let users know what is happening.

This can be as simple as displaying static text to the user, or to let the user know that we are requesting for the user to enter their username or password. Alternatively, we can use the **Label** control to inform them whenever something has gone terribly wrong.

Let's start by ensuring that our **Toolbox** window is currently open and performing the following steps:

1. Ensure the **SlidingTiles** solution is currently open in the Visual Studio for Mac IDE.
2. Next, select the **View | Pads | Toolbox** menu option, as shown in the following screenshot:

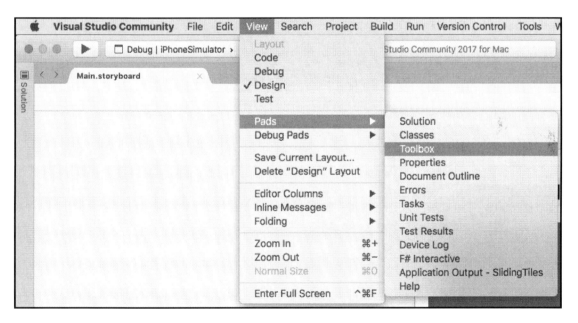

Displaying the Toolbox Pane

As you can see from the preceding screenshot, this will bring up the **Toolbox** window, which will allow you to choose from a number of controls and View Controllers that you can drag to your Storyboard to construct your user interface. There is even a search field, which you can use to search for the item you want to use, rather than scrolling through the list.

3. Then, from the **Toolbox Library**, drag a **Label** control onto the **View Controller**.
4. Next, resize the **Label** control so that it fills the width of the **View Controller**:

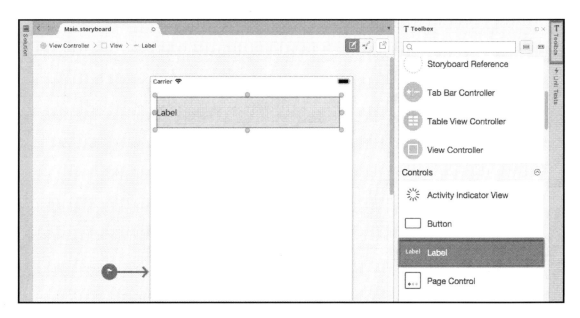

Dragging a Label Control to the ViewController

5. Then, select the **Label** control in the **View Controller** to bring up the **Properties** window and ensure that the **Widget** tab has been selected, as shown in the following screenshot:

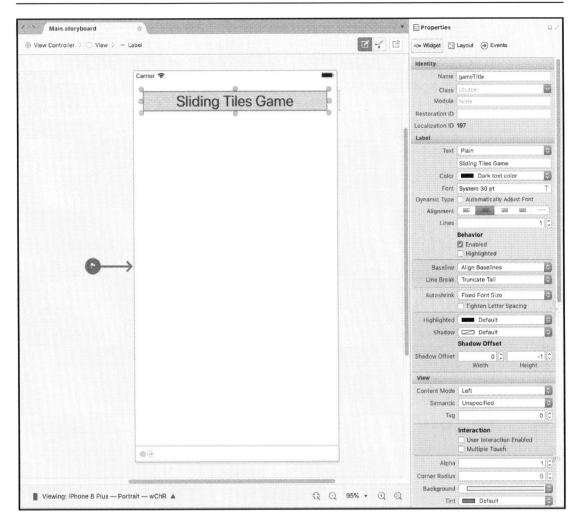

Properties window for the Label Control

You can display the **Properties** window by selecting the
View|Pads|Properties menu option, as you did previously to display the
Toolbox window.

6. Next, modify the **Name** property, which is located in the **Identity** section, to read
   gameTitle.
7. Then, from the **Properties** window, modify the **Label Text** property, which is
   located in the **Label** section, to read **Sliding Tiles Game**.

8. Next, modify the **Font** property to be **System 30 pt**.

9. Then, set the **Alignment** property to be **Center** and the **Background** property to be **Yellow**.

10. Next, select the **Label** control in the **View Controller** to bring up the **Properties** window and select the **Layout** tab, as shown in the following screenshot:

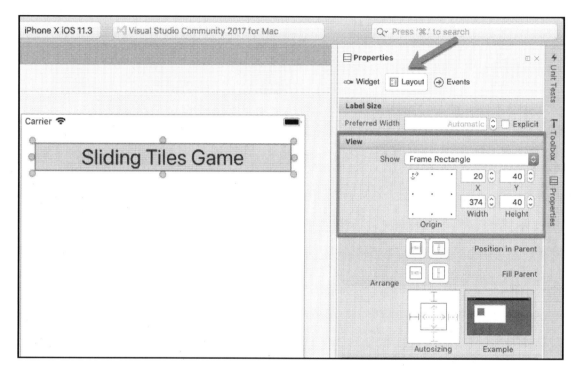

Layout Section of the Properties window

11. Then, modify the **X** property to read **20** and the **Y** property to read **40**, which are located in the **View** section.

12. Next, modify the **Width** property to read **374** and the **Height** property to read **40**, which are located in the **View** section.

At this point, all we have done is add a **Label** control, but it is good to save our **Storyboard** by selecting **File | Save** from the menu bar or alternatively by pressing *command + S*. Our next step is to add a **View** control to our **View Controller**, which will act as the GameBoard for our game.

Adding a View to our View Controller in the Storyboard

In this section, we will take a look at how we can use **Views** to act as a means of defining places where we need to present content differently than standard views allow. The advantage of creating custom views is that they allow you to handle interactions with any object that is added to that interface, which you can use to animate things quite easily.

Let's start adding a **View** object to our **View Controller** by performing the following steps:

1. Ensure the **SlidingTiles** solution is currently open in the **Visual Studio for Mac IDE.**
2. Then, from the **Toolbox** Library, drag a **View** control onto the **View Controller**.
3. Next, resize the **View** control so that it fills the width of the **View Controller** and matches the width of the **Label** control that we added previously:

Adding a View within the View Controller

4. Then, select the **View** control in the **View Controller** to bring up the **Properties** window and ensure that the **Widget** tab has been selected, as shown in the following screenshot:

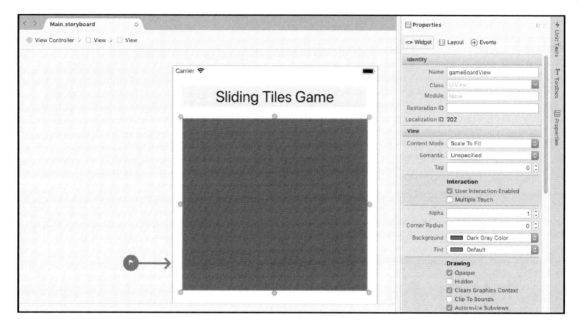

Modifying the properties for the View control

5. Next, from the **Properties** window, modify the **Name** property, which is located in the **Identity** section, to read **gameBoardView**.
6. Then, set the **Content Mode** property to be **Scale To Fill**, and set the **Background** property to be **Dark Gray Color**.
7. Next, select the **View** control in the **View Controller** to bring up the **Properties** window and select the **Layout** tab, as shown in the following screenshot:

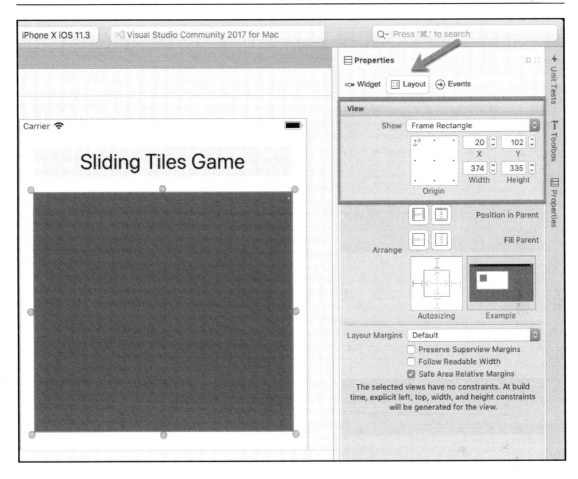

Updating Layout properties for the View control

8. Then, modify the X property to read 20 and the Y property to read 102, which are located in the View section.
9. Next, modify the Width property to read 374 and the Height property to read 335, which are located in the View section.

Excellent, the user interface for our Sliding Tiles game is coming along quite nicely; we have added a **Label** control as well as a **View** control. Before we proceed with adding the remaining controls to our **View Controller** in our Storyboard, it would be good to save our Storyboard. Our next step is to add a **Button** control to our **View Controller**, which will reset the game in progress.

Adding a reset button to our View Controller in the Storyboard

In this section, we will take a look at how we can use **Buttons** to respond to user actions when they are tapped on in the **View Controller**. Buttons contain numerous properties that can be set, as well as things called **Control Events** and **Target/Action Events**.

Control Events are executed and respond to actions whenever they are tapped. An example would be when you want to change the color of a button when it has been tapped or play some sound. On the other hand, Target/Action Events calls the underlying instance method to perform the action that is associated with that button where the code resides.

Let's start by adding a **Button** object to our **View Controller**, performing the following steps:

1. Ensure the **SlidingTiles** solution is currently open in the **Visual Studio for Mac IDE.**
2. Then, from the **Toolbox** library, drag a **Button** control onto the **View Controller**.
3. Next, resize the **Button** control so that it fills the width of the **View Controller** and matches the **Width** of the **View** control that we added previously:

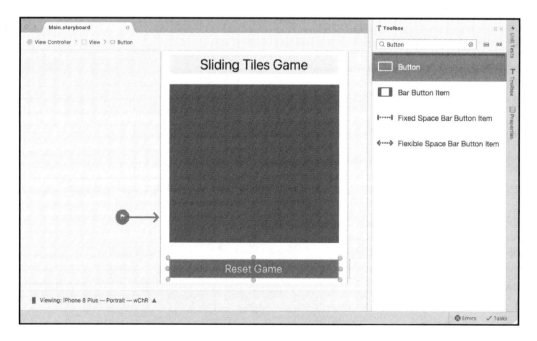

Adding the Reset Game button to the View Controller

4. Then, select the **Button** control in the **View Controller** to bring up the **Properties** window and ensure that the **Widget** tab has been selected, as shown in the following screenshot:

Modifying the Reset Game button properties

5. Next, from the **Properties** window, modify the **Name** property, which is located in the **Identity** section, to read **resetGameButton** and ensure that the **Type** property, which is located in the **Button** section, reads **System**.

6. Then, modify the **Label Text** property for the **Title** field, which is located in the **Button** section, to read **Reset Game**.

7. Next, modify the **Font** property to be **System 24 pt.** and set the **Text Color** property to be **White Color**, and ensure that you set the **Background** property to be **Red**.

Now that we have set up the properties for our **Button** control, we need to modify the **Layout** properties for our **Reset Game** button:

8. Select the **Button** control in the **View Controller** to bring up the **Properties** window and select the **Layout** tab, as shown in the following screenshot:

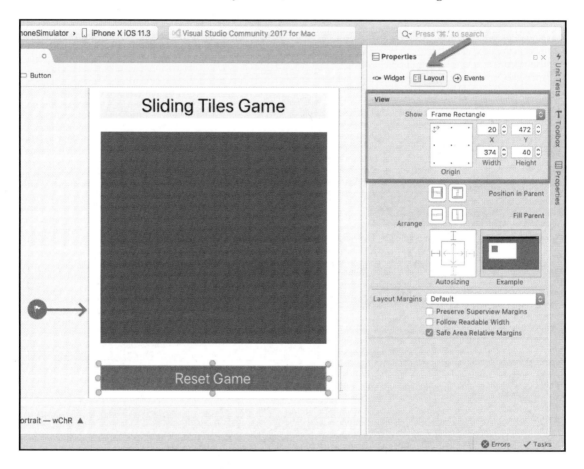

Modifying Layout properties for the Reset Game button

9. Next, modify the **X** property to read **20** and the **Y** property to read **472**, which are located in the **View** section.

10. Next, modify the **Width** property to read **374** and the **Height** property to read **40**, which are located in the **View** section.

Up to now, we have specified properties for our **Button** control to change the appearance, positioning, and size of the control. Our next step is to set up events for our **Button** control so that it can respond to actions whenever the button has been pressed, which we will cover next.

11. Select the **Button** control in the **View Controller** to bring up the **Properties** window and select the **Events** tab, as shown in the following screenshot:

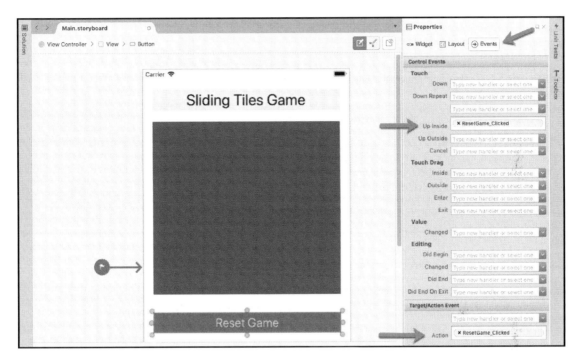

Assigning an Event Action to the Reset Game button

12. Next, modify the **Up Inside** property of the button to read **ResetGame_Clicked**, which is located in the **Touch** section of the **Control Events** pane.

13. Then, modify the **Action** property of the button to read **ResetGame_Clicked**, which is located in the **Target/Action Event** pane.

Now, we have added our **Button** control to our **Storyboard** and have specified the **Control Events** and **Target/Action Event** properties for our control, which will respond whenever the user taps on this button. As we progress through this chapter, we will be implementing the code for the **ResetGame_Clicked** instance method. Our next step is to add one more **Button** control to our **View Controller**, which will complete our user interface for our **Sliding Tiles Game** and will be responsible for shuffling each of our tiles on the game board.

Adding the Shuffle Button to our View Controller in the Storyboard

In this section, we will take a look at how we can add our final button to our **View Controller** in our **Storyboard**, which will complete the construction of our user interface for our **Sliding Tiles Game**. We will also be modifying properties for this control, applying **Layout** attributes, and specifying **Control Events** and **Target/Action Events**.

Let's start by adding a **Button** object to our **View Controller**, performing the following steps:

1. Ensure the **SlidingTiles** solution is currently open in the **Visual Studio for Mac IDE.**
2. Then, from the **Toolbox** Library, drag a **Button** control onto the **View Controller**.
3. Next, resize the **Button** control so that it fills the width of the **View Controller** and matches the **Width** of the **View** control that we added previously.
4. Then, select the **Button** control in the **View Controller** to bring up the **Properties** window and ensure that the **Widget** tab has been selected, as shown in the following screenshot:

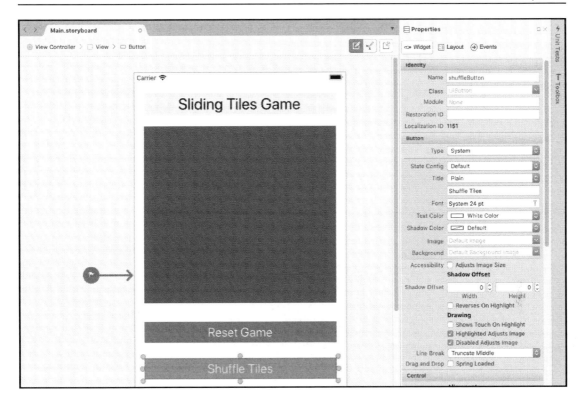

Adding the Shuffle Tiles button to our View Controller

5. Next, from the **Properties** window, modify the **Name** property, which is located in the **Identity** section, to read **shuffleButton** and ensure that the **Type** property, which is located in the **Button** section, reads **System**.

6. Then, modify the **Label Text** property for the **Title** field, which is located in the **Button** section, to read **Shuffle Tiles**.

7. Next, modify the **Font** property to be **System 24 pt.**, set the **Text Color** property to be **White Color**, and ensure that you set the **Background** property to be **Orange**.

Now that we have set up the properties for our **Button** control, we need to modify the **Layout** properties for our **Shuffle Tiles** button and adjust the layout properties for our button.

8. Select the **Button** control in the **View Controller** to bring up the **Properties** window and select the **Layout** tab, as shown in the following screenshot:

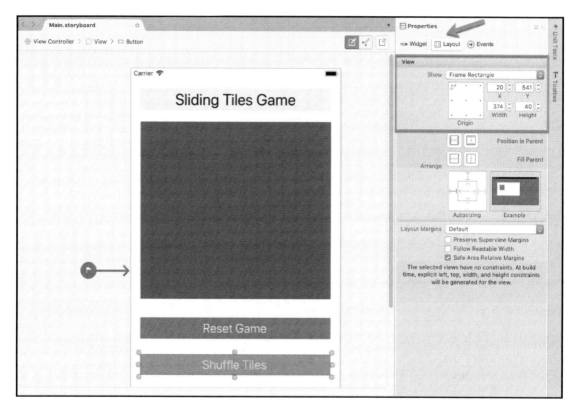

Modifying Layout properties for the Shuffle Tiles button

9. Next, modify the **X** property to read **20** and the **Y** property to read **541**, both of which are located in the **View** section.

10. Next, modify the **Width** property to read **374** and the **Height** property to read **40**, which are located in the **View** section.

Up to now, we have specified properties for our **Button** control to change the appearance and the positioning and size of the control. Our next step is to set up events for our **Button** control so that it can respond to actions whenever the button has been pressed, which we will cover next.

11. Select the **Button** control in the **View Controller** to bring up the **Properties** window and select the **Events** tab, as shown in the following screenshot:

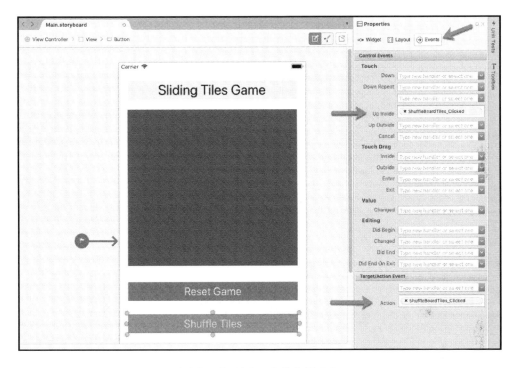

Assigning an Event Action to the Shuffle Tiles button

12. Next, modify the **Up Inside** property of the button to read **ShuffleBoardTiles_Clicked**, which is located in the **Touch** section of the **Control Events** pane.
13. Then, modify the **Action** property of the button to read **ShuffleBoardTiles_Clicked**, which is located in the **Target/Action Event** pane.

We have finally added our final **Button** control to our **Storyboard**, as well as specifying the **Control Events** and **Target/Action Event** properties that will respond whenever the user taps on this button. As we progress through this chapter, we will be implementing the code for the `ShuffleBoardTiles_Clicked` instance method.

Adding the GameTile image to our SlidingTiles game

In this section, we will take a look at how we can add the image that will be used for our Game Tiles, which will be displayed in the GameBoard.

Before we can proceed, we need to add the GameTile image to our **SlidingTiles** project by performing the following steps:

1. Ensure the **SlidingTiles** solution is currently open in the **Visual Studio for Mac IDE.**
2. Then, **unzip** the **Assets.zip** file that comes as part of the accompanying code bundle.
3. Next, double-click on the **Assets** folder to display the folder's contents.
4. Then, drag the `game_tile.png` image from the `Assets` folder to the `Resources` folder contained in the **SlidingTiles** project, as shown in the following screenshot:

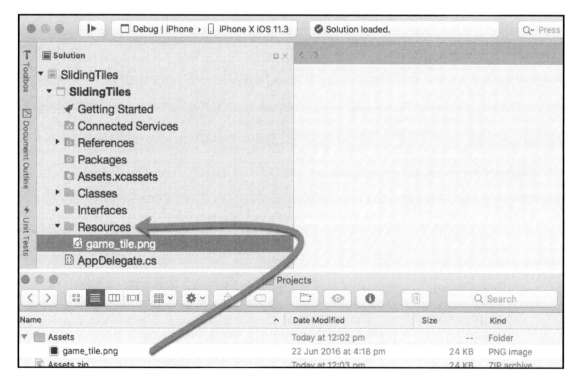

Adding the Game Tile image to the Resources folder

If you want to use your own game tile images, you will need to ensure that the image dimensions are **141 x 141** for the width and height; otherwise, you will experience issues when the tiles are placed on the GameBoard.

Now that we have added the game tile image to our **SlidingTiles** project solution, we can start to implement the game logic for our Sliding Tiles game.

Implementing the game logic for our SlidingTiles Game

In this section, we will start by creating and implementing the logic needed to complete our **SlidingTiles** game. We will start by creating and implementing a `GameTile` Interface and Class, which will be used to create and store each of our GameTiles.

We will then move on to implementing the required code, as well as the necessary instance method implementations that will make up and complete our game.

Creating and implementing the GameTile Interface class

As explained in the introduction to this section, we will start by creating the `GameTile` interface class for our SlidingTiles game, which will be used to create instances of each game tile that will be displayed in the `gameboard` View control we added to our ViewController contained in our Storyboard.

Let's start by creating the `IGameTile` interface for our **SlidingTiles** app by performing the following steps:

1. Ensure that the **SlidingTiles** solution is open in the Visual Studio for Mac IDE.

2. Next, right-click on the **SlidingTiles** project and choose **Add|New Folder** from the pop up menu, as shown in the following screenshot:

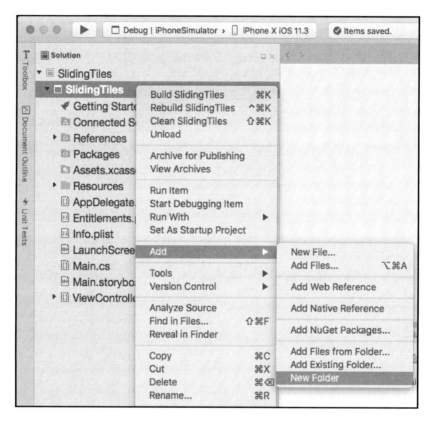

Creating a new Folder within the SlidingTiles solution

3. Then, enter **Interfaces** for the name of the new folder to be created, then right-click on the **Interfaces** folder and choose **Add|New File...** from the pop up menu, as shown in the following screenshot:

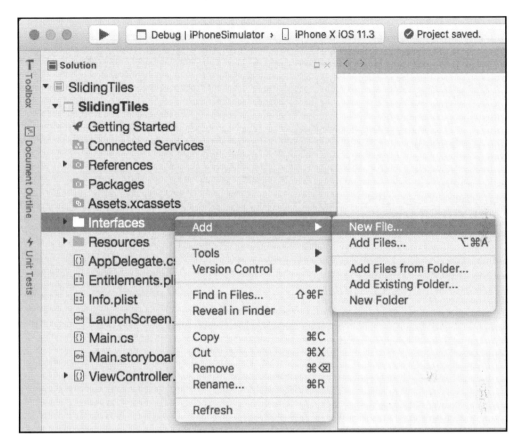

Creating a new Empty Interface within the Interfaces folder

4. Next, choose the **Empty Interface** option under the **General** section and enter
   IGameTile for the name of the new **Interface** file to be created, as shown in the
   following screenshot:

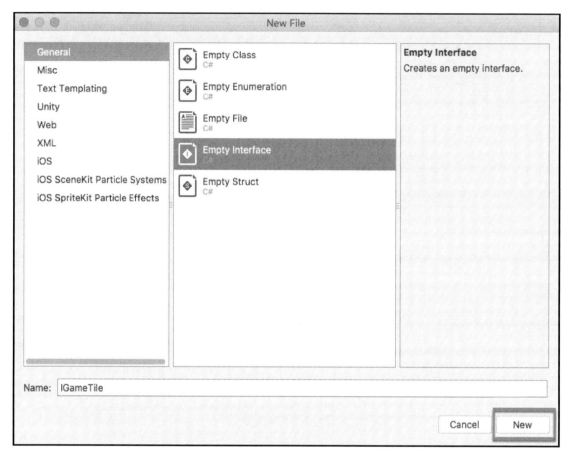

Creating the IGameTile Interface

5. Next, click on the **New** button to allow the wizard to proceed and create the new
   file, as shown in the preceding screenshot. Now that we have created our
   IGameTile interface file, we can proceed with implementing the required code
   for our Interface class.

6. Locate and open the `IGameTile.cs` file, which is located as part of the
   SlidingTiles group, ensure that it is displayed in the code editor, and enter the
   following code snippet:

```
//
// IGameTile.cs
// Interface class for the GameTile class
//
// Created by Steven F. Daniel on 24/04/2018.
// Copyright © 2018 GENIESOFT STUDIOS. All rights reserved.
//
using UIKit;

namespace SlidingTiles.Interfaces
{
    public interface IGameTile
    {
        UIImage DrawTileText(UIImage uiImage, string sText,
                             UIColor textColor, int iFontSize);
    }
}
```

Let's take a look at what we covered in the preceding code snippet:

1. First, we started by including a reference to the `UIKit` namespace that will be
   used to allow us to access iOS-specific user interface components, such as
   `UIButton`, `UIView`, `UIImageView`, and so on
2. Next, we declared an instance method called `DrawTileText`, which contains a
   number of parameters that will be used to draw text onto a specified image
3. Then, we declared a `uiImage` parameter that is the image that we want to use
4. Next, we declared an `sText` parameter that will be the text we want to place in
   the image

Creating and implementing the GameTile class

Now that we have created our `GameTile` Interface class, our next step is to proceed with
creating the `GameTile` class and then implement the underlying code for our
`DrawTileText` instance method.

Let's start by creating the `GameTile` class for our **SlidingTiles** app, performing the following steps:

1. Right-click on the **SlidingTiles** project and create a new folder called **Classes** by choosing **Add | New Folder** from the pop up menu, like you did in the previous section.

2. Next, right-click on the **Classes** folder and choose **Add | New File...** from the pop up menu, as shown in the following screenshot:

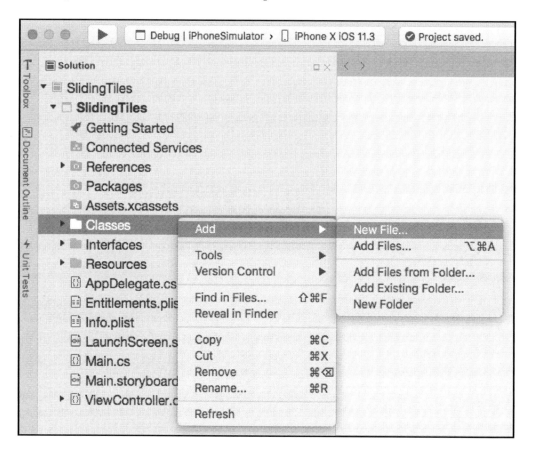

Creating a new Empty Class within the Classes folder

3. Next, choose the **Empty Class** option under the **General** section and enter **GameTile** for the name of the new **Class** file to be created, as shown in the following screenshot:

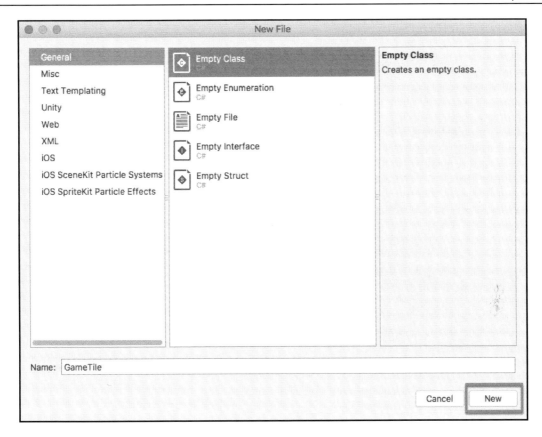

Creating the GameTile Class

4. Next, click on the **New** button to allow the wizard to proceed and create the new file, as shown in the preceding screenshot. Now that we have created our **GameTile** Class file, we can proceed with implementing the required code for our class.

5. Locate and open the `GameTile.cs` file, which is part of the **SlidingTiles** group, ensure that it is displayed in the code editor, and enter the following code snippet:

```
//
//  GameTile.cs
//  Creates each of our tile images for our Tile Slider Game.
//
//  Created by Steven F. Daniel on 24/04/2018.
//  Copyright © 2018 GENIESOFT STUDIOS. All rights reserved.
//
using UIKit;
```

```
using SlidingTiles.Interfaces;
using CoreGraphics;
using System;

namespace SlidingTiles.Classes
{
```

6. Next, underneath `namespace`, we need to ensure that our `GameTile` class inherits from the `UIImageView` class, as well as our `IGameTile` interface, by updating the class declaration:

```
public class GameTile : UIImageView, IGameTile
{
```

7. Then, underneath the `GameTile` class declaration, we need to create two `GameTile` class constructors; one that accepts no parameters, and an other that accepts `Row` and `Col`, as well as defining two `integer` properties for our `Row` and `Col` that will be used by our class:

```
// GameTile Class Constructor
public GameTile()
{
}

// Overload GameTile Class Constructor
public GameTile(int row, int col)
{
    this.Row = row;
    this.Col = col;
}

// Define the properties that will be used by our class
public int Row { private set; get; }
public int Col { private set; get; }
```

8. Next, we need to create the `DrawTileText` instance method that will be used to draw text onto the supplied image, which is passed in to the instance method declaration:

```
// Instance method to draw our tile with additional text
public UIImage DrawTileText(UIImage uiImage, string sText,
                            UIColor textColor, int iFontSize)
{
    nfloat fWidth = uiImage.Size.Width;
    nfloat fHeight = uiImage.Size.Height;
    CGColorSpace colorSpace = CGColorSpace.CreateDeviceRGB();
    using (CGBitmapContext ctx = new CGBitmapContext(IntPtr.Zero,
```

```
                                    (nint)fWidth,
                                    (nint)fHeight, 8, 4 * (nint)fWidth,
                                    CGColorSpace.CreateDeviceRGB(),
CGImageAlphaInfo.PremultipliedFirst))
            {
                ctx.DrawImage(new CGRect(0, 0,
(double)fWidth,(double)fHeight), uiImage.CGImage);
                ctx.SelectFont("HelveticaNeue-Bold", iFontSize,
CGTextEncoding.MacRoman);

                // Measure the text's width - This involves drawing an
                // invisible string to calculate the X position difference
                float start, end, textWidth;

                // Get the texts current position
                start = (float)ctx.TextPosition.X;

                // Set the drawing mode to invisible
                ctx.SetTextDrawingMode(CGTextDrawingMode.Invisible);

                // Draw the text at the current position
                ctx.ShowText(sText);

                // Get the end position
                end = (float)ctx.TextPosition.X;

                // Subtract start from end to get the text's width
                textWidth = end - start;
                nfloat fRed, fGreen, fBlue, fAlpha;

                // Set the fill color to black. This is the text color.
                textColor.GetRGBA(out fRed, out fGreen, out fBlue, out
fAlpha);
                ctx.SetFillColor(fRed, fGreen, fBlue, fAlpha);

                // Set the drawing mode back to something that will actually
draw
                // Fill for example
                ctx.SetTextDrawingMode(CGTextDrawingMode.Fill);

                // Draw the text at given coords.
                ctx.ShowTextAtPoint(50, 50, sText);
                return UIImage.FromImage(ctx.ToImage());
            }
        }
    }
    }
```

Let's take a look at what we covered in the preceding code snippet:

1. First, we started by including a reference to the `UIKit` namespace that will be used to allow us to access **iOS**-specific user interface components, such as `UIButton`, `UIView`, `UIImageView`, and so on.

2. Next, we included a reference to our `SlidingTiles.Interface` namespace so that our `GameTile` class can inherit the instance methods contained in the interface.

3. Then, we included references to both the `CoreGraphics` and `System` namespaces, so that we have access to graphics capabilities for image manipulation. We then modified the `GameTile` class declaration to inherit from both the `UIImageView` and `IGameTile` interfaces. It will become clear why we need to inherit from `UIImageView` as we progress through this chapter.

4. Next, we defined two **Class Constructors** for our `GameTile` class, one where we instantiate our class without parameters, and one where we need to pass in the `row` and `column` for each tile that will be placed in the `GameBoard` **View** control.

5. Then, we declared a `CGColorSpace colorSpace` variable that creates and returns a device-dependent RGB color space, and we created a `CGBitmapContext ctx` variable that creates an in-memory bitmap.

6. Next, we use the `DrawImage` method of the `CGBitmapContext` class to create our image in memory and draw the text on the image using the `HelveticaNeue-Bold` font, with the font size that we passed into our `DrawTileText` instance method.

7. Then, we measured the width of the text that we wanted to place in the image, calculated the starting position of the text, and set the drawing mode to invisible by using the `CGTextDrawingMode.Invisible` property. We then called the `ShowText` method of `CGBitmapContext` to draw the text at the current position.

8. Next, we calculated the ending position of the text that we wanted to place in the image, and then calculated the width of the text by subtracting the starting and ending positions for the text's width.

9. Then, we set the fill color to black and set the drawing mode to Fill using the `CGTextDrawingMode` class, before drawing the text at the given coordinates and returning the modified image using the `FromImage` method of the `UIImage` class.

For more information on the CGBitmapContext and CGColorSpace classes, as well as the various types of different class available, refer to the Xamarin Developer documentation at https://developer.xamarin.com/api/type/CoreGraphics.CGBitmapContext/.

Updating the ViewController class to implement our class methods

In this section, we will look at updating our ViewController class and start to implement each of the class methods that will make up our Sliding Tiles game. If you remember, the **ViewController** class is essentially a C# class file that is bound to our View Controller contained in our **Main.storyboard** file, which we saw when we were designing the user interface for our game.

As you start to build your own projects, your **Storyboard** will essentially contain more than one **View Controller**, and each **View Controller** will have its own associated **ViewController** class, as well as the instance methods that make up the class.

Let's start by modifying the **ViewController** class for our **SlidingTiles** app, performing the following steps:

1. Locate and open the ViewController.cs file, which is located as part of the **SlidingTiles** group, ensure that it is displayed in the code editor, and enter the following code snippet:

```
//
//  ViewController.cs
//  Main game logic for the Letter Tiles Sliding game
//
//  Created by Steven F. Daniel on 24/04/2018.
//  Copyright © 2018 GENIESOFT STUDIOS. All rights reserved.
//
using System;
using System.Collections.Generic;
using CoreGraphics;
using Foundation;
using SlidingTiles.Classes;
using UIKit;

namespace SlidingTiles
{
    public partial class ViewController : UIViewController
    {
```

2. Next, we need to declare each of the game variables that will be used by our game; we use the #region and #endregion tags to ensure that all variable declarations are contained in these tags:

```
#region 1 - Declare our game variables for our game
float gameViewWidth;
float gameViewHeight;
float tileWidth;
float tileHeight;

// Declare size of each of our grid cells
int gridCellSize = 5;

// Declare and set up our tiles array
GameTile[,] tiles = new GameTile[5, 5];

// Declare an array for our game tile images and game tile indexes
List<UIImageView> gameTileImagesArray = new List<UIImageView>();
List<CGPoint> GameTileCoords = new List<CGPoint>();
// Declare our empty tile position
CGPoint emptyTilePos;
#endregion

protected ViewController(IntPtr handle) : base(handle)
{
    // Note: this .ctor should not contain any initialization logic.
}

public override void ViewDidLoad()
{
    base.ViewDidLoad();
    // Perform any additional setup after loading the view, typically
from a nib.
}
```

3. Next, we need to update the ViewDidAppear method, which will be called whenever our view appears onscreen; enter the following code snippet:

```
#region 2 - Layout our Game Board
public override void ViewDidAppear(bool animated)
{
    base.ViewDidAppear(animated);

    // Obtain the Width and Height for our GameBoard
    gameViewWidth = (float)gameBoardView.Frame.Size.Width;
    gameViewHeight = (float)gameBoardView.Frame.Size.height;
```

```
      // call our method to start a new game
      startNewGame();
  }
  #endregion
```

Let's take a look at what we covered in the preceding code snippets:

1. First, we started by including various references to the `System`, `CoreGraphics`, `Foundation`, `SlidingTiles.Classes`, and `UIKit` namespaces, which will allow us to access .NET-specific and iOS-specific methods and so on.

2. Next, we declared the game variables that will be used by our **SlidingTiles** game. We declared variables for our game board view and tile widths, as well as declaring the size that each of our game board tiles will be.

3. Then, we declared and set up our tiles array using our `GameTile` class, defined our tiles to be 5 x 5 (Rows, Columns), and then declared two arrays that will store our game tile images, as well as the index positions of each tile that is placed on the game board.

4. Next, we declared an empty tile position variable, which will place an empty tile on the game board.

5. Then, we modified the `ViewDidAppear` method to ensure that our game board view has been displayed correctly in the GameBoard `View`.

6. Next, we assigned the width and height of the `gameBoardView` to our `gameViewWidth` and `gameViewHeight`, and then called our `startNewGame` instance method, which we will be creating as we progress through this section.

 For more information on the `UIImageView` class, as well as the various types of different class available, refer to the Xamarin Developer documentation at `https://developer.xamarin.com/api/type/UIKit.UIImageView/`.

Creating and implementing the CreateGameBoard method

In this section, we will look at implementing the `CreateGameBoard` instance method in our `ViewController` class. The `CreateGameBoard` instance method will be responsible for creating our game board and placing each of the tiles in our GameBoard View, using the `GameTile` class that we created previously.

Let's start by modifying the ViewController class for our **SlidingTiles** app by performing the following steps:

1. Ensure that the ViewController.cs file is currently displayed in the code editor.

2. Next, underneath the ViewDidAppear method, we need to create a new instance method called CreateGameBoard that will be called whenever our view appears onscreen; enter the following code snippet:

```
#region 3 - Instance method to create our Game Board and Game Tiles
public void CreateGameBoard()
{
    // Specify the Width and Heights for each of our Tiles
    tileWidth = this.gameViewWidth / this.gridCellSize;
    tileHeight = this.gameViewHeight / this.gridCellSize;

    // Specify our tile width and tile centre values
    float tileCenterX = tileWidth / 2;
    float tileCenterY = tileHeight / 2;
    // Initialise our tile counter value
    int counter = 65;

    // Build our game board with images from our array
    for (int row = 0; row < this.gridCellSize; row++)
    {
        for (int column = 0; column < this.gridCellSize; column++)
        {
            // Create a new tile by instantiating a new instance of our
            // GameTile class
            GameTile tile = new GameTile(row, column);
            tile.Frame = new CGRect(0, 0, tileWidth, tileHeight);
            tile.Image =
tile.DrawTileText(UIImage.FromFile("game_tile.png"),
                Convert.ToChar(counter).ToString(), UIColor.White, 65);

            tile.Center = new CGPoint(tileCenterX, tileCenterY);
            tile.UserInteractionEnabled = true;

            // Store our Tile Coordinates in our ArrayList object
            GameTileCoords.Add(new CGPoint(tileCenterX,
tileCenterY));

            // Add the tile to our Tile Images
            gameTileImagesArray.Add(tile);
            gameBoardView.AddSubview(tile);
```

```
                    // Increment to the next tile position and image in
array.
                    tileCenterX = tileCenterX + tileWidth;
                    counter = counter + 1;
                }
                tileCenterX = tileWidth / 2;
                tileCenterY = tileCenterY + tileHeight;
            }
            // Remove the last tile from the gameBoard and our
gameTileImagesArray
            var emptyTile = gameTileImagesArray[gameTileImagesArray.Count -
1];
            emptyTile.RemoveFromSuperview();
            gameTileImagesArray.RemoveAt(gameTileImagesArray.Count - 1);
        }
        #endregion
```

Let's take a look at what we covered in the preceding code snippet:

1. Firstly, in the `CreateGameBoard` instance method, we started by creating two floating point variables, `tileCenterX` and `tileCenterY`, which will be used to specify the width and height of each tile that is placed on the game board.

2. Next, we calculated the width of each tile, using the width of our `gameViewWidth` divided by the `gridCellSize`, which is the size of each tile.

3. Then, we initialized our tile counter value, which will start from the letter **A**.

4. Next, we created a loop to build our game board with images from our array, iterating from zero to the total number of tiles that we want to have in each row and column.

5. Then, we created a new tile instance by instantiating a new instance of our `GameTile` class, using the row and column and defining the frame width and height. We then set the image to use for our `GameTile` using the `DrawTileText` instance method. You will notice that we use the `Convert.ToChar` method to convert the value of our counter to a character, and then we set the text color and font size to use.

6. Next, we set the `Center` property to where we wanted to place the tile on our game board using the `CGPoint` method and passing in the `tileCenterX` and `tileCenterY` values, as well as setting the `UserInteractionEnabled` property to `true`, which will allow the user to tap on the tile in the game board.

7. Then, we stored the tile coordinates in our `GameTileCoords List` object and added this tile to our `gameTileImagesArray`, as well as our `gameBoardView`, using the `AddSubview` method.

8. Next, we removed the last tile from our game board using the
`RemoveFromSuperview` method, and removed the tile from our
`gameTileImagesArray` so that we have an empty spot on our game board and
we can shift tiles around.

For more information on the `AddSubView` and `CGPoint` classes, as well as
the various types of different class available, refer to the Xamarin
Developer documentation at `https://developer.xamarin.com/api/type/`
`CoreGraphics.CGPoint/` and
`https://developer.xamarin.com/api/member/UIKit.UIView.`
`AddSubview/`.

Creating and implementing the ResetGame_Clicked method

In this section, we will look at implementing the `ResetGame_Clicked` instance method in
our `ViewController` class. The `ResetGame_Clicked` instance method will be responsible
for resetting the game in progress, which, if you remember when we were constructing our
user interface for our game, we created an event for with our **Reset Game** button.

Let's start by modifying the `ViewController` class for our **SlidingTiles** app by performing
the following steps:

1. Ensure that the `ViewController.cs` file is currently displayed in the code
   editor.
2. Next, underneath the `CreateGameBoard` instance method, we need to create an
   event method called `ResetGame_Clicked` that will be called whenever the user
   taps on this button; enter the following code snippet:

```
#region 4 - Instance method that will reset the current game in
progress
    partial void ResetGame_Clicked(UIButton sender)
    {
       // Set up our UIAlertController as well as the Action methods
       UIApplication.SharedApplication.InvokeOnMainThread(new Action(() =>
       {
          var alert = UIAlertController.Create("Reset Game",
                                        "Are you sure you want to
start again?",
UIAlertControllerStyle.Alert);

          // set up button event handlers
```

```
        alert.AddAction(UIAlertAction.Create("OK",
UIAlertActionStyle.Default, a =>
        {
            startNewGame();
        }));
        alert.AddAction(UIAlertAction.Create("Cancel",
UIAlertActionStyle.Default, null));

        // Display the UIAlertController to the current view
        this.ShowViewController(alert, sender);
    }));
}
#endregion
```

Let's take a look at what we covered in the preceding code snippet:

1. Firstly, in the `ResetGame_Clicked` instance method, we started by setting up our `UIAlertController` class and used the `InvokeOnMainThread` method, which will wait for your code running on the main thread to execute before continuing. If we didn't use the `InvokeOnMainThread` method, our dialog would not be displayed to the user.

2. Next, we called the `Create` method on the `UIAlertController` class to create a `UIAlertController` object, which will display an alert to the user that includes a title, a message, and the `UIAlertControllerStyle` preferred style, and then returns that `UIAlertController` object.

3. Then, we set up our button event handlers, using the `AddAction` method, calling the `UIAlertAction.Create` action, and setting the `UIAlertActionStyle` that is required by the controller to display a button for the user to choose.

4. Finally, we displayed the `UIAlertController` to the current view using the `ShowViewController` method, passing in the `UIAlertController` and the `sender` object, which in this case is the **Reset Game** button.

 For more information on the `UIAlertController` class, as well as the various types of different class available, refer to the Xamarin Developer documentation at `https://developer.xamarin.com/api/type/UIKit.UIAlertController/`.

Randomly shuffling our Game Tiles on the Game Board

In this section, we will look at implementing the ShuffleBoardTiles_Clicked instance method in our ViewController class. The ShuffleBoardTiles_Clicked instance method will be responsible for randomly shuffling our GameTiles on the game board, which, if you remember when we were constructing our user interface for our game, we created an event for with our **Shuffle Tiles** button.

We will use the Random class to generate a random number that will be used to specify a new location to place each of our GameTile images on the game board.

Let's start by modifying the ViewController class for our **SlidingTiles** app by performing the following steps:

1. Ensure that the ViewController.cs file is currently displayed in the code editor.

2. Next, underneath the ResetGame_Clicked event method, we need to create an event method called ShuffleBoardTiles_Clicked that will be called whenever the user taps on this button; enter the following code snippet:

```
#region 5 - Instance method to randomly shuffle our game tiles
partial void ShuffleBoardTiles_Clicked(UIButton sender)
{
    var tempGameTileCoords = new List<CGPoint>(GameTileCoords);
    foreach (UIImageView any in gameTileImagesArray)
    {
        var randGen = new Random();
        int randomIndex = randGen.Next(0, tempGameTileCoords.Count);
        any.Center = (CGPoint)tempGameTileCoords[randomIndex];
        tempGameTileCoords.RemoveAt(randomIndex);
    }
    emptyTilePos = (CGPoint)tempGameTileCoords[0];
    tempGameTileCoords.Clear();
}
#endregion
```

Let's take a look at what we covered in the preceding code snippet:

1. Firstly, in the `ShuffleBoardTiles_Clicked` instance method, we started by creating a new `tempGameTileCoords` variable that creates an array of `CGPoints` and stores them in a `List` object.
2. Next, we iterated through all images in our `gameTileImagesArray` of type `UIImageView`, and then used the `Random` class to create a random number that will be used to specify a new location to place each of our **GameTile** images by setting the `Center` property.
3. Then, we removed `randomIndex` from our `tempGameTileCoords` array and set our `emptyTilePos` variable to point to the first location in our `tempGameTileCoords` array.

> For more information on the `Random` class, refer to the Xamarin Developer documentation at `https://developer.xamarin.com/api/type/System.Random/`.

Implementing the StartNewGame Instance method

In this section, we will look at implementing the `startNewGame` instance method in our `ViewController` class. The `startNewGame` instance method will be responsible for starting a new game whenever the `ViewDidAppear` method is fired or the user taps on the **Reset Game** button.

Let's start by modifying the `ViewController` class for our **SlidingTiles** app by performing the following steps:

1. Ensure that the `ViewController.cs` file is currently displayed in the code editor.
2. Next, underneath the `ShuffleBoardTiles_Clicked` event method, we need to create an event method called `startNewGame` that will be called whenever a new game is required; enter the following code snippet:

```
#region 6 – Instance method to end the current game and start a new game
void startNewGame()
{
    // Remove remnants of our ImageViews from our GameBoard
```

```
foreach (UIImageView any in gameBoardView.Subviews)
{
    any.RemoveFromSuperview();
}
// Clear out our game tile arrays
gameTileImagesArray.Clear();
GameTileCoords.Clear();

// Initialise our grid cell size
gridCellSize = 5;
CreateGameBoard();
shuffleBoardTiles_Clicked(shuffleButton);
}
#endregion
```

Let's take a look at what we covered in the preceding code snippet:

1. Firstly, in the `startNewGame` instance method, we started by creating a loop that will iterate through all subviews that are contained in the **gameBoardView** and remove them from the **ViewControllers** superview hierarchy

2. Next, we cleared out both of our `gameTileImagesArray` and `GameTileCoords` arrays, so that we don't end up with duplicate tiles appearing

3. Then, we initialized our `gridCellSize` to the default size of each game tile

4. Next, we called our `CreateGameBoard` instance method to randomly create each of our `GameTiles`

5. Finally, we called the `ShuffleBoardTiles_Clicked` event method to shuffle each of our game tiles, so that they will be randomly placed on the game board

 For more information on the `RemoveFromSuperview` class, refer to the Xamarin Developer documentation at `https://developer.xamarin.com/api/member/UIKit.UIView.RemoveFromSuperview/`.

Handling touch events in the Game Board user interface

In this section, we will look at implementing the necessary logic in our `ViewController` class and learn how to work with the `UITouch` class to handle touch events to determine when a Game Tile has been tapped on the Game Board.

Let's start by modifying the `ViewController` class for our **SlidingTiles** app by performing the following steps:

1. Ensure that the `ViewController.cs` file is currently displayed in the code editor.
2. Next, underneath the `startNewGame` instance method, we need to create and implement an event method called `TouchesEnded` that will be called whenever a touch has happened in the game board view; enter the following code snippet:

```
#region 7 - Handling touch events in the Game Board
public override void TouchesEnded(NSSet touches, UIEvent evt)
{
    base.TouchesEnded(touches, evt);

    if (touches.Count == 1)
    {
        try
        {
            // Get the touch that was activated in the view
            var myTouch = (UITouch)touches.AnyObject;
            var touchedView = (UIImageView)myTouch.View;

            if (gameTileImagesArray.Contains(touchedView))
            {
                var thisCenter = touchedView.Center;
                touchedView.Center = emptyTilePos;
                emptyTilePos = thisCenter;
            }
        }
        catch (Exception e)
        {
            Console.WriteLine("touchedView is not a UIImageView: " +
e.Message);
        }
    }
}
#endregion
```

Let's take a look at what we covered in the preceding code snippet:

1. Firstly, in the `TouchesEnded` event method, we started by checking the number of touches that have been detected in the `ViewController`, and then we obtained the touch location that was activated in the gameboard `View`.
2. Next, we declared a `touchedView` variable that returns the `View` (our Game Tile) that was touched on the `GameBoard`.

3. Then, we used the `Contains` property method of our `gameTileImagesArray` to check to see whether the `GameTile` that was tapped on our `GameBoard` is indeed in our array.

4. Next, if we have determined that the view is in our `gameTileImagesArray`, we get the center location of the View and declare a number of floating point variables, calculate the horizontal and vertical distance of the View, as well as the distance between each tile.

5. Finally, we set the `center` point of the view to be that of the empty tile position, and then set the empty tile position to be the tile that was tapped in the `GameBoard` view.

> For more information on the `UITouch` class, refer to the Xamarin Developer documentation at `https://developer.xamarin.com/guides/ios/application_fundamentals/touch/touch_in_ios/`.

Working with and applying animations to your app

In this section, you'll learn how to work with **CoreAnimation** so that you can apply simple animations to your `UIViews` by using **View Transitions** in an animation block.

Core Animation is essentially a graphics rendering and animation framework that is available on both the iOS and Mac OS X platforms and allows you to animate visual elements of your app, providing rich and smooth animation without having any impact on CPU performance.

Creating and implementing animations for the SlidingTiles game

In this section, we will look at how easy it is to implement animations in our **SlidingTiles** game. You'll work with **CoreAnimation** and the `Animate` property of the `UIView` class to handle animations, which will make our game come alive whenever a Game Tile is tapped on the Game Board.

So, let's start by applying the final touches to our **SlidingTiles** game by modifying the `ViewController` class, performing the following steps:

1. Ensure that the `ViewController.cs` file is currently displayed in the code editor.

2. Next, locate the `TouchesEnded` event method and enter the following code snippet:

```
#region 7 - Handling touch events in the Game Board
public override void TouchesEnded(NSSet touches, UIEvent evt)
{
    base.TouchesEnded(touches, evt);

    if (touches.Count == 1)
    {
        try
        {
            // Get the touch that was activated in the view
            var myTouch = (UITouch)touches.AnyObject;
            var touchedView = (UIImageView)myTouch.View;

            if (gameTileImagesArray.Contains(touchedView))
            {
                var thisCenter = touchedView.Center;
                UIView.Animate(.15f, () => // animation
                {
                    touchedView.Center = emptyTilePos;
                },
                () => // completion
                {
                    emptyTilePos = thisCenter;
                });
            }
        }
        catch (Exception e)
        {
            Console.WriteLine("touchedView is not a UIImageView: " +
e.Message);
        }
    }
}
#endregion
```

In the preceding code snippet, we modified the `TouchesEnded` event method to include additional functionality that will execute our **GameTile** once it has been tapped on the **GameBoard**. We encapsulated `touchedView.Center` in a `UIView.Animate` animation block that will execute for a period of 15 seconds. Once completed, the completion block will then be called and we set the empty tile position to be the tile that was tapped in the **GameBoard** view.

> For more information on the **CoreAnimation** class, refer to the Xamarin Developer documentation at https://developer.xamarin.com/guides/ios/platform_features/graphics_animation_ios/core_animation/.

Now that you have created all of the necessary **C#** code and implemented the necessary instance methods in our `GameTile` Interface and Class, as well as updating the `ViewController` class to include all of the necessary instance and event methods for our game, our next step is to compile, build, and run the **SlidingTiles** game using the **iOS Simulator**.

Launching the SlidingTiles game using the iOS simulator

In this section, we will take a look at how to compile and run our **SlidingTiles** game. You have the option of choosing to run your application using an actual device or choosing from a list of iOS simulators that mimic each of the different types of iOS device.

Let's begin by performing the following steps:

1. Ensure that you have chosen **Debug|iPhoneSimulator** from the drop-down menu.

2. Next, choose your preferred device from the list of available **iOS Simulators.**

3. Then, select the **Run | Start Debugging** menu option, as shown in the following screenshot:

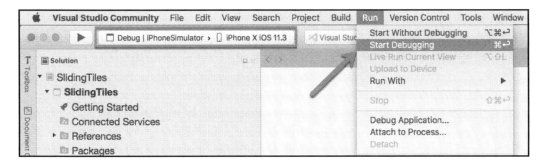

Launching the SlidingTiles game within the iOS Simulator

4. Alternatively, you can also build and run the **SlidingTiles** application by pressing *Command + Enter*.

When the compilation is complete, the iOS Simulator will appear automatically and the **SlidingTiles** application will be displayed, as shown in the following screenshot:

The Sliding Tiles Game running within the iOS Simulator

As you can see from the preceding screenshot, this currently displays our SlidingTiles game. Clicking on the **Reset Game** button will display the dialog, and when clicking on the **Shuffle Tiles** button, it will randomly shuffle our tiles in our `View` control.

Summary

In this chapter, we focused primarily on how to develop a native iOS app using Visual Studio for Mac, Xamarin.iOS, and C#. You learned how to work with **Storyboards** in the Visual Studio for Mac IDE to construct the user interface for our **SlidingTiles** game, and then learned how to create the `GameTile` Interface and Class that will be used to create each of the tiles for our game.

Next, we implemented the remaining logic in our `ViewController` class that completed our **SlidingTiles** game. We created an instance method that is used to build our game board, created each of our game tiles using the images from our Array, and also created an instance method that randomly shuffles and arranges each of our game tiles on our game board.

Lastly, we learned how to work with the `UITouch` class to handle touch events to determine when a game tile has been tapped on the Game Board. You learned about **CoreAnimation** and how you can apply simple animations to your **UIViews** by using View Transitions in an animation block before deploying and launching the app in the iOS Simulator.

In the next chapter, you will learn how to create and set up a basic cross-platform native app using Microsoft Visual Studio for Mac and Xamarin.Forms.

You'll also learn how to create **C#** classes that will act as the model, and then create the various content pages that will form the user interface for your app. We will also cover how to add new, and update existing, NuGet packages to your solutions.

4
Creating the TrackMyWalks Native App

In the previous chapter, we learned how to develop a native iOS app using Visual Studio for Mac, Xamarin.iOS, and C#. You learned how to use and work with Storyboards within the Visual Studio for Mac IDE to construct the user interface for our **SlidingTiles** game by dragging a number of Labels, Views, and Buttons that will make up our game.

We also covered how to work with interfaces and classes and how you can use them to create the GameTile interface and class, which will be used to create each of the tiles for our game. We then implemented the remaining logic within the ViewController class to build the game board and created each of our game tiles using the images from an array. We learned how to create an instance method that randomly shuffled each of the game tiles within the game board by using the Random class, and used the UITouch class to handle touch events to determine when a game tile has been tapped within the game board's UIView.

Finally, we learned how to work with Core Animation to apply simple animations to our UIViews using View Transitions within an animation block, before deploying and launching the app within the iOS Simulator.

This chapter will focus on how to develop a cross-platform app using Visual Studio for Mac, Xamarin.Forms, and C#. This native app will form the basic foundation for the subsequent chapters, where we will continually build upon this application and apply new concepts, such as implementing MVVM, Animations, DataTemplates, PlatformEffects, Location-based services, Microsoft Azure, and Facebook Integrations.

By the end of this chapter, you will have learned how to create a C# class that will act as the data model for our application, as well as learned how to create content pages that will form the user interface for our app using XAML.

This chapter will cover the following topics:

- Creating a cross-platform TrackMyWalks app using Visual Studio for Mac
- Creating the data model that will form the basis for the TrackMyWalks app
- Creating the user interfaces for the TrackMyWalks app using XAML
- Creating the underlying C# code for the TrackMyWalks `ContentPages`
- Launching the TrackMyWalks app using the iOS Simulator

Creating the TrackMyWalks project solution

In this section, we will take a look at how to create a cross-platform Xamarin.Forms solution. We will begin by developing the basic structure for our application, as well as adding the necessary data model and designing the user interface files using XAML.

Before we can proceed, we need to create our `TrackMyWalks` project. It is very simple to create this using Visual Studio for Mac. Simply follow these steps:

1. First, launch the Visual Studio for Mac application.
2. Next, choose the **New Solution...** option, or alternatively choose **File | New | Solution...**, or simply press *Shift + command + N*.
3. Then, choose the **Blank Forms App** option, which is located under the **Multiplatform | App** section. Ensure that you have selected **C#** as the programming language to use:

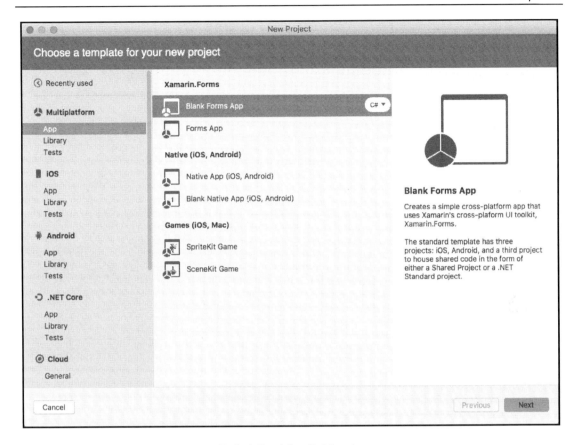

Creating the Xamarin.Forms Blank Forms App

4. Next, enter `TrackMyWalks` as the name for your app in the **App Name** field, and then specify a name for the **Organization Identifier** field.

5. Then, ensure that both **Android** and **iOS** have been selected for the **Target Platforms** field.

6. Next, ensure that you have selected **Use .NET Standard** for the **Shared Code** field, as shown in the following screenshot:

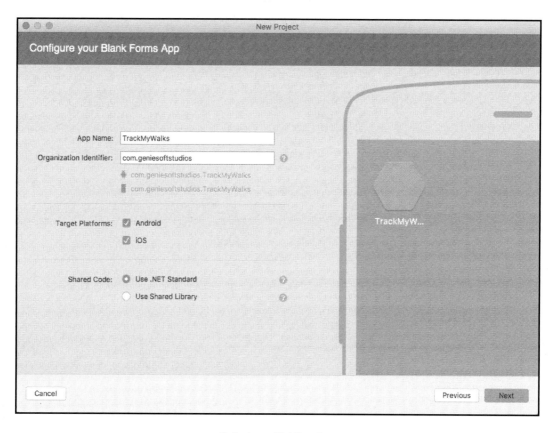

Configuring your Blank Forms App

 The **Organization Identifier** option for your app needs to be unique. Xamarin recommends that you use the reverse domain style (for example, `com.domainName.appName`).

7. Then, click on the **Next** button to proceed to the next step in the wizard:

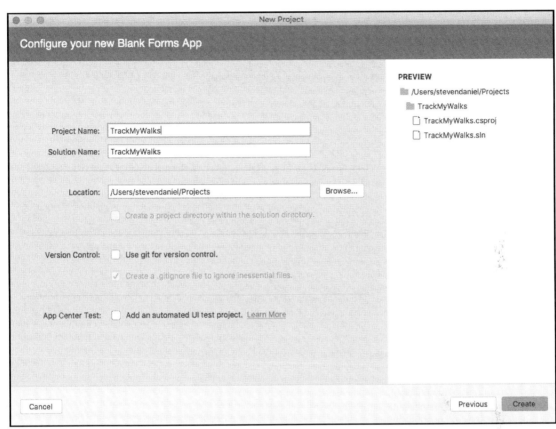

Configuring your new Blank Forms App

8. Finally, click on the **Create** button to save your project at the specified location.

Once your project has been created, you will be presented with the Visual Studio for Mac Community development environment, which contains several project files that the template wizard has created for you.

To find out what each of the project files are used for and the roles each play within the solution, refer to the section on *Creating a Xamarin Project for both iOS and Android*, which is located within `Chapter 1`, *Setting up Visual Studio for Mac*.

Now that we have created our TrackMyWalks solution, our next step is to update the NuGet packages that are contained within our solution, which we will cover in the next section.

Updating the NuGet packages within our solution

In this section, we will take a look at how to update each of the NuGet packages that are contained within the TrackMyWalks solution.

You'll notice that within each project that is contained within our solution, that it will contain a Packages folder, with the exception that our **.NET Standard shared-code project** contains a **Dependencies | NuGet** folder, as well as an SDK folder.

Whenever you create a new Xamarin.Forms project, you will notice that if you expand the Packages folder within each of your Android or iOS solutions, the Xamarin.Forms NuGet package will automatically be included.

 A NuGet package is essentially the package manager for the Microsoft Development Platform that contains the client tools which provide the capability for producing and consuming .NET packages.

Let's take a look at how to go about updating the NuGet packages within the TrackMyWalks solution to ensure that we are running the latest Xamarin.Forms packages. Follow these steps to do so:

Right-click on the **TrackMyWalks** solution and choose the **Update NuGet Packages** menu option, as shown in the following screenshot:

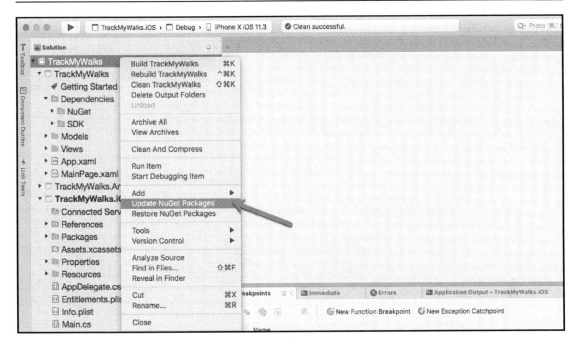

Updating the NuGet Packages within the TrackMyWalks solution

Once you have selected this option, Microsoft Visual Studio for Mac will proceed to update each package that is contained within the TrackMyWalks solution for each of the platform-specific projects. It will require you to accept their license terms for each of the packages prior to installing them.

Up until this point, all we have done is create our solution and updated the NuGet packages contained within our solution. The next step is to start creating the data model that will be used to represent each of our trail walks, as well as create each of the ContentPages that will be used to represent our user interface for our TrackMyWalks app using XAML.

Creating and implementing our data model

In this section, we will take a look at how to create the data model that will be used to define information that's related to our trail entries. The advantage of creating a data model is that it is much easier to add additional properties to this model, and then implement these in the relevant class files.

Another advantage of using a data model is that you can bind this model to a database or bind this to data that's stored within a Microsoft Azure database. As we progress through this chapter, you'll see how you can use this model to set up and initialize walk entries for our TrackMyWalks page using a `ListView` control to display trail information for each row contained within the `ListView`.

Let's start by creating the `WalkDataModel` class for our TrackMyWalks app by performing the following steps:

1. Ensure that the TrackMyWalks solution is open within the Visual Studio for Mac IDE.

2. Next, right-click on the TrackMyWalks project, and choose **Add** | **New Folder** from the pop-up menu, as shown in the following screenshot:

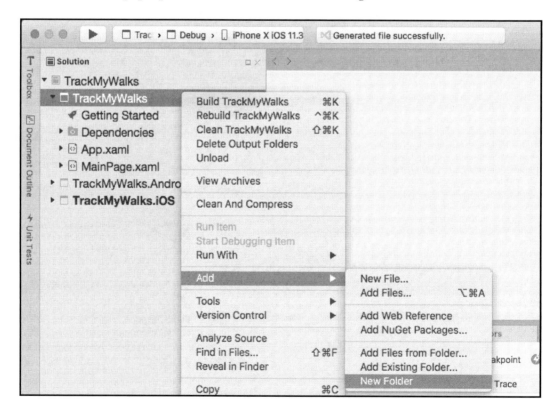

Creating the Models folder within the TrackMyWalks solution

3. Then, enter `Models` for the name of the new folder to be created, and then right-click on the `Models` folder.

4. Next, choose **Add | New File...** from the pop-up menu, as shown in the following screenshot:

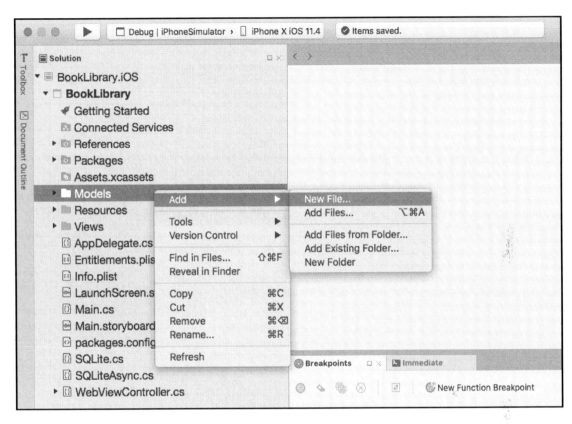

Creating a New File within the Models folder

5. Then, choose the **Empty Class** option under the **General** section and enter `WalkDataModel` for the name of the class to be created, as shown in the following screenshot:

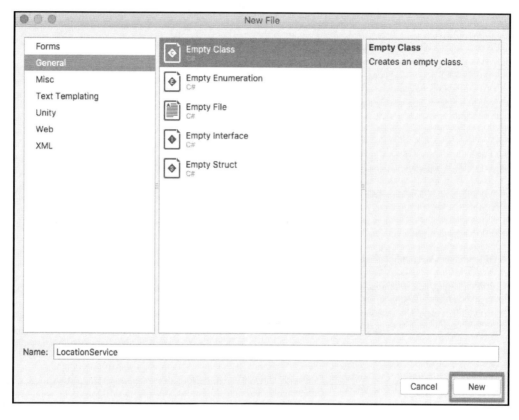

Creating the WalkDataModel Class

6. Next, click on the **New** button to allow the wizard to proceed and create the new file, as shown in the preceding screenshot. Now that we have created our `WalkDataModel` class file, we can proceed with implementing the required code for our class.

7. Locate and open the `WalkDataModel.cs` file, which is located as part of the `TrackMyWalks` group, and ensure that it is displayed within the code editor. Enter the following code snippet:

```
//
//   WalkDataModel.cs
//   The TrackMyWalks Database Model
```

```
//
//   Created by Steven F. Daniel on 14/05/2018
//   Copyright © 2018 GENIESOFT STUDIOS. All rights reserved.
//
using System;

namespace TrackMyWalks.Models
{
    public class WalkDataModel
    {
        public int Id { get; set; }
        public string Title { get; set; }
        public string Description { get; set; }
        public double Latitude { get; set; }
        public double Longitude { get; set; }
        public double Distance { get; set; }
        public string Difficulty { get; set; }
        public string ImageUrl { get; set; }
    }
}
```

Now, let's start by taking a look at what we covered in the preceding code snippet:

1. First, we started by including a reference to the `System` namespace that will be used to ensure that our `WalkDataModel` class allows single inheritance. We don't need to specify or inherit from the `object` class, as the `System.Object` class is inherited implicitly by your class and will be taken care of by the compiler so that you don't need to explicitly say `WalkDataModels : System.Object` (though you can if you want to).

2. Next, we defined a number of properties that will be used to define and describe our `WalkDataModel` and store all of the trail information that will be displayed within the `ListView` control for our TrackMyWalks `ContentPage`.

Creating the WalksMainPage interface using XAML

In this section, we will begin by defining the user interface for our `WalksMainPage` using XAML. This page will be used to display a list of trail walks information, as well as information relating to the distance and difficulty of each trail. There are a number of ways you can go about presenting this information, but for the purposes of our app, we will be using a `ListView` to present this information.

Let's start by creating the user interface for our `WalksMainPage` by performing the following steps:

1. First, create a new folder within the **TrackMyWalks** project called `Views`, as you did in the previous section for **Models**.
2. Next, right-click on the `Views` folder, and choose **Add** | **New File...** from the pop-up menu.
3. Then, choose the **Forms ContentPage XAML** option under the **Forms** section and enter `WalksMainPage` for the name of the XAML file to be created, as shown in the following screenshot:

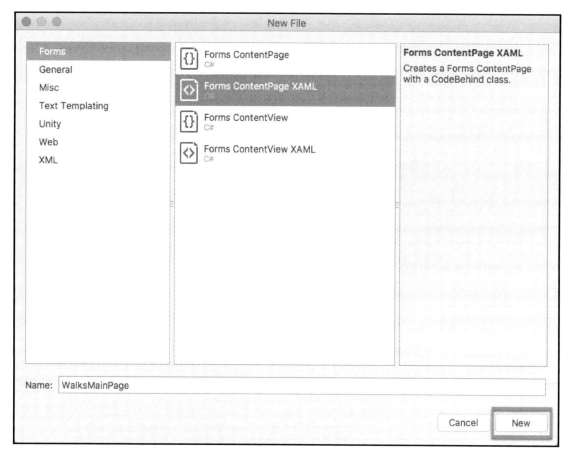

Creating the WalksMainPage Forms ContentPage XAML

4. Then, click on the **New** button to allow the wizard to proceed and create the new file, as shown in the preceding screenshot. Now that we have created our `WalksMainPage` XAML file, we can proceed with defining the user interface and implementing the underlying code for our class.

5. Locate and open the `WalksMainPage.xaml` file, which is located in the `Views` folder, and ensure that it is displayed within the code editor. Enter the following code snippet:

```xml
<?xml version="1.0" encoding="UTF-8"?>
<ContentPage xmlns="http://xamarin.com/schemas/2014/forms"
xmlns:x="http://schemas.microsoft.com/winfx/2009/xaml"
             x:Class="TrackMyWalks.Views.WalksMainPage">
    <ContentPage.ToolbarItems>
        <ToolbarItem Text="Add" Clicked="AddWalk_Clicked" />
    </ContentPage.ToolbarItems>
    <ContentPage.Content>
        <StackLayout>
            <ListView x:Name="WalkEntriesListView"
RowHeight="80" HasUnevenRows="true"
                SeparatorColor="#ddd"
ItemTapped="myWalkEntries_ItemTapped">
                <ListView.ItemTemplate>
                    <DataTemplate>
                        <ImageCell ImageSource="{Binding
ImageUrl}" Text="{Binding Title}"
                            Detail="{Binding Description}"/>
                    </DataTemplate>
                </ListView.ItemTemplate>
            </ListView>
        </StackLayout>
    </ContentPage.Content>
</ContentPage>
```

Now, let's start by taking a look at what we defined within the preceding XAML:

1. We started by defining `ContentPage.ToolbarItems` and specified the `ToolbarItem Text` property as well as the associated `Clicked` event for the toolbar item called `AddWalk_Clicked`.

2. Next, we defined a `StackLayout` control that will be used to stack each of our `WalkEntries` on top of each other, and a `ListView` control that will be used to display the data items. We also specified the `RowHeight` for each of the rows within the `ListView`.

3. Then, we specified the `SeperatorColor` to use and the `ItemTapped` property that will be called whenever an item has been tapped within the `ListView` control. Then, we defined a `DataTemplate` property, which will be used to handle the displaying of data from a collection of objects within our `ListView`.

4. Finally, we used the `ImageCell` control and then set the `ImageSource` property to bind to our `ImageUrl` property. We also set the `Text` property to bind to our `Title`, and the `Detail` property to bind to our `Description` property within our `WalkDataModel`.

Implementing the WalksMainPage code using C#

Now that we have defined our user interface for our `ContentPage` using XAML, the next step is to begin creating the underlying C# code within our `WalksMainPage` code-behind file, which will be used to populate our data model with static data. This will then display this information within our `ListView`.

Let's take a look at how we can achieve this by following these steps:

Open the `WalksMainPage.xaml.cs` code-behind file, ensuring that it is displayed within the code editor, and enter in the following code snippet:

```
//
//  WalksMainPage.xaml.cs
//  Displays Walk Information within a ListView control from
an array
//
//  Created by Steven F. Daniel on 14/05/2018
//  Copyright © 2018 GENIESOFT STUDIOS. All rights reserved.
//
using System;
using System.Collections.ObjectModel;
using TrackMyWalks.Models;
using Xamarin.Forms;

namespace TrackMyWalks.Views
{
    public partial class WalksMainPage : ContentPage
    {
        public WalksMainPage()
        {
            InitializeComponent();
```

```
                    // Update the page title for our Main Page
                    Title = "Track My Walks";
                    this.InitialiseWalks();
          }

          public void InitialiseWalks()
          {
                    // Create a collection that will raise an event,
                    // whenever an object is added or removed from
                    // our WalksListModel collection.
                    var WalksListModel = new
ObservableCollection<WalkDataModel> {
                    // Populate our collection with some dummy data
that will be used
                    // to populate our ListView
                    new WalkDataModel
                    {
                        Id = 1,
                        Title = "10 Mile Brook Trail, Margaret River",
                        Description = "The 10 Mile Brook Trail starts
in the Rotary Park
                        near Old Kate, a preserved steam engine at the
northern edge of
                        Margaret River. ",
                        Latitude = -33.9727604,
                        Longitude = 115.0861599,
                        Distance = 7.5,
                        Difficulty = "Medium",
                        ImageUrl =
"http://trailswa.com.au/media/cache/media/images/
trails/_mid/FullSizeRender1_600_480_c1.jpg"
                    },
                    new WalkDataModel
                    {
                        Id = 2,
                        Title = "Ancient Empire Walk, Valley of the
Giants",
                        Description = "The Ancient Empire is a 450
metre walk trail that
                        takes you around and through some of the giant
tingle trees
                        including the most popular of the gnarled
veterans, known
                        as Grandma Tingle.",
                        Latitude = -34.9749188,
                        Longitude = 117.3560796,
                        Distance = 450,
                        Difficulty = "Hard",
```

```
                            ImageUrl =
        "http://trailswa.com.au/media/cache/media/images/
        trails/_mid/Ancient_Empire_534_480_c1.jpg"
                        }};
                    // Populate our ListView with entries from our
        WalksListModel
                    WalkEntriesListView.ItemsSource = WalksListModel;
                }

                    // Instance method to call the WalkEntryPage to add a
        Walk Entry
                    public void AddWalk_Clicked(object sender, EventArgs
        e)
                    {
                        App.SelectedItem = null;
                        Navigation.PushAsync(new WalkEntryPage());
                    }

                    // Instance method to call the WalkTrailInfoPage using
        the selected item
                    public void myWalkEntries_ItemTapped(object sender,
        ItemTappedEventArgs e)
                    {
                        // Get the selected item from our ListView
                        App.SelectedItem = e.Item as WalkDataModel;
                        Navigation.PushAsync(new WalkTrailInfoPage());
                    }
                }
            }
```

Now, let's start by taking a look at what we covered in the preceding code snippet:

1. First, we started by including references to both the
   `System.Collections.ObjectModel` and `TrackMyWalks.Models` namespaces
   so that we can access the classes that are defined within these namespaces.
2. Next, we modified the `Title` property for our `ContentPage`, and then created
   our `InitialiseWalks` instance method and created an
   `ObservableCollection` called `WalksListModel`, which essentially is a
   collection that will raise an event whenever an object is added or removed from
   our `WalksListModel` collection.
3. Then, we used the `Add` method to add values to each of our properties contained
   within our `WalkDataModel`, before finally setting the `WalksListModel`
   collection to the `ItemsSource` property of the `WalkEntriesListView` property
   that is contained within the `WalksMainPage.xaml` file.

4. Next, we created the `AddWalk_Clicked` event method that will be called whenever the `Add` button is tapped. We initialized our `App.SelectedItem` variable to `null` since we are creating a new walk entry, and then we used the `PushAsync` method of the `Navigation` class to navigate to our `WalkEntryPage`.

5. Finally, we created the `myWalkEntries_ItemTapped` event method, which will be responsible for displaying the `WalkTrailInfoPage` when a row has been tapped on within the `WalkEntriesListView` and using the `ItemTappedEventArgs` parameter to determine the item that has been tapped within the `ListView`, before calling the `WalkTrailInfoPage` using the `Navigation.PushAsync` method.

Creating the WalkEntryPage interface using XAML

In this section, we will begin by defining the user interface for our `WalkEntryPage` using XAML. This page is called whenever the user taps on the `Add` button from the `WalksMainPage` and will be used to allow the user to add new walk trail information.

There are a number of ways you can go about presenting this information to collect data, but for the purpose of our app, we will be using a `TableView` and a number of `EntryCell` fields, as well as a `Picker` control.

Let's start by creating the user interface for our `WalkEntryPage` by performing the following steps:

1. First, create a new **Forms ContentPage XAML** called `WalkEntryPage`, as you did in the section entitled *Creating the WalksMainPage interface using XAML*, located within this chapter.

2. Next, ensure that the `WalkEntryPage.xaml` file is displayed within the code editor, and enter the following code snippet:

```
<?xml version="1.0" encoding="UTF-8"?>
<ContentPage xmlns="http://xamarin.com/schemas/2014/forms"
xmlns:x="http://schemas.microsoft.com/winfx/2009/xaml"
             x:Class="TrackMyWalks.Views.WalkEntryPage">
  <ContentPage.ToolbarItems>
     <ToolbarItem Text="Save" Clicked="SaveWalkItem_Clicked" />
  </ContentPage.ToolbarItems>
  <ContentPage.Content>
      <TableView Intent="Form">
```

```
                    <TableView.Root>
                        <TableSection Title="Enter Walk Trail
Information">
                            <EntryCell Label="Title:"
Placeholder="Provide a Title for this trail" />
                            <EntryCell Label="Description:"
Placeholder="Provide trail description" />
                            <EntryCell Label="Latitude:"
Placeholder="Provide latitude coordinates"
                                      Keyboard="Numeric" />
                            <EntryCell Label="Longitude:"
Placeholder="Provide longitude coordinates"
                                      Keyboard="Numeric" />
                            <EntryCell Label="Distance:"
Placeholder="Provide trail distance"
                                      Keyboard="Numeric"/>
                        <ViewCell>
                            <StackLayout Orientation="Horizontal"
Margin="15,0">
                                <Label Text="Trail Difficulty
Level:" VerticalOptions="Center" />
                                <Picker Title="Choose Difficulty"
VerticalOptions="Center"
HorizontalOptions="EndAndExpand">
                                    <Picker.ItemsSource>
                                        <x:Array Type="{x:Type
x:String}">
<x:String>Easy</x:String>
<x:String>Medium</x:String>
<x:String>Hard</x:String>
<x:String>Extreme</x:String>
                                        </x:Array>
                                    </Picker.ItemsSource>
                                </Picker>
                            </StackLayout>
                        </ViewCell>
                        <EntryCell Label="Image URL:"
Placeholder="Provide an Image URL" />
                    </TableSection>
                </TableView.Root>
            </TableView>
        </ContentPage.Content>
    </ContentPage>
```

Now, let's start by taking a look at what we defined within the preceding XAML:

1. We started by defining `ContentPage.ToolbarItems` and specified the `ToolbarItem Text` property as well as the associated `Clicked` event for the toolbar item called `SaveWalkItem_Clicked`.

2. Next, we defined a `TableView` control and set the `Intent` to `Form` so that our `TableView` will act as a Form, and we set the `TableRoot` for our `TableView` that will be the parent to one or more `TableSections`. We then proceeded to add each of our `EntryCell` fields to our `TableSection` property of our `TableView` control, with each `TableSection` defined within the `TableView` consisting of a heading and one or more `ViewCells`, which in our case are the `EntryCell` fields.

3. We then defined a `StackLayout` control as well as a `Label` control and `Picker` control, which will be used to display and allow the user to choose the level of difficulty for the trail. Then, we set the `ItemsSource` property for our `Picker` control to include an array of strings containing the various difficulty levels.

4. Finally, we declared an `EntryCell` property that will allow the user to specify the URL location for the image to use for the trail.

Implementing the WalkEntryPage code using C#

Now that we have defined our user interface for our `ContentPage` using XAML, the next step is to begin creating the underlying C# code within our `WalkEntryPage` code-behind file, which will eventually be used to save all information entered within this page to a database and refresh our `ListView` that's contained within our `WalksMainPage`.

Let's take a look at how we can achieve this by following these steps:

Open the `WalkEntryPage.xaml.cs` code-behind file, ensuring that it is displayed within the code editor, and enter the following code snippet:

```
//
//  WalkEntryPage.xaml.cs
//  Data Entry screen that allows new walk information to be added
//
//  Created by Steven F. Daniel on 14/05/2018
//  Copyright © 2018 GENIESOFT STUDIOS. All rights reserved.
//
using System;
```

```
using Xamarin.Forms;

namespace TrackMyWalks.Views
{
    public partial class WalkEntryPage : ContentPage
    {
        public WalkEntryPage()
        {
            InitializeComponent();

            // Update the page title for our Walks Entry Page
            Title = "New Walk Entry Page";
        }
        // Instance method that saves the new walk entry
        public void SaveWalkItem_Clicked(object sender, EventArgs e)
        {
            Navigation.PopToRootAsync(true);
        }
    }
}
```

Now, let's start by taking a look at what we covered in the preceding code snippet:

1. First, we modified the `Title` property for our `ContentPage`, within our `WalkEntryPage` constructor.

2. Next, we created the `SaveWalkItem_Clicked` event method, which will be called whenever the **Save** button is tapped to save the walk information that's entered into the `WalksMainPage`. Obviously, we will be refactoring the `WalkEntryPage` throughout this book, which will actually send the information entered to the server using a RESTful API and refresh the `WalksMainPage`.

3. Finally, we used the `PopToRootAsync` method of the `Navigation` class to remove the `WalkEntryPage` from the navigation stack and return to the calling page.

Creating the WalkTrailInfoPage interface using XAML

In this section, we will begin by defining the user interface for our `WalkTrailInfoPage` using XAML. This page will be used to display information relating to the chosen trail from the `ListView` contained within our `WalksMainPage`.

Let's start by creating the user interface for our `WalkTrailInfoPage` by performing the following steps:

1. First, create a new **Forms ContentPage XAML** called `WalkTrailInfoPage`, like you did in the section entitled *Creating the WalksMainPage interface using XAML*, located within this chapter.

2. Next, ensure that the `WalkTrailInfoPage.xaml` file is displayed within the code editor and enter the following code snippet:

```xml
<?xml version="1.0" encoding="UTF-8"?>
<ContentPage xmlns="http://xamarin.com/schemas/2014/forms"
xmlns:x="http://schemas.microsoft.com/winfx/2009/xaml"
        x:Class="TrackMyWalks.Views.WalkTrailInfoPage">
    <ContentPage.Content>
        <ScrollView Padding="10">
            <StackLayout Orientation="Vertical"
HorizontalOptions="FillAndExpand">
                <Image x:Name="TrailImage" Aspect="AspectFill"
Source="{Binding ImageUrl}"
                        HorizontalOptions="FillAndExpand"
VerticalOptions="FillAndExpand" />
                <Label x:Name="TrailName" FontSize="28"
FontAttributes="Bold" TextColor="Black"
                        Text="{Binding Title}" />
                <Label x:Name="TrailKilometers" FontSize="12"
TextColor="Black"
                        Text="{Binding Distance,
StringFormat='Kilometers: {0} km'}" />
                <Label x:Name="TrailDifficulty" FontSize="12"
TextColor="Black"
                        Text="{Binding Difficulty,
StringFormat='Difficulty: {0}'}" />
                <Label x:Name="TrailFullDescription"
FontSize="11" TextColor="Black"
                        Text="{Binding Description}"
HorizontalOptions="FillAndExpand" />
                <Button x:Name="BeginTrailWalk" Text="Begin
this Trail" TextColor="White"
                        BackgroundColor="#008080"
Clicked="BeginTrailWalk_Clicked"/>
            </StackLayout>
        </ScrollView>
    </ContentPage.Content>
</ContentPage>
```

Now, let's start by taking a look at what we defined within the preceding XAML:

1. We started by defining a `ScrollView` control that will allow our `ContentPage` to scroll its contents, if the information being displayed is too big to fit within actual devices' screen real estate. Then, we specified the `Padding` property to represent the distance between an element as well as its child elements.

2. Next, we defined a `StackLayout` control as well as defined the `Image` and `Label` fields. We also set the `Text` properties to each of the properties defined within our `WalkDataItem` class and then declared a `Button` control called `BeginTrailWalk`.

3. Finally, we updated the `Text` and `TextColor` controls, and the `BackgroundColor` property, as well as the associated `Clicked` event for the `Button` called `BeginTrailWalk_Clicked`.

Implementing the WalkTrailInfoPage code using C#

Now that we have defined our user interface for our `ContentPage` using XAML, our next step is to begin creating the underlying C# code within our `WalkTrailInfoPage` code-behind file, which will populate each of our Bindings with the chosen trail information from the `WalksMainPage`, which will be passed in as a parameter to this class.

Let's take a look at how we can achieve this by following these steps:

Open the `WalkTrailInfoPage.xaml.cs` code-behind file, ensuring that it is displayed within the code editor, and enter the following code snippet:

```
//
// WalkTrailInfoPage.xaml.cs
// Displays related trail information chosen from the WalksMainPage
//
// Created by Steven F. Daniel on 14/05/2018
// Copyright © 2018 GENIESOFT STUDIOS. All rights reserved.
//
using System;
using Xamarin.Forms;
using TrackMyWalks.Models;

namespace TrackMyWalks.Views
{
    public partial class WalkTrailInfoPage : ContentPage
```

```
        {
            public WalkTrailInfoPage()
            {
                InitializeComponent();

                // Update the page title for our Walk Information Page
                Title = "Trail Walk Information";

                // Set the Binding Context for our ContentPage
                this.BindingContext = App.SelectedItem;
            }
            // Instance method that proceeds to begin a new walk trail
            public void BeginTrailWalk_Clicked(object sender, EventArgs e)
            {
                if (App.SelectedItem == null)
                    return;
                Navigation.PushAsync(new WalkDistancePage());
                Navigation.RemovePage(this);
            }
        }
    }
}
```

Now, let's start by taking a look at what we covered in the preceding code snippet:

1. First, we started by including a reference to our `TrackMyWalks.Models` namespace so that we can access our `WalkDataModel` class as well as the properties.
2. Next, within the `WalkTrailInfoPage` constructor, we modified the `Title` property for our `ContentPage`, and then we set the binding context for our `ContentPage` using the `App.SelectedItem` which points to our data-model, containing our walk entry information for the chosen item from the `ListView` on the `WalksMainPage`.
3. Finally, we created the `BeginTrailWalk_Clicked` event method, which will be called whenever the `BeginTrailWalk` button is tapped. We checked to ensure that our `App.SelectedItem` object is valid and then called the `WalkDistancePage`, using the `Navigation.PushAsync` method and then calling the `RemovePage` method of the `Navigation` class to remove the `WalkTrailInfoPage` from the navigation stack.

Integrating and implementing maps within your app

In this section, we will be taking a look at how to work with and integrate mapping capabilities for our **TrackMyWalks** application. We will learn how to add the `NuGet` package in `Xamarin.Forms.Maps` to our shared-code project.

The main purpose of the `Xamarin.Forms.Maps` control is to allow you to display a map inside your `Xamarin.Forms` application or within a `ContentPage`. You can see a map of your current location, add pin placeholders within the map, and also provide a route between two locations.

Let's take a look at how we can achieve this by following these steps:

1. Right-click on the **TrackMyWalks** solution and choose the **Add Packages...** menu option, as shown in the following screenshot:

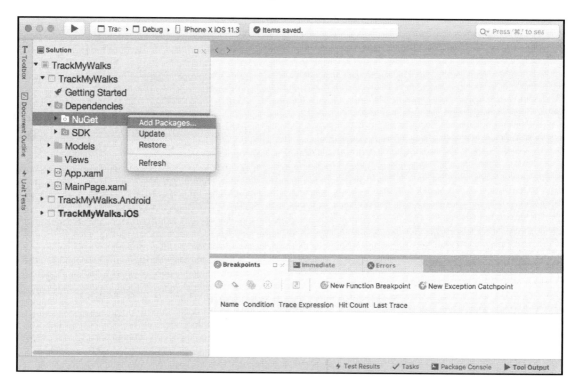

Adding Packages to the NuGet Folder

2. Next, enter `maps` within the Search field located within the **Add Package** dialog and then select the `Xamarin.Forms.Maps` option within the list, as shown in the following screenshot:

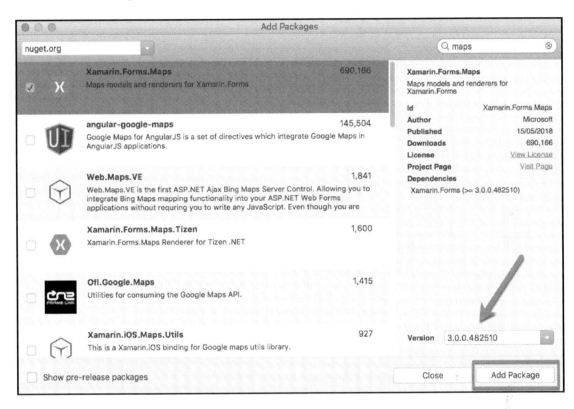

Adding the Xamarin.Forms.Maps NuGet Package

3. Then, ensure that you choose the latest version to install for the **Version** field (this will be displayed by default). It must match the version of `Xamarin.Forms` that you are using, otherwise, you will experience issues when you compile and run your solution.

4. Finally, click on the **Add Package** button to add the `NuGet` package in **Xamarin.Forms.Maps** to the **TrackMyWalks** shared-core solution.

5. Repeat this process to add the **Xamarin.Forms.Maps** NuGet package for both the iOS and Android projects that are contained within the Packages folder within the TrackMyWalks solution, as shown in the following screenshot:

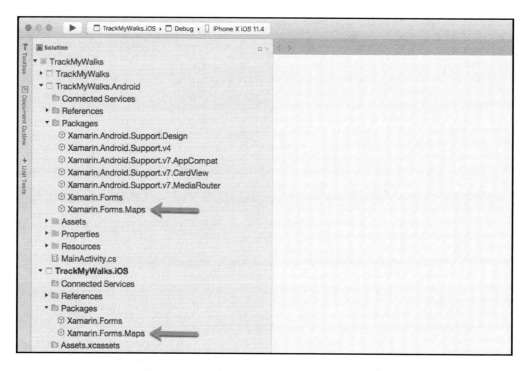

Adding the Xamarin.Forms.Maps NuGet Package to the iOS and Android projects

Now that you have added the NuGet package for Xamarin.Forms.Maps, we can begin utilizing this control within the WalkDistancePage ContentPage, which we will be covering in the next section.

Creating the WalkDistancePage interface using XAML

In this section, we will begin by defining the user interface for our WalkDistancePage using XAML. This page will be used to display a full-screen map with a pin placeholder that, when tapped, will display information relating to the chosen trail from the ListView that's contained within our WalksMainPage.

Let's start by creating the user interface for our WalkDistancePage by performing the following steps:

1. First, create a new **Forms ContentPage XAML** called WalkDistancePage, like you did in the section entitled *Creating the WalksMainPage interface using XAML*, located within this chapter.

2. Next, ensure that the WalkDistancePage.xaml file is displayed within the code editor and enter the following code snippet:

```
<?xml version="1.0" encoding="UTF-8"?>
<ContentPage xmlns="http://xamarin.com/schemas/2014/forms"
xmlns:x="http://schemas.microsoft.com/winfx/2009/xaml"
          xmlns:maps="clr-
namespace:Xamarin.Forms.Maps;assembly=Xamarin.Forms.Maps"
            x:Class="TrackMyWalks.Views.WalkDistancePage">
     <ContentPage.Content>
         <ScrollView Padding="10">
             <StackLayout Orientation="Vertical"
HorizontalOptions="FillAndExpand">
                 <maps:Map WidthRequest="320"
HeightRequest="200" x:Name="MyCustomTrailMap"
                          IsShowingUser="true"
MapType="Street" />
                 <Button x:Name="EndThisTrail" Text="End this
Trail" TextColor="White"
                          BackgroundColor="#008080"
Clicked="EndThisTrailButton_Clicked" />
             </StackLayout>
         </ScrollView>
     </ContentPage.Content>
</ContentPage>
```

Now, let's start by taking a look at what we defined within the preceding XAML:

1. We started by defining a ScrollView control that will allow our ContentPage to scroll its contents if the information being displayed is too big to fit within the actual devices' screen real-estate. Then, we specified the Padding property to represent the distance between an element as well as its child elements.

2. Next, we defined a StackLayout control as well as defined the <maps:Map field, which will be used to represent our map. We also set the WidthRequest and HeightRequest properties, which will be used to define our map control.

3. Then, we specified a name for our map control called MyCustomTrailMap so that we can reference this within our code-behind file, and then set the IsShowingUser and MapType properties that will display the user's current location within the map control, as well as set the type of map to use.

4. Finally, we declared a Button control called EndThisTrail and updated the Text and TexColor controls, and the BackgroundColor property, as well as the associated Clicked event for the Button called EndThisTrailButton_Clicked.

For more information on the different MapTypes that are available within Xamarin.Forms, refer to the Xamarin Developer Documentation at https://docs.microsoft.com/en-us/dotnet/api/xamarin.forms.maps. maptype?view=xamarin-forms.

Implementing the WalkDistancePage code using C#

Now that we have defined our user interface for our ContentPage using XAML, the next step is to begin creating the underlying C# code within our WalkDistancePage code-behind file, which will be used to interact with our Map control and place a pin placeholder that will contain information relating to the chosen trail from the ListView control that is contained within our WalksMainPage.

Let's take a look at how we can achieve this by following these steps:

Open the WalkDistancePage.xaml.cs code-behind file, ensuring that it is displayed within the code editor, and enter the following code snippet:

```
//
//   WalkDistancePage.xaml.cs
//   Displays related trail information within a map using a pin
placeholder
//
//   Created by Steven F. Daniel on 14/05/2018
//   Copyright © 2018 GENIESOFT STUDIOS. All rights reserved.
//
using System;
using TrackMyWalks.Models;
using Xamarin.Forms;
using Xamarin.Forms.Maps;
```

```
namespace TrackMyWalks.Views
{
    public partial class WalkDistancePage : ContentPage
    {
        public WalkDistancePage()
        {
            InitializeComponent();

            // Update the page title for our Distance Travelled Page
            Title = "Distance Travelled Information";

            // Place a pin on the map for the chosen walk type
            MyCustomTrailMap.Pins.Add(new Pin
            {
                Type = PinType.Place,
                Position = new Position(
                        App.SelectedItem.Latitude,
                        App.SelectedItem.Longitude),
                Label = App.SelectedItem.Title,
                Address = "Difficulty: " +
                App.SelectedItem.Difficulty + "
                Total Distance: " +
                App.SelectedItem.Distance,
                Id = App.SelectedItem.Title
            });

            // Create a region around the map within a one-kilometer
radius
MyCustomTrailMap.MoveToRegion(MapSpan.FromCenterAndRadius(new
                Position(App.SelectedItem.Latitude,
                App.SelectedItem.Longitude),
Distance.FromKilometers(1.0)));
        }

        // Instance method that ends the current trail and returns back
to the main screen.
        public void EndThisTrailButton_Clicked(object sender, EventArgs
e)
        {
            App.SelectedItem = null;
            Navigation.PopToRootAsync(true);
        }
    }
}
```

Now, let's start by taking a look at what we covered in the preceding code snippet:

1. First, we started by including a reference to `TrackMyWalks.Models` so that we can access our `WalkDataItem` class as well as the properties defined within that class. We also included a reference to the `Xamarin.Forms.Maps` namespace so that we can access all of the features of our `Map` control that we defined within our XAML.

2. Next, within the `WalkDistancePage` constructor, we modified the `Title` property for our `ContentPage`, and then placed a pin on the map by using the `Position` property of the `MyCustomTrailMap`. We did the same for the `Latitude` and `Longitude` coordinates by using `App.SelectedItem`, which points to our data model, containing our walk entry information for the chosen walk trail.

3. Next, we assigned values for the `Title` and `Address`, as well as an `Id` for our pin placeholder, and then called the `MoveToRegion` method to create a region around the map within a 1-k radius around the trail walk area.

4. Finally, we created the `EndThisTrailButton_Clicked` event method, which will be called whenever the `EndThisTrail` button is tapped. We then initialized our `App.SelectedItem` object to `null`, prior to calling the `PopToRootAsync` method of the `Navigation` class to remove the `WalkDistancePage` from the navigation stack and return to our main `WalksMainPage`.

Updating the TrackMyWalks.iOS AppDelegate

In this section, we need to make changes to the `AppDelegate` class for our `TrackMyWalks.iOS` project so that we can initialize our `Xamarin.FormsMaps` library, otherwise we won't be able to use any of the map features.

The `AppDelegate` class gets notified whenever the object to which it is connected to reaches certain events or states. In this case, the *Application Delegate* is an object which receives notifications whenever the `UIApplication` object reaches certain states. In many respects, it is a specialized one-to-one `Observer` pattern.

Let's take a look at how we can achieve this by following these steps:

1. First, expand the `TrackMyWalks.iOS` solution project that is contained within the `TrackMyWalks` solution.

2. Next, double-click on the `AppDelegate.cs` file, ensuring that it is displayed within the code editor, and enter the following highlighted code sections:

```
//
//  AppDelegate.cs
//  Application Delegate class for the TrackMyWalks.iOS Project
//
//  Created by Steven F. Daniel on 14/05/2018
//  Copyright © 2018 GENIESOFT STUDIOS. All rights reserved.
//
using Foundation;
using UIKit;

namespace TrackMyWalks.iOS
{
    // The UIApplicationDelegate for the application. This
class is responsible for launching the
    // User Interface of the application, as well as listening
(and optionally responding) to
    // application events from iOS.
    [Register("AppDelegate")]
    public partial class AppDelegate :
global::Xamarin.Forms.Platform.iOS.FormsApplicationDelegate
    {
        //
        // This method is invoked when the application has
loaded and is ready to run. In this
        // method you should instantiate the window, load the
UI into it and then make the window
        // visible.
        //
        // You have 17 seconds to return from this method, or
iOS will terminate your application.
        //
        public override bool FinishedLaunching(UIApplication
app, NSDictionary options)
        {
            global::Xamarin.Forms.Forms.Init();
            // Initialise our Xamarin.FormsMaps library
            Xamarin.FormsMaps.Init();
            LoadApplication(new App());
            return base.FinishedLaunching(app, options);
        }
    }
}
```

In the preceding code snippet, we began by making some changes to the `FinishedLaunching` method within the `AppDelegate` class to initialize our `Xamarin.FormsMaps` library by making a call to the `Xamarin.FormsMaps.Init()` method. The `FinishedLaunching` method is called whenever your application launches. If we forget to reference our `Xamarin.FormsMaps.Init()` method, the `WalkDistancePage` content page will cause issues when running the app.

Updating the TrackMyWalks.Android MainActivity

In this section, we need to make changes to the `MainActivity` class for our `TrackMyWalks.Android` project so that we can initialize our `Xamarin.FormsMaps` library, otherwise we won't be able to use any of the map features.

The `MainActivity` class begins immediately after your app launches. Once the main activity is running, it can launch other activities, which in turn can launch subactivities. When the application exits, it does so by terminating the main activity and any other activities terminate in a cascade form from within the main activity.

Let's take a look at how we can achieve this by following these steps:

1. First, expand the `TrackMyWalks.Android` solution project that is contained within the **TrackMyWalks** solution.
2. Next, double-click on the `MainActivity.cs` file, ensuring that it is displayed within the code editor, and enter the following highlighted code sections:

```
//
// MainActivity.cs
// MainActivity class for the TrackMyWalks.Android Project
//
// Created by Steven F. Daniel on 14/05/2018
// Copyright © 2018 GENIESOFT STUDIOS. All rights reserved.
//
using Android.App;
using Android.Content.PM;
using Android.OS;

namespace TrackMyWalks.Droid
{
    [Activity(Label = "TrackMyWalks", Icon = "@mipmap/icon",
     Theme = "@style/MainTheme",
     MainLauncher = true,
```

```
            ConfigurationChanges = ConfigChanges.ScreenSize |
    ConfigChanges.Orientation)]
            public class MainActivity :
    global::Xamarin.Forms.Platform.Android.FormsAppCompatActivity
        {
            protected override void OnCreate(Bundle bundle)
            {
                TabLayoutResource = Resource.Layout.Tabbar;
                ToolbarResource = Resource.Layout.Toolbar;

                base.OnCreate(bundle);
                // Initialise our Xamarin.FormsMaps library
                Xamarin.FormsMaps.Init(this, bundle);
                global::Xamarin.Forms.Forms.Init(this, bundle);
                LoadApplication(new App());
            }
        }
    }
```

In the preceding code snippet, we began by making changes to the OnCreate method within the MainActivity class to initialize our Xamarin.Forms.Maps library by making a call to the Xamarin.FormsMaps.Init() method, which accepts two parameters, the first one being the current class instance, and the second one being the bundle identifier. The OnCreate method is called whenever your application launches. If we forget to reference our Xamarin.FormsMaps.Init() method, the WalkDistancePage content page will cause issues when running the app.

 For more information on the Xamarin.Forms.Maps library, as well as the various types of classes that are available, please refer to the Xamarin developer documentation at https://developer.xamarin.com/api/namespace/Xamarin.Forms.Maps/.

Creating the SplashPage interface using XAML

In this section, we will begin by defining the user interface for our SplashPage using XAML. This page will only be used and displayed whenever we launch our TrackMyWalks.Android project and will essentially display an image that fills the whole screen.

Let's start by creating the user interface for our `SplashPage` by performing the following steps:

1. First, create a new **Forms ContentPage XAML** called `SplashPage`, like you did in the section entitled *Creating the WalksMainPage interface using XAML*, located within this chapter.

2. Next, ensure that the `SplashPage.xaml` file is displayed within the code editor and enter the following code snippet:

```xml
<?xml version="1.0" encoding="UTF-8"?>
<ContentPage xmlns="http://xamarin.com/schemas/2014/forms"
xmlns:x="http://schemas.microsoft.com/winfx/2009/xaml"
             x:Class="TrackMyWalks.Views.SplashPage">
    <ContentPage.Content>
        <StackLayout x:Name="ImageFrame"
Orientation="Vertical"
                         AbsoluteLayout.LayoutBounds="0, 0, 1, 1"
AbsoluteLayout.LayoutFlags="All">
            <Image Source="icon.png" Aspect="AspectFill"
VerticalOptions="FillAndExpand"
                     HorizontalOptions="FillAndExpand">
            </Image>
        </StackLayout>
    </ContentPage.Content>
</ContentPage>
```

Now, let's start by taking a look at what we defined within the preceding XAML:

1. First, we defined a `StackLayout` control as well as specified a name for our `StackLayout` control called `ImageFrame`. Then, we set the `Orientation` and layout information using the `LayoutBounds` and `LayoutFlags` properties on the `AbsoluteLayout` class so that the image resizes within the view.

2. Finally, we declared an `Image` control and then assigned the `Source` property to the image that we would like to use and set the `Aspect` property so that our image fills and expands within the `ContentPage`.

Implementing the SplashPage code using C#

Now that we have defined our user interface for our `ContentPage` using XAML, the next step is to begin creating the underlying C# code within our `SplashPage` code-behind file, which will be used to handle applying a 3-s timer on our splash screen, before navigating to our **WalksMainPage**.

Let's take a look at how we can achieve this by following these steps:

Open the `SplashPage.xaml.cs` code-behind file, ensuring that it is displayed within the code editor, and enter the following code snippet:

```
//
//  SplashPage.xaml.cs
//  Displays a timed splash screen for the TrackMyWalks application
//
//  Created by Steven F. Daniel on 14/05/2018
//  Copyright © 2018 GENIESOFT STUDIOS. All rights reserved.
//
using System.Threading.Tasks;
using Xamarin.Forms;

namespace TrackMyWalks.Views
{
    public partial class SplashPage : ContentPage
    {
        public SplashPage()
        {
            InitializeComponent();
        }

        protected override async void OnAppearing()
        {
            base.OnAppearing();

            // Set a wait delay of 3 seconds on our Splash Screen
            await Task.Delay(3000);

            // Create a new navigation page, using the WalksMainPage
            Application.Current.MainPage = new NavigationPage(new
WalksMainPage());
        }
    }
}
```

In the preceding code snippet, we began by including a reference to the `System.Threading.Tasks` namespace and then we used the `Task.Delay` method which will create a task that will complete after a specified time has passed, which in our case is 3 seconds. The parameter that this method accepts is specified in milliseconds. Once the specified amount of time has passed, we modify the `Application.Current.MainPage` property to call our **WalksMainPage** by creating a new instance of the `NavigationPage` class.

For more information about the `Task.Delay` class, refer to the Microsoft Developer Documentation at `https://msdn.microsoft.com/en-us/library/hh194873(v=vs.110).aspx`.

Updating the App.xaml class to target various platforms

Now that we have successfully created all of the `ContentPages` that make up the user interface for our **TrackMyWalks** app using XAML, as well as implemented the code within the code-behind files for each of the user interfaces, the next step is to make some changes to our `App.xaml.cs` file.

The `App.xaml.cs` file is essentially the main class for the `Xamarin.Forms` application and is called whenever our **TrackMyWalks** app is started. Within this class, we will make some changes to the `OnStart` method to check what target OS platform we are running on and then call and display our `SplashPage` for our `TrackMyWalks.Android` app. Alternatively, if we are running on iOS, we will display the main page for our application.

Let's take a look at how we can achieve this by following these steps:

1. Open the `App.xaml.cs` located within the `TrackMyWalks` group and ensure that it is displayed within the code editor.

2. Next, locate the `OnStart` method and enter the following highlighted code sections, as shown in the following code snippet:

```
//
// App.xaml.cs
// Main class that gets called whenever our TrackMyWalks app
is started
//
// Created by Steven F. Daniel on 14/05/2018
// Copyright © 2018 GENIESOFT STUDIOS. All rights reserved.
```

```
        //
        using Xamarin.Forms;
        using Xamarin.Forms.Xaml;
        using TrackMyWalks.Views;
        using TrackMyWalks.Models;

        [assembly: XamlCompilation(XamlCompilationOptions.Compile)]
        namespace TrackMyWalks
        {
            public partial class App : Application
            {
                public App()
                {
                    InitializeComponent();
                }

                protected override void OnStart()
                {
                    // Check what Target OS Platform we are running on
whenever the app starts
                    if (Device.RuntimePlatform.Equals(Device.Android))
                    {
                        MainPage = new SplashPage();
                    }
                    else
                    {
                        // Set the root page for our application
                        MainPage = new NavigationPage(new
WalksMainPage());
                    }
                }

                // Declare our WalkDataModel that will store our Walk
Trail Details
                public static WalkDataModel SelectedItem { get; set; }

                protected override void OnSleep()
                {
                    // Handle when your app sleeps
                }

                protected override void OnResume()
                {
                    // Handle when your app resumes
                }
            }
        }
```

Now, let's start by taking a look at what we defined within the preceding XAML:

1. First, we started by including a reference to our `TrackMyWalks.Views` and `TrackMyWalks.Models` namespaces, and then within the `OnStart` method, we checked to see what OS platform we are running on when the application starts.

2. Next, we used the `Device.RuntimePlatform` method to check if we are running on the Android platform by using the `Device` class, and if we are, we set the `MainPage` property to a new instance of our `SplashPage` to display the splash screen for our Android app.

3. Then, if we are running on the iOS platform, we simply set the root page for our application by creating a new instance of the `NavigationPage` class and pass in the **WalksMainPage** `ContentPage`.

4. Finally, we declared a static variable called `SelectedItem` that points to the `WalkDataModel` data model, which will be used to store our walk trail details.

Now that you have created all of the necessary user interface files using XAML and the underlying C# code, as well as implemented the necessary instance and event methods for our app, the next step is to compile, build, and run the TrackMyWalks application within the iOS simulator.

Launching TrackMyWalks using the iOS simulator

In this section, we will take a look at how to compile and run the TrackMyWalks application. You have the option of choosing to run your application by using an actual device or choosing from a list of iOS simulators that mimic each of the different types of iOS devices.

Let's begin by performing the following steps:

1. Ensure that you have chosen the **Debug | iPhone Simulator** from the drop-down menu.

2. Next, choose your preferred device from the list of available iOS Simulators.

3. Then, select the **Run | Start Debugging** menu option, as shown in the following screenshot:

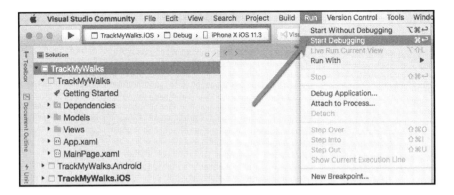

Launching the TrackMyWalks app within the iOS Simulator

4. Alternatively, you can also build and run the TrackMyWalks application by pressing the *Command + Return* key combinations.

5. When the compilation is complete, the iOS Simulator will appear automatically and the TrackMyWalks application will be displayed, as shown in the following screenshot:

Creating a New Walk Entry within the Track My Walks app

As you can see from the preceding screenshot, this currently displays our **TrackMyWalks** application, displaying a list of static walk entries within our `ListView`. Clicking on the **Add** button will display the **New Walk Entry Page**, where you can begin entering information relating to the trail.

Currently, any information that is entered within this page will not be saved. As we progress throughout this book, we will be refactoring these pages to allow this to happen. When you click on the **Save** button, the user will be redirected to the **Track My Walks** screen:

Displays the navigation flow whenever a walk trail has been selected

The preceding screenshot shows you the navigation flow between each of the pages whenever a trail has been selected from the `ListView`, with the final screen showing the **Distance Travelled Information** ContentPage, along with a marker pinpointing information related to the trail within the map.

Summary

In this chapter, we created a cross-platform `Xamarin.Forms` application for both iOS and Android platforms, and then created a data model that will be used to store information related to trails that will be used by our application. We then created a number of content pages that were populated with static data using our data model. Finally, we looked at how to use the navigation APIs that are included as part of the `Xamarin.Forms` platform to help navigate between each of the different content pages, before running the **TrackMyWalks** application within the iOS Simulator.

As we progress through this book, we will be enhancing our app to include better architectural design patterns, nicer looking user interface elements, as well as real-time data that is to be synchronized through the use of RESTful web service APIs.

In the next chapter, you'll learn about the concepts behind the MVVM architectural pattern as well as how to implement the MVVM architectural pattern within the TrackMyWalks application. You'll learn how to create a `BaseViewModel` class that each of our ViewModels will inherit from, as well as create each of the associated C# class files for each of our ViewModels that will data-bind to each of the properties that are defined within our XAML pages.

5
MVVM and Data Binding

In the previous chapter, we created a cross-platform `Xamarin.Forms` application for both iOS and Android platforms, and then created a data model that stored information relating to walking trails used by our application. We then created a number of content pages using XAML that were populated with static data using our data model. Finally, we looked at how to use the navigation APIs included as part of the `Xamarin.Forms` platform to help navigate between each of the different content pages, before running the TrackMyWalks application within the iOS Simulator.

The **Model-View-ViewModel** (**MVVM**) architectural pattern was invented with the XAML in mind, which was created by Microsoft back in 2008. It is well-suited for use with the MVVM architectural pattern, as it enforces a separation of the XAML user interface from the underlying data model, through a class that will act as a connection between the View and the ViewModel, which can be connected through data bindings, which have been defined within the XAML file.

This chapter teaches you the concepts behind the MVVM architectural pattern, as well as how to implement the MVVM architectural pattern within the TrackMyWalks application. You'll learn how to create a BaseViewModel base class that every ViewModel will inherit from, as well as create the associated C# class files for each of our ViewModels that will data-bind to each of the properties defined within our XAML pages.

The associated properties that we define within the ViewModel for the `ContentPage` will be used to represent the information that will be displayed within the user interface for our application. We will learn how to add `ContextActions` to our XAML content pages, and how to implement the code action events within our code, so that we can respond to those actions.

This chapter will cover the following topics:

- Understanding the MVVM architectural pattern as well as data binding
- Creating and implementing the Base-Model class that the ViewModels will inherit
- Updating the user interface pages using XAML to include data binding
- Creating and implementing the underlying ViewModels using C# code
- Implementing the data bindings within our user interfaces using XAML
- Launching the TrackMyWalks app using the iOS Simulator

Understanding the MVVM architectural pattern

In this section, we will take a look at the MVVM architectural pattern and the communication between the components that make up the architecture.

The MVVM design pattern is designed to control the separation between the user interfaces (Views), the ViewModels that contain the actual binding to the model, and the models that contain the actual structure of the entities, which represent information that's stored on a database or from a web service.

The following diagram shows the communication between each of the components contained within the MVVM architectural pattern:

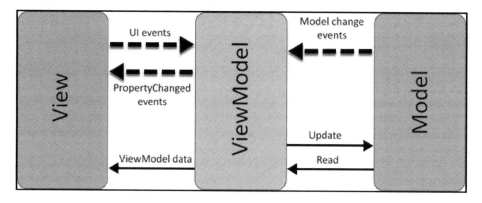

Components of the MVVM architectural pattern

As you can see from the preceding diagram, the MVVM architectural design pattern is divided into three main areas. The following table provides a brief description of what each area is used for:

Type	Description
Model	The Model is basically a representation of business-related entities that are used by an application. It is responsible for fetching data from either a database or web service, and then deserialised to the entities contained within the Model.
View	The View component of the MVVM model represents the actual screens that make up the application, along with any custom control components and control elements, such as Buttons, Labels, and EntryCells. The views contained within the MVVM pattern are platform-specific, which means that they are dependent on the platform APIs that render the information contained within the application's user interface.
ViewModel	The ViewModel controls and manipulates each of the views by acting as their main data context. The ViewModel contains various properties that are bound to the information contained within each model, that are then bound to each of the views to represent this information within the user interface. ViewModels can also contain command objects that provide action-based events to trigger the execution of event methods that occur within the View. An example could be whenever the user taps on a `ToolBar` item or button. ViewModels generally implement the `INotifyPropertyChanged` interface, which will then fire a `PropertyChanged` event whenever changes to a collection occur.

Now that you have a reasonably good understanding of each of the components that are contained within the MVVM architectural pattern, our next step is to begin creating and implementing the `BaseViewModel`, as well as updating each of our XAML user interface files for our TrackMyWalks application, so that it can bind to each of the entities contained within our data model.

Creating and implementing the BaseViewModel

In this section, we will take a look at how to create the `BaseViewModel` class that will essentially be an `abstract` class containing basic functionality that each of our ViewModels will inherit from and implement the `INotifyPropertyChanged` interface. The advantage of creating a `BaseViewModel` class is that it is much easier to add additional functionality to this model, and then implement these in the relevant class files.

Let's start by creating the `BaseViewModel` class for our **TrackMyWalks** application by performing the following steps:

1. Ensure that the **TrackMyWalks** solution is open within the Visual Studio for Mac IDE.

2. Next, right-click on the **TrackMyWalks** project, and choose **Add | New Folder** from the pop-up menu, as shown in the following screenshot:

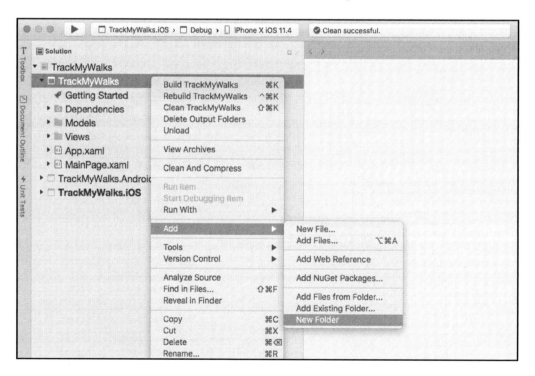

Creating the ViewModels Folder within the TrackMyWalks project

3. Then, enter **ViewModels** for the name of the new folder to be created. After, right-click on the **ViewModels** folder and choose **Add|New File...** from the pop-up menu, as shown in the following screenshot:

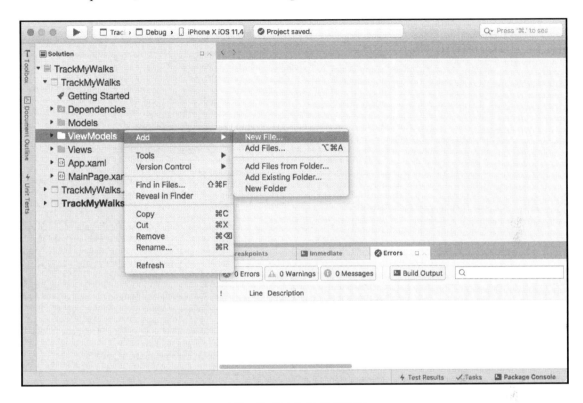

Adding a New File to the ViewModels folder

4. Next, choose the **Empty Class** option under the **General** section and enter **BaseViewModel** for the name of the class to be created, as shown in the following screenshot:

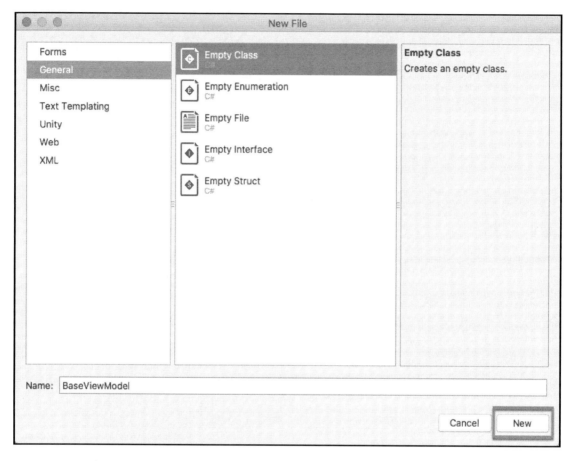

Creating the BaseViewModel Class

5. Next, click on the **New** button to allow the wizard to proceed and create the new file, as shown in the preceding screenshot. Now that we have created our `BaseViewModel` class file, we can proceed with implementing the required code for our class.

6. Locate and open the `BaseViewModel.cs` file, which is located as part of the **TrackMyWalks** group, and ensure that it is displayed within the code editor. Then, enter the following code snippet:

```
// BaseViewModel.cs
```

```csharp
//  BaseView Model Class that each of our ViewModels will
inherit from
//
//  Created by Steven F. Daniel on 5/06/2018
//  Copyright © 2018 GENIESOFT STUDIOS. All rights reserved.
//
using System.ComponentModel;
using System.Runtime.CompilerServices;
using System.Threading.Tasks;

namespace TrackMyWalks.ViewModels
{
    public abstract class BaseViewModel :
INotifyPropertyChanged
    {
        public const string PageTitlePropertyName =
"PageTitle";
        string pageTitle;
        public string PageTitle
        {
            get => pageTitle;
            set { pageTitle = value; OnPropertyChanged(); }
        }
        protected BaseViewModel()
        {
        }

        public abstract Task Init();
        public event PropertyChangedEventHandler
PropertyChanged;
        protected virtual void
OnPropertyChanged([CallerMemberName] string propertyName = null)
        {
            PropertyChangedEventHandler handler =
PropertyChanged;
            PropertyChanged?.Invoke(this, new
PropertyChangedEventArgs(propertyName));
        }
    }
    public abstract class BaseViewModel<TParam> :
BaseViewModel
    {
        protected BaseViewModel()
        {
        }
    }
}
```

Now, let's start by taking a look at what we covered in the preceding code snippet:

1. First, we started by creating an `abstract` class that inherits from the `INotifyPropertyChanged` interface, which allows the View (content page) to be notified whenever properties contained within the ViewModel change.

2. Next, we declared a string constant `PageTitlePropertyName`, as well as a getter and setter called `PageTitle` that will be used to reference the current page.

3. Then, we declared an `Init` method that will be used to initialize the ViewModel, as well as declared a `PropertyChanged` variable that will be used to indicate whenever properties on the object have changed.

4. Next, we created the `OnPropertyChanged` instance method, which will be called when it has determined that a change has occurred on a property within the ViewModel from a child class.

5. Finally, we declared an abstract class `BaseViewModel` that inherits from the `BaseViewModel` and accepts a parameter called `TParam`.

 The `INotifyPropertyChanged` interface is used to notify whenever the value of a property has changed within the ViewModel.

Creating the WalksMainPageViewModel using C#

Now that we have created our `BaseViewModel` class which will be used and inherited by each of the ViewModels that we create, the next step is to start creating the `WalksMainPageViewModel` class that will be used by our `WalksMainPage`.

The `WalksMainPageViewModel` ViewModel class will be used to populate our data model and display the information within our `ListView` by setting the `BindingContext` within the ContentPage.

Let's take a look at how we can achieve this by following these steps:

1. Ensure that the **TrackMyWalks** solution is open within the Visual Studio for Mac IDE.

2. Next, right-click on the `ViewModels` folder and choose **Add | New File...** from the pop-up menu.

3. Then, choose the **Empty Class** option under the **General** section and enter **WalksMainPageViewModel** for the name of the class to be created, as shown in the following screenshot:

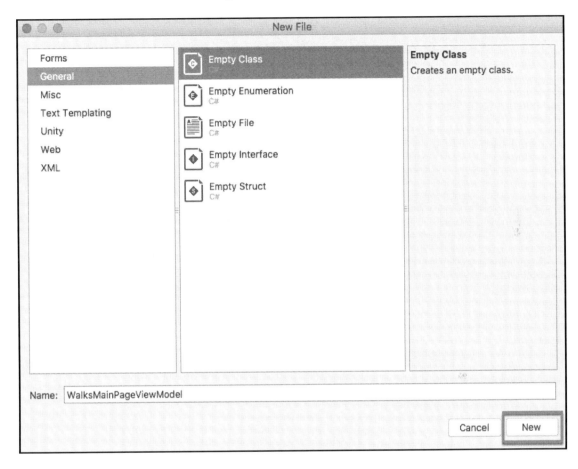

Creating the WalksMainPageViewModel Class

4. Next, click on the **New** button to allow the wizard to proceed and create the new file, as shown in the preceding screenshot. Now that we have created our `WalksMainPageViewModel` class file, we can proceed with implementing the underlying code for our class.

5. Open the `WalksMainPageViewModel.cs` class and ensure that it is displayed within the code editor. Then, enter the following code snippet:

```
//
//  WalksMainPageViewModel.cs
```

```
//   The ViewModel for our WalksMainPage ContentPage
//
//   Created by Steven F. Daniel on 5/06/2018.
//   Copyright © 2018 GENIESOFT STUDIOS. All rights reserved.
//
using System.Collections.ObjectModel;
using System.Threading.Tasks;
using TrackMyWalks.Models;

namespace TrackMyWalks.ViewModels
{
    public class WalksMainPageViewModel : BaseViewModel
    {
        // Create our WalksListModel Observable Collection
        public ObservableCollection<WalkDataModel>
WalksListModel;

        public WalksMainPageViewModel()
        {
        }

        // Instance method to add and retrieve our  Walk Trail
items
        public void GetWalkTrailItems()
        {
            // Specify our List Collection to store the items
being read
            WalksListModel = new
ObservableCollection<WalkDataModel> {
            // Populate our collection with some dummy data
that will be
            // used to populate our ListView
            new WalkDataModel
            {
                Id = 1,
                Title = "10 Mile Brook Trail, Margaret River",
                Description = "The 10 Mile Brook Trail starts
in the Rotary Park near
                Old Kate, a preserved steam engine at the
northern edge of Margaret River.",
                Latitude = -33.9727604,
                Longitude = 115.0861599,
                Distance = 7.5,
                Difficulty = "Medium",
                ImageUrl =
"http://trailswa.com.au/media/cache/media/images/trails/_mid/
                FullSizeRender1_600_480_c1.jpg"
            },
```

```
                         new WalkDataModel
                         {
                             Id = 2,
                             Title = "Ancient Empire Walk, Valley of the
Giants",
                             Description = "The Ancient Empire is a 450
metre walk trail that takes
                             you around and through some of the giant
tingle trees including the most
                             popular of the gnarled veterans, known as
Grandma Tingle.",
                             Latitude = -34.9749188,
                             Longitude = 117.3560796,
                             Distance = 450,
                             Difficulty = "Hard",
                             ImageUrl =
"http://trailswa.com.au/media/cache/media/images/trails/_mid/
                             Ancient_Empire_534_480_c1.jpg"
                         }};
                 }
                 // Instance method to initialise the
WalksMainPageViewModel
                 public override async Task Init()
                 {
                     await Task.Factory.StartNew(() =>
                     {
                         // Call our GetWalkTrailItems method to
populate our collection
                         GetWalkTrailItems();
                     });
                 }
             }
         }
```

Now, let's start by taking a look at what we covered in the preceding code snippet:

1. We started by including references to the `System.Collections.ObjectModel`, `System.Threading.Tasks`, and the `TrackMyWalks.Models` namespaces so that we can access the classes that are defined within these namespaces.

2. Next, we ensured that our `WalksMainPageViewModel` inherits from our `BaseViewModel` class, and then created an `ObservableCollection` called `WalksListModel`, which is essentially a collection that will raise an event whenever an object is added or removed from our `WalksListModel` collection.

3. Then, we created an instance method called `GetWalkTrailItems` and used the `Add` method to add values to each of the properties contained within our `WalkDataModel`.

4. Finally, we created the `Init` instance method that we defined within our `BaseViewModel` to initialize our ViewModel and then called the `GetWalkTrailItems` instance method to populate our `WalksListModel` collection.

Updating the WalksMainPage user interface using XAML

In this section, we will begin by updating the user interface for our **WalksMainPage** using XAML in order to define a series of `ContextActions` menu items that the user can choose from, as well as display a list of trails walks as well as the **Image**, **Title**, and **Description** associated with the walk trail by using a `ListView` to present this information.

Let's start by updating the user interface for our **WalksMainPage** by performing the following steps:

1. Locate and open the `WalksMainPage.xaml` file which is located in the `Views` folder.

2. Next, ensure that it is displayed within the code editor and enter the following highlighted code sections:

```xml
<?xml version="1.0" encoding="UTF-8"?>
<ContentPage xmlns="http://xamarin.com/schemas/2014/forms"
  xmlns:x="http://schemas.microsoft.com/winfx/2009/xaml"
x:Class="TrackMyWalks.Views.WalksMainPage">
    <ContentPage.ToolbarItems>
        <ToolbarItem Text="Add" Clicked="AddWalk_Clicked" />
    </ContentPage.ToolbarItems>
    <ContentPage.Content>
        <StackLayout>
            <ListView x:Name="WalkEntriesListView" RowHeight="80"
HasUnevenRows="true"
                SeparatorColor="#ddd"
ItemTapped="myWalkEntries_ItemTapped">
                <ListView.ItemTemplate>
                    <DataTemplate>
                        <ViewCell>
                            <ViewCell.ContextActions>
                                <MenuItem Clicked="OnEditItem"
CommandParameter="{Binding .}"
                                    Text="Edit" IsDestructive="False"
/>

                                <MenuItem Clicked="OnDeleteItem"
```

```
                CommandParameter="{Binding .}"
                                        Text="Delete"
        IsDestructive="True" />
                                    </ViewCell.ContextActions>
                                    <StackLayout x:Name="cellLayout"
        Padding="10,5,10,5"
                                        Orientation="Horizontal"
        HorizontalOptions="FillAndExpand">
                                        <Image Aspect="AspectFit"
        Source="{Binding ImageUrl}"
                                            VerticalOptions="FillAndExpand" />
                                        <StackLayout
        x:Name="DetailsLayout" Padding="10,0,0,0"
        HorizontalOptions="FillAndExpand">
                                            <Label Text="{Binding Title}"
        FontAttributes="Bold"
                                                FontSize="16"
        TextColor="Black" />
                                            <Label Text="{Binding
        Description}" FontAttributes="None"
                                                FontSize="12"
        TextColor="Blue" />
                                        </StackLayout>
                                    </StackLayout>
                                </ViewCell>
                        </DataTemplate>
                    </ListView.ItemTemplate>
                </ListView>
            </StackLayout>
        </ContentPage.Content>
    </ContentPage>
```

Now, let's start by taking a look at what we've updated within the preceding XAML:

1. We started by defining a `ViewCell` as well as a `ViewCell.ContextActions` that will contain two `MenuItems`, as well as assigned the associated `Clicked` event for editing and deleting items from the `ListView` and/or our `WalkDataModel` data model.

2. Next, we defined a `StackLayout` control called `x:Name="cellLayout"` and used the `Image` control, and then set the `Source` property to bind to our `ImageUrl` property from our data model. Then, we set our `Padding`, as well as the `Orientation` and `HorizontalOptions`.

3. Finally, we created another `StackLayout` control called `x:Name="DetailsLayout"` that will be used to display our walk trail details by setting the `Text` property to bind to our `Title` and `Description` data bindings within our `WalkDataModel`.

Updating the WalksMainPage code-behind using C#

Now that we have updated our user interface to include our `ContextActions` as well as each of the menu item choices that we would like to appear, including each of the various data bindings, the next step is to begin updating the underlying C# code within our `WalksMainPage` code-behind file so that it can communicate with our ViewModel and populate our `ListView` with information from our `WalkDataModel`.

Let's take a look at how we can achieve this by following these steps:

Open the `WalksMainPage.xaml.cs` code-behind file, ensuring that it is displayed within the code editor, and enter the following highlighted code sections:

```
//
//  WalksMainPage.xaml.cs
//  Displays Walk Information within a ListView control from an
array//
//  Created by Steven F. Daniel on 14/05/2018
//  Copyright © 2018 GENIESOFT STUDIOS. All rights reserved.
//
using System;
using TrackMyWalks.Models;
using TrackMyWalks.ViewModels;
using Xamarin.Forms;

namespace TrackMyWalks.Views
{
    public partial class WalksMainPage : ContentPage
    {
        // Return the Binding Context for the ViewModel
        WalksMainPageViewModel _viewModel =>
                                BindingContext as
WalksMainPageViewModel;

        public WalksMainPage()
        {
            InitializeComponent();
```

```
            // Update the Title and Initialise our BindingContext
for
            // the Page
            this.Title = "Track My Walks Listing";
            this.BindingContext = new WalksMainPageViewModel();
        }

        // Instance method to call the WalkEntryPage to add a Walk
Entry
        public void AddWalk_Clicked(object sender, EventArgs e)
        {
            App.SelectedItem = null;
            Navigation.PushAsync(new WalkEntryPage());
        }

        // Instance method to call the WalkTrailInfoPage using the
        // selected item
        public void myWalkEntries_ItemTapped(object sender,
ItemTappedEventArgs e)
        {
            // Get the selected item from our ListView
            App.SelectedItem = e.Item as WalkDataModel;
            Navigation.PushAsync(new WalkTrailInfoPage());
        }

        // Instance method to call the WalkEntryPage to allow item
        // to be edited
        public async void OnEditItem(object sender, EventArgs e)
        {
          // Get the selected item to be edited from our ListView
          var selectedItem =
(WalkDataModel)((MenuItem)sender).CommandParameter;
            App.SelectedItem = selectedItem;
            await Navigation.PushAsync(new WalkEntryPage());
        }

        // Instance method to remove the trail item from our
        // collection
        public async void OnDeleteItem(object sender, EventArgs e)
        {
            // Get the selected item to be deleted from our
ListView
            var selectedItem =
(WalkDataModel)((MenuItem)sender).CommandParameter;

            // Prompt the user with a confirmation dialog to confirm
            if (await DisplayAlert("Delete Walk Entry Item",
                "Are you sure you want to delete this Walk Entry
```

```
Item?",
                        "OK", "Cancel"))
            {
                // Remove Walk Item from our WalkListModel collection
                _viewModel.WalksListModel.Remove(selectedItem);
            }
            else
                return;
        }

        // Method to initialise our View Model when the ContentPage
        // appears
        protected override async void OnAppearing()
        {
            base.OnAppearing();
            if (_viewModel != null)
            {
                // Call the Init method to initialise the ViewModel
                await _viewModel.Init();
            }

            // Set up and initialise the binding for our ListView
    WalkEntriesListView.SetBinding(ItemsView<Cell>.ItemsSourceProperty,
                                        new Binding("."));
            WalkEntriesListView.BindingContext =
    _viewModel.WalksListModel;
        }
    }
}
```

Now, let's start by taking a look at what we covered in the preceding code snippet:

1. We started by including a reference to the `TrackMyWalks.ViewModels` namespace so that we can access the classes and instance methods that are defined within the namespace.

2. Next, we returned the `BindingContext` that will be used by our `WalksMainPage` ContentPage by defining a `getter` property that points to our `WalksMainPageViewModel`.

3. Then, we modified the `Title` property for our ContentPage, and then initialized and set the `BindingContext` of our `WalksMainPage` ContentPage to a new instance of our `WalksMainPageViewModel`.

4. Next, we created the `OnEditItem` instance method that will be called whenever the **Edit** context-menu item is tapped within the `ListView`. We get the selected item to be edited by using the `CommandParameter` of the `sender` object from the `MenuItem` class and assign this to our `App.SelectedItem` property and then call the `PushAsync` method of the `Navigation` class to navigate to our **WalkEntryPage**.

5. Then, we created the `OnDeleteItem` instance method that will be called whenever the **Delete** context-menu item is tapped within the `ListView`. We get the selected item to be deleted by using the `CommandParameter` of the `sender` object from the `MenuItem` class and display a confirmation dialog that will prompt the user to confirm the deletion, and if **OK** has been selected, we remove the walk information from our `WalkListModel` object collection within our ViewModel by using the `Remove` method. Alternatively, we just return from the `OnDeleteItem` instance method.

6. Then, we created the `OnAppearing` method, which will be used to initialize our ViewModel whenever the `ContentPage` appears on screen. We checked to see if our `_viewModel` contains a value, and then called the `Init` instance method so that we could initialize our ViewModel.

7. Finally, we set up and initialize the binding for our `ListView` by setting the `ItemsSourceProperty` and `BindingContext` to our `WalksListModel`, which we defined within our `WalksMainPageViewModel`.

Creating the WalkEntryPageViewModel using C#

Now that we have updated the `WalksMainPage` code-behind file so that it communicates with our `WalksMainPageViewModel` as well as each of the associated data bindings for the ContentPage that will be used by the ViewModel, the next step is to create and implement the underlying C# code for our ViewModel that will be used by our `WalkEntryPage` code-behind file. This allows the user to add or edit walk trail information within our `WalkDataModel` data model, as well as validate the information that's provided.

Let's take a look at how we can achieve this by following these steps:

1. First, create a new **Empty Class** called `WalkEntryPageViewModel`, like you did in the section entitled *Creating the WalksMainPageViewModel using C#*, located within this chapter.

2. Next, ensure that the `WalkEntryPageViewModel.cs` file is displayed within the code editor and enter the following code snippet:

```
//
//  WalkEntryPageViewModel.cs
//  The ViewModel for our WalkEntryPage ContentPage
//
//  Created by Steven F. Daniel on 5/06/2018.
//  Copyright © 2018 GENIESOFT STUDIOS. All rights reserved.
//
using System;
using System.Threading.Tasks;
using TrackMyWalks.Models;

namespace TrackMyWalks.ViewModels
{
    public class WalkEntryPageViewModel : BaseViewModel
    {
        public WalkEntryPageViewModel()
        {
            // Update the title if we are creating a new Walk
Entry
            if (App.SelectedItem == null)
            {
                PageTitle = "Adding Trail Details";
                App.SelectedItem = new WalkDataModel();

                // Set the default values when creating a new
Trail
                Title = "New Trail Entry";
                Difficulty = "Easy";
                Distance = 1.0;
            }
            else
            {
                // Otherwise, we must be editing an existing
entry
                PageTitle = "Editing Trail Details";
            }
        }

        // Checks to see if we have provided a Title and
Description
        public bool ValidateFormDetailsAndSave()
        {
            if (App.SelectedItem != null &&
!string.IsNullOrEmpty(App.SelectedItem.Title) &&
!string.IsNullOrEmpty(App.SelectedItem.Description))
```

```
                {
                    // Save the selected item to our database
and/or model
                }
                else
                {
                    return false;
                }
                return true;
            }

            // Update each EntryCell on the WalkEntryPage with
values from our Model
            public string Title
            {
                get => App.SelectedItem.Title;
                set { App.SelectedItem.Title = value;
OnPropertyChanged(); }
            }
            public string Description
            {
                get => App.SelectedItem.Description;
                set { App.SelectedItem.Description = value;
OnPropertyChanged(); }
            }
            public double Latitude
            {
                get => App.SelectedItem.Latitude;
                set { App.SelectedItem.Latitude = value;
OnPropertyChanged(); }
            }
            public double Longitude
            {
                get => App.SelectedItem.Longitude;
                set { App.SelectedItem.Longitude = value;
OnPropertyChanged(); }
            }
            public double Distance
            {
                get => App.SelectedItem.Distance;
                set { App.SelectedItem.Distance = value;
OnPropertyChanged(); }
            }
            public String Difficulty
            {
                get => App.SelectedItem.Difficulty;
                set { App.SelectedItem.Difficulty = value;
OnPropertyChanged(); }
```

```
        }
        public String ImageUrl
        {
            get => App.SelectedItem.ImageUrl;
            set { App.SelectedItem.ImageUrl = value;
OnPropertyChanged(); }
        }

        // Instance method to initialise the
WalkEntryPageViewModel
        public override async Task Init()
        {
            await Task.Factory.StartNew(() =>
            {
            });
        }
    }
}
```

Now, let's start by taking a look at what we covered in the preceding code snippet:

1. We started by including references to the `System.Collections.ObjectModel`, `System.Threading.Tasks`, and `TrackMyWalks.Models` namespaces so that we can access the classes that are defined within these namespaces.

2. Next, we ensured that our `WalkEntryPageViewModel` inherits from our `BaseViewModel` class. Then, within our class constructor, we checked the value for our `App.SelectedItem` property to see if we were creating a new walk entry, and proceeded to update the `PageTitle`, as well as initialize the `App.SelectedItem` property to a new instance of our `WalkDataModel` class.

3. Then, we initialized our ViewModel with default values whenever we created a new trail item. Alternatively, if we were editing an existing walk trail item, we updated the `PageTile` to reflect this.

4. Next, we created an instance method called `ValidateFormDetailsAndSave` and checked to see if we had a value for our `App.SelectedItem`, as well as see if we had provided values for both our `Title` and `Description` properties, prior to saving the details either to a database, or back to the data model. Alternatively, if any validation errors had been detected, we returned a value of `false`.

5. Finally, we created a number of properties that were to be bound to each of the `EntryCell` fields within our `WalkEntryPage` and created the `Init` instance method that we defined within our `BaseViewModel`, which can be used to initialize our ViewModel.

Updating the WalkEntryPage user interface using XAML

In this section, we will begin by updating the user interface for our `WalkEntryPage` using XAML to specify the `Binding Modes` for each of our `EntryCell` fields, which will be used to allow the user to add new walk trail information whenever the user taps on the **Add** button or chooses the **Edit** menu context action from the `WalksMainPage`.

Let's start by updating the user interface for our `WalkEntryPage` by performing the following steps:

Locate and open the `WalkEntryPage.xaml` file which is located in the `Views` folder, ensuring that it is displayed within the code editor, and enter the following highlighted code sections:

```xml
<?xml version="1.0" encoding="UTF-8"?>
 <ContentPage xmlns="http://xamarin.com/schemas/2014/forms"
xmlns:x="http://schemas.microsoft.com/winfx/2009/xaml"
x:Class="TrackMyWalks.Views.WalkEntryPage">
     <ContentPage.ToolbarItems>
         <ToolbarItem Text="Save" Clicked="SaveWalkItem_Clicked" />
     </ContentPage.ToolbarItems>
     <ContentPage.Content>
         <TableView Intent="Form">
             <TableView.Root>
                 <TableSection Title="Enter Walk Trail
Information">
                     <EntryCell Label="Title:" Text="{Binding
Title, Mode=TwoWay}"
                         Placeholder="Provide a Title for this trail"
/>
                     <EntryCell Label="Description:" Text="{Binding
Description, Mode=TwoWay}"
                         Placeholder="Provide trail description" />
                     <EntryCell Label="Latitude:" Text="{Binding
Latitude, Mode=TwoWay}"
                         Placeholder="Provide latitude coordinates"
Keyboard="Numeric" />
                     <EntryCell Label="Longitude:" Text="{Binding
Longitude, Mode=TwoWay}"
                         Placeholder="Provide longitude coordinates"
Keyboard="Numeric" />
                     <EntryCell Label="Distance:" Text="{Binding
Distance, Mode=TwoWay}"
                         Placeholder="Provide trail distance"
```

```
                    Keyboard="Numeric" />
                                <ViewCell>
                                    <StackLayout Orientation="Horizontal"
Margin="15,0">
                                        <Label Text="Trail Difficulty Level:"
VerticalOptions="Center" />
                                        <Picker Title="Choose Difficulty"
VerticalOptions="Center"
HorizontalOptions="FillAndExpand"
                                                SelectedItem="{Binding
Difficulty, Mode=TwoWay}">
                                            <Picker.ItemsSource>
                                                <x:Array Type="{x:Type
x:String}">
                                                    <x:String>Easy</x:String>
<x:String>Medium</x:String>
                                                    <x:String>Hard</x:String>
<x:String>Extreme</x:String>
                                                </x:Array>
                                            </Picker.ItemsSource>
                                        </Picker>
                                    </StackLayout>
                                </ViewCell>
                                <EntryCell Label="Image URL:" Text="{Binding
ImageUrl, Mode=TwoWay}"
                                           Placeholder="Provide an Image URL"
/>
                            </TableSection>
                        </TableView.Root>
                    </TableView>
                </ContentPage.Content>
            </ContentPage>
```

Now, let's start by taking a look at what we defined within the preceding XAML:

1. We started by specifying the Binding as well as the binding Mode that we would like to set for each of our EntryCell fields. Here, we used the TwoWay binding to indicate that the binding should propagate any changes from the ViewModel to each of the bindable objects that we have specified, in both directions.

2. Finally, we updated the Binding and binding Mode for our Picker control, as well as specified the Binding and binding Mode for our Image URL EntryCell property that will allow the user to specify the URL location for the image to use for the trail.

The following table provides a brief description of the different binding types, and when you should use these within your applications:

Binding Mode	Description
OneWay	The OneWay binding indicates that the binding should only propagate changes from a source (usually the ViewModel) to target the BindableObject. This is the default mode for most BindableProperty values.
OneWayToSource	The OneWayToSource binding indicates that the binding only propagates changes from the target BindableObject to the ViewModel and is mainly used for read-only BindableProperty values.
TwoWay	The TwoWay binding indicates that the binding should propagate the changes from the ViewModel to the target BindableObject in both directions.

Updating the WalkEntryPage code-behind using C#

Now that we have updated our WalkEntryPage user interface to include the various data bindings and the different binding modes for each of our EntryCell fields, the next step is to begin updating the underlying C# code within our WalkEntryPage code-behind file so that it can communicate with our WalkEntryPageViewModel. This will eventually be used to save all information entered within this page to a database and to refresh the ListView contained within our WalksMainPage.

Let's take a look at how we can achieve this by following these steps:

Open the WalkEntryPage.xaml.cs code-behind file, ensuring that it is displayed within the code editor, and enter the following code snippet:

```
//
// WalkEntryPage.xaml.cs
// Data Entry screen that allows new walk information to be added
//
// Created by Steven F. Daniel on 14/05/2018
// Copyright © 2018 GENIESOFT STUDIOS. All rights reserved.
//
using System;
using TrackMyWalks.ViewModels;
```

```csharp
using Xamarin.Forms;

namespace TrackMyWalks.Views
{
    public partial class WalkEntryPage : ContentPage
    {
        // Return the Binding Context for the ViewModel
        WalkEntryPageViewModel _viewModel => BindingContext as
WalkEntryPageViewModel;

        public WalkEntryPage()
        {
            InitializeComponent();

            // Update the Title and Initialise our BindingContext
for the Page
            Title = "New Walk Entry Page";
            BindingContext = new WalkEntryPageViewModel();
            SetBinding(TitleProperty, new
Binding(BaseViewModel.PageTitlePropertyName));
        }

        // Instance method that saves the new walk entry
        public async void SaveWalkItem_Clicked(object sender,
EventArgs e)
        {
            // Prompt the user with a confirmation dialog to
confirm
            if (await DisplayAlert("Save Walk Entry Item",
                                    "Proceed and save changes?",
"OK", "Cancel"))
            {
                // Attempt to save and validate our Walk Entry
Item
                if (!_viewModel.ValidateFormDetailsAndSave())
                    // Error Saving - Must have Title and
description
                    await DisplayAlert("Validation Error",
                                        "Title and Description are
required.", "OK");
                else
                    // Navigate back to the Track My Walks Listing
page
                    await Navigation.PopToRootAsync(true);
            }
            else
            {
                // Navigate back to the Track My Walks Listing
```

```
page
                    await Navigation.PopToRootAsync(true);
              }
         }
     }
}
```

Now, let's start by taking a look at what we covered in the preceding code snippet:

1. We started by including a reference to the `TrackMyWalks.ViewModels` namespace so that we can access the classes and instance methods that are defined within the namespace, and then return the `BindingContext` that will be used by our `WalkEntryPage` ContentPage by defining a `getter` property that points to our `WalkEntryPageViewModel`.

2. Then, we modified the `Title` property and initialized and set the `BindingContext` of our `WalkEntryPage` to a new instance of our `WalkEntryPageViewModel`. Then, we modified the `BaseViewModel.PageTitlePropertyName` using the `TitleProperty` property of the `WalkEntryPage` ContentPage.

3. Next, within the `SaveWalkItem_Clicked` instance method, we displayed a confirmation dialog that prompts the user to confirm the saving of the walk entry, and if **OK** has been selected, we attempt to validate and save the walk entry item by calling the `ValidateFormDetailsAndSave` instance method that we declared within our ViewModel.

4. Finally, we check to see if there are any validation errors. We display an alert using the `DisplayAlert` method, otherwise, we use the `PopToRootAsync` method of the `Navigation` class to remove the `WalkEntryPage` from the navigation stack. Alternatively, if no validation errors have occurred, or we click **Cancel** within the confirmation dialog, we use the `PopToRootAsync` method of the `Navigation` class to remove the `WalkEntryPage` from the navigation stack.

Creating the WalkTrailInfoPageViewModel using C#

Now that we have updated the `WalkEntryPage` code-behind file so that it communicates with `WalkEntryPageViewModel` as well as each of the associated data bindings for the ContentPage that'll be used by ViewModel, the next step is to create and implement the underlying C# code for ViewModel. This'll be used by `WalkTrailInfoPage` code-behind file so that it can display information related to the chosen walk trail from `WalksMainPage`.

Let's take a look at how we can achieve this by following these steps:

1. First, create a new **Empty Class** called `WalkTrailInfoPageViewModel`, like you did in the section entitled *Creating the WalksMainPageViewModel using C#*, located within this chapter.

2. Next, ensure that the `WalkTrailInfoPageViewModel.cs` file is displayed within the code editor and enter the following code snippet:

```
//
//   WalkTrailInfoPageViewModel.cs
//   The ViewModel for our WalkTrailInfoPage ContentPage
//
//   Created by Steven F. Daniel on 5/06/2018.
//   Copyright © 2018 GENIESOFT STUDIOS. All rights reserved.
//
using System;
using System.Threading.Tasks;

namespace TrackMyWalks.ViewModels
{
    public class WalkTrailInfoPageViewModel : BaseViewModel
    {
        public WalkTrailInfoPageViewModel()
        {
        }

        // Update each control on the WalkTrailInfoPage with
values from our Model
        public string Title => App.SelectedItem.Title;
        public string Description =>
App.SelectedItem.Description;
        public double Distance => App.SelectedItem.Distance;
        public String Difficulty =>
App.SelectedItem.Difficulty;
        public String ImageUrl => return
App.SelectedItem.ImageUrl;

        // Instance method to initialise the
WalkTrailInfoPageViewModel
        public override async Task Init()
        {
            await Task.Factory.StartNew(() =>
            {
            });
        }
    }
}
```

Now, let's start by taking a look at what we covered in the preceding code snippet:

1. We started by including references to the `System` and the `System.Threading.Tasks` namespaces so that we can access the classes that are defined within these namespaces.
2. Next, we ensured that our `WalkTrailInfoPageViewModel` inherits from our `BaseViewModel` class, and then we created a number of properties that will be bound to each control that is located within the `WalkTrailInfoPage` ContentPage by using the values from our `App.SelectedItem` property.
3. Finally, we created the `Init` instance method that we defined within our `BaseViewModel`, which can be used to initialize our ViewModel.

Updating the WalkTrailInfoPage user interface using XAML

In this section, we will begin by updating the user interface for our `WalkTrailInfoPage`, using XAML to make some minor changes to our `ScrollView` control `Padding` property. We do this in order to adjust the layout space and the bounding region of how the child elements should be displayed when displaying the chosen walk trail information from the `ListView` control that is contained within the `WalksMainPage`.

Let's start by updating the user interface for our `WalkTrailInfoPage` by performing the following steps:

Locate and open the `WalkTrailInfoPage.xaml` file which is located in the `Views` folder, ensuring that it is displayed within the code editor, and enter the following highlighted code sections:

```
<?xml version="1.0" encoding="UTF-8"?>
 <ContentPage xmlns="http://xamarin.com/schemas/2014/forms"
xmlns:x="http://schemas.microsoft.com/winfx/2009/xaml"
x:Class="TrackMyWalks.Views.WalkTrailInfoPage">
     <ContentPage.Content>
        <ScrollView Padding="5,0,2,5">
            <StackLayout Orientation="Vertical"
HorizontalOptions="FillAndExpand">
                <Image x:Name="TrailImage" Aspect="AspectFill"
Source="{Binding ImageUrl}"
                        HorizontalOptions="FillAndExpand"
VerticalOptions="FillAndExpand" />
```

```xml
                    <Label x:Name="TrailName" FontSize="20"
        FontAttributes="Bold"
                                    TextColor="Black" Text="{Binding Title}"
        />
                    <Label x:Name="TrailKilometers" FontSize="12"
        TextColor="Black"
                                    Text="{Binding Distance,
        StringFormat='Kilometers: {0} km'}" />
                    <Label x:Name="TrailDifficulty" FontSize="12"
        TextColor="Black"
                                    Text="{Binding Difficulty,
        StringFormat='Difficulty: {0}'}" />
                    <Label x:Name="TrailFullDescription" FontSize="11"
        TextColor="Black"
                                    Text="{Binding Description}"
        HorizontalOptions="FillAndExpand" />
                    <Button x:Name="BeginTrailWalk" Text="Begin this
        Trail" TextColor="White"
                                    BackgroundColor="#008080"
        Clicked="BeginTrailWalk_Clicked" Margin="20"/>
                </StackLayout>
            </ScrollView>
        </ContentPage.Content>
    </ContentPage>
```

In the preceding code snippet, we began by making some minor changes to our
`ScrollView` control that will allow our `ContentPage` to scroll its contents if the
information being displayed is too big to fit within actual devices' screen real estate. We
updated the `Padding` property to represent the layout space and the bounding region into
which each of the child elements should be arranged by specifying values for the `Left`,
`Top`, `Right`, and `Bottom` values.

Updating the WalkTrailInfoPage code-behind using C#

Now that we have updated our `WalkTrailInfoPage` user interface to include the updated
`Padding` property that will represent the layout space and the bounding region into which
each of the child elements should be arranged when displaying our walk trail information,
the next step is to begin updating the underlying **C#** code within our `WalkTrailInfoPage`
code-behind file. We do this so that it can communicate with our
`WalkTrailInfoPageViewModel`, which will be used to display information associated
with the chosen walk trail.

Let's take a look at how we can achieve this by following these steps:

Open the `WalkTrailInfoPage.xaml.cs` code-behind file, ensuring that it is displayed within the code editor, and enter the following code snippet:

```
//
//  WalkTrailInfoPage.xaml.cs
//  Displays related trail information chosen from the WalksMainPage
//
//  Created by Steven F. Daniel on 14/05/2018
//  Copyright © 2018 GENIESOFT STUDIOS. All rights reserved.
//
using System;
using Xamarin.Forms;
using TrackMyWalks.ViewModels;

namespace TrackMyWalks.Views
{
    public partial class WalkTrailInfoPage : ContentPage
    {
        // Return the Binding Context for the ViewModel
        WalkTrailInfoPageViewModel _viewModel =>
                                  BindingContext as
WalkTrailInfoPageViewModel;

        public WalkTrailInfoPage()
        {
            InitializeComponent();

            // Update the Title and Initialise our BindingContext for the
Page
            this.Title = "Trail Walk Information";
            this.BindingContext = new WalkTrailInfoPageViewModel();
        }

        // Instance method that proceeds to begin a new walk trail
        public void BeginTrailWalk_Clicked(object sender, EventArgs e)
        {
            if (App.SelectedItem == null)
                return;
            Navigation.PushAsync(new WalkDistancePage());
            Navigation.RemovePage(this);
        }
    }
}
```

Now, let's start by taking a look at what we covered in the preceding code snippet:

1. We started by including a reference to the `TrackMyWalks.ViewModels` namespace so that we can access the classes and instance methods that are defined within the namespace, and then return the `BindingContext` that will be used by our `WalkTrailInfoPage` ContentPage by defining a `getter` property that points to our `WalkTrailInfoPageViewModel`.

2. Finally, we modified the `Title` property and initialized and set the `BindingContext` of our `WalkTrailInfoPage` to a new instance of our `WalkTrailInfoPageViewModel`.

Creating the WalkDistancePageViewModel using C#

Now that we have updated the `WalkTrailInfoPage` code-behind file so that it communicates with our `WalkTrailInfoPageViewModel` as well as each of the associated data bindings for the ContentPage that will be used by the ViewModel, the next step is to create and implement the underlying C# code for our ViewModel. This will be used by our `WalkDistancePage` code-behind file so that it can display information related to the chosen walk trail from our `WalksMainPage`.

Let's take a look at how we can achieve this by following these steps:

1. First, create a new **Empty Class** called `WalkDistancePageViewModel`, like you did in the section entitled *Creating the WalksMainPageViewModel using C#*, located within this chapter.

2. Next, ensure that the `WalkDistancePageViewModel.cs` file is displayed within the code editor and enter the following code snippet:

```
//
//  WalkDistancePagePageViewModel.cs
//  The ViewModel for our WalkDistancePage ContentPage
//
//  Created by Steven F. Daniel on 5/06/2018
//  Copyright © 2018 GENIESOFT STUDIOS. All rights reserved.
//
using System;
using System.Threading.Tasks;

namespace TrackMyWalks.ViewModels
{
```

```
public class WalkDistancePageViewModel : BaseViewModel
{
    public WalkDistancePageViewModel()
    {
    }

    // Update each control on the WalkDistancePage with
values from our Model
    public string Title => App.SelectedItem.Title;
    public string Description =>
App.SelectedItem.Description;
    public double Latitude => App.SelectedItem.Latitude;
    public double Longitude => App.SelectedItem.Longitude;
    public double Distance => App.SelectedItem.Distance;
    public String Difficulty =>
App.SelectedItem.Difficulty;
    public String ImageUrl => App.SelectedItem.ImageUrl;

    // Instance method to initialise the
WalkDistancePageViewModel
    public override async Task Init()
    {
        await Task.Factory.StartNew(() =>
        {
        });
    }
}
```

Now, let's start by taking a look at what we covered in the preceding code snippet:

1. We started by including references to the `System` and the `System.Threading.Tasks` namespaces so that we can access the classes that are defined within these namespaces.

2. Next, we ensured that our `WalkDistancePageViewModel` inherits from our `BaseViewModel` class. Then, we created a number of properties that will be bound to each control that is located within the `WalkDistancePage` ContentPage, using the values from our `App.SelectedItem` property.

3. Finally, we created the `Init` instance method that we defined within our `BaseViewModel`, which can be used to initialize our ViewModel.

Updating the WalkDistancePage user interface using XAML

In this section, we will begin by updating the user interface for our `WalkDistancePage` by using XAML. This will be used to display a full-screen map with a pin placeholder that, when tapped, will display information related to the chosen trail from the `ListView` contained within our `WalksMainPage`.

Let's start by updating the user interface for our `WalkTrailInfoPage` by performing the following steps:

Locate and open the `WalkDistancePage.xaml` file which is located in the **Views** folder, ensuring that it is displayed within the code editor, and enter the following highlighted code sections:

```xml
<?xml version="1.0" encoding="UTF-8"?>
 <ContentPage xmlns="http://xamarin.com/schemas/2014/forms"
xmlns:x="http://schemas.microsoft.com/winfx/2009/xaml"
xmlns:maps="clr-
namespace:Xamarin.Forms.Maps;assembly=Xamarin.Forms.Maps"
x:Class="TrackMyWalks.Views.WalkDistancePage">
    <ContentPage.Content>
        <ScrollView Padding="2,0,2,2">
            <StackLayout Orientation="Vertical"
HorizontalOptions="FillAndExpand"
                         VerticalOptions="FillAndExpand">
                <maps:Map x:Name="customMap" IsShowingUser="true"
MapType="Street" />
                <Button x:Name="EndThisTrail" Text="End this
Trail" TextColor="White"
                        BackgroundColor="#008080"
Clicked="EndThisTrailButton_Clicked"
                        Margin="20" />
            </StackLayout>
        </ScrollView>
    </ContentPage.Content>
 </ContentPage>
```

Now, let's start by taking a look at what we defined within the preceding XAML:

1. We began by making some minor changes to our `ScrollView` control, which will allow our ContentPage to scroll its contents if the information being displayed is too big to fit within the actual devices' screen real-estate.

2. Next, we updated the `Padding` property to represent the layout space and the bounding region into which each of the child elements should be arranged by specifying values for the left, top, right, and bottom values. Then,we defined a `StackLayout` control as well as defined the `<maps:Map>` field, which will be used to represent our map. Finally, we specified a name for our map control called `CustomMap` so that we can reference this within our code-behind file.

3. Finally, we set the `IsShowingUser` and `MapType` properties that will display the user's current location within the map control, as well as set the type of map to use.

Updating the WalkDistancePage code-behind using C#

Now that we have updated our user interface for our ContentPage using XAML, to include minor changes to our `ScrollView` control, as well as specify the Padding layout values for the arrangement of our child elements and specify properties for our `CustomMap` control, the next step is to begin updating the underlying C# code within our `WalkDistancePage` code-behind file in order to communicate with our `WalkDistancePageViewModel`. This will be used to interact with our `Map` control and place a pin placeholder that will contain information associated with the chosen walk trail from the `ListView` contained within our `WalksMainPage`.

Let's take a look at how we can achieve this by following these steps:

Open the `WalkDistancePage.xaml.cs` code-behind file, ensuring that it is displayed within the code editor, and enter the following code snippet:

```
//
//  WalkDistancePage.xaml.cs
//  Displays related trail information within a map using a
//  pin placeholder
//
//  Created by Steven F. Daniel on 14/05/2018
//  Copyright © 2018 GENIESOFT STUDIOS. All rights reserved.
//
using System;
```

```
using TrackMyWalks.ViewModels;
using Xamarin.Forms;
using Xamarin.Forms.Maps;

namespace TrackMyWalks.Views
{
    public partial class WalkDistancePage : ContentPage
    {
        // Return the Binding Context for the ViewModel
        WalkDistancePageViewModel _viewModel =>
                                    BindingContext as
WalkDistancePageViewModel;

        public WalkDistancePage()
        {
            InitializeComponent();

            // Update the Title and Initialise our BindingContext
            // for the Page
            Title = "Distance Travelled Information";
            this.BindingContext = new WalkDistancePageViewModel();

            // Create a pin placeholder within the map containing
the
            // walk information
            customMap.Pins.Add(new Pin
            {
                Type = PinType.Place,
                Position = new Position(_viewModel.Latitude,
_viewModel.Longitude),
                Label = _viewModel.Title,
                Address = "Difficulty: " + _viewModel.Difficulty +
" Total Distance: " +
                                _viewModel.Distance, Id =
_viewModel.Title
            });

            // Create a region around the map within a one-
kilometer radius
            customMap.MoveToRegion(MapSpan.FromCenterAndRadius(new
                    Position(_viewModel.Latitude,
_viewModel.Longitude),
                            Distance.FromKilometers(1.0)));
        }

        // Instance method that ends the current trail and returns
        // back to the main screen
        public void EndThisTrailButton_Clicked(object sender,
```

```
EventArgs e)
        {
            App.SelectedItem = null;
            Navigation.PopToRootAsync(true);
        }
    }
}
```

Now, let's start by taking a look at what we covered in the preceding code snippet:

1. We started by including a reference to the `TrackMyWalks.ViewModels` namespace so that we can access the classes and instance methods that are defined within the namespace, and then return the `BindingContext` that will be used by our `WalkDistancePage` ContentPage by defining a `getter` property that points to our `WalkDistancePageViewModel`.

2. Next, we modified the `Title` property and initialized and set the `BindingContext` of our `WalkDistancePage` to a new instance of our `WalkDistancePageViewModel`.

3. Then, we created a pin placeholder within our map by using the `Pins.Add` method of our `CustomMap`, and then specified the `Type` and `Position` properties of the `CustomMap` by using the `Latitude` and `Longitude` coordinates of the chosen walk trail.

4. Finally, we assigned values for the `Title` and `Address`, as well as an `Id` for our pin placeholder, and then called the `MoveToRegion` method to create a region around the map within a 1-k radius around the trail walk area.

You have created all of the necessary ViewModels and have updated each of the user interface files using XAML, as well as implemented the necessary instance and event methods and have made the necessary changes to the underlying C# code for our app. The next step is to compile, build, and run the TrackMyWalks application within the iOS simulator.

Launching the TrackMyWalks app using the iOS simulator

In this section, we will take a look at how to compile and run the **TrackMyWalks** application. You have the option of choosing to run your application using an actual device or choosing from a list of iOS simulators that mimic each of the different types of iOS devices.

Let's begin by performing the following steps:

1. Ensure that you have chosen the **Debug | iPhone Simulator** from the drop-down menu.
2. Next, choose your preferred device from the list of available iOS Simulators.
3. Then, select the **Run | Start Debugging** menu option, as shown in the following screenshot:

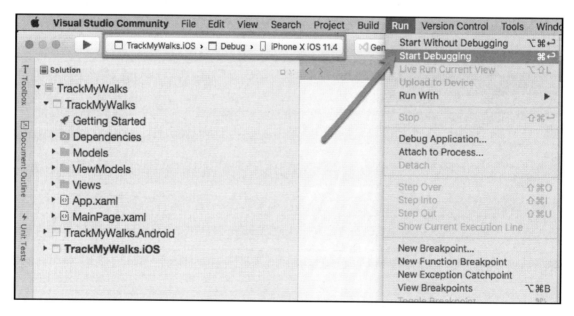

Launching the TrackMyWalks app within the iOS Simulator

4. Alternatively, you can also build and run the **TrackMyWalks** application by pressing the *Command + Return* key combinations.

When the compilation is complete, the iOS Simulator will appear automatically and the **TrackMyWalks** application will be displayed, as shown in the following screenshot:

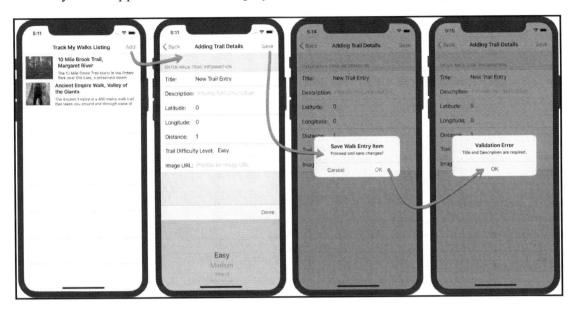

Adding of new Trail details with Validation

As you can see from the preceding screenshot, it displays our TrackMyWalks application, along with a list of static walk entries that have been defined within our `WalksMainPageViewModel` and displayed within our `ListView`. Clicking on the **Add** button will display the **Adding Trail Details**, where you can begin entering information related to the trail. You will notice that, since we are creating a new trail walk entry, our **Title, Trail Difficulty Level**, as well as the **Distance** `EntryCell` fields have been populated with the default values that we specified within our `WalkEntryPageViewModel`.

Clicking on the **Save** button will display a dialog asking the user if they would like to proceed and save changes. When clicking on the **OK** button without specifying values for both the **Title** and **Description** EntryCell fields, they will receive the **Validation Error** dialog. Alternatively, clicking on the **Cancel** button from the **Save Walk Entry Item** dialog will redirect the user back to the **Track My Walks Listing** screen:

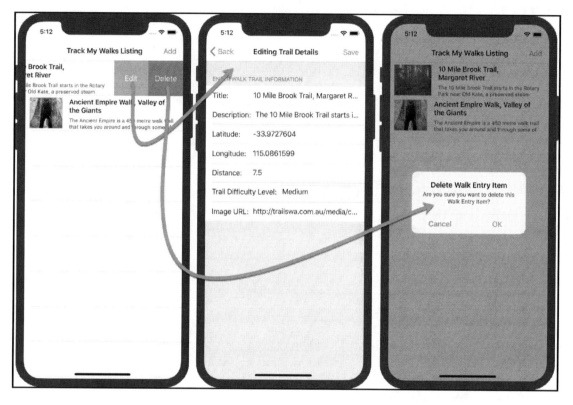

Deleting an existing Walk Entry Item

The preceding screenshot shows you the navigation flow between each of the pages whenever a trail item that needs to be edited has been selected from the ContextActions MenuItems. When the **Edit** option has been selected, this will display the **Editing Trail Details** screen, where the user can make changes and save this back to the model. Alternatively, if the user chooses the **Delete** button, this will display the **Delete Walk Entry Item** dialog, asking the user if they would like to proceed with the deletion.

Clicking on the **OK** button, the code will proceed and remove the item from the `WalksListModel` within our ViewModel, but will reappear when the `ListView` is refreshed the next time round. As we progress throughout this book, we will be refactoring these pages to allow this to happen. Alternatively, clicking on the **Cancel** button will dismiss the dialog:

Navigation flow whenever a walk trail has been selected

The preceding screenshot shows the navigation flow between each of the pages whenever a trail has been selected from the `ListView`, with the final screen showing the **Distance Travelled Information** ContentPage, along with a marker pinpointing the coordinates related to the chosen trail, along with its associated information.

Summary

In this chapter, we learned about the architecture behind the MVVM architecture pattern, as well as the different components and roles that they play. You then learned how to create an abstract `BaseViewModel` class that contained various properties with additional class methods.

We then created various ViewModel classes that inherited the properties and methods from our `BaseViewModel` class, and then proceeded to make some additional changes to each of the user interface ContentPages using XAML. Next, we updated each of the code-behind files for each of our ContentPages in order to implement the ViewModels so that the `bindable` object properties defined within the XAML could be bound to those properties defined within the associated ViewModel.

Lastly, you learned how to work with `ContextActions` and specified the associated `Clicked` method event for each menu item within the `WalksMainPage` XAML. You also implemented the instance methods to the `MenuItems` when they were clicked, before running the **TrackMyWalks** app within the iOS Simulator.

In the next chapter, you'll build upon your working knowledge of the MVVM architectural design pattern and learn how to navigate smoothly between each ViewModel by creating a C# class that will act as a navigation service for our app, and then refactor the existing ViewModels to allow navigation between these views to happen.

6
Navigating Within the Mvvm Model

In the previous chapter, you learned about the **Model-View-ViewModel (MVVM)** architecture, as well as how to implement the MVVM pattern within the TrackMyWalks application. You learned how to create a BaseViewModel base class that each of our ViewModels will inherit from, as well as how to go about creating the associated C# class files for each of our ViewModels that will data bind to each of the properties defined within our XAML Pages. Finally, you learned how to add ContextActions to your (XAML) content pages, and how to implement the code action events within your code, so that you can respond to those actions.

In this chapter, you'll learn how to leverage what you already know about the MVVM architectural design pattern to learn how to navigate between each of the ViewModels within our TrackMyWalks application.

You'll learn how to create a NavigationService Interface and Class, as well as update our BaseViewModel base class, which will include a reference to our NavigationService class that each of our ViewModels will utilize. Finally, you will update each of the ViewModels as well as each of the XAML pages to allow navigation between these pages to happen.

This chapter will cover the following points:

- Understanding the Xamarin.Forms Navigation API
- Creating and implementing a NavigationService class that each of our ViewModels will use
- Updating the XAML code-behind pages to use the NavigationService class
- Updating the underlying ViewModels to use the NavigationService class
- Implementing the data bindings within our user interfaces using XAML

Understanding the Xamarin.Forms Navigation API

In this section, we will take a look at the `Xamarin.Forms` Navigation API architectural pattern, as well as gain an understanding of the different types of navigation patterns that are available for us. The `Xamarin.Forms` Navigation API is exposed through the `Xamarin.Forms.INavigation` interface, and is implemented by using the `Navigation` property. This can be called from any `Xamarin.Forms` object, typically from the `Xamarin.Forms.Page`, which inherits from the `ContentPage` class that is part of the `Xamarin.Forms.Core` assembly namespace.

The `Xamarin.Forms` Navigation API supports two different types of navigation: **Hierarchical** and **Modal**. The following table provides a brief description of what each area is used for:

Type	Description
Hierarchical	The **Hierarchical** navigation type is basically a **stack-based** navigation pattern that enables users to move iteratively through each of the **Views** within the hierarchy, and then navigate back out again, one screen at a time, thus removing them from the **navigation stack.**
Modal	The **Modal** navigation type is a single pop-up screen that interrupts the hierarchical navigation by requiring that the user respond to an action, prior to the screen or popup being dismissed.

The Hierarchical navigation provides a means of navigating through the navigational structure and is the most widely used approach. This involves the user tapping their way forward through a series of pages and navigating back through the navigation stack, using the navigation methods available on Android or iOS devices.

The following diagram shows the process of moving from one page to another within the Hierarchical model, and what happens when popping pages from the navigation stack:

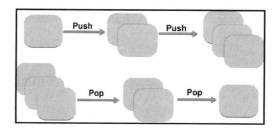

Navigating within the Hierarchical model

As you can see from the preceding screenshot, whenever a View is pushed onto the navigation stack, this will become the most active page. Alternatively, when you want to return to the previous page, the application will start to Pop the current page from the navigation stack, and the new top-most View will then become the active View. The Modal navigation pattern displays a View on top of the current View that prevents the user from interacting with the View underneath it. This approach provides the user with choices for what they want to do prior to the Modal View being closed.

The INavigation interface, which is part of the Xamarin.Forms.NavigationPage, implements and exposes two separate read-only properties: NavigationStack and ModalStack. This will allow you to view both the Hierarchical and Modal navigation stacks. The INavigation interface provides you with a number of methods that allow you to asynchronously **Push** (Add) and **Pop** (Remove) **Views** onto the navigation stack and modal stacks, which are explained in the following table, along with a brief description of what each area is used for:

Type	Description
PushAsync(Page page)	The PushAsync(Page page) method adds a new Page to the top of the navigation stack that enables users to move deeper within the View hierarchy.
PopAsync()	The PopAsync() method allows you to navigate back through the navigation stack to the previous page, but only if one has previously been added to the navigation stack.
PushModalAsync(Page page)	The PushModalAsync(Page page) method allows you to display the **Page** modally whenever you need to display an informational message to the user, or to request information from the user. A good example of a **Modal** page would be a sign-in page where you need to get the user's credentials.
PopModalAsync()	The PopModalAsync() method allows you to dismiss the currently displayed Page and returns you through the navigation stack to the Page that is displayed underneath.

As well as the aforementioned navigational methods, the `Xamarin.Forms.INavigation` interface provides you with a number of additional methods that will help you manipulate the navigation stack, which are explained in the following table, along with a brief description of what each area is used for:

Type	Description
`InsertPageBefore(Page page, Page before)`	The `InsertPageBefore(Page page, Page before)` method allows you to insert a new Page before a specific Page that has already been added to the navigation stack.
`RemovePage(Page page)`	The `RemovePage(Page page)` method allows you to remove a specific Page within the navigation stack.
`PopToRootAsync()`	The `PopToRootAsync()` method allows you to navigate back to the first Page that is contained within the navigation stack, as well as remove all of the other Pages contained within the navigation stack hierarchy.

Now that you have a reasonably good understanding of each of the components that are contained within the Navigation API architectural pattern, our next step is to begin learning about some of the different approaches for navigating between Views and ViewModels.

Differences between the Navigation and ViewModel approaches

In this section, we will take a look at the different approaches when performing navigation within your ViewModels that are contained within a `Xamarin.Forms` application. Whenever you navigate between your ViewModels, there are a couple of approaches you should consider before going down this path.

One approach would be to use the `View` (Page) navigation approach, which involves navigating to another `View` by using a direct reference to that page, for example, using `Navigation.PushAsync(new WalksMainPage());`. Alternatively, if you want to use the ViewModel approach to navigate to a `View` (Page) using the associated `Views` (Page) ViewModel, you would first need to form some sort of mapping between each of the `Views` (Page) as well as their associated ViewModels.

By creating a `Dictionary` or key-value type property within the `NavigationService`, this will maintain a one-to-one mapping for each of the `Views` and their associated ViewModel. In the MVVM architectural pattern, any actions that are taken by the user on a particular `View` (Page) are bound to commands that are part of the `View` (Page), as well as the ViewModels, and so this process needs to be thought through differently when navigating to another `View` (Page), or even the previous `View` (Page) within the navigation stack, when performing such tasks as saving data or updating a map's location.

As such, we need to rethink how we can achieve navigating through our ViewModels, which leverages the MVVM architectural design pattern within our app, so that it can be controlled by the ViewModels and not by the underlying `Views` (Pages).

Now that you have a good understanding of the different ways in which you can navigate through your `Views` (Pages), by either using the Navigation approach or using the ViewModel approach that leverages the MVVM architectural design pattern approach, our next step is to begin creating and implementing the `NavigationService` class, which will be used to help you navigate within the ViewModels for our `TrackMyWalks` application.

Creating and implementing the NavigationService interface

In this section, we will take a look at how to create the `INavigationService` class, which will essentially contain various instance methods that will be used by our `BaseViewModel` class, that each of our `ViewModels` class constructors will implement in the `INavigationService` interface. The advantage of creating an `INavigationService` class is that it's much easier to add additional class instance methods that will be used by those ViewModels that utilize this interface.

Let's start by creating the `NavigationService` class for our `TrackMyWalks` app by performing the following steps:

1. Ensure that the `TrackMyWalks` solution is open within the Visual Studio for Mac IDE.

2. Next, right-click on the `TrackMyWalks` project, and choose **Add|New Folder** from the pop-up menu, as shown in the following screenshot:

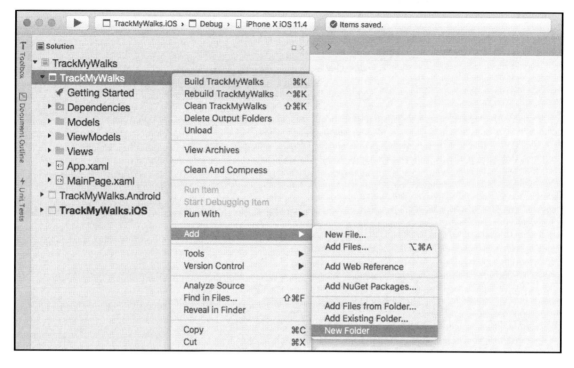

Creating the Services folder within the TrackMyWalks project

3. Then, enter **Services** for the name of the new folder to be created, right-click on the `Services` folder, and choose **Add|New File...** from the pop-up menu, as shown in the following screenshot:

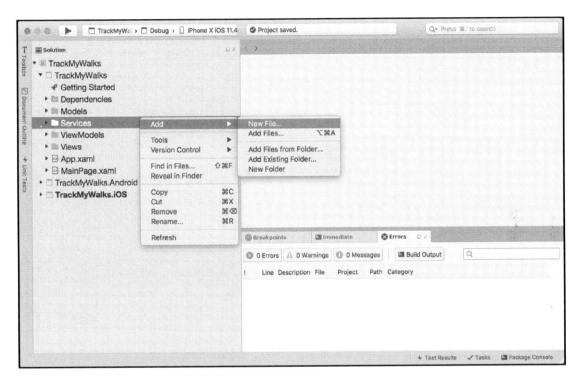

Adding a New File to the Services folder

4. Next, choose the **Empty Interface** option under the **General** section and enter **INavigation** for the name of the class to be created, as shown in the following screenshot:

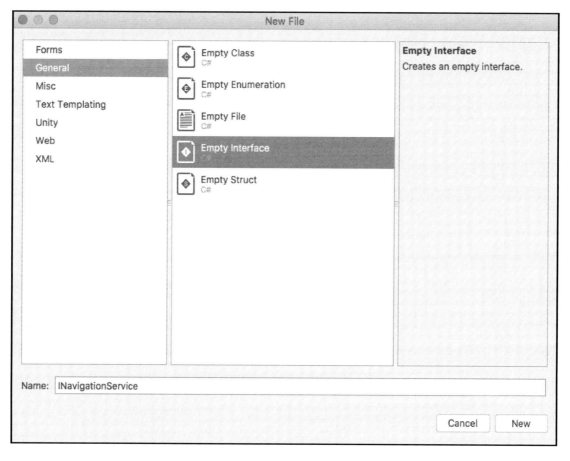

Creating the INavigationService Interface

5. Next, click on the **New** button to allow the wizard to proceed and create the new file, as shown in the preceding screenshot. Now that we have created our INavigationService interface, we can proceed with implementing the required code for our class.

6. Locate and open the INavigationService.cs file, which is located as part of the TrackMyWalks group, and ensure that it is displayed within the code editor. Enter the following code snippet:

```
//
//   INavigationService.cs
//   Navigation Service Interface that each of our ViewModels will use
//
//   Created by Steven F. Daniel on 16/06/2018.
//   Copyright © 2018 GENIESOFT STUDIOS. All rights reserved.
//
using System;
using System.Threading.Tasks;
using TrackMyWalks.ViewModels;
using Xamarin.Forms;

namespace TrackMyWalks.Services
{
    public interface INavigationService
    {
        // Asynchronously removes the most recent page from the
navigation stack.
        Task<Page> RemoveViewFromStack();

        // Returns to the Root Page after removing the current page
from the
        // navigation stack
        Task BackToMainPage();

        // Navigate to a particular ViewModel within our MVVM Model
        Task NavigateTo<TVM>() where TVM : BaseViewModel;
    }
}
```

Now, let's start by taking a look at what we covered in the preceding code snippet:

1. First, we started by creating an interface class that will contain various class instance methods that will be utilized by our NavigationService class, as well as our Views (Content Page) and within our ViewModels.

2. Then, we declared a RemoveViewFromStack instance method, which will be responsible for removing the most recent page from within the navigation stack.

3. Next, we declared a `BackToMainPage` instance method, which will be responsible for returning the user back to the Root main page, after removing the current page from the navigation stack.

4. Finally, we declared our `NavigateTo` instance method, which declares a generic type that will be used to restrict the ViewModel to only use objects of the `BaseViewModel` base class.

The `Task` class is essentially used to handle asynchronous operations, which is done by ensuring that the method you initiated will eventually finish, thus completing the task and returning a `Task` object, almost instantaneously, although the underlying work within the method could likely finish later.

 Whenever you use the `Task` object, you can use the await keyword to wait for the task to complete, which will essentially block the current thread, and wait until the `asynchronous` method has completed.

Creating and implementing the NavigationService class

In this section, we will take a look at how to create the `NavigationService` class, which will inherit from our `INavigationService` interface and implement the underlying instance methods that we declared within our interface class to help navigate between our ViewModels.

Let's start by creating the `NavigationService` class for our `TrackMyWalks` app by performing the following steps:

1. Ensure that the `TrackMyWalks` solution is open within the Visual Studio for Mac IDE.

2. Next, right-click on the `Services` folder, and choose **Add | New File...** from the pop-up menu.

3. Then, choose the **Empty Class** option under the **General** section and enter `NavigationService` for the name of the class to be created, as shown in the following screenshot:

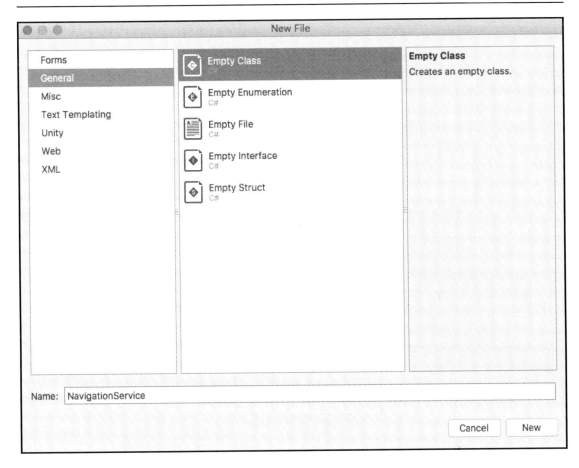

Creating the NavigationService Class

4. Next, click on the **New** button to allow the wizard to proceed and create the new file, as shown in the preceding screenshot. Now that we have created our NavigationService class, we can proceed with implementing the required code for our class.

5. Locate and open the NavigationService.cs file, which is located as part of the TrackMyWalks group, and ensure that it is displayed within the code editor. Enter the following code snippet:

```
//
//   NavigationService.cs
//   Navigation Service Class that each of our ViewModels will utilise
//
//   Created by Steven F. Daniel on 16/06/2018.
//   Copyright © 2018 GENIESOFT STUDIOS. All rights reserved.
```

```
//
using System;
using System.Collections.Generic;
using System.Linq;
using System.Reflection;
using System.Threading.Tasks;
using TrackMyWalks.Services;
using TrackMyWalks.ViewModels;
using Xamarin.Forms;

[assembly: Dependency(typeof(NavigationService))]
namespace TrackMyWalks.Services
{
    public class NavigationService : INavigationService
    {
        public INavigation XFNavigation { get; set; }
        readonly IDictionary<Type, Type> _viewMapping = new
Dictionary<Type, Type>();

        // Register our ViewModel and View within our Dictionary
        public void RegisterViewMapping(Type viewModel, Type view)
        {
            _viewMapping.Add(viewModel, view);
        }
        // Removes the most recent Page from the navigation stack.
        public Task<Page> RemoveViewFromStack()
        {
            return XFNavigation.PopAsync();
        }
        // Returns to the Root Page after removing the current page
        // from the navigation stack
        public Task BackToMainPage()
        {
            return XFNavigation.PopToRootAsync(true);
        }
        // Navigates navigates to a specific ViewModel
        public async Task NavigateTo<TVM>() where TVM : BaseViewModel
        {
            await NavigateToView(typeof(TVM));
            if (XFNavigation.NavigationStack.Last().BindingContext is
BaseViewModel)
                await
((BaseViewModel)(XFNavigation.NavigationStack.Last().
                    BindingContext)).Init();
        }
        // Navigates to a specific ViewModel within our dictionary
        // viewMapping
        public async Task NavigateToView(Type viewModelType)
```

```
        {
            Type viewType;
            if (!_viewMapping.TryGetValue(viewModelType, out
viewType))
                throw new ArgumentException("No view found in View
Mapping
                    for " + viewModelType.FullName + ".");

            var constructor = viewType.GetTypeInfo().
                DeclaredConstructors.FirstOrDefault(
                dc =>!dc.GetParameters().Any());

            var view = constructor.Invoke(null) as Page;
            await XFNavigation.PushAsync(view, true);
        }
    }
}
```

Now, let's start by taking a look at what we covered in the preceding code snippet:

1. First, we started by initializing our `NavigationService` class to be marked as a dependency by adding the `Dependency` metadata attribute so that it can be resolved by the Xamarin.Forms `DependencyService` class. This will enable our class to find and use the method implementations defined by our `INavigationService` interface.

2. Next, we need to ensure that our `NavigationService` class inherits from the `INavigationService` interface so that it can access the instance methods, as well as any getters and setters.

3. Then, we created an `INavigationService` property called `XFNavigation`, which will provide our class with a reference to the current navigation instance that will need to be set up when the navigation service class is first initialized within our `App.xaml.cs` file.

4. Next, we declared a `_viewMapping` variable, which will be used to store all of the ViewModel and `Views` (Pages) mappings, prior to declaring a `RegisterViewMapping` instance method, which will be used to register each of our ViewModels and `Views` (Pages) within our `Dictionary _viewMapping` object.

5. Next, we created our `RemoveViewFromStack` instance method, which will be responsible for removing the most recently added page from within our navigation stack, and created a `BackToMainPage` instance method, which will be responsible for removing all of the pages from the navigation stack, including the current page, and display the Root page.

6. Then, we created our `NavigateTo` instance method, which will be used to navigate to a specific ViewModel that is contained within our `_viewMapping` `Dictionary` object, by calling the `NavigateToView` instance method, and then calling the `Init` method within the associated ViewModel to initialize the `BindingContext`.

7. Finally, we created our `NavigateToView` instance method, which accepts the ViewModel as a parameter, and which will be used to navigate to the specified ViewModel within our `_viewMapping` object. We used the `TryGetValue` method to check to see whether the view can be found within the `_viewMapping` `Dictionary`. Then, we navigate to the ViewModel if it is found.

For more information on the `DependencyService` class, refer to the Microsoft Developer Documentation at `https://docs.microsoft.com/en-us/xamarin/xamarin-forms/app-fundamentals/dependency-service/introduction`.

Updating the BaseViewModel to use the navigation service

Now that we have created both our `NavigationService` Interface and Class, we will be able to navigate within our ViewModels. The next step is to update the underlying C# code within our `BaseViewModel` class. Since our `BaseViewModel` class is used by each of our ViewModels, it makes sense to add these additional properties and instance methods within the `BaseViewModel` class.

Let's take a look at how we can achieve this by following these steps:

1. Open the `BaseViewModel.cs` class, ensuring that it is displayed within the code editor, and enter the following highlighted code sections:

```
//
//  BaseViewModel.cs
//  BaseView Model Class that each of our ViewModels will inherit from
//
```

```
//  Created by Steven F. Daniel on 5/06/2018
//  Copyright © 2018 GENIESOFT STUDIOS. All rights reserved.
//
using System.ComponentModel;
using System.Runtime.CompilerServices;
using System.Threading.Tasks;
using TrackMyWalks.Services;

namespace TrackMyWalks.ViewModels
{
    public abstract class BaseViewModel : INotifyPropertyChanged
    {
        public INavigationService Navigation { get; set; }
        public const string PageTitlePropertyName = "PageTitle";

        string pageTitle;
        public string PageTitle
        {
            get => pageTitle;
            set { pageTitle = value; OnPropertyChanged(); }
        }
        protected BaseViewModel(INavigationService navService)
        {
            Navigation = navService;
        }
        public abstract Task Init();
        public event PropertyChangedEventHandler PropertyChanged;

        protected virtual void OnPropertyChanged([CallerMemberName]
                                        string propertyName =
null)
        {
            PropertyChanged?.Invoke(this, new
PropertyChangedEventArgs(propertyName));
        }
    }
    public abstract class BaseViewModel<TParam> : BaseViewModel
    {
        protected BaseViewModel(INavigationService navService) :
base(navService)
        {
        }
    }
}
```

Now, let's start by taking a look at what we covered in the preceding code snippet:

1. We started by including a reference to the `TrackMyWalks.Services` namespace so that we can access the classes and instance methods that are defined within the namespace.

2. Finally, we created a `Navigation` property that points to our `INavigationService` class and defines the getter and setter properties. We also modified the `BaseViewModel` class constructor to include a parameter called `navService`, which will be required by each of the ViewModels that inherit from this class.

Updating the WalksMainPageViewModel using C#

Now that we have updated our `BaseViewModel` class to reference our `NavigationService` class, which will be used and inherited by each of the ViewModels that we create, we can now proceed and start updating the `WalksMainPageViewModel` class so that it can use our navigation service.

Let's take a look at how we can achieve this by following these steps:

1. Ensure that the `TrackMyWalks` solution is open within the Visual Studio for Mac IDE.

2. Open the `WalksMainPageViewModel.cs` class, ensuring that it is displayed within the code editor, and enter the following highlighted code sections within the code snippet:

```
//
//   WalksMainPageViewModel.cs
//   The ViewModel for our WalksMainPage ContentPage
//
//   Created by Steven F. Daniel on 5/06/2018.
//   Copyright © 2018 GENIESOFT STUDIOS. All rights reserved.
//
using System.Collections.ObjectModel;
using System.Threading.Tasks;
using TrackMyWalks.Models;
using TrackMyWalks.Services;

namespace TrackMyWalks.ViewModels
{
```

```
public class WalksMainPageViewModel : BaseViewModel
{
    // Create our WalksListModel Observable Collection
    public ObservableCollection<WalkDataModel> WalksListModel;
    public WalksMainPageViewModel(INavigationService navService) :
base(navService)
    {
    }

    // Instance method to add and retrieve our  Walk Trail items
    public void GetWalkTrailItems()
    {
        // Specify our List Collection to store the items being
read
        WalksListModel = new ObservableCollection<WalkDataModel>();

        // Populate our collection with some dummy data that will
be
        // used to populate our ListView
        ...
        ...
        // Instance method to initialise the WalksMainPageViewModel
        public override async Task Init()
        {
            await Task.Factory.StartNew(() =>
            {
                // Call our GetWalkTrailItems method to populate our
                // collection
                GetWalkTrailItems();
            });
        }
    }
}
```

Now, let's start by taking a look at what we covered in the preceding code snippet:

1. We started by including a reference to the `TrackMyWalks.Services` namespace so that we can access the classes and instance methods that are defined within the namespace.

2. Finally, we modified the `WalksMainPageViewModel` class constructor to include a parameter called `navService` that references our `INavigationService` interface. Since our ViewModel inherits from the `BaseViewModel` class, we have to honor this agreement.

Updating the WalksMainPage code-behind using C#

Now that we have updated our `WalksMainPageViewModel` to take advantage of our `NavigationService`, which will enable our ViewModel to navigate within the navigation stack, the next step is to begin updating the underlying C# code within our `WalksMainPage` code-behind file so that it will communicate with our ViewModel so that we can navigate.

Let's take a look at how we can achieve this by following these steps:

1. Open the `WalksMainPage.xaml.cs` code-behind file, ensuring that it is displayed within the code editor, and enter the following highlighted code sections:

```
//
//  WalksMainPage.xaml.cs
//  Displays Walk Information within a ListView control from an array
//
//  Created by Steven F. Daniel on 14/05/2018
//  Copyright © 2018 GENIESOFT STUDIOS. All rights reserved.
//
using System;
using TrackMyWalks.Models;
using TrackMyWalks.Services;
using TrackMyWalks.ViewModels;
using Xamarin.Forms;

namespace TrackMyWalks.Views
{
    public partial class WalksMainPage : ContentPage
    {
        // Return the Binding Context for the ViewModel
        WalksMainPageViewModel _viewModel => BindingContext as
WalksMainPageViewModel;

        public WalksMainPage()
        {
            InitializeComponent();

            // Update the Title and Initialise our BindingContext for
the Page
            this.Title = "Track My Walks Listing";
            this.BindingContext = new
WalksMainPageViewModel(DependencyService.
```

```
                                    Get<INavigationService>());
        }

        // Instance method to call the WalkEntryPage to add a Walk
Entry
        public async void AddWalk_Clicked(object sender, EventArgs e)
        {
            App.SelectedItem = null;
            await
_viewModel.Navigation.NavigateTo<WalkEntryPageViewModel>();
        }

        // Instance method to call the WalkTrailInfoPage using the
selected item
        public async void myWalkEntries_ItemTapped(object sender,
ItemTappedEventArgs e)
        {
            // Get the selected item from our ListView
            App.SelectedItem = e.Item as WalkDataModel;
            await
_viewModel.Navigation.NavigateTo<WalkTrailInfoPageViewModel>();
        }

        // Instance method to call the WalkEntryPage to allow item to
be edited
        public async void OnEditItem(object sender, EventArgs e)
        {
            // Get the selected item to be edited from our ListView
            var selectedItem =
(WalkDataModel)((MenuItem)sender).CommandParameter;
            App.SelectedItem = selectedItem;
            await
_viewModel.Navigation.NavigateTo<WalkEntryPageViewModel>();
        }

        // Instance method to remove the trail item from our
collection
        public async void OnDeleteItem(object sender, EventArgs e)
        {
            // Get the selected item to be deleted from our ListView
            var selectedItem =
(WalkDataModel)((MenuItem)sender).CommandParameter;

            // Prompt the user with a confirmation dialog to confirm
            if (await DisplayAlert("Delete Walk Entry Item", "Are you
sure you want
                to delete this Walk Entry Item?", "OK", "Cancel"))
            {
```

```
            // Remove Walk Item from our WalkListModel collection
            _viewModel.WalksListModel.Remove(selectedItem);
        }
        else
            return;
    }

    // Method to initialise our View Model when the ContentPage
appears
    protected override async void OnAppearing()
    {
        base.OnAppearing();

        if (_viewModel != null)
        {
            // Call the Init method to initialise the ViewModel
            await _viewModel.Init();
        }

        // Set up and initialise the binding for our ListView
WalkEntriesListView.SetBinding(ItemsView<Cell>.ItemsSourceProperty,
                                    new Binding("."));
        WalkEntriesListView.BindingContext =
_viewModel.WalksListModel;
    }
  }
}
```

Now, let's start by taking a look at what we covered in the preceding code snippet:

1. We started by including a reference to the `TrackMyWalks.Services` namespace so that we can access the classes and instance methods that are defined within the namespace.
2. Next, we modified the `BindingContext` of our **WalksMainPage** to a new instance of our `WalksMainPageViewModel`, which uses the `DependencyService` class and includes our `INavigationService` interface.
3. Then, we updated the `AddWalk_Clicked` instance method to use the `NavigateTo` instance method of the `_viewModel.Navigation` property that takes the `WalkEntryPageViewModel` as the ViewModel to navigate within the navigation stack.
4. Next, we updated the `myWalkEntries_ItemTapped` instance method to use the `NavigateTo` instance method of the `_viewModel.Navigation` property that takes the `WalkTrailInfoPageViewModel` as the ViewModel to navigate within the navigation stack.

5. Finally, we updated the `OnEditItem` instance method that will be called whenever the **Edit** context menu item is tapped within the `ListView`. We use the `NavigateTo` instance method of the `_viewModel.Navigation` property that accepts the `WalkEntryPageViewModel` as the ViewModel to navigate within the navigation stack.

Updating the WalkEntryPageViewModel using C#

Now that we have updated our `WalksMainPage` code-behind file so that it can reference our `NavigationService` class, thereby enabling it to navigate to our ViewModels within our navigation stack, we can proceed and start updating the `WalksEntryPageViewModel` class so that it can use our navigation service.

Let's take a look at how we can achieve this by following these steps:

1. Ensure that the `WalkEntryPageViewModel.cs` file is displayed within the code editor and enter in the following highlighted code sections within the code snippet:

```
//
//   WalkEntryPageViewModel.cs
//   The ViewModel for our WalkEntryPage ContentPage
//
//   Created by Steven F. Daniel on 5/06/2018.
//   Copyright © 2018 GENIESOFT STUDIOS. All rights reserved.
//
using System;
using System.Threading.Tasks;
using TrackMyWalks.Models;
using TrackMyWalks.Services;

namespace TrackMyWalks.ViewModels
{
    public class WalkEntryPageViewModel : BaseViewModel
    {
        public WalkEntryPageViewModel(INavigationService navService) :
base(navService)
        {
            // Update the title if we are creating a new Walk Entry
            if (App.SelectedItem == null)
            {
                PageTitle = "Adding Trail Details";
```

```
            App.SelectedItem = new WalkDataModel();

            // Set the default values when creating a new Trail
            Title = "New Trail Entry";
            Difficulty = "Easy";
            Distance = 1.0;
        }
        else
        {
            // Otherwise, we must be editing an existing entry
            PageTitle = "Editing Trail Details";
        }
    }
    ...
    ...
}
}
```

Now, let's start by taking a look at what we covered in the preceding code snippet:

1. We started by including a reference to the `TrackMyWalks.Services` namespace so that we can access the classes and instance methods that are defined within the namespace.
2. Finally, we modified the `WalkEntryPageViewModel` class constructor to include a parameter called `navService` that references our `INavigationService` interface. Since our ViewModel inherits from the `BaseViewModel` class, we have to honor this agreement.

Updating the WalkEntryPage code-behind using C#

Now that we have updated our `WalkEntryPageViewModel` to take advantage of the `NavigationService` that will enable our ViewModel to navigate within the navigation stack, the next step is to begin updating the underlying C# code within our `WalkEntryPage` code-behind file so that it will communicate with our ViewModel to allow for navigation.

Let's take a look at how we can achieve this by following these steps:

1. Open the `WalkEntryPage.xaml.cs` code-behind file, ensuring that it is displayed within the code editor, and enter the following highlighted code sections:

```
//
// WalkEntryPage.xaml.cs
// Data Entry screen that allows new walk information to be added
//
// Created by Steven F. Daniel on 14/05/2018
// Copyright © 2018 GENIESOFT STUDIOS. All rights reserved.
//
using System;
using TrackMyWalks.Services;
using TrackMyWalks.ViewModels;
using Xamarin.Forms;

namespace TrackMyWalks.Views
{
    public partial class WalkEntryPage : ContentPage
    {
        // Return the Binding Context for the ViewModel
        WalkEntryPageViewModel _viewModel => BindingContext as
WalkEntryPageViewModel;

        public WalkEntryPage()
        {
            InitializeComponent();

            // Update the Title and Initialise our BindingContext
            // for the Page
            Title = "New Walk Entry Page";
            BindingContext = new
WalkEntryPageViewModel(DependencyService.
                            Get<INavigationService>());
            SetBinding(TitleProperty, new
Binding(BaseViewModel.PageTitlePropertyName));
        }

        // Instance method that saves the new walk entry
        public async void SaveWalkItem_Clicked(object sender,
EventArgs e)
        {
            // Prompt the user with a confirmation dialog to confirm
            if (await DisplayAlert("Save Walk Entry Item",
                    "Proceed and save changes?", "OK", "Cancel"))
            {
```

```
                          // Attempt to save and validate our Walk Entry Item
                          if (!_viewModel.ValidateFormDetailsAndSave())
                              // Error Saving - Must have Title and description
                              await DisplayAlert("Validation Error", "Title and
                                  Description are required.", "OK");
                          else
                            // Navigate back to the Track My Walks Listing page
                            await _viewModel.Navigation.RemoveViewFromStack();
                      }
                      else
                      {
                          // Navigate back to the Track My Walks Listing page
                          await _viewModal.Navigation.RemoveViewFromStack();
                      }
                  }
              }
          }
```

Now, let's start by taking a look at what we covered in the preceding code snippet:

1. We started by including a reference to the `TrackMyWalks.Services` namespace so that we can access the classes and instance methods that are defined within the namespace.

2. Next, we modified the `BindingContext` of our `WalkEntryPage` to a new instance of our `WalkEntryPageViewModel` that uses the `DependencyService` class and includes our `INavigationService` interface.

3. Finally, we updated the `SaveWalkItem_Clicked` instance method to use the `PopToRootAsync` instance method of the `_viewModel.Navigation` property to remove the `WalkEntryPage` from the navigation stack. Alternatively, if no validation errors have occurred, or we click `Cancel` within the confirmation dialog, we can use the `PopToRootAsync` method of the `_viewModel.Navigation` property to remove the `WalkEntryPage` from the navigation stack.

Updating the WalkTrailInfoPageViewModel using C#

Now that we have updated our `WalkEntryPage` code-behind file so that it can reference our `NavigationService` class so that it can navigate to our ViewModels within our navigation stack, we can now proceed and start updating the `WalkTrailInfoPageViewModel` class so it can use our navigation service.

Let's take a look at how we can achieve this by following these steps:

1. Ensure that the `WalkTrailInfoPageViewModel.cs` file is displayed within the code editor and enter the following highlighted code sections within the code snippet:

```
//
//   WalkTrailInfoPageViewModel.cs
//   The ViewModel for our WalkTrailInfoPage ContentPage
//
//   Created by Steven F. Daniel on 5/06/2018.
//   Copyright © 2018 GENIESOFT STUDIOS. All rights reserved.
//
using System;
using System.Threading.Tasks;
using TrackMyWalks.Services;

namespace TrackMyWalks.ViewModels
{
    public class WalkTrailInfoPageViewModel : BaseViewModel
    {
        public WalkTrailInfoPageViewModel(INavigationService
navService) : base(navService)
        {
        }
        // Update each control on the WalkTrailInfoPage with values
        // from our Model
        ...

        ...
        // Instance method to initialise the
WalkTrailInfoPageViewModel
        public override async Task Init()
        {
            await Task.Factory.StartNew(() =>
            {
            });
        }
    }
}
```

Now, let's start by taking a look at what we covered in the preceding code snippet:

1. We started by including a reference to the `TrackMyWalks.Services` namespace so that we can access the classes and instance methods that are defined within the namespace.

2. Finally, we modified the `WalkTrailInfoPageViewModel` class constructor to include a parameter called `navService` that references our `INavigationService` interface. Since our ViewModel inherits from the `BaseViewModel` class, we have to honor this agreement.

Updating the WalkTrailInfoPage code-behind using C#

Now that we have updated our `WalkTrailInfoPageViewModel` to take advantage of the `NavigationService` that will enable our ViewModel to navigate within the navigation stack, the next step is to begin updating the underlying **C#** code within our `WalkTrailInfoPage` code-behind file so that it will communicate with our ViewModel to allow for navigation.

Let's take a look at how we can achieve this by following these steps:

1. Open the `WalkTrailInfoPage.xaml.cs` code-behind file, ensuring that it is displayed within the code editor, and enter the following highlighted code sections:

```
//
//  WalkTrailInfoPage.xaml.cs
//  Displays related trail information chosen from the WalksMainPage
//
//  Created by Steven F. Daniel on 14/05/2018
//  Copyright © 2018 GENIESOFT STUDIOS. All rights reserved.
//
using System;
using Xamarin.Forms;
using TrackMyWalks.ViewModels;
using TrackMyWalks.Services;

namespace TrackMyWalks.Views
{
    public partial class WalkTrailInfoPage : ContentPage
    {
        // Return the Binding Context for the ViewModel
        WalkTrailInfoPageViewModel _viewModel => BindingContext as
WalkTrailInfoPageViewModel;

        public WalkTrailInfoPage()
        {
            InitializeComponent();
```

```
            // Update the Title and Initialise our BindingContext for the
Page
            this.Title = "Trail Walk Information";
            this.BindingContext = new
WalkTrailInfoPageViewModel(DependencyService.
                            Get<INavigationService>());
        }

        // Instance method that proceeds to begin a new walk trail
        public async void BeginTrailWalk_Clicked(object sender, EventArgs
e)
        {
            if (App.SelectedItem == null)
                return;
            await
_viewModel.Navigation.NavigateTo<WalkDistancePageViewModel>();
        }
    }
}
```

Now, let's start by taking a look at what we covered in the preceding code snippet:

1. We started by including a reference to the `TrackMyWalks.Services` namespace so that we can access the classes and instance methods that are defined within the namespace.

2. Next, we modified the `BindingContext` of our `WalkTrailInfoPage` to a new instance of our `WalkTrailInfoPageViewModel` that uses the `DependencyService` class and includes our `INavigationService` interface.

3. Finally, we updated the `BeginTrailWalk_Clicked` instance method to use the `NavigateTo` instance method of the `_viewModel.Navigation` property that takes the `WalkDistancePageViewModel` as the ViewModel to navigate to within the navigation stack.

Updating the WalkDistancePageViewModel using C#

Now that we have updated our `WalkTrailInfoPage` code-behind file so that it can reference the `NavigationService` class, thereby enabling it to navigate to our ViewModels within our navigation stack, we can proceed and start updating the `WalkDistancePageViewModel` class so that it can use our navigation service.

Let's take a look at how we can achieve this by following these steps:

1. Ensure that the `WalkDistancePageViewModel.cs` file is displayed within the code editor and enter the following highlighted code sections within the code snippet:

```
//
//   WalkDistancePagePageViewModel.cs
//   The ViewModel for our WalkDistancePage ContentPage
//
//   Created by Steven F. Daniel on 5/06/2018
//   Copyright © 2018 GENIESOFT STUDIOS. All rights reserved.
//
using System;
using System.Threading.Tasks;
using TrackMyWalks.Services;

namespace TrackMyWalks.ViewModels
{
    public class WalkDistancePageViewModel : BaseViewModel
    {
        public WalkDistancePageViewModel(INavigationService
navService) : base(navService)
        {
        }
        // Update each control on the WalkDistancePage with values
        // from our Model
        ...
        ...
        // Instance method to initialise the WalkDistancePageViewModel
        public override async Task Init()
        {
            await Task.Factory.StartNew(() =>
            {
            });
        }
    }
}
```

Now, let's start by taking a look at what we covered in the preceding code snippet:

1. We started by including a reference to the `TrackMyWalks.Services` namespace so that we can access the classes and instance methods that are defined within the namespace.
2. Finally, we modified the `WalkDistancePageViewModel` class constructor to include a parameter called `navService` that references our `INavigationService` interface. Since our ViewModel inherits from the `BaseViewModel` class, we have to honor this agreement.

Updating the WalkDistancePage code-behind using C#

Now that we have updated our `WalkDistancePageViewModel` to take advantage of the `NavigationService` that will enable our ViewModel to navigate within the navigation stack, the next step is to begin updating the underlying C# code within our `WalkDistancePage` code-behind file so that it will communicate with our ViewModel to allow for navigation.

Let's take a look at how we can achieve this by following these steps:

1. Open the `WalkDistancePage.xaml.cs` code-behind file, ensuring that it is displayed within the code editor, and enter the following highlighted code sections:

```
//
//  WalkDistancePage.xaml.cs
//  Displays related trail information within a map using a pin
placeholder
//
//  Created by Steven F. Daniel on 14/05/2018
//  Copyright © 2018 GENIESOFT STUDIOS. All rights reserved.
//
using System;
using TrackMyWalks.Services;
using TrackMyWalks.ViewModels;
using Xamarin.Forms;
using Xamarin.Forms.Maps;

namespace TrackMyWalks.Views
{
    public partial class WalkDistancePage : ContentPage
```

```
        {
            // Return the Binding Context for the ViewModel
            WalkDistancePageViewModel _viewModel => BindingContext as
WalkDistancePageViewModel;

            public WalkDistancePage()
            {
                InitializeComponent();

                // Update the Title and Initialise our BindingContext for the
Page
                Title = "Distance Travelled Information";
                this.BindingContext = new
WalkDistancePageViewModel(DependencyService.
                                        Get<INavigationService>());

                // Create a pin placeholder within the map containing the walk
information
                customMap.Pins.Add(new Pin
                {
                    Type = PinType.Place,
                    Position = new Position(_viewModel.Latitude,
_viewModel.Longitude),
                            Label = _viewModel.Title,
                            Address = "Difficulty: " + _viewModel.Difficulty
+
                            "  Total Distance: " + _viewModel.Distance, Id =
_viewModel.Title
                });

                // Create a region around the map within a one-kilometer
radius
                customMap.MoveToRegion(MapSpan.FromCenterAndRadius(new
                            Position(_viewModel.Latitude,
_viewModel.Longitude),
                            Distance.FromKilometers(1.0)));
            }

            // Instance method that ends the current trail and returns
            // back to the main screen
            public async void EndThisTrailButton_Clicked(object sender,
EventArgs e)
            {
                App.SelectedItem = null;
                await _viewModel.Navigation.BackToMainPage();
            }
        }
    }
```

Now, let's start by taking a look at what we covered in the preceding code snippet:

1. We started by including a reference to the `TrackMyWalks.Services` namespace so that we can access the classes and instance methods that are defined within the namespace.

2. Next, we modified the `BindingContext` of our `WalkDistancePage` to a new instance of our `WalkDistancePageViewModel` that uses the `DependencyService` class and includes our `INavigationService` interface.

3. Finally, we updated the `EndThisTrailButton_Clicked` instance method to use the `PopToRootAsync` instance method of the `_viewModel.Navigation` property to remove the `WalkDistancePage` from the navigation stack.

Updating the SplashPage code-behind using C#

Now that we have updated each of our ViewModels so that they can take advantage of our `NavigationService` class, as well as updating each of the underlying C# code, contained within the `ContentPages` for our `TrackMyWalks` application, the next step is to begin updating the underlying C# code within our `SplashPage` code-behind file. We do this in order to update the `MainPage` and `NavigationBar` color, as well as initialize the navigation service property for our application.

Let's take a look at how we can achieve this by following these steps:

1. Open the `SplashPage.xaml.cs` code-behind file, ensuring that it is displayed within the code editor, and enter the following highlighted code sections:

```
//
//  SplashPage.xaml.cs
//  Displays a timed splash screen for the TrackMyWalks application
//
//  Created by Steven F. Daniel on 14/05/2018
//  Copyright © 2018 GENIESOFT STUDIOS. All rights reserved.
//
using System.Threading.Tasks;
using Xamarin.Forms;

namespace TrackMyWalks.Views
{
    public partial class SplashPage : ContentPage
    {
```

```
public SplashPage()
{
    InitializeComponent();
}

protected override async void OnAppearing()
{
    base.OnAppearing();

    // Set a wait delay of 3 seconds on our Splash Screen
    await Task.Delay(3000);

    // Update the Main Page and update the NavigationBar
    // color for our app
    Application.Current.MainPage = new NavigationPage(
                              new WalksMainPage())
    {
        BarBackgroundColor = Color.CadetBlue,
        BarTextColor = Color.White,
    };
    // Update the Application's Navigation Service property
    App.NavService.XFNavigation =
Application.Current.MainPage.Navigation;
    }
  }
}
```

Now, let's start by taking a look at what we covered in the preceding code snippet:

1. We began by updating the `OnAppearing` method, which will initialize our `ContentPage` whenever it appears on-screen. Then, we modified the `Application.Current.MainPage` property to call our `WalksMainPage` by creating a new instance of the `NavigationPage` class, and then specified values for the `BarBackgroundColor` and `BarTextColor` properties of the `NavigationPage` class.

2. Finally, we updated the application's `App.NavService.XFNavigation` property to point to the `Navigation` property of our `MainPage` object for our `ContentPage`.

Updating the App.xaml class to use the navigation service

Now that we have successfully updated each of our `ViewModels` and `ContentPages` to take advantage of our `NavigationService` so that our ViewModels will be able to navigate to each ViewModel and `ContentPage` within the navigation stack, the next step is to make some additional changes within our `OnStart` method. We do this in order to declare a `NavService` property that will be used to navigate between each of our ViewModels, as well as create an instance of our navigation service class.

Finally, we will see how to register each of our ViewModels and `ContentPages` on our navigation stack and check to see what Target OS Platform we are running on so that we can call the appropriate `NavigationPage`.

Let's take a look at how we can achieve this by following these steps:

1. Open the `App.xaml.cs` file, ensuring that it is displayed within the code editor, and enter the following highlighted code sections:

```
//
// App.xaml.cs
// Main class that gets called whenever our TrackMyWalks app is
started
//
// Created by Steven F. Daniel on 14/05/2018
// Copyright © 2018 GENIESOFT STUDIOS. All rights reserved.
//
using Xamarin.Forms;
using Xamarin.Forms.Xaml;
using TrackMyWalks.Views;
using TrackMyWalks.Models;
using TrackMyWalks.Services;
using TrackMyWalks.ViewModels;

[assembly: XamlCompilation(XamlCompilationOptions.Compile)]
namespace TrackMyWalks
{
    public partial class App : Application
    {
        public App()
        {
            InitializeComponent();

            // Initialise and create an instance of our navigation
```

```
                        // service class
                        NavService = DependencyService.Get<INavigationService>()
    as NavigationService;
                    }
                protected override void OnStart()
                {
                        // Check what Target OS Platform we are running on
    whenever the app starts
                        if (Device.RuntimePlatform.Equals(Device.Android))
                        {
                            // Set the Root Page for our Application
                            MainPage = new NavigationPage(new SplashPage());
                        }
                        else
                        {
                            // Set the Root Page and update the NavigationBar
    color for our app
                            MainPage = new NavigationPage(new WalksMainPage())
                            {
                                BarBackgroundColor = Color.IndianRed,
                                BarTextColor = Color.White,
                            };
                        }

                        // Set the current main page to our Navigation Service
                        NavService.XFNavigation = MainPage.Navigation;

                        // Register each of our View Models on our Navigation
    Stack
    NavService.RegisterViewMapping(typeof(WalksMainPageViewModel),
                                            typeof(WalksMainPage));
    NavService.RegisterViewMapping(typeof(WalkEntryPageViewModel),
                                            typeof(WalkEntryPage));
    NavService.RegisterViewMapping(typeof(WalkTrailInfoPageViewModel),
                                            typeof(WalkTrailInfoPage));
    NavService.RegisterViewMapping(typeof(WalkDistancePageViewModel),
                                            typeof(WalkDistancePage));
                }

                // Declare our SelectedItem property that will store our
                // Walk Trail details
                public static WalkDataModel SelectedItem { get; set; }

                // Declare our NavService property that will be used to
                // navigate between ViewModels
                public static NavigationService NavService { get; set; }

                protected override void OnSleep()
```

```
        {
            // Handle when your app sleeps
        }

        protected override void OnResume()
        {
            // Handle when your app resumes
        }
    }
}
```

Now, let's start by taking a look at what we defined within the preceding XAML:

1. We started by including a reference to the `TrackMyWalks.Services` namespace, and then, within the `App` constructor, we updated the `NavService` property to an instance of our `NavigationService` class. We did this by using the `DependencyService` class, which includes our `INavigationService` interface.

2. Next, within the `OnStart` method, we checked to see what OS Platform we were running on when the application started using the `Device.RuntimePlatform` method. We performed a check to see whether we were running on the Android platform using the `Device` class and set the `MainPage` class to a new `NavigationPage` instance of our `SplashPage`.

3. Then, we created a new instance of the `NavigationPage` class and set the `Navigation` property of the `MainPage` class to our `XFNavigation.NavService` property, prior to updating `BarBackgroundColor` and `BarTextColor` of the `NavigationBar` class.

4. Next, we called the `RegisterViewMapping` instance method on the `NavService` property to register each of our ViewModels and the associated XAML `ContentPages` to our navigation stack.

5. Finally, we declared a static variable called `NavService` that points to our `NavigationService`, which will be used to handle all of the navigation within our navigation stack.

Summary

In this chapter, we learned about the architecture behind the Xamarin.Forms Navigation API architecture, which provides us with a better method of performing navigation within the ViewModel. Then, we learned the differences between navigating using the Navigation and the ViewModel approaches.

You then learned how to create and implement a Navigation Interface and Class that will be used by each of our ViewModels to handle the navigation between our Views and ViewModels. We then updated our BaseViewModel class to include a property to our INavigationService interface.

Lastly, we updated each of our ViewModels to make use of the INavigation interface, as well as the code-behind files for each of our ContentPages that will implement the ViewModels, so that the bindable object properties defined within the XAML can be bound to those properties that are defined within the associated ViewModel.

In the next chapter, you'll learn how to incorporate platform-specific features within your app, depending on the mobile platform that is being run, as well as learn how to incorporate the Xam.Plugin.Geolocator NuGet package that you will use in order to create a LocationService Interface and Class. This will include a number of class instance methods that both our iOS and Android platforms will use to obtain current GPS coordinates and handle location updates in the background on the device.

7
Adding Location-based Features Within Your App

In the previous chapter, we learned how to leverage what we already know about the **Model-View-ViewModel (MVVM)** architectural design pattern and learned how to navigate between each of our ViewModels within our `TrackMyWalks` application. You learned how to create a `BaseViewModel` base class that each of our ViewModels will inherit from, as well as how to go about creating the associated C# class files for each of our ViewModels that will data bind to each of the properties defined within our XAML pages.

To end the chapter, you learned how to add `ContextActions` to your (XAML) content pages, and how to implement the code action events within your code so that you can respond to those actions.

In this chapter, you'll learn how to incorporate platform-specific features within your application, dependent on the mobile platform that is being run, as well as learn how to incorporate the `Xam.Plugin.Geolocator` NuGet package that you will use in order to create a `LocationService` Interface and Class, which will include a number of class instance methods that both our iOS and Android platforms will use to obtain current GPS coordinates and hande location updates in the background on the device.

You'll update both the `WalkEntryPageViewModel` and `WalkDistancePageViewModel` classes to allow location-based features to happen and create a `CustomMapOverlay` class that will be used to display a native Map control, based on the platform.

Finally, you'll make some minor changes to the `WalkDistancePage.xaml` file so that it can use the `CustomMapOverlay` class and then make changes within the `WalkDistancePage.xaml.cs` code-behind file to handle location updates, as well as perform location updates in the background to update the native Map control automatically, whenever new location coordinates are obtained.

This chapter will cover the following topics:

- The benefits of using and implementing platform-specific services within your application
- Incorporating the `Xam.Plugin.Geolocator` NuGet package within our shared-core solution
- Creating and implementing a `LocationService` class using C#
- Creating and implementing a `CustomMapOverlay` class using C#
- Updating the `WalkEntryPageViewModel` to use the `LocationService` class
- Updating the `WalkDistancePageViewModel` to use the `LocationService` class
- Updating the `WalkDistancePage` XAML page to use our `CustomMapOverlay` class
- Updating the `WalkDistancePage` code-behind to use the `LocationService` class
- Enabling location-based background updates for both our iOS and Android projects

Creating and using platform-specific services within your app

As mentioned in the introduction to this chapter, we created a customized `NavigationService` Interface and Class and then updated our `BaseViewModel` to include a property reference to our `INavigationService` so that each of our ViewModels can reference it.

The benefits of using an interface and class to define a platform-specific service is that they can be used within each of your ViewModels. Then, the implementations of the service can be provided using dependency injection.

This is achieved by declaring the `DependencyService` meta tag, with each of those implementations being actual services, or even Mock services that can be used to unit test your ViewModels, which we will be covering in `Chapter 13`, *Unit Testing your Xamarin.Forms Apps*.

In addition to the `NavigationService` interface and class that we created within our previous chapter, we can use a couple of other platform-specific feature services to enrich the data and user experience. In this section, we'll take a look at how to create a `LocationService` class that will enable us to get specific geolocation coordinates from the actual device for both our iOS and Android platforms.

Adding the plugin geolocator NuGet package to our solution

In this section, we will begin by adding the `Xam.Plugin.Geolocator` NuGet package to our `TrackMyWalks` shared-core solution, which is essentially a cross-platform library that you can use to obtain current device GPS location coordinates, as well as perform location updates within the background by writing a few lines of code to access the various Properties and Methods available within this class.

Let's start by adding the `Xam.Plugin.Geolocator` NuGet package to our TrackMyWalks app by performing the following the steps:

1. Right-click on the **Dependencies|NuGet** folder, located within the `TrackMyWalks` solution, and choose the **Add Packages...** menu option, as you did in `Chapter 4`, *Creating the TrackMyWalks Native app*.

2. Next, within the **Search** field located within the **Add Packages** dialog, you need to enter in **Plugin.Geolocator** and select the **Xam.Plugin.Geolocator** option within the list, as shown in the following screenshot:

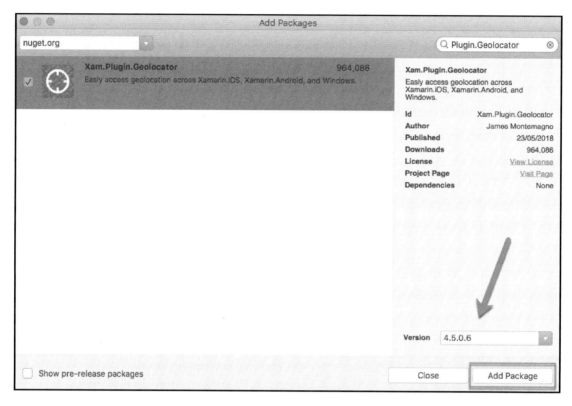

Adding the Xam.Plugin.Geolocator NuGet Package

3. Then, make sure that you choose the latest version to install from the dropdown list for the **Version** field (*this will be displayed by default*).

4. Finally, click on the **Add Package** button to add the **Xam.Plugin.Geolocator** NuGet package to the **TrackMyWalks** shared-core solution.

Now that you have added the NuGet package for the **Xam.Plugin.Geolocator**, we can begin utilizing this control by creating a `LocationService` Interface and Class that will be used by our ViewModels and ContentPages (Views).

Creating and implementing the ILocationService interface

In this section, we'll take a look at how to create the ILocationService class, which will essentially contain various instance methods that will be used by our LocationService class. The advantage of creating an ILocationService class is that it's much easier to add additional class instance methods that will be used by those ViewModels and ContentPages (Views) that utilize this interface.

Let's start by creating the ILocationService interface for our TrackMyWalks app by performing the following steps:

1. Ensure that the **TrackMyWalks** solution is open within the Visual Studio for Mac IDE.
2. Next, right-click on the Services folder, and choose **Add|New File...** from the pop-up menu, as shown in the following screenshot:

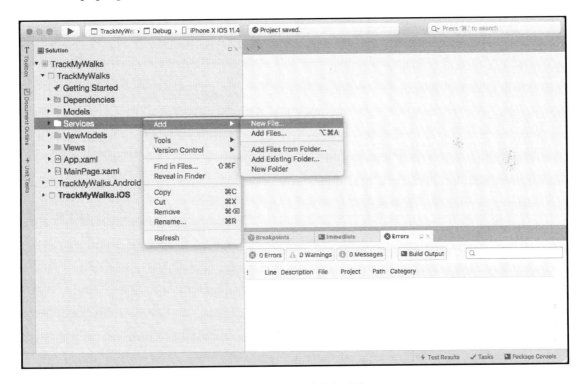

Creating a New File within the Services Folder

3. Next, choose the **Empty Interface** option under the **General** section and enter **ILocationService** for the name of the interface to be created, as shown in the following screenshot:

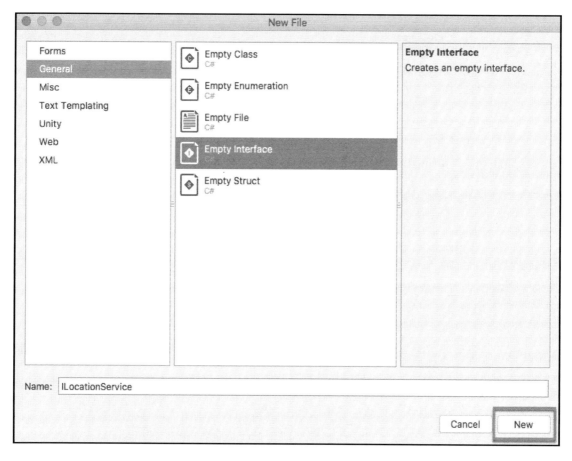

Creating the ILocationService Interface

4. Next, click on the **New** button to allow the wizard to proceed and create the new file, as shown in the preceding screenshot. Now that we have created our ILocationService interface, we can proceed with implementing the required code for our class.

5. Locate and open the `ILocationService.cs` file, which is located as part of the **TrackMyWalks** group, and ensure that it is displayed within the code editor. Then, enter the following code snippet:

```
//
//   ILocationService.cs
//   Location Service Interface used by our Location Service Class
//
//   Created by Steven F. Daniel on 28/06/2018.
//   Copyright © 2018 GENIESOFT STUDIOS. All rights reserved.
//
using System.Threading.Tasks;
using Plugin.Geolocator.Abstractions;

namespace TrackMyWalks.Services
{
    public interface ILocationService
    {
        // Asynchronously gets the current GPS location from the
device.
        Task<Position> GetCurrentPosition();

        // Asynchronously listens for changes in the GPS coordinates
        Task StartListening();

        // Stops listening for changes in GPS location updates
        void StopListening();
    }
}
```

Now, let's start by taking a look at what we covered in the preceding code snippet:

1. We started by including references to the `System.Threading.Tasks` and `Plugin.Geolocator.Abstractions` namespaces so that we can access the classes that are defined within these namespaces. We included the `Plugin.Geolocator.Abstractions` namespace, so that we can listen to changes within our GPS coordinates, as well as retrieve the current location's position.

2. Next, we created an `interface` class that will contain various class instance methods that will be utilized by our `LocationService` class, as well as our **Views** (Content Page) and within our ViewModels.

3. Then, we declared a `GetCurrentPosition` instance method that will be responsible for asynchronously retrieving the current GPS location from the device.

4. Next, we declared a `StartListening` instance method that will essentially listen for changes in the GPS coordinates from the device and return the position.

5. Finally, we declared our `StopListening` instance method that will essentially cease listening for changes in GPS location updates.

The `Task` class is essentially used to handle **asynchronous** operations, which is done by ensuring that the method you initiated will eventually finish, thus completing the task and returning back a `Task` object, almost instantaneously, although the underlying work within the method could likely finish later.

> Whenever you use the `Task` object, you can use the `await` keyword to wait for the task to complete, which will essentially block the current **thread** and wait until the asynchronous method has completed.

Creating and implementing the LocationService class

In this section, we will take a look at how to create the `LocationService` class that will inherit from our `ILocationService` interface, and implement the underlying instance methods that we declared within our `interface` class. We did this to help us retrieve and continually listen for changes within the GPS location coordinates which will be used by our ViewModels and ContentPages (**Views**).

Let's start by creating the `LocationService` class for our TrackMyWalks app by performing the following steps:

1. Ensure that the **TrackMyWalks** solution is open within the Visual Studio for Mac IDE.

2. Next, right-click on the `Services` folder and choose **Add | New File...** from the pop-up menu.

3. Then, choose the **Empty Class** option under the **General** section and enter `LocationService` for the name of the class to be created, as shown in the following screenshot:

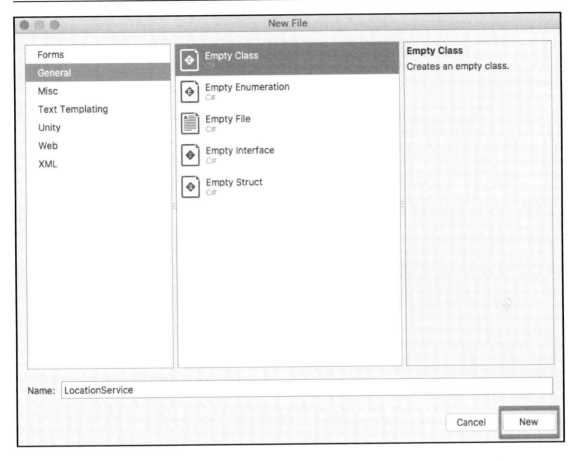

Creating the LocationService Class

4. Next, click on the **New** button to allow the wizard to proceed and create the new file, as shown in the preceding screenshot. Now that we have created our LocationService class, we can proceed with implementing the required code for our class.

5. Locate and open the LocationService.cs file, which is located as part of the TrackMyWalks group, and ensure that it is displayed within the code editor. Then, enter the following code snippet:

```
//
// LocationService.cs
// Location Service Class that will be used retrieve GPS Coordinates
//
// Created by Steven F. Daniel on 28/06/2018.
// Copyright © 2018 GENIESOFT STUDIOS. All rights reserved.
```

```
        //
        using System;
        using System.Threading.Tasks;
        using TrackMyWalks.Services;
        using Xamarin.Forms;
        using Plugin.Geolocator;
        using Plugin.Geolocator.Abstractions;
        using System.Diagnostics;

        [assembly: Dependency(typeof(LocationService))]
        namespace TrackMyWalks.Services
        {
            public class LocationService : ILocationService
            {
                // Declare our EventHandler that can be referenced within the
App
                public event EventHandler<PositionEventArgs> PositionChanged;

                // Retrieves the current GPS Coordinates for the device
                public async Task<Position> GetCurrentPosition()
                {
                    Position position = null;
                    try
                    {
                        // Initialise our current location and set the
accuracy in Meters
                        var locator = CrossGeolocator.Current;
                        locator.DesiredAccuracy = 200;

                        // Check and get a cached position if we have one
                        position = await locator.GetLastKnownLocationAsync();
                        if (position != null) return position;

                        // Check to see if Location Services are available /
enabled
                        if (!locator.IsGeolocationAvailable ||
                            !locator.IsGeolocationEnabled)
                        {
                            return null;
                        }
                        // Call the GetPositionAsync to retrieve the GPS
Coordinates
                        position = await
locator.GetPositionAsync(TimeSpan.FromSeconds(1),
                                        null, true);
                    }
                    catch (Exception ex)
                    {
```

```
                        Debug.WriteLine("There was a problem getting the
location: " + ex);
                }
                // Return the current location coordinates
                return position;
        }
        // Asynchronously listens for changes in GPS location updates
        public async Task StartListening()
        {
                // Check to see if we are currently listening for updates
                if (CrossGeolocator.Current.IsListening)
                    return;

                // Check what Target OS Platform we are running on
whenever
                // the app starts
                if (Device.RuntimePlatform.Equals(Device.Android))
                {
                    await CrossGeolocator.Current.StartListeningAsync(
                    TimeSpan.FromSeconds(5), 10, true);
                }
                else
                {
                    // Start listening for changes in location within the
                    // Background for iOS
                    await CrossGeolocator.Current.StartListeningAsync(
                    TimeSpan.FromSeconds(1), 100, true, new
ListenerSettings
                        {
                            ActivityType = ActivityType.AutomotiveNavigation,
                            AllowBackgroundUpdates = true,
                            DeferLocationUpdates = true,
                            DeferralDistanceMeters = 500,
                            DeferralTime = TimeSpan.FromSeconds(1),
                            ListenForSignificantChanges = false,
                            PauseLocationUpdatesAutomatically = false
                        });
                }
                // EventHandler to determine whenever the GPS
                // position changes
                CrossGeolocator.Current.PositionChanged += (sender, e) =>
                {
                    // Raise our PositionChanged EventHandler,
                    // using the Coordinates
                    PositionChanged.Invoke(sender, e);
                };
        }
        // Stops listening for location service updates on the device
```

```
        public async void StopListening()
        {
            // Checks to see if we are currently listening for updates
            if (!CrossGeolocator.Current.IsListening)
                return;

            // Stops listening for updates, and removes our
            // PositionChanged EventListener
            await CrossGeolocator.Current.StopListeningAsync();
            CrossGeolocator.Current.PositionChanged -=
PositionChanged;
        }
    }
}
```

Now, let's start by taking a look at what we covered in the preceding code snippet:

1. First, we started by including references to the `System.Threading.Tasks`, `Plugin.Geolocator`, and the `Plugin.Geolocator.Abstractions` namespaces so that we can access the classes that are defined within these namespaces. We need to include the `Plugin.Geolocator` and `Plugin.Geolocator.Abstractions` namespaces so that we can listen to changes within our GPS coordinates, as well as retrieve the current location's position.

2. Next, we started by initializing our `LocationService` class to be marked as a dependency by adding the `Dependency` metadata attribute so that it can be resolved by the `Xamarin.Forms DependencyService` class. This will enable our class to find and use the method implementations defined by our `ILocationService` interface.

3. Then, we needed to ensure that our `LocationService` class inherited from the `ILocationService` interface, so that it can access the instance methods, as well as any getters and setters.

4. Then, we created an `EventHandler` property called `PropertyChanged`, that will store the GPS location coordinates whenever the location changes so that we can reference it within our ViewModels.

5. Next, we created our `GetCurrentPosition` instance method, which will be responsible for retrieving the current device's GPS location. We initialized our current location object and set the accuracy to check within meters, prior to checking for and getting the cached position, if we have one.

6. Then, we checked to see if we had location services enabled by calling both the `IsGeolocationAvailable` and `IsGeolocationEnabled` methods of the `CrossGeolocator` class. We return `null` if they have been disabled. Alternatively, we could call `GeoPositionAsync` to retrieve and return the current GPS geo coordinates.

7. Next, we created our `StartListening` instance method, which will be responsible for asynchronously listening for changes in GPS location updates. We check to see if we were currently listening for updates by calling the `IsListening` property of the `CrossGeolocator` class, and returned our instance method if we were.

8. Then, we proceeded to check what target OS platform we are running on and start listening for changes in the location for Android, and listened for changes within the background for iOS.

9. Next, we created and subscribed to our `EventHandler` to determine whenever the GPS position changes using the `PositionChanged` property of the `CrossGeolocator` class, and then used the `Invoke` method on the main UI `Thread` and passed the GPS coordinates.

10. Finally, we created our `StopListening` instance method, which will be responsible for stopping listening for location service and background updates on the device. We checked to see if we were currently listening for updates, prior to calling the `StopListeningAsync` method on our `CrossGeolocator` class, and then unsubscribed from our `EventListener`.

> For more information on the `DependencyService` class, refer to the Microsoft Developer Documentation at `https://docs.microsoft.com/en-us/xamarin/xamarin-forms/app-fundamentals/dependency-service/introduction`.

Updating the WalkEntryPageViewModel using C#

Now that we have created our `ILocationService` interface, as well as implemented the instance methods and `EventHandlers` within our `LocationService` class, we can now proceed and start updating the `WalksEntryPageViewModel` class so that it can use our `LocationService` to populate our `Latitude` and `Longitude` properties with the determined device's GPS coordinates.

Let's take a look at how we can achieve this by following these steps:

1. Ensure that the `WalkEntryPageViewModel.cs` file is displayed within the code editor and enter the following highlighted code sections within the code snippet:

```
//
//   WalkEntryPageViewModel.cs
//   The ViewModel for our WalkEntryPage ContentPage
//
//   Created by Steven F. Daniel on 5/06/2018.
//   Copyright © 2018 GENIESOFT STUDIOS. All rights reserved.
//
using System;
using System.Threading.Tasks;
using TrackMyWalks.Models;
using TrackMyWalks.Services;

namespace TrackMyWalks.ViewModels
{
    public class WalkEntryPageViewModel : BaseViewModel
    {
        public WalkEntryPageViewModel(INavigationService navService)
    : base(navService)
        {
            // Update the title if we are creating a new Walk Entry
            if (App.SelectedItem == null)
            {
                PageTitle = "Adding Trail Details";
                App.SelectedItem = new WalkDataModel();

                // Set the default values when creating a new Trail
                Title = "New Trail Entry";
                Difficulty = "Easy";
                Distance = 1.0;
            }
            else
            {
                // Otherwise, we must be editing an existing entry
                PageTitle = "Editing Trail Details";
            }
        }

        // Checks to see if we have provided a Title and Description
        public bool ValidateFormDetailsAndSave()
        {
            if (App.SelectedItem != null &&
                !string.IsNullOrEmpty(App.SelectedItem.Title) &&
                !string.IsNullOrEmpty(App.SelectedItem.Description))
```

```
                {
                    // Save the selected item to our database and/or
model
                }
                else
                {
                    return false;
                }
                return true;
            }

            // Get the current device GPS location Coordinates
            public async Task GetMyLocation()
            {
                // Get the current determined GPS position coordinates
                // from the device
                var position = await new
LocationService().GetCurrentPosition();

                if (position == null) return;

                // If we are Adding a new Walk Entry, update the Latitude
                // and Longitude Coordinates
                if (App.SelectedItem.Latitude.Equals(0) &&
                    App.SelectedItem.Longitude.Equals(0))
                {
                    Latitude = position.Latitude;
                    Longitude = position.Longitude;
                }
            }
            ...
            ...
            // Instance method to initialise the WalkEntryPageViewModel
            public override async Task Init()
            {
                await Task.Factory.StartNew(async () =>
                {
                    // Call our GetMyLocation method to obtain our
                    // GPS Coordinates
                    await GetMyLocation();
                });
            }
        }
    }
```

Now, let's start by taking a look at what we covered in the preceding code snippet:

1. We started by creating our `GetMyLocation` instance method, which will be responsible for asynchronously obtaining the current device GPS location coordinates. We then got the current determined GPS position coordinates from the device by calling the `GetCurrentPosition` instance method.

2. Next, we checked to see if we were adding a new walk entry by checking the values of the `Latitude` and `Longitude` properties, and then updated the properties using the determined GPS device coordinates.

3. Finally, we modified the `Init` instance method to initialize our ViewModel. Then, we called the `GetMyLocation` instance method to obtain our GPS coordinates and update our `Latitude` and `Longitude` ViewModel properties.

Updating the WalkDistancePageViewModel using C#

Now that we have updated our `WalkEntryPageViewModel` ViewModel so that it can communicate with our `LocationService` class to obtain the current GPS `Latitude` and `Longitude` coordinates of the device, we can now proceed to start updating the `WalkDistancePageViewModel` class. We are doing this so that it can use our location service to obtain the current GPS device location, as well as handle checking for changes in GPS location in the background and raising an `EventHandler` containing the updated coordinates that we can reference within our `WalkDistancePage.xaml.cs` code-behind file.

Let's take a look at how we can achieve this by following these steps:

1. Ensure that the `WalkDistancePageViewModel.cs` file is displayed within the code editor and enter the following highlighted code sections within the code snippet:

```
//
//  WalkDistancePagePageViewModel.cs
//  The ViewModel for our WalkDistancePage ContentPage
//
//  Created by Steven F. Daniel on 5/06/2018
//  Copyright © 2018 GENIESOFT STUDIOS. All rights reserved.
//
using System;
using System.Threading.Tasks;
```

```
using TrackMyWalks.Services;
using Plugin.Geolocator.Abstractions;

namespace TrackMyWalks.ViewModels
{
    public class WalkDistancePageViewModel : BaseViewModel
    {
        // Initialise our location service variable that points to
        // our LocationService class
        LocationService location;
        public event EventHandler<PositionEventArgs> CoordsChanged;

        public WalkDistancePageViewModel(INavigationService
navService) : base(navService)
        {
        }

        // Instance method to get the current GPS location
        // Coordinates from device
        public async Task<Position> GetCurrentLocation()
        {
            // Initialise our location service variable that points
to
            // our LocationService class
            location = new LocationService();
            location.PositionChanged += (sender, e) =>
            {
                // Raise our PositionChanged EventHandler, using
                // the Coordinates
                CoordsChanged.Invoke(sender, e);
            };

            // Get the current device GPS location coordinates
            var position = await location.GetCurrentPosition();
            return position;
        }

        // Instance method to begin listening for changes in
        // GPS coordinates
        public async void OnStartUpdate()
        {
            await location.StartListening();
        }

        // Instance method to stop listening for changes
        // in location
        public void OnStopUpdate()
        {
```

```
            location.StopListening();
        }
        . . .
        . . .
    }
}
```

Now, let's start by taking a look at what we covered in the preceding code snippet:

1. First, we started by including a reference to the `Plugin.Geolocator.Abstractions` namespace so that we can listen to changes within our GPS coordinates, as well as retrieve the current location position and continually listen for background updates.

2. Next, we created an `EventHandler` property called `CoordsChanged`, which will store the GPS location coordinates whenever the location changes so that we can reference it within our ViewModels.

3. Then, we created our `GetCurrentLocation` instance method, which will be responsible for retrieving the current device's GPS location. We created and initialized our location object and subscribed to our `EventHandler` to determine whenever the GPS position changes by using the `PositionChanged` property of the `CrossGeolocator` class. Then, we raised our `CoordsChanged` `EventHandler` by using the `Invoke` method on the main UI `Thread` and passed the GPS coordinates.

4. Finally, we created our `OnStartUpdate` instance method, which will be responsible for listening for the location service and background updates on the device. We then created our `OnStopUpdate` instance method, which will stop listening for background updates on the device, as well as unsubscribe from our `EventHandler`.

Creating the CustomMapOverlay class using C#

In this section, we will take a look at how to create the `CustomMapOverlay` class that will inherit from our `Xamarin.Forms.Maps` namespace and implement the underlying properties and instance methods. These will be used to create a native map overlay using a `CustomRenderer` class for both our iOS and Android platforms.

Let's start by creating the `CustomMapOverlay` class by performing the following steps:

1. First, create a new **Empty Class** called **CustomMapOverlay** within the `Views` folder, as you did in the section entitled *Creating and implementing the LocationService class*, located within this chapter.

2. Next, ensure that the `CustomMapOverlay.cs` file is displayed within the code editor and enter the following code snippet:

```
//
//  CustomMapOverlay.cs
//  Displays a custom map overlay using the stored Route Coordinates
//
//  Created by Steven F. Daniel on 28/06/2018
//  Copyright © 2018 GENIESOFT STUDIOS. All rights reserved.
//
using System.Collections.Generic;
using Xamarin.Forms.Maps;

namespace TrackMyWalks.Views.MapOverlay
{
    public class CustomMapOverlay : Map
    {
        public List<Position> RouteCoordinates { get; set; }
        public CustomMapOverlay()
        {
            RouteCoordinates = new List<Position>();
        }
    }
}
```

Now, let's start by taking a look at what we covered in the preceding code snippet:

1. First, we started by ensuring that our class inherits from the `Xamarin.Forms.Maps Map` interface so that it can access the instance methods as well as any getter and setter implementations.

2. Next, we declared a property instance variable called `RouteCoordinates`, which will be used to store the route coordinates. These will be used by our `CustomRenderer` classes for our iOS and Android platforms.

3. Finally, within the `CustomOverlay` class constructor, we set our `RouteCoordinates` property to a new instance of the `List` class, passing in the `Position` of the `Xamarin.Forms.Maps` namespace.

Updating the WalkDistancePage user interface using XAML

In this section, we will begin by updating the user interface for our **WalkDistancePage**, using XAML, which will use our `CustomOverlay` class to display a full-screen map with pin placeholders that will mark the starting and ending positions for the chosen trail from the `ListView` contained within our **WalksMainPage**. We will also remove our **End this Trail** button and add this as a `ToolbarItem` to the `NavigationBar` of our `WalkDistancePage.xaml` file.

Let's start by updating the user interface for our **WalkDistancePage** by performing the following steps:

1. Open the `WalkDistancePage.xaml` file, which is located in the `Views` folder, and ensure that it is displayed within the code editor. Then, enter the following highlighted code sections:

```xml
<?xml version="1.0" encoding="UTF-8"?>
<ContentPage xmlns="http://xamarin.com/schemas/2014/forms"
             xmlns:x="http://schemas.microsoft.com/winfx/2009/xaml"
             xmlns:local="clr-
namespace:TrackMyWalks.Views.MapOverlay;assembly=TrackMyWalks"
             x:Class="TrackMyWalks.Views.WalkDistancePage">
    <ContentPage.ToolbarItems>
        <ToolbarItem Text="End Trail"
Clicked="EndTrailButton_Clicked" />
    </ContentPage.ToolbarItems>
    <ContentPage.Content>
        <ScrollView Padding="2,0,2,2">
            <StackLayout Orientation="Vertical"
                         HorizontalOptions="FillAndExpand"
                         VerticalOptions="FillAndExpand">
                <local:CustomMapOverlay x:Name="customMap"
                    IsShowingUser="true" MapType="Street" />
            </StackLayout>
        </ScrollView>
    </ContentPage.Content>
</ContentPage>
```

Now, let's start by taking a look at what we defined within the preceding XAML:

1. We began by making some minor changes to our `ContentPage` so that we could include a `xmlns:local` namespace that will point to our `CustomMapOverlay` `MapOverlay` namespace.

2. Next, we added a `ToolBarItem` for our `End Trail` button to our `NavigationBar`, and set up the `Clicked` event to our `EndTrailButton_Clicked` instance method, which will return to the **WalksMainPage** when clicked.

3. Finally, we defined a `<local:CustomMapOverlay` namespace, which will be used to represent our `CustomMapOverlay` class. Then, we specified a name for our `CustomMapOverlay` control called `customMap` so that we can reference this within our code-behind file.

> For more information on the different `MapTypes` that are available within `Xamarin.Forms`, refer to the Xamarin Developer documentation at `https://docs.microsoft.com/en-us/dotnet/api/xamarin.forms.maps.maptype?view=xamarin-forms`.

Updating the WalkDistancePage code-behind using C#

Now that we have updated our user interface for our `ContentPage` using XAML to include minor changes to our `ContentPage` control, as well as specify properties for our `CustomMapOverlay` local namespace, the next step is to begin updating the underlying C# code within our `WalkDistancePage` code-behind file. We will do this to communicate with our `WalkDistancePageViewModel`, which will be used to interact with our `CustomMapOverlay` control, and place a pin placeholder that will contain information associated with the chosen walk trail from the `ListView` contained within our **WalksMainPage**.

Let's take a look at how we can achieve this by following these steps:

Open the `WalkDistancePage.xaml.cs` code-behind file, ensuring that it is displayed within the code editor, and enter the following highlighted code sections:

```
//
// WalkDistancePage.xaml.cs
// Displays related trail information within a map using a pin
```

```
placeholder
    //
    //   Created by Steven F. Daniel on 14/05/2018
    //   Copyright © 2018 GENIESOFT STUDIOS. All rights reserved.
    //
    using System;
    using Plugin.Geolocator.Abstractions;
    using TrackMyWalks.Services;
    using TrackMyWalks.ViewModels;
    using Xamarin.Forms;
    using Xamarin.Forms.Maps;
    using System.Threading.Tasks;
    using TrackMyWalks.Views.MapOverlay;

    namespace TrackMyWalks.Views
    {
        public partial class WalkDistancePage : ContentPage
        {
            // Return the Binding Context for the ViewModel
            WalkDistancePageViewModel _viewModel =>
                                BindingContext as
    WalkDistancePageViewModel;

            // Create a variable that will store our original saved
    Position
            Task<Plugin.Geolocator.Abstractions.Position> origPosition;

            public WalkDistancePage()
            {
                InitializeComponent();

                // Update the Title and Initialise our BindingContext
                // for the Page
                Title = "Distance traveled Information";
                this.BindingContext = new
    WalkDistancePageViewModel(DependencyService.
                                    Get<INavigationService>());

                // Get the current GPS location coordinates and listen
                // for updates
                origPosition = _viewModel.GetCurrentLocation();
                _viewModel.CoordsChanged += Location_CoordsChanged;
                _viewModel.OnStartUpdate();

                // Instantiate our Custom Map Overlay
                customMap = new CustomMapOverlay
                {
                    MapType = MapType.Street
```

```
            };

            // Clear all previously created Pins on our CustomMap
            customMap.Pins.Clear();

            // Create the Pin placeholder that will represent our
            // current location
            CreatePinPlaceholder(PinType.Place,
                                 origPosition.Result.Latitude,
                                 origPosition.Result.Longitude,
                                 "",
                                 "My Location", 1);

            // Create the Pin placeholder that will represent our
            // ending location
            CreatePinPlaceholder(PinType.Place,
                                 _viewModel.Latitude,
                                 _viewModel.Longitude,
                                 _viewModel.Title,
                                 "Difficulty: " +
_viewModel.Difficulty +
                                 " Total Distance: " +
_viewModel.Distance, 2);

            // Add the Starting and Ending Latitude and Longitude
            // Coordinates
            customMap.RouteCoordinates.Add(new
Xamarin.Forms.Maps.Position(
                                 origPosition.Result.Latitude,
                                 origPosition.Result.Longitude));
            customMap.RouteCoordinates.Add(new
Xamarin.Forms.Maps.Position(
                                 _viewModel.Latitude,
                                 _viewModel.Longitude));

            // Create and Initialise a map region within a
            // one-kilometre radius
            customMap.MoveToRegion(MapSpan.FromCenterAndRadius(
                        new Xamarin.Forms.Maps.Position(
                        origPosition.Result.Latitude,
                        origPosition.Result.Longitude),
                        Distance.FromKilometers(1)));

            // Display our Custom Map for the detected device
            // Platform
            Content = customMap;
        }
```

```
        // Instance method to handle updating the UI whenever the
        // location changes
        void Location_CoordsChanged(object sender, PositionEventArgs
e)
        {
            Device.BeginInvokeOnMainThread(() =>
            {
                // Calculate the total distance traveled from the
                // origPosition to the Current GPS Coordinate
                var distancetraveled =
origPosition.Result.CalculateDistance(
                                        e.Position,
GeolocatorUtils.DistanceUnits.Kilometers);

                // Create a new Pin Placeholder, showing the current
GPS
                // Coordinate and the distance traveled
                CreatePinPlaceholder(PinType.SavedPin,
                                    e.Position.Latitude,
                                    e.Position.Longitude,
                                    String.Format("traveled: {0:0.00}
KM",
                                    distancetraveled), "", 3);
            });
        }

        // Instance method to create a pin placeholder to the custom
map
        public void CreatePinPlaceholder(PinType pinType, double
latitude,
                                        double longitude,
                                        String label,
                                        String address, int Id)
        {
            customMap.Pins.Add(new Pin
            {
                Type = pinType,
                Position = new Xamarin.Forms.Maps.Position(latitude,
longitude),
                Label = label,
                Address = address,
                Id = Id
            });

            // Show the users current location on the map
            customMap.IsShowingUser = true;
        }
```

```
            // Instance method that ends the current trail and returns
            // back to the main screen
            public async void EndTrailButton_Clicked(object sender,
EventArgs e)
            {
                // Stop listening for location updates prior to navigating
                App.SelectedItem = null;
                _viewModel.OnStopUpdate();
                await _viewModel.Navigation.BackToMainPage();
            }
        }
    }
```

Now, let's start by taking a look at what we covered in the preceding code snippet:

1. We started by including a reference to the `Plugin.Geolocator.Abstractions` and `TrackMyWalks.Views.MapOverlay` namespaces so that we can access the classes and instance methods that are defined within the namespaces.

2. Next, we created a variable called `origPosition` that will be used to store our original saved GPS coordinates and make a call to our `GetCurrentLocation` instance method to get the current GPS location coordinates, and subscribed to our `CoordsChanged` property `EventHandler`. This will start listening for location updates by calling the `OnStartUpdate` instance method within our ViewModel.

3. Then, we instantiated a new instance of our `CustomMapOverlay` class and set the default `MapType` to be used, prior to calling the `Clear` method to clear all previously created Pins on our `CustomMap`.

4. Next, we created a pin placeholder that will be used to represent our current location within the `Map` by calling the `CreatePinPlaceholder` instance method. Then, we created another pin placeholder that will represent our ending location.

5. Then, we called our `RouteCoordinates` instance method within our `CustomMapOverlay` class to add the starting and ending `Latitude` and `Longitude` coordinates, and then created and initialized a map region within a one-kilometers radius using the `origPosition` coordinates and set the `ContentPage` for our `WalkDistancePage` to use our `customMap`.

6. Next, we created our `Location_CoordsChanged` instance method, which will be called by our `CoordsChanged` property whenever the device's GPS location coordinates have changed. We used the `BeginInvokeOnMainThread` method of the `Device` class to update the `Map` using the main UI `Thread`.

7. Then, we created a variable called `distancetraveled` that will calculate the total distance traveled from the `origPosition` to the current GPS coordinate in Kilometres. This will use the `CalculateDistance` method and create a new pin placeholder to show the current GPS coordinate and the distance traveled, which will be displayed when the pin is tapped.

8. Next, we created our `CreatePinPlaceholder` instance method which will be used to create a pin placeholder within the `customMap` using the `Latitude` and `Longitude` coordinates, and call the `IsShowingUser` property of the `customMap` to show the user's current location continually as their location changes.

9. Finally, we modified the name of our `EndThisTrailButton_Clicked` instance method to `EndTrailButton_Clicked`, and added the `async` and `await` keywords to the method. The `EndTrialButton_Clicked` instance method is responsible for stopping listening for location updates using the `OnStopUpdate` instance method, prior to navigating to the **WalksMainPage**.

Creating and implementing the CustomMapRenderer (iOS)

In this section, we will begin by creating the `CustomMapRenderer` class for the **iOS** section of our **TrackMyWalks** solution, which will essentially contain various instance methods that will be used by our `LocationService` class. The advantage of creating a `CustomMapRenderer` class is that it's much easier to add additional class instance methods that will be used by those ViewModels that utilize this interface.

Let's start by creating the `CustomMapRenderer` class for our **TrackMyWalks** app by performing the following steps:

1. Ensure that the **TrackMyWalks** solution is open within the Visual Studio for Mac IDE.

2. Next, right-click on the `TrackMyWalks.iOS` project and choose **Add | New Folder** from the pop-up menu. Then, enter `CustomRenderers` for the name of the new folder to be created.

3. Afterwards, right-click on the `CustomRenderers` folder and choose **Add | New File...** from the pop-up menu, as shown in the following screenshot:

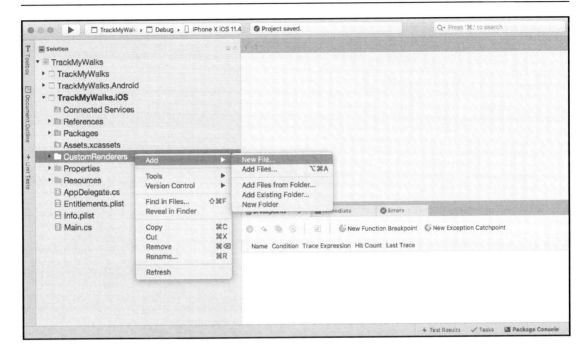

Creating a New File within the CustomRenderers folder

4. Next, create a new **Empty Class** called `CustomMapRenderer` within the `CustomRenderers` folder, as you did in the section entitled *Creating and implementing the LocationService class*, located within this chapter.

5. Then, ensure that the `CustomMapRenderer.cs` file which is located as part of the `TrackMyWalks.iOS` group is displayed within the code editor and enter the following code snippet:

```
//
// CustomMapRenderer.cs
// Draws an overlay onto a Custom Native Map that maps out the route
// taken
//
// Created by Steven F. Daniel on 28/06/2018
// Copyright © 2018 GENIESOFT STUDIOS. All rights reserved.
//
using CoreLocation;
using MapKit;
using ObjCRuntime;
using TrackMyWalks.iOS;
using TrackMyWalks.Views.MapOverlay;
using UIKit;
```

```
using Xamarin.Forms;
using Xamarin.Forms.Maps.iOS;
using Xamarin.Forms.Platform.iOS;

[assembly: ExportRenderer(typeof(CustomMapOverlay),
typeof(CustomMapRenderer))]
namespace TrackMyWalks.iOS
{
    public class CustomMapRenderer : MapRenderer
    {
        MKPolylineRenderer polylineRenderer;
        protected override void
OnElementChanged(ElementChangedEventArgs<View> e)
        {
            base.OnElementChanged(e);

            // Redraw the map whenever the RouteCoordinates property
has
            // changed to draw the line from PointA to PointB
            if (e.OldElement == null)
            {
                var formsMap = (CustomMapOverlay)e.NewElement;
                var nativeMap = Control as MKMapView;

                nativeMap.OverlayRenderer = GetOverlayRenderer;
                CLLocationCoordinate2D[] coords = new
CLLocationCoordinate2D[
formsMap.RouteCoordinates.Count];

                int index = 0;
                foreach (var position in formsMap.RouteCoordinates)
                {
                    coords[index] = new CLLocationCoordinate2D(
                                  position.Latitude,
position.Longitude);
                    index++;
                }
                var routeOverlay = MKPolyline.FromCoordinates(coords);
                nativeMap.AddOverlay(routeOverlay);
            }
        }

        // Customize the rendering of our Polyline overlay within the
map
        MKOverlayRenderer GetOverlayRenderer(MKMapView mapView,
IMKOverlay overlayWrapper)
        {
            if (polylineRenderer == null && !Equals(overlayWrapper,
```

```
null))
                   {
                       var overlay =
Runtime.GetNSObject(overlayWrapper.Handle) as IMKOverlay;
                       polylineRenderer = new MKPolylineRenderer(overlay as
MKPolyline)
                       {
                           FillColor = UIColor.Red,
                           StrokeColor = UIColor.Red,
                           LineWidth = 3,
                           Alpha = 0.4f
                       };
                   }
                   return polylineRenderer;
               }
           }
       }
```

Now, let's start by taking a look at what we covered in the preceding code snippet:

1. First, we started by adding the `ExportRenderer` assembly attribute to our `CustomMapRenderer` class to register the custom renderer with `Xamarin.Forms`.

2. Then, we ensured that our `CustomMapRenderer` class inherits from the `Xamarin.Forms MapRenderer` class, prior to creating a `polylineRenderer` variable by using the `MKPolylineRenderer` class of the `MapKit` namespace for the iOS platform.

3. Next, we created and overridden the `OnElementChanged` method to add the polyline overlay within the native `MKMapView` control for the iOS platform. We did this by using the `AddOverlay` class by converting the `Latitude` and `Longitude` coordinates from the `RouteCoordinates` collection into a `CLLocationCoordinate2D` class.

4. Finally, we created the `GetOverlayRenderer` method, which will be used to customize the rendering of our polyline overlay within the `MKMapView` control. We did this by creating and using the `MKPolylineRenderer` instance and passing in the overlay parameter, as well as setting the properties for the line to be drawn.

Creating and implementing the CustomMapRenderer (Android)

In this section, we will begin creating the `CustomMapRenderer` class for the Android section of our **TrackMyWalks** solution, which will essentially contain various instance methods that will be used by our `LocationService` class. The advantage of creating a `CustomMapRenderer` class is that it's much easier to add additional class instance methods that will be used by those ViewModels that utilize this interface.

Let's start by creating the `CustomMapRenderer` class for our `TrackMyWalks.Android` app by performing the following steps:

1. First, create a new folder called `CustomRenderers` within the `TrackMyWalks.Android` folder, as you did in the section entitled *Creating and implementing the CustomMapRenderer (iOS)*, located within this chapter.

2. Next, create a new **Empty Class** called `CustomRenderer` within the `CustomRenderers` folder.

3. Then, open the `CustomMapRenderer.cs` file, which is located as part of the `TrackMyWalks.Android` group and ensure that it is displayed within the code editor. Then, enter the following code snippet:

```
//
//   CustomMapRenderer.cs
//   Draws an overlay onto a Custom Native Map that maps out the route
//   taken
//
//   Created by Steven F. Daniel on 28/06/2018
//   Copyright © 2018 GENIESOFT STUDIOS. All rights reserved.
//
using Android.Content;
using Android.Gms.Maps.Model;
using TrackMyWalks.Droid;
using TrackMyWalks.Views.MapOverlay;
using Xamarin.Forms;
using Xamarin.Forms.Maps;
using Xamarin.Forms.Maps.Android;

[assembly: ExportRenderer(typeof(CustomMapOverlay),
typeof(CustomMapRenderer))]
    namespace TrackMyWalks.Droid
    {
        public class CustomMapRenderer : MapRenderer
        {
```

```
            CustomMapOverlay formsMap;

            public CustomMapRenderer(Context context) : base(context)
            {
            }

            // Redraw the map whenever the RouteCoordinates property has
            // changed to draw the line from PointA to PointB
            protected override void
OnElementChanged(Xamarin.Forms.Platform.Android.
ElementChangedEventArgs<Map> e)
            {
                base.OnElementChanged(e);

                if (e.OldElement == null)
                {
                    formsMap = (CustomMapOverlay)e.NewElement;
                    Control.GetMapAsync(this);
                }
            }

            // Customize the rendering of our Polyline overlay within the
map
            protected override void OnMapReady(Android.Gms.Maps.GoogleMap
map)
            {
                base.OnMapReady(map);

                var polylineOptions = new PolylineOptions();
                polylineOptions.InvokeColor(0x66FF0000);

                // Extract each position from our RouteCoordinates List
                foreach (var position in formsMap.RouteCoordinates)
                {
                    // Add each Latitude and Longitude position to our
                    // PolylineOptions
                    polylineOptions.Add(new LatLng(position.Latitude,
                                                    position.Longitude));
                }

                // Finally, add the Polyline to our map
                NativeMap.AddPolyline(polylineOptions);
            }
        }
    }
```

Now, let's start by taking a look at what we covered in the preceding code snippet:

1. We started by adding the `ExportRenderer` assembly attribute to our `CustomMapRenderer` class to register the custom renderer with `Xamarin.Forms`, prior to ensuring that our `CustomMapRenderer` class inherits from the `Xamarin.Forms MapRenderer` class. Then, we created a `formsMap` variable that points to our `CustomMapOverlay` class.

2. Next, we created and overridden the `OnElementChanged` method to redraw the map whenever the element within the map changes. We also initialized our `formsMap` variable to an instance of our `CustomMapOverlay` class and called the `GetMapAsync` method, which will raise an event to the `OnMapReady` method.

3. Then, we created and overridden the `OnMapReady` method, which will be used to customize the rendering of our polyline overlay within the `GoogleMap` control by creating and using the `PolylineOptions` instance, and setting the color for our line by using the `InvokeColor` method which will execute on the main UI Thread.

4. Finally, we iterated through our `RouteCoordinates` collection to extract each of our `Latitude` and `Longitude` coordinates and added these to our `polylineOptions` variable, prior to drawing the Polyline to our map using the `AddPolyline` method.

Enabling background location updates and permissions

In this section, we will take a look at how we can enable background location updates and set the required permissions within our iOS and Android subprojects. We will start by making the necessary changes to our `TrackMyWalks.iOS` solution, and then move on to applying the changes for the `TrackMyWalks.Android` solution.

Let's see how we can achieve this by performing the following steps:

1. First, double-click on the `Info.plist` file within the `TrackMyWalks.iOS` project solution, and ensure that the **Application** tab is displayed, as shown in the following screenshot:

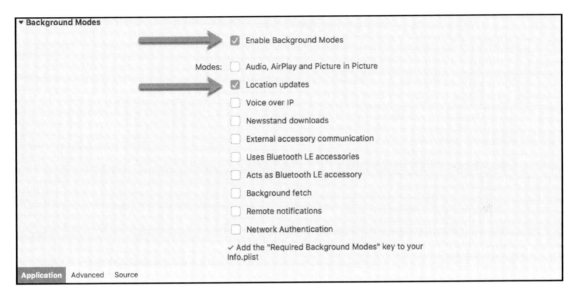

Enabling Background Modes and Location updates

2. Next, scroll down to the **Background Modes** section, and ensure that both the **Enable Background Modes** and **Location updates** checkboxes are checked, as shown in the preceding screenshot.

3. Our next step is to begin creating additional **key-entries**. Ensure that the **Info.plist** file is displayed, and then click on the **Source** tab, as shown in the following screenshot:

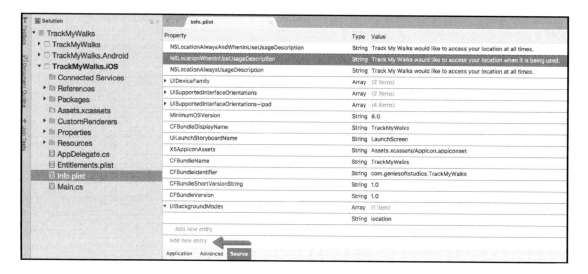

Adding Location specific key entries to the Info.plist

4. Next, create each of the key properties and their associated descriptions within the **Source** tab, as shown in the following table, by clicking within the **Add new entry** section of the Info.plist file, as shown in the preceding screenshot:

Key	Description
NSLocationAlwaysAndWhenInUseUsageDescription	TrackMyWalks would like to access your location at all times.
NSLocationWhenInUseUsageDescription	TrackMyWalks would like to access your location when it is being used.
NSLocationAlwaysUsageDescription	TrackMyWalks would like to access your location at all times.

Next, we also need to configure our Android portion of our TrackMyWalks.Android project by modifying the AndroidManifest.xml file.

5. Double-click on the `AndroidManifest.xml` file, which is contained within the `Properties` folder within the `TrackMyWalks.Android` solution, and ensure that the **Application** tab is selected, as shown in the following screenshot:

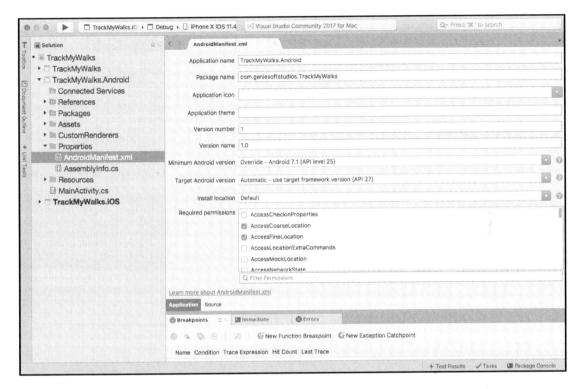

Adding Location specific permissions to the AndroidManifest.xml

6. Next, ensure that both the `AccessCoarseLocation` and `AccessFineLocation` checkboxes are ticked, as shown in the preceding screenshot.

7. Then, ensure that the **Source** tab is currently selected and that the `AndroidManifest.xml` file is displayed within the code-editor window, as shown in the following screenshot:

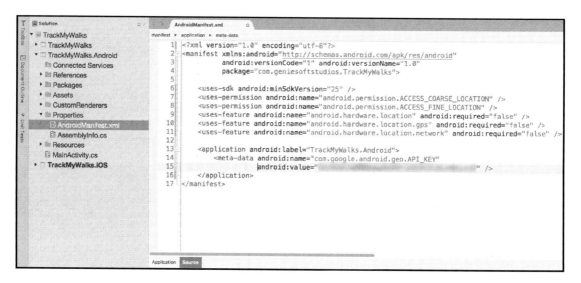

Adding Location specific permissions to the AndroidManifest.xml

8. Next, within the `AndroidManifest.xml` file, enter the following highlighted code sections:

```
<?xml version="1.0" encoding="utf-8"?>
<manifest xmlns:android="http://schemas.android.com/apk/res/android"
          android:versionCode="1"
          android:versionName="1.0"
          package="com.geniesoftstudios.TrackMyWalks">

    <uses-sdk android:minSdkVersion="25" />
    <uses-permission
android:name="android.permission.ACCESS_COARSE_LOCATION"/>
    <uses-permission
android:name="android.permission.ACCESS_FINE_LOCATION"/>
    <uses-feature android:name="android.hardware.location"
                  android:required="false"/>
    <uses-feature android:name="android.hardware.location.gps"
                  android:required="false"/>
    <uses-feature android:name="android.hardware.location.network"
                  android:required="false"/>
    <application android:label="TrackMyWalks.Android">
        <meta-data android:name="com.google.android.geo.API_KEY"
```

```
                  android:value="<PROVIDE YOUR API_KEY HERE>"/>
        </application>
    </manifest>
```

Now, let's start by taking a look at what we covered in the preceding code snippet:

1. First, we started by adding permissions that will allow our `TrackMyWalks.Android` app to access location information and handle updates within the background by using the `ACCESS_COARSE_LOCATION` and `ACCESS_FINE_LOCATION` permissions.

2. Next, we specified the different types of features that we would like our Android app to utilize. Here, we used the `<uses-feature` tag and specified that we wanted to access location features to monitor changes in location coordinates over the cellular network.

3. Finally, we needed to specify an `API_KEY` value that is required for our `TrackMyWalks.Android` app to function correctly. If you don't include this, your application won't work, and your app will crash when trying to obtain a geolocation.

 For more information on how to create a Google Maps API Key for the `TrackMyWalks.Android` app, refer to the Xamarin Developer documentation at `https://xamarinhelp.com/google-maps-api-key-xamarin-android-app/`.

Now that you have made all of the necessary changes to the user interface files by using XAML and ViewModels, which will make use of our `LocationService` class, as well as implement the necessary instance and event methods and have made the necessary changes to the underlying C# code for our app, our next step is to compile, build, and run the **TrackMyWalks** application within the iOS simulator.

Launching the TrackMyWalks app using the iOS simulator

In this section, we will begin by compiling and running the **TrackMyWalks** application to see how our application looks, since we have made changes to our XAML and ViewModels, as well as the underlying C# code within our code-behind files to utilize our `LocationService` class.

Let's see how we can achieve this by performing the following steps:

1. Ensure that you have chosen the `TrackMyWalks.iOS` platform from the dropdown menu.

2. Next, ensure that you have chosen the **Debug** option from the dropdown menu.

3. Then, choose your preferred device from the list of available **iOS Simulators**.

4. Next, select the **Run|Start Debugging** menu option, as shown in the following screenshot:

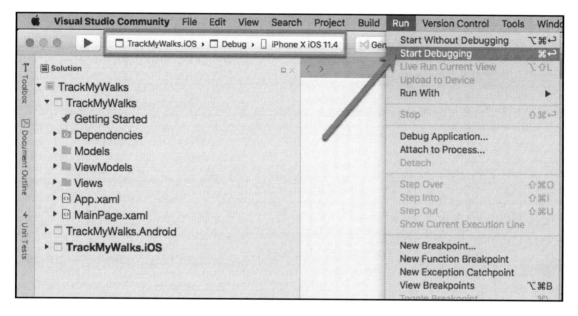

Launching the TrackMyWalks app within the iOS Simulator

5. Alternatively, you can also build and run the **TrackMyWalks** application by pressing the *Command + Return* key combinations.

When the compilation is complete, the iOS Simulator will appear automatically and the **TrackMyWalks** application will be displayed, as shown in the following screenshot:

Adding Trail Details screen displaying Latitude and Longitude coordinates

As you can see from the preceding screenshot, it displays our **TrackMyWalks** application, along with a list of static walk entries that have been defined within our `WalksMainPageViewModel` and displayed within our `ListView`. Clicking on the **Add** button will display the **Adding Trail Details**, where you can begin entering information relating to the trail. This screen also displayed the `Latitude` and `Longitude` coordinates which were obtained from our `LocationService` class, and have been blurred out:

Navigation flow between each screen for the chosen Walk Trail

The preceding screenshot shows the navigation flow between each of the pages whenever a trail has been selected from the `ListView`, with the final screen showing the **Distance traveled Information** ContentPage, along with our oolyline drawn between our starting and ending position. It also shows the markers pinpointing the coordinates relating to the chosen trail, along with the distance traveled for each pin when tapped.

Since we are running this within the iOS Simulator, you can simulate various locations to display within the Map by choosing the **Debug|Location** menu option, as shown in the following screenshot:

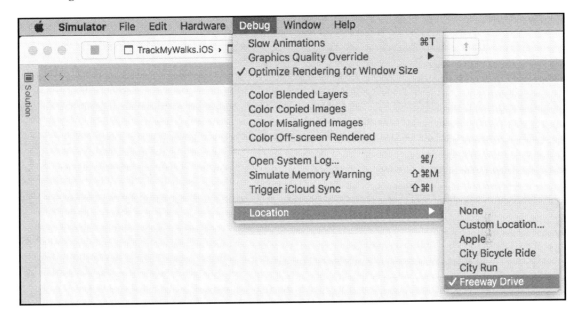

Simulating various locations within the iOS Simulator

As you can see from the preceding screenshot, we have chosen the **Freeway Drive** simulated location to show each of our pin markers, as well as calculate the distance that has been traveled from the starting GPS coordinate location.

Summary

In this chapter, you learned how to incorporate platform-specific features within the **TrackMyWalks** application, dependent on the mobile platform that is being run, as well as how to incorporate the `Xam.Plugin.Geolocator` NuGet package within the shared-core project solution.

You also learned how to create a `LocationService` Interface and Class, which included a number of class instance methods that our iOS and Android platforms will use to handle location-based features, like obtaining current GPS coordinates and handling location updates in the background on the device. You then updated the `WalkEntryPageViewModel` and `WalkDistancePageViewModel` classes to allow location-based features to happen and created a `CustomMapOverlay` class that will be used to display a native **Map** control, based on the platform. Lastly, you updated the `WalkDistancePage.xaml` and the code-behind file to handle location updates as well as perform location updates in the background and update the native `Map` control automatically whenever new location coordinates are obtained.

In the next chapter, you'll work with `DataTemplates` to layout your `Views` beautifully and neatly within your application's user interface by modifying your ContentPages (**Views**). You will also get accustomed to working with the `Xamarin.Forms PlatformEffects` API to customize the appearance, as well as learn how to style native control elements for each platform.

Finally, you'll learn how to set up your margins and padding for each platform using the `OnPlatform` XAML tag, before moving on to learning how to manipulate the visual appearance of data-bound fields using `ValueConverters` and `ImageConverters`.

Customizing the User Interface

8

In the previous chapter, we learned how to incorporate platform-specific features into the `TrackMyWalks` application, depending on the mobile platform that is being run, as well as how to incorporate the NuGet package into the shared-core project solution.

You learned how to create a `LocationService` Interface and Class, which included a number of class instance methods used by our iOS and Android platforms to handle location-based features and obtain current GPS coordinates, as well as handling location updates in the background on the mobile device. You learned how to make relevant changes to both `WalkEntryPageViewModel` and `WalkDistancePageViewModel` to allow for location-based features to work, before moving on to creating a `CustomMapOverlay` class that will be used to display a native Map control, based on the current platform.

Lastly, you updated `WalkDistancePage.xaml` and the code-behind file to handle location updates so that it will automatically update the native Map control whenever new location coordinates are obtained.

In this chapter, you'll learn how to customize `DataTemplates` to lay out your Views beautifully and neatly in your application's user interface by modifying your `ContentPages` (Views). You will also learn how to create and implement various styles in your XAML pages, prior to getting accustomed to working with the `PlatformEffects` API to customize the appearance, as well as styling native control elements for each platform.

Finally, you'll learn how to set up your margins and padding for each platform using the `OnPlatform` XAML tag, before moving on to learning how to manipulate the visual appearance of data-bound fields using `ValueConverters` and `ImageConverters`.

This chapter will cover the following points:

- Customizing the `DataTemplate` in the `WalksMainPage` to lay out content neatly
- Customizing `Padding` and `Margins` in your XAML pages

- Creating and implementing various Xamarin.Forms Styles in your XAML Pages
- Implementing RoutingEffects to access platform-specific PlatformEffects using C#
- Implementing PlatformEffects to customize the appearance of control elements using C#
- Implementing ValueConverters and ImageConverters in your app using C#
- Updating the BaseViewModel class to include additional properties using C#

Customizing the DataTemplate in the WalksMainPage

One of the features that comes as part of the Xamarin.Forms platform is the ability to manipulate the user interface by leveraging the various platform-specific APIs that are available, whether it be manipulating the appearance of controls and their elements using custom renderers or changing the appearance and styling of native control elements.

In this section, we will begin by updating the DataTemplate in our WalksMainPage, using XAML to apply additional features to change the appearance of control elements, such as updating font sizes based on the platform that our app is running on and using the OnPlatform argument.

Let's start by updating the user interface for our WalksMainPage by performing the following steps:

1. Locate and open the WalksMainPage.xaml file, which is located in the Views folder, ensure that it is displayed in the code editor, and enter the following highlighted code sections:

```
<?xml version="1.0" encoding="UTF-8"?>
<ContentPage xmlns="http://xamarin.com/schemas/2014/forms"
             xmlns:x="http://schemas.microsoft.com/winfx/2009/xaml"
             x:Class="TrackMyWalks.Views.WalksMainPage">
    <ContentPage.ToolbarItems>
        <ToolbarItem Text="Add" Clicked="AddWalk_Clicked" />
    </ContentPage.ToolbarItems>
    <StackLayout>
        <ListView x:Name="WalkEntriesListView" HasUnevenRows="true"
                  SeparatorColor="#ddd"
ItemTapped="myWalkEntries_ItemTapped">
```

```
                <ListView.ItemTemplate>
                    <DataTemplate>
                        <ViewCell>
                            <ViewCell.ContextActions>
                                <MenuItem Clicked="OnEditItem"
                                 CommandParameter="{Binding .}"
Text="Edit"
                                 IsDestructive="False" />
                                <MenuItem Clicked="OnDeleteItem"
                                 CommandParameter="{Binding .}"
Text="Delete"
                                 IsDestructive="True" />
                            </ViewCell.ContextActions>
                            <StackLayout x:Name="cellLayout" Padding="2,2"
                                Orientation="Horizontal"
HorizontalOptions="FillAndExpand">
                                <Image Aspect="AspectFill" Source="{Binding
ImageUrl}"
                                    WidthRequest="140" HeightRequest="140"
                                    VerticalOptions="FillAndExpand"
                                    HorizontalOptions="FillAndExpand" />
                                <StackLayout x:Name="DetailsLayout"
Padding="5,0"
                                    HorizontalOptions="FillAndExpand">
                                    <Label Text="{Binding Title}"
                                        FontAttributes="Bold"
                                        TextColor="Black">
                                    <Label.FontSize>
                                        <OnPlatform
x:TypeArguments="x:Double">
                                            <On Platform="Android,
WinPhone" Value="14" />
                                            <On Platform="iOS"
Value="16" />
                                        </OnPlatform>
                                    </Label.FontSize>
                                    </Label>
                                    <Label Text="{Binding Distance,
                                        StringFormat='Kilometers: {0}
km'}"
                                        FontAttributes="Bold"
FontSize="12"
                                        TextColor="#666" />
                                    <Label Text="{Binding Difficulty,
                                        StringFormat='Difficulty:
{0}'}"
                                        FontAttributes="Bold"
FontSize="12"
```

```
                                              TextColor="Black" />
                                   <StackLayout Spacing="3"
   Orientation="Vertical">

                                      <Label Text="{Binding
   Description}"

                                         FontAttributes="None"
   FontSize="12"

                                         TextColor="Blue"
   VerticalOptions="FillAndExpand" />

                                   </StackLayout>
                                   </StackLayout>
                           </StackLayout>
                       </ViewCell>
                   </DataTemplate>
               </ListView.ItemTemplate>
           </ListView>
       </StackLayout>
   </ContentPage>
```

Let's now take a look at what we defined in the preceding XAML:

1. We started by making some minor changes to our `DataTemplate` by defining a `Label.FontSize` attribute, which will set the `FontSize` based on the platform that our app is running on using the `OnPlatform` and specifying the `x:TypeArguments` of `Double`

2. We used the `On Platform` attribute, passed in each platform that we want to check for, and assigned the font size value for each platform prior to defining the `Spacing` and `Orientation` values for our `StackLayout` to display the `Description` that is associated with each trail

Applying padding and margins to XAML layouts

In this section, we will take a look at how to apply and set `Padding` and `Margins` in each of your XAML Pages. The advantage of applying padding and setting margins in your XAML pages is that it allows you to customize the presentation of your control elements, so that those elements will display nicely in your user interface, based on the platform that your app is being run on.

Updating the WalksMainPage user interface using XAML

In this section, we will take a look at how to update the user interface for our `WalksMainPage` to apply padding and set margins in your XAML, so that our control elements will display neatly in our user interface, based on the platform that is being run and using the `OnPlatform` tag.

Let's start by updating the user interface for our `WalksMainPage` by performing the following steps:

1. Locate and open the `WalksMainPage.xaml` file, which is located in the `Views` folder, ensure that it is displayed in the code editor, and enter the following highlighted code sections:

```xml
<?xml version="1.0" encoding="UTF-8"?>
<ContentPage xmlns="http://xamarin.com/schemas/2014/forms"
        xmlns:x="http://schemas.microsoft.com/winfx/2009/xaml"
            x:Class="TrackMyWalks.Views.WalksMainPage">
    <ContentPage.ToolbarItems>
    <ToolbarItem Text="Add" Clicked="AddWalk_Clicked" />
    </ContentPage.ToolbarItems>
<StackLayout>
    <ListView x:Name="WalkEntriesListView" HasUnevenRows="true"
SeparatorColor="#ddd"
        ItemTapped="myWalkEntries_ItemTapped">
        <ListView.ItemTemplate>
            <DataTemplate>
                <ViewCell>
                    <ViewCell.ContextActions>
                        <MenuItem Clicked="OnEditItem"
                         CommandParameter="{Binding .}" Text="Edit"
                         IsDestructive="False" />
                        <MenuItem Clicked="OnDeleteItem"
                         CommandParameter="{Binding .}" Text="Delete"
                         IsDestructive="True" />
                    </ViewCell.ContextActions>
                    <StackLayout x:Name="cellLayout"
Orientation="Horizontal"
                                    HorizontalOptions="FillAndExpand">
                    <StackLayout.Padding>
                        <OnPlatform x:TypeArguments="Thickness">
                            <On Platform="Android, WinPhone"
                                Value="0,0" />
                            <On Platform="iOS" Value="2,2" />
```

```
                          </OnPlatform>
                      </StackLayout.Padding>
                          <Image Aspect="AspectFill" Source="{Binding
ImageUrl}" WidthRequest="140"
                               HeightRequest="140"
VerticalOptions="FillAndExpand"
                               HorizontalOptions="FillAndExpand" />
                      <StackLayout x:Name="DetailsLayout"
HorizontalOptions="FillAndExpand">
                      <StackLayout.Padding>
                         <OnPlatform
x:TypeArguments="Thickness">
                              <On Platform="Android, WinPhone"
                                   Value="5,0" />
                              <On Platform="iOS" Value="5,0" />
                         </OnPlatform>
                      </StackLayout.Padding>
                      <Label Text="{Binding Title}"
FontAttributes="Bold" TextColor="Black">
                          <Label.FontSize>
                             <OnPlatform
x:TypeArguments="x:Double">
                                 <On Platform="Android,
WinPhone"
                                     Value="14" />
                                 <On Platform="iOS" Value="16"
/>
                             </OnPlatform>
                          </Label.FontSize>
                      </Label>
                      <Label Text="{Binding Distance,
                          StringFormat='Kilometers: {0} km'}"
                          FontAttributes="Bold" FontSize="12"
                          TextColor="#666" />
                      <Label Text="{Binding Difficulty,
                          StringFormat='Difficulty: {0}'}"
                          FontAttributes="Bold" FontSize="12"
                          TextColor="Black" />
                      <StackLayout Spacing="3"
Orientation="Vertical">
                          <Label Text="{Binding Description}"
                              FontAttributes="None"
                              FontSize="12" TextColor="Blue"
                              VerticalOptions="FillAndExpand" />
                      </StackLayout>
                      </StackLayout>
                  </StackLayout>
              </ViewCell>
```

```
            </DataTemplate>
          </ListView.ItemTemplate>
      </ListView>
  </StackLayout>
</ContentPage>
```

Let's now take a look at what we defined in the preceding XAML:

1. We started by adding the `StackLayout.Padding` for our `cellLayout` and specifying the `OnPlatform` and `TypeArguments`, as well as specifying the `Thickness` parameter since we are working with the `Padding` feature of the `StackLayout` control

2. We used the `On Platform` attribute, which is used to specify each of the platforms that we want to target and provide a value for the `Value` property

3. We defined the `StackLayout.Padding` for our `DetailsLayout`, and also specified `OnPlatform` and `TypeArguments`, then specify the `Thickness` parameter, since we are working with the `Padding` feature of the `StackLayout` control

4. Finally, we used the `<On Platform` tag to specify each of the platforms that we want to target and provide a value for the `Value` property

Updating the WalkEntryPage user interface using XAML

In this section, we will take a look at how to update the user interface for our `WalkEntryPage` to define `Margins` in your XAML, so that our control elements will display neatly in our user interface, based on the platform that is being run and using the `OnPlatform` attribute.

Let's start by updating the user interface for our `WalkEntryPage` by performing the following steps:

1. Locate and open the `WalkEntryPage.xaml` file, which is located in the `Views` folder, ensure that it is displayed in the code editor, and enter the following highlighted code sections:

```
<?xml version="1.0" encoding="UTF-8"?>
<ContentPage xmlns="http://xamarin.com/schemas/2014/forms"
             xmlns:x="http://schemas.microsoft.com/winfx/2009/xaml"
             x:Class="TrackMyWalks.Views.WalkEntryPage">
    <ContentPage.ToolbarItems>
```

```xml
                <ToolbarItem Text="Save" Clicked="SaveWalkItem_Clicked" />
            </ContentPage.ToolbarItems>
            <ContentPage.Content>
                <TableView Intent="Form">
                    <TableView.Root>
                        <TableSection Title="Enter Walk Trail Information">
                            <EntryCell Label="Title:" Text="{Binding Title,
Mode=TwoWay}"
                                Placeholder="Provide a Title for this trail" />
                            <EntryCell Label="Description:" Text="{Binding
Description, Mode=TwoWay}"
                                Placeholder="Provide trail description" />
                            <EntryCell Label="Latitude:" Text="{Binding
Latitude, Mode=TwoWay}"
                                Placeholder="Provide latitude coordinates"
Keyboard="Numeric" />
                            <EntryCell Label="Longitude:" Text="{Binding
Longitude, Mode=TwoWay}"
                                Placeholder="Provide longitude coordinates"
Keyboard="Numeric" />
                            <EntryCell Label="Distance:" Text="{Binding
Distance, Mode=TwoWay}"
                                Placeholder="Provide trail distance"
Keyboard="Numeric" />
                            <ViewCell>
                                <StackLayout Orientation="Horizontal">
                                    <StackLayout.Margin>
                                        <OnPlatform
x:TypeArguments="Thickness">
                                            <On Platform="Android, WinPhone"
                                                Value="15,0" />
                                            <On Platform="iOS"
                                                Value="15,0" />
                                        </OnPlatform>
                                    </StackLayout.Margin>
                                    <Label Text="Trail Difficulty Level:"
VerticalOptions="Center" />
                                    <Picker Title="Choose Difficulty"
                                        VerticalOptions="Center"
                                        HorizontalOptions="FillAndExpand"
                                        SelectedItem="{Binding Difficulty,
Mode=TwoWay}">
                                        <Picker.ItemsSource>
                                            <x:Array Type="{x:Type x:String}">
                                                <x:String>Easy</x:String>
                                                <x:String>Medium</x:String>
                                                <x:String>Hard</x:String>
                                                <x:String>Extreme</x:String>
```

```
            </x:Array>
          </Picker.ItemsSource>
        </Picker>
      </StackLayout>
    </ViewCell>
    <EntryCell Label="Image URL:" Text="{Binding
ImageUrl, Mode=TwoWay}"
          Placeholder="Provide an Image URL" />
  </TableSection>
 </TableView.Root>
 </TableView>
 </ContentPage.Content>
</ContentPage>
```

Let's now take a look at what we defined in the preceding XAML:

1. We start by adding the `<StackLayout.Margin` for our `StackLayout` and specifying the `OnPlatform` and `TypeArguments`, as well as specifying the `Thickness` parameter, since we are working with the `Margin` feature of the `StackLayout` control

2. Finally, we use the `<On Platform` attribute to specify each of the platforms that we want to target and provided a value for the `Value` property

Updating the WalkTrailInfoPage user interface using XAML

In this section, we will take a look at how to update the user interface for our `WalkTrailInfoPage` to define padding in your XAML, so that our control elements will display neatly in our user interface, based on the platform that is being run and using the `OnPlatform` tag.

Let's start by updating the user interface for our `WalkTrailInfoPage` by performing the following steps:

1. Locate and open the `WalkTrailInfoPage.xaml` file, which is located in the `Views` folder, ensure that it is displayed in the code editor, and enter the following highlighted code sections:

```
<?xml version="1.0" encoding="UTF-8"?>
<ContentPage xmlns="http://xamarin.com/schemas/2014/forms"
        xmlns:x="http://schemas.microsoft.com/winfx/2009/xaml"
        x:Class="TrackMyWalks.Views.WalkTrailInfoPage">
  <ContentPage.Content>
```

```xml
<ScrollView>
    <StackLayout.Padding>
        <OnPlatform x:TypeArguments="Thickness">
            <On Platform="Android, WinPhone" Value="2,0" />
            <On Platform="iOS" Value="2,0" />
        </OnPlatform>
    </StackLayout.Padding>
    <StackLayout Orientation="Vertical"
HorizontalOptions="FillAndExpand">
        <Image x:Name="TrailImage" Aspect="AspectFill"
        Source="{Binding ImageUrl}"
        HorizontalOptions="FillAndExpand"
        VerticalOptions="FillAndExpand" />
        <Label x:Name="TrailName" FontSize="20"
FontAttributes="Bold"
         TextColor="Black" Text="{Binding Title}"/>
        <Label x:Name="TrailKilometers" FontSize="12"
TextColor="Black"
         Text="{Binding Distance, StringFormat='Kilometers:
{0} km'}" />
        <Label x:Name="TrailDifficulty" FontSize="12"
TextColor="Black"
         Text="{Binding Difficulty, StringFormat='Difficulty:
{0}'}" />
        <Image Aspect="AspectFill" HeightRequest="50"
        WidthRequest="50" HorizontalOptions="Start"
        Source="{Binding Difficulty,
        Converter={StaticResource imageConverter}}" />
        <Label x:Name="TrailFullDescription" FontSize="11"
TextColor="Black"
         Text="{Binding Description}"
HorizontalOptions="FillAndExpand" />
        <Button x:Name="BeginTrailWalk" Text="Begin this
Trail"
         TextColor="White" BackgroundColor="#008080"
         Clicked="BeginTrailWalk_Clicked" Margin="20">
        </Button>
    </StackLayout>
</ScrollView>
</ContentPage.Content>
</ContentPage>
```

Let's now take a look at what we defined in the preceding XAML:

1. We started by adding the `StackLayout.Padding` for our `StackLayout` and specifying the `OnPlatform` and `TypeArguments`, as well as specifying the `Thickness` parameter, since we are working with the `Padding` feature of the `StackLayout` control

2. We use the `On Platform` attribute to specify each of the platforms that we want to target and provided a value for the `Value` property

Creating and implementing Styles in your App

In this section, we will be taking a look at the various styles that are offered by the `Xamarin.Forms` platform, which you can implement in your XAML pages. `Styles` can be created to customize each control's appearance, and we will look at how to create Global Styles, which are made available globally by adding them into the application's `ResourceDictionary`, to avoid duplication of styles across your XAML pages and controls.

Lastly, we will also look at how we can define **Implicit** and **Explicit** Styles, how we can apply these to controls in your XAML pages, and how we can work with `Device` styles that come as part of the `Xamarin.Forms` platform and apply these to your `Label` controls in your XAML pages.

Creating and implementing Global Styles using XAML

In this section, we will take a look at how to update our application's `App.xaml` file and define a Global Style that can be used by each of our XAML pages in our `TrackMyWalks` app. The advantage of declaring a Global Style in your application's `App.xaml` file is that it helps avoid duplication of styles across each of your pages or the controls that you have defined in these pages.

Whenever you create a `Xamarin.Forms` application, it is created from a template that uses the `App` class and implements the `Application` subclass. In order to create a Global style at the application level, you declare a style in the `ResourceDictionary` using XAML.

Let's take a look at how we can achieve this by following these steps:

1. Open the `App.xaml` file and ensure that it is displayed in the code editor, then enter the following highlighted code sections:

```xml
<?xml version="1.0" encoding="utf-8"?>
<Application xmlns="http://xamarin.com/schemas/2014/forms"
             xmlns:x="http://schemas.microsoft.com/winfx/2009/xaml"
             x:Class="TrackMyWalks.App">
    <Application.Resources>
        <ResourceDictionary>
            <Style x:Key="buttonStyle" TargetType="Button">
                <Setter Property="HorizontalOptions"
Value="CenterAndExpand" />
                <Setter Property="BorderColor" Value="Black" />
                <Setter Property="BorderRadius" Value="2" />
                <Setter Property="BorderWidth" Value="2" />
                <Setter Property="WidthRequest" Value="300" />
                <Setter Property="TextColor" Value="White" />
                <Setter Property="BackgroundColor"
Value="MediumSeaGreen"/>
            </Style>
        </ResourceDictionary>
    </Application.Resources>
</Application>
```

Let's now take a look at what we covered in the preceding code snippet:

1. We declared a `ResourceDictionary` and created a single explicit `buttonStyle`, then set the `TargetType`, which will be used to set the appearance of all `Button` instances in a XAML page.
2. We created a number of setter properties that we can apply to our `Button` control. Here, we specified the `HorizontalOptions` to be `CenteredAndExpand`, which will center our button control in our XAML and expand it so that it takes up the width of the XAML page.
3. We applied properties to set the `BorderColor`, as well as defining the `BorderRadius`, `BorderWidth`, and requested `Width` to use for our `Button`, as well as its `TextColor` and `BackgroundColor`.

Updating our WalksMainPage to use the Device Style

In this section, we will take a look at how to update the user interface for our `WalksMainPage` to

apply `Device` Styles to our XAML elements using the `Device.Styles` class so that our control elements will take on each of the platform-specific styles of the platforms that our app is running on.

Let's start by updating the user interface for our `WalksMainPage` by perf

orming the following steps:

1. Locate and open the `WalksMainPage.xaml` file, which is located in the `Views` folder, ensure that it is displayed in the code editor, and enter the following highlighted code sections:

```xml
<?xml version="1.0" encoding="UTF-8"?>
<ContentPage xmlns="http://xamarin.com/schemas/2014/forms"
             xmlns:x="http://schemas.microsoft.com/winfx/2009/xaml"
             x:Class="TrackMyWalks.Views.WalksMainPage">
    <ContentPage.ToolbarItems>
        <ToolbarItem Text="Add" Clicked="AddWalk_Clicked" />
    </ContentPage.ToolbarItems>
    <StackLayout>
        <ListView x:Name="WalkEntriesListView" HasUnevenRows="true"
                  SeparatorColor="#ddd"
ItemTapped="myWalkEntries_ItemTapped">
            <ListView.ItemTemplate>
                <DataTemplate>
                    <ViewCell>
                        <ViewCell.ContextActions>
                            <MenuItem Clicked="OnEditItem"
                              CommandParameter="{Binding .}"
Text="Edit"
                                IsDestructive="False" />
                            <MenuItem Clicked="OnDeleteItem"
                              CommandParameter="{Binding .}"
Text="Delete"
                                IsDestructive="True" />
                        </ViewCell.ContextActions>
                        <StackLayout x:Name="cellLayout"
Orientation="Horizontal"
                                    HorizontalOptions="FillAndExpand">
```

```
                                        <StackLayout.Padding>
                                            <OnPlatform
x:TypeArguments="Thickness">

                                                <On Platform="Android, WinPhone"
                                                    Value="0,0" />
                                                <On Platform="iOS"
                                                    Value="2,2" />
                                            </OnPlatform>
                                        </StackLayout.Padding>
                                        <Image Aspect="AspectFill"
Source="{Binding ImageUrl}"

                                            WidthRequest="140"

HeightRequest="140"

                                            VerticalOptions="FillAndExpand"
                                            HorizontalOptions="FillAndExpand"
/>
                                        <StackLayout x:Name="DetailsLayout"
HorizontalOptions="FillAndExpand">
                                            <StackLayout.Padding>
                                                <OnPlatform
x:TypeArguments="Thickness">

                                                    <On Platform="Android,
WinPhone"

                                                        Value="5,0" />
                                                    <On Platform="iOS"
                                                        Value="5,0" />
                                                </OnPlatform>
                                            </StackLayout.Padding>
                                            <Label Text="{Binding Title}"
FontAttributes="Bold"

                                                TextColor="Black"

Style="{DynamicResource TitleStyle}">
                                                <Label.FontSize>
                                                    <OnPlatform
x:TypeArguments="x:Double">

                                                        <On Platform="Android,
WinPhone"

                                                            Value="14" />
                                                        <On Platform="iOS"
                                                            Value="16" />
                                                    </OnPlatform>
                                                </Label.FontSize>
                                            </Label>
                                            <Label Text="{Binding Distance,
                                                StringFormat='Kilometers: {0}
km'}"

                                                FontAttributes="Bold"

TextColor="#666"
```

```
                                                Style="{DynamicResource
CaptionStyle}" />
                                    <Label Text="{Binding Difficulty,
                                            StringFormat='Difficulty:
{0}'}"
                                        FontAttributes="Bold"
TextColor="Black"
                                        Style="{DynamicResource
ListItemTextStyle}" />
                                <StackLayout Spacing="3"
Orientation="Vertical">
                                    <Label Text="{Binding
Description}" FontAttributes="None"
                                        TextColor="Blue"
VerticalOptions="FillAndExpand"
                                        Style="{DynamicResource
BodyStyle}" />
                                    </StackLayout>
                                </StackLayout>
                            </StackLayout>
                        </ViewCell>
                    </DataTemplate>
                </ListView.ItemTemplate>
            </ListView>
        </StackLayout>
    </ContentPage>
```

Let's now take a look at what we covered in the preceding code snippet:

1. First, we started by adding the Style property to our Title and using the DynamicResource to apply the device-specific TitleStyle
2. We proceeded to add the Style property to our Distance bindable property and use the DynamicResource to apply the device-specific CaptionStyle
3. We added the Style property to our Difficulty bindable property to use the DynamicResource to apply the device-specific ListItemTextStyle
4. We added the Style property to our Description bindable property and used the DynamicResource to apply the device-specific BodyStyle

 For more information on the Device.Styles class, please refer to the Microsoft Developer Documentation at https://docs.microsoft.com/ en-us/dotnet/api/xamarin.forms.device.styles?view=xamarin-forms.

Updating our WalkTrailInfoPage to use Explicit and Global Styles

In this section, we will take a look at how to update the user interface for our `WalkTrailInfoPage`, to apply Explicit Styles to our XAML elements so that our control elements will take on each of the platform-specific styles that our app is running on.

Whenever you use Explicit Styles, these must be declared in your XAML pages using a `ResourceDictionary`, and unlike Global Styles, they must be added to the XAML page using one or more `Style` declarations.

A `Style` is made Explicit by giving its declaration an `x:Key` attribute, which provides it with a descriptive key in the `ResourceDictionary`. These will then need to be applied to specific visual elements by setting their `Style` properties, as we will see in this section.

Let's start by updating the user interface for our `WalkTrailInfoPage` by performing the following steps:

1. Locate and open the `WalkTrailInfoPage.xaml` file, which is located in the `Views` folder, ensure that it is displayed in the code editor, and enter the following highlighted code sections:

```xml
<?xml version="1.0" encoding="UTF-8"?>
<ContentPage xmlns="http://xamarin.com/schemas/2014/forms"
             xmlns:x="http://schemas.microsoft.com/winfx/2009/xaml"
             x:Class="TrackMyWalks.Views.WalkTrailInfoPage">
    <ContentPage.Resources>
        <ResourceDictionary>
            <Style x:Key="labelTrailName" TargetType="Label">
                <Setter Property="HorizontalOptions" Value="Start" />
                <Setter Property="FontAttributes" Value="Bold" />
                <Setter Property="Style" Value="{DynamicResource
TitleStyle}" />
                <Setter Property="TextColor" Value="Black" />
            </Style>
            <Style x:Key="labelTrailKilometers" TargetType="Label">
                <Setter Property="HorizontalOptions" Value="Start" />
                <Setter Property="FontAttributes" Value="Bold" />
                <Setter Property="Style" Value="{DynamicResource
CaptionStyle}" />
                <Setter Property="TextColor" Value="Black" />
            </Style>
            <Style x:Key="labelTrailDifficulty" TargetType="Label">
                <Setter Property="HorizontalOptions" Value="Start" />
```

```xml
                <Setter Property="FontAttributes" Value="Bold" />
                <Setter Property="Style" Value="{DynamicResource
ListItemTextStyle}" />
                <Setter Property="TextColor" Value="Black" />
            </Style>
            <Style x:Key="labelTrailDescription" TargetType="Label">
                <Setter Property="HorizontalOptions" Value="Start" />
                <Setter Property="Style" Value="{DynamicResource
BodyStyle}" />
                <Setter Property="TextColor" Value="MidnightBlue" />
            </Style>
        </ResourceDictionary>
    </ContentPage.Resources>
    <ScrollView>
        <StackLayout.Padding>
            <OnPlatform x:TypeArguments="Thickness">
                <On Platform="Android, WinPhone" Value="2,0" />
                <On Platform="iOS" Value="2,0" />
            </OnPlatform>
        </StackLayout.Padding>
        <StackLayout Orientation="Vertical"
HorizontalOptions="FillAndExpand">
            <Image x:Name="TrailImage" Aspect="AspectFill"
                Source="{Binding ImageUrl}"
HorizontalOptions="FillAndExpand"
                VerticalOptions="FillAndExpand" />
            <Label x:Name="TrailName" Text="{Binding Title}"
                Style="{DynamicResource labelTrailName}">
            </Label>
            <Label x:Name="TrailKilometers" Text="{Binding Distance,
                StringFormat='Kilometers: {0} km'}"
                Style="{StaticResource labelTrailKilometers}" />
            <Label x:Name="TrailDifficulty" Text="{Binding Difficulty,
                StringFormat='Difficulty: {0}'}"
                Style="{StaticResource labelTrailDifficulty}" />
            <Label x:Name="TrailFullDescription" Text="{Binding
Description}"
                HorizontalOptions="FillAndExpand"
                Style="{StaticResource labelTrailDescription}" />
            <Button x:Name="BeginTrailWalk" Text="Begin this Trail"
                Clicked="BeginTrailWalk_Clicked" Margin="20"
                Style="{StaticResource buttonStyle}">
            </Button>
        </StackLayout>
    </ScrollView>
</ContentPage>
```

Let's now take a look at what we covered in the preceding code snippet:

1. We declared the `ResourceDictionary` in our `ContentPage.Resources` attribute, and then we created a single Explicit `labelTrailName` and set the `TargetType`, which will be used to set the appearance of `Label` instances in the XAML page that we apply this attribute to, using the descriptive Key.

2. We created a number of setter properties that we can apply to our `Label` control. Here, we specified the `HorizontalOptions` to be `Start`, which will left-align our button control in our XAML page prior to setting `FontAttributes`, as well as defining `Style` using the `Device.Styles` class and the device-specific class type and specifying `TextColor` to use for this control element.

3. We added the `Style` property to each of our `Label` control elements using `StaticResource` to apply the Explicit Style.

4. We added the `Style` property to our `Button` using `StaticResource` to apply the Global Style to our control element, which we defined in our `App.xaml` file. If you remember, Global Styles can also be referred to as Explicit or Implicit Styles.

 For more information on the `Style` class, please refer to the Microsoft Developer Documentation at `https://docs.microsoft.com/en-us/dotnet/api/xamarin.forms.style?view=xamarin-forms`.

Updating our WalksEntryPage to use our Implicit Style

In this section, we will take a look at how to update the user interface for our `WalksEntryPage`, to apply Implicit Styles to each of the XAML element controls that are of the same type without requiring each control to reference the style.

Implicit Styles are very different from Global and Explicit Styles, as they don't require you to specify the `x:Key` declaration attribute. The `Style` will then be applied to all visual elements that match the `TargetType`, as we will see in this section.

Let's start by updating the user interface for our `WalkTrailInfoPage` by performing the following steps:

1. Locate and open the `WalkTrailInfoPage.xaml` file, which is located in the `Views` folder, ensure that it is displayed in the code editor, and enter the following highlighted code sections:

```xml
<?xml version="1.0" encoding="UTF-8"?>
<ContentPage xmlns="http://xamarin.com/schemas/2014/forms"
             xmlns:x="http://schemas.microsoft.com/winfx/2009/xaml"
             xmlns:valueConverters="clr-
namespace:TrackMyWalks.ValueConverters"
             x:Class="TrackMyWalks.Views.WalkEntryPage">
    <ContentPage.ToolbarItems>
        <ToolbarItem Text="Save" Clicked="SaveWalkItem_Clicked" />
    </ContentPage.ToolbarItems>
    <ContentPage.Resources>
        <ResourceDictionary>
            <Style TargetType="Picker">
                <Setter Property="VerticalOptions" Value="Center"/>
                <Setter Property="HorizontalOptions"
Value="FillAndExpand"/>
                <Setter Property="TextColor" Value="Red"/>
                <Setter Property="FontSize" Value="{DynamicResource
CaptionStyle}"/>
                <Setter Property="BackgroundColor"
Value="LightGoldenrodYellow"/>
            </Style>
        </ResourceDictionary>
    </ContentPage.Resources>
    <ContentPage.Content>
        <TableView Intent="Form">
            <TableView.Root>
                <TableSection Title="Enter Walk Trail Information">
                    <EntryCell Label="Title:"
                     Text="{Binding Title, Mode=TwoWay}"
                     Placeholder="Provide a Title for this trail" />
                    <EntryCell Label="Description:"
                     Text="{Binding Description, Mode=TwoWay}"
                     Placeholder="Provide trail description" />
                    <EntryCell Label="Latitude:"
                     Text="{Binding Latitude, Mode=TwoWay}"
                     Placeholder="Provide latitude coordinates"
Keyboard="Numeric" />
                    <EntryCell Label="Longitude:"
                     Text="{Binding Longitude, Mode=TwoWay}"
                     Placeholder="Provide longitude coordinates"
```

```
Keyboard="Numeric" />
                    <EntryCell Label="Distance:"
                     Text="{Binding Distance, Mode=TwoWay}"
                     Placeholder="Provide trail distance"
Keyboard="Numeric" />
                    <ViewCell>
                        <StackLayout Orientation="Horizontal">
                            <StackLayout.Margin>
                                <OnPlatform
x:TypeArguments="Thickness">
                                    <On Platform="Android, WinPhone"
                                        Value="15,0" />
                                    <On Platform="iOS"
                                        Value="15,0" />
                                </OnPlatform>
                            </StackLayout.Margin>
                            <Label Text="Difficulty:"
VerticalOptions="Center" />

                            <Picker Title="Choose Difficulty"
                             SelectedItem="{Binding Difficulty,
Mode=TwoWay}">

                                <Picker.ItemsSource>
                                    <x:Array Type="{x:Type x:String}">
                                        <x:String>Easy</x:String>
                                        <x:String>Medium</x:String>
                                        <x:String>Hard</x:String>
                                        <x:String>Extreme</x:String>
                                    </x:Array>
                                </Picker.ItemsSource>
                            </Picker>
                        </StackLayout>
                    </ViewCell>
                    <EntryCell Label="Image URL:"
                     Text="{Binding ImageUrl, Mode=TwoWay}"
                     Placeholder="Provide an Image URL" />
                </TableSection>
            </TableView.Root>
        </TableView>
    </ContentPage.Content>
</ContentPage>
```

Let's now take a look at what we covered in the preceding code snippet:

1. We declared the `ResourceDictionary` in our `ContentPage.Resources` tag, and then we created and set the `TargetType`, which will be used to set the appearance of all `Picker` instances that are declared in our XAML page.
2. We created a number of setter properties that we can apply to our picker control. Here, we specified `VerticalOptions` to be `Center`, which will center our control in our XAML page.
3. We set the `HorizontalOptions` and specified `TextColor`, `FontSize`, and `BackgroundColor` to use for this control element.

Now that you have created and implemented the necessary Global, Implicit, Explicit, and Device Styles in your XAML pages, our next step is to take a look at how we can use and work with the `PlatformEffects` API to create and implement `ButtonShadowEffects` and `LabelShadowEffects` for both iOS and Android platforms.

Creating and using PlatformEffects in your app

In this section, we will see how we can work with the `PlatformEffects` API, which will allow us to customize the appearance and styling of our `Xamarin.Forms` native control elements for both the iOS and Android platforms. You will notice that these implementations have the same class names, but will be implemented completely differently, as you will see once we start.

We will look at how to create two completely different platform-effects, `ButtonShadowEffect` and `LabelShadowEffect`, for both iOS and Android platforms.

Creating and Implementing the ButtonShadowEffect (iOS)

In this section, we will begin creating the `ButtonShadowEffect` class for the iOS section of our `TrackMyWalks` solution, which will essentially contain platform-specific methods that will be used by our `ButtonShadowEffect` class. The advantage of creating a `ButtonShadowEffect` class is that it's much easier to modify or add additional control properties that will be used by the XAML pages that utilize this class.

Let's start by creating the `ButtonShadowEffect` class for our `TrackMyWalks` app by performing the following the steps:

1. Ensure that the `TrackMyWalks` solution is open in the **Visual Studio for Mac IDE**.

2. Right-click on the `TrackMyWalks.iOS` project, choose **Add|New Folder** from the pop-up menu, and enter `CustomEffects` for the name of the new folder to be created.

3. Right-click on the `CustomEffects` folder and choose **Add|New File...** from the pop-up menu, as shown in the following screenshot:

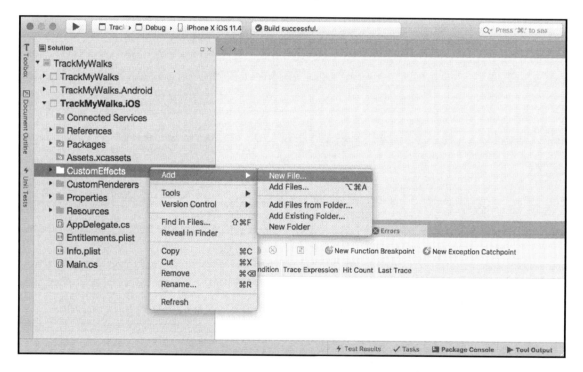

Creating a New File within the CustomEffects folder

4. Create a new **Empty Class** called `ButtonShadowEffect` in the `CustomEffects` folder, as shown in the following screenshot:

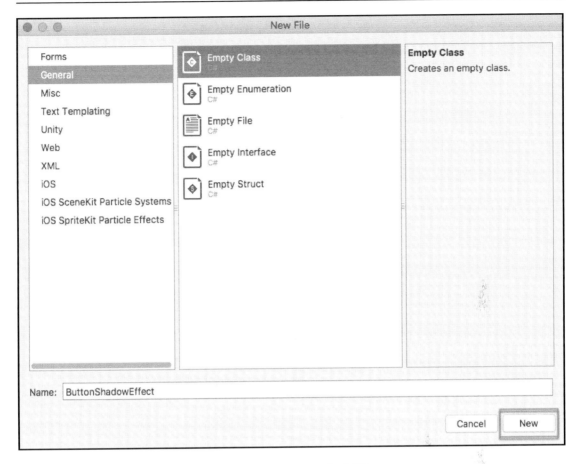

Creating the ButtonShadowEffect Class for iOS

5. Ensure that the `ButtonShadowEffect.cs` file, which is located as part of the `TrackMyWalks.iOS` group, is displayed in the code editor and enter the following code snippet:

```
//
//  ButtonShadowEffect.cs
//  Creates a custom Button Shadow Effect using
//  PlatformEffects (iOS)
//
//  Created by Steven F. Daniel on 16/07/2018.
//  Copyright © 2018 GENIESOFT STUDIOS. All rights reserved.
//
using System;
using UIKit;
```

```
using Xamarin.Forms;
using Xamarin.Forms.Platform.iOS;

[assembly: ResolutionGroupName("GeniesoftStudios")]
[assembly: ExportEffect(
            typeof(TrackMyWalks.iOS.CustomEffects.ButtonShadowEffect),
            "ButtonShadowEffect")]
namespace TrackMyWalks.iOS.CustomEffects
{
    public class ButtonShadowEffect : PlatformEffect
    {
        protected override void OnAttached()
        {
            try
            {
                Container.Layer.ShadowOpacity = 0.5f;
                Container.Layer.ShadowColor = UIColor.Black.CGColor;
                Container.Layer.ShadowRadius = 2;
            }
            catch (Exception ex)
            {
                Console.WriteLine("Cannot set property on attached
control.
                                    Error: " + ex.Message);
            }
        }

        protected override void OnDetached()
        {
            Container.Layer.ShadowOpacity = 0;
        }
    }
}
```

Let's now take a look at what we covered in the preceding code snippet:

1. We started by including references to the `System`, `UIKit`, `Xamarin.Forms`, and `Xamarin.Forms.Platform.iOS` namespaces so that we can access the classes that are defined in these namespaces

2. We added the `ResolutionGroupName` and `ExportEffect` assembly attribute to our `ButtonShadowEffect` class, to register the custom effect with `Xamarin.Forms` so that we can reference this in our XAML pages

3. Then, we ensured that our `ButtonShadowEffect` class inherits from the `PlatformEffect` class, so that we can access each of the platform-specific method implementations of the `PlatFormEffect` class

4. We created and implemented the `OnAttached` method, used the `Container` property to reference the platform-specific `Button` control, and applied shadowing effects to our button control by updating the properties for our control

5. We created the `OnDetached` method, which will be used to perform any cleanup whenever the control is detached from a `Xamarin.Forms Button` control

Creating and implementing the LabelShadowEffect (iOS)

In this section, we will begin creating the `LabelShadowEffect` class for the iOS section of our `TrackMyWalks` solution, which will essentially contain platform-specific methods that will be used by our `LabelShadowEffect` class. The advantage of creating a `LabelShadowEffect` class is that it's much easier to modify or add additional control properties that will be used by those XAML pages that utilize this class.

Let's start creating the `LabelShadowEffect` class for our `TrackMyWalks` app by performing the following the steps:

1. Ensure that the `TrackMyWalks` solution is open in the **Visual Studio for Mac IDE**.
2. In the `TrackMyWalks.iOS` project, right-click on the `CustomEffects` folder and choose **Add | New File...** from the pop-up menu.
3. Create a new **Empty Class** called `ButtonShadowEffect` in the `CustomEffects` folder, as you did in the section of this chapter entitled *Creating and Implementing the ButtonShadowEffect (iOS)* of this chapter.
4. Ensure that the `LabelShadowEffect.cs` file, which is located as part of the `TrackMyWalks.iOS` group, is displayed in the code editor and enter the following code snippet:

```
//
//  LabelShadowEffect.cs
//  Creates a custom Label Shadow Effect using
//  PlatFormEffects (iOS)
//
//  Created by Steven F. Daniel on 16/07/2018.
//  Copyright © 2018 GENIESOFT STUDIOS. All rights reserved.
//
using System;
using CoreGraphics;
```

```csharp
using Xamarin.Forms;
using Xamarin.Forms.Platform.iOS;

[assembly: ExportEffect(
        typeof(TrackMyWalks.iOS.CustomEffects.LabelShadowEffect),
        "LabelShadowEffect")]

namespace TrackMyWalks.iOS.CustomEffects
{
    public class LabelShadowEffect : PlatformEffect
    {
        protected override void OnAttached()
        {
            try
            {
                Control.Layer.CornerRadius = 5;
                Control.Layer.ShadowColor = Color.Black.ToCGColor();
                Control.Layer.ShadowOffset = new CGSize(4, 4);
                Control.Layer.ShadowOpacity = 0.5f;
            }
            catch (Exception ex)
            {
                Console.WriteLine("Cannot set property on attached
control.
                                Error: " + ex.Message);
            }
        }

        protected override void OnDetached()
        {
        }
    }
}
```

Let's now take a look at what we covered in the preceding code snippet:

1. We started by including references to the `System`, `CoreGraphics`, `Xamarin.Forms`, and `Xamarin.Forms.Platform.iOS` namespaces, so that we can access the classes that are defined in these namespaces.
2. We added the `ExportEffect` assembly attribute to our `LabelShadowEffect` class to register the custom effect with `Xamarin.Forms`, so that we can reference this in our XAML pages. You will have noticed that we don't need to add the `ResolutionGroupName` assembly attribute, as there can only be one declaration of this for the iOS platform, and any attempt to add the assembly attribute again will result in a compilation error occurring.

3. We ensured that our `LabelShadowEffect` class inherits from the `PlatformEffect` class, so that we can access each of the platform-specific method implementations of the `PlatFormEffect` class.

4. We created and implemented the `OnAttached` method, and used the `Container` property to reference the platform-specific `Label` control, then apply shadowing effects to our button control by updating the properties for our control.

5. We created the `OnDetached` method that will be used to perform any cleanup whenever the control is detached from a `Xamarin.Forms Label` control.

Creating and implementing the ButtonShadowEffect (Android)

In this section, we will begin creating the `ButtonShadowEffect` class for the Android section of our `TrackMyWalks` solution, which will essentially contain platform-specific methods that will be used by our `ButtonShadowEffect` class. The advantage of creating a `ButtonShadowEffect` class is that it's much easier to modify or add additional control properties that will be used by those XAML pages that utilize this class.

Let's start by creating the `ButtonShadowEffect` class for our `TrackMyWalks` app by performing the following the steps:

1. Ensure that the `TrackMyWalks` solution is open in the **Visual Studio for Mac IDE**.

2. Right-click on the `TrackMyWalks.Android` project, choose **Add | New Folder** from the pop-up menu, and enter `CustomEffects` for the name of the new folder to be created.

3. Right-click on the `CustomEffects` folder and choose **Add | New File...** from the pop-up menu, as shown in the following screenshot:

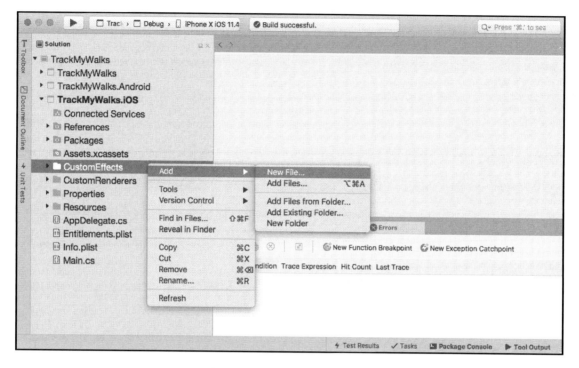

Creating the ButtonShadowEffect Class for Android

4. Next, create a new **Empty Class** called `ButtonShadowEffect` in the `CustomEffects` folder, as you did in the section entitled *Creating and Implementing the ButtonShadowEffect (iOS)* in this chapter.

5. Then, ensure that the `ButtonShadowEffect.cs` file, which is located as part of the `TrackMyWalks.Android` group, is displayed in the code editor and enter the following code snippet:

```
//
//   ButtonShadowEffect.cs
//   Creates a custom Button Shadow Effect using
//   PlatformEffects (Android)
//
//   Created by Steven F. Daniel on 16/07/2018.
//   Copyright © 2018 GENIESOFT STUDIOS. All rights reserved.
//
using Xamarin.Forms;
```

```
using Xamarin.Forms.Platform.Android;
using System;

[assembly: ResolutionGroupName("GeniesoftStudios")]
[assembly: ExportEffect(
typeof(TrackMyWalks.Droid.CustomEffects.ButtonShadowEffect),
           "ButtonShadowEffect")]

namespace TrackMyWalks.Droid.CustomEffects
{
    public class ButtonShadowEffect : PlatformEffect
    {
        protected override void OnAttached()
        {
            try
            {
                var control = Control as Android.Widget.Button;
                Android.Graphics.Color color =
Android.Graphics.Color.Red;
                control.SetShadowLayer(12, 4, 4, color);
            }
            catch (Exception ex)
            {
                Console.WriteLine("Cannot set property on attached
control.
                                  Error: " + ex.Message);
            }
        }

        protected override void OnDetached()
        {
            throw new NotImplementedException();
        }
    }
}
```

Let's now take a look at what we cover in the preceding code snippet:

1. We started by including references to the `Xamarin.Forms`,
   `Xamarin.Forms.Platform.Android`, and `System` namespaces so that we can
   access the classes that are defined in these namespaces.
2. We added the `ResolutionGroupName` and `ExportEffect` assembly attributes
   to our `ButtonShadowEffect` class, to register the custom effect with
   `Xamarin.Forms` so that we can reference this in our XAML pages.

3. We ensured that our `ButtonShadowEffect` class inherits from the `PlatformEffect` class, so that we can access each of the platform-specific method implementations of the `PlatFormEffect` class.

4. We created and implemented the `OnAttached` method, used the `Container` property to reference the platform-specific `Button` control, and apply shadowing effects to our button control by updating the properties for our control.

5. We created the `OnDetached` method, which will be used to perform any cleanup whenever the control is detached from a `Xamarin.Forms Button` control.

Creating and implementing the LabelShadowEffect (Android)

In this section, we will begin creating the `LabelShadowEffect` class for the Android section of our `TrackMyWalks` solution, which will essentially contain platform-specific methods that will be used by our `LabelShadowEffect` class. The advantage of creating a `LabelShadowEffect` class is that it's much easier to modify or add additional control properties that will be used by those XAML pages that utilize this class.

Let's start creating the `LabelShadowEffect` class for our `TrackMyWalks` app by performing the following the steps:

1. Ensure that the `TrackMyWalks` solution is open in the **Visual Studio for Mac IDE**.

2. In the `TrackMyWalks.Android` project, right-click on the `CustomEffects` folder and choose **Add | New File...** from the pop-up menu.

3. Create a new **Empty Class** called `LabelShadowEffect` in the `CustomEffects` folder, as you did in the section entitled *Creating and Implementing the ButtonShadowEffect (Android)* in this chapter.

4. Ensure that the `LabelShadowEffect.cs` file, which is located as part of the `TrackMyWalks.Android` group, is displayed in the code editor and enter the following code snippet:

```
//
//  LabelShadowEffect.cs
//  Creates a custom Label Shadow Effect using
//  PlatformEffects (Android)
//
//  Created by Steven F. Daniel on 16/07/2018.
//  Copyright © 2018 GENIESOFT STUDIOS. All rights reserved.
//
```

```
using System;
using Xamarin.Forms;
using Xamarin.Forms.Platform.Android;

[assembly: ExportEffect(
            typeof(TrackMyWalks.Droid.CustomEffects.LabelShadowEffect),
            "LabelShadowEffect")]

namespace TrackMyWalks.Droid.CustomEffects
{
    public class LabelShadowEffect : PlatformEffect
    {
        protected override void OnAttached()
        {
            try
            {
                var control = Control as Android.Widget.TextView;
                float radius = 5;
                float distanceX = 4;
                float distanceY = 4;
                Android.Graphics.Color color =
Color.White.ToAndroid();
                control.SetShadowLayer(radius, distanceX, distanceY,
color);
            }
            catch (Exception ex)
            {
                Console.WriteLine("Cannot set property on attached
control.
                                  Error: " + ex.Message);
            }
        }

        protected override void OnDetached()
        {
        }
    }
}
```

Let's now take a look at what we covered in the preceding code snippet:

1. We started by including references to the System, Xamarin.Forms, and Xamarin.Forms.Platform.Android namespaces, so that we can access the classes that are defined in these namespaces.

2. We added the ExportEffect assembly attribute to our LabelShadowEffect class, to register the custom effect with Xamarin.Forms so that we can reference this in our XAML pages. You will have noticed that we don't need to add the ResolutionGroupName assembly attribute, as there can only be one declaration of this for the Android platform, and any attempt to add the assembly attribute again will result in a compilation error occurring.

3. We ensured that our LabelShadowEffect class inherits from the PlatformEffect class, so that we can access each of the platform-specific method implementations of the PlatFormEffect class.

4. We created and implemented the OnAttached method, used the Container property to reference the platform-specific Label control, and applied shadowing effects to our button control by updating the properties for our control.

5. We created the OnDetached method that will be used to perform any cleanup whenever the control is detached from a Xamarin.Forms Label control.

Implementing the ButtonShadowEffect RoutingEffect class

In this section, we will begin creating the ButtonShadowEffect class for the shared project section of our TrackMyWalks solution. This class will essentially contain a routing reference to our platform-specific class used by our ButtonShadowEffect class. Since we cannot directly reference PlatformEffects classes that have been created for each platform, we will need to create a RoutingEffect class, referencing the same name as we defined in each platform, so that it will make it much easier to access these in our XAML pages that utilize this effect.

Let's start by creating the `ButtonShadowEffect RoutingEffect` class for our `TrackMyWalks` app by performing the following steps:

1. Ensure that the `TrackMyWalks` solution is open in the **Visual Studio for Mac IDE**.
2. Right-click on the `TrackMyWalks` shared project and choose **Add | New Folder** from the pop-up menu and enter `CustomEffects` for the name of the new folder to be created.
3. Right-click on the `CustomEffects` folder and choose **Add | New File...** from the pop-up menu, as shown in the following screenshot:

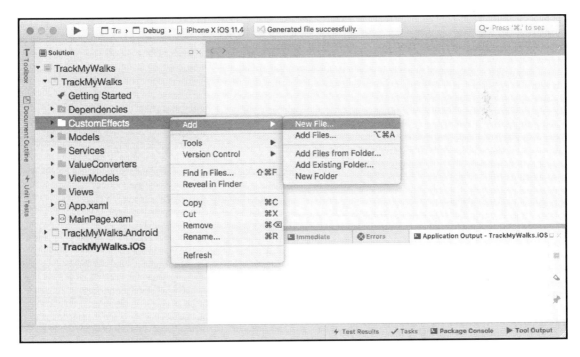

Creating a New File within the CustomEffects Folder

4. Create a new **Empty Class** called `ButtonShadowEffect` in the `CustomEffects` folder, as shown in the following screenshot:

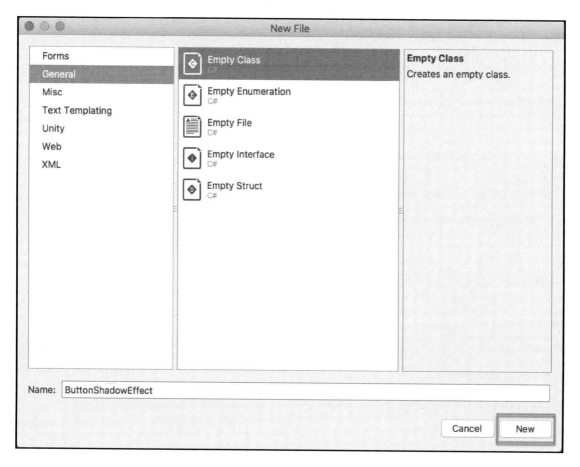

Creating the ButtonShadowEffect Class

5. Ensure that the `ButtonShadowEffect.cs` file, which is located as part of the `TrackMyWalks` group, is displayed in the code editor and enter the following code snippet:

```
//
//  ButtonShadowEffect.cs
//  Creates a Button Shadow Effect using the
//  RoutingEffect Class
//
//  Created by Steven F. Daniel on 16/07/2018.
//  Copyright © 2018 GENIESOFT STUDIOS. All rights reserved.
```

```
//
using Xamarin.Forms;

namespace TrackMyWalks.CustomEffects
{
    public class ButtonShadowEffect : RoutingEffect
    {
        public ButtonShadowEffect() :
                base("GeniesoftStudios.ButtonShadowEffect")
        {
        }
    }
}
```

Let's now take a look at what we covered in the preceding code snippet:

1. We started by including references to the `Xamarin.Forms` namespace, so that we can access the classes that are defined in these namespaces.
2. We ensured that our `ButtonShadowEffect` class inherits from the `RoutingEffect` class, so that we can access each of the platform-specific method implementations of the `PlatFormEffect` class.
3. We created the `ButtonShadowEffect` class constructor and ensured that this inherits from the base class that points to the `ResolutionGroupName` and `PlatformEffect` assembly attributes in our platform-specific `ButtonShadowEffect` class, so that we can reference this in our XAML pages.

Implementing the LabelShadowEffect RoutingEffect class

In this section, we will begin creating the `LabelShadowEffect` class for the shared project section of our `TrackMyWalks` solution. This class will essentially contain a routing reference to our platform-specific class used by our `LabelShadowEffect` class. Since we cannot directly reference `PlatformEffects` classes that have been created for each platform, we will need to create a `RoutingEffect` class, referencing the same name as we defined in each platform, so that it will make it much easier to access these in our XAML pages that utilize this effect.

Let's start by creating the `LabelShadowEffect` `RoutingEffect` class for our `TrackMyWalks` app by performing the following the steps:

1. Ensure that the `TrackMyWalks` solution is open in the **Visual Studio for Mac IDE**.
2. In the `TrackMyWalks` project, right-click on the `CustomEffects` folder and choose **Add | New File...** from the pop-up menu.
3. Create a new **Empty Class** called `LabelShadowEffect` in the `CustomEffects` folder, as you did in the section entitled *Implementing the ButtonShadowEffect RoutingEffect Class* in this chapter.
4. Ensure that the `LabelShadowEffect.cs` file, which is located as part of the `TrackMyWalks` group, is displayed in the code editor and enter the following code snippet:

```
//
//  LabelShadowEffect.cs
//  Creates a Label Shadow Effect using the
//  RoutingEffect Class
//
//  Created by Steven F. Daniel on 16/07/2018.
//  Copyright © 2018 GENIESOFT STUDIOS. All rights reserved.
//
using Xamarin.Forms;

namespace TrackMyWalks.CustomEffects
{
    public class LabelShadowEffect : RoutingEffect
    {
        public LabelShadowEffect() :
            base("GeniesoftStudios.LabelShadowEffect")
        {
        }
    }
}
```

Let's now take a look at what we covered in the preceding code snippet:

1. We started by including references to the `Xamarin.Forms` namespace, so that we can access the classes that are defined there
2. We ensured that our `LabelShadowEffect` class inherits from the `RoutingEffect` class, so that we can access each of the platform-specific method implementations of the `PlatFormEffect` class

3. We created the `LabelShadowEffect` class constructor, and ensured that this inherits from the base class that points to the `ResolutionGroupName` and `PlatformEffect` assembly attributes in our platform-specific `LabelShadowEffect` class, so that we can reference this in our XAML pages

Updating the WalksMainPage to use the LabelShadowEffect

In this section, we will take a look at how to update the user interface for our `WalksMainPage` to apply `PlatformEffects` and utilize our `LabelShadowEffect` in your XAML, so that our control elements will take on our custom effect based on the platform that is being run.

Let's start by updating the user interface for our `WalksMainPage` by performing the following steps:

1. Locate and open the `WalksMainPage.xaml` file, which is located in the `Views` folder, ensure that it is displayed in the code editor, and enter the following highlighted code sections:

```xml
<?xml version="1.0" encoding="UTF-8"?>
<ContentPage xmlns="http://xamarin.com/schemas/2014/forms"
             xmlns:x="http://schemas.microsoft.com/winfx/2009/xaml"
             xmlns:customEffect="clr-
namespace:TrackMyWalks.CustomEffects"
             x:Class="TrackMyWalks.Views.WalksMainPage">
    <ContentPage.ToolbarItems>
        <ToolbarItem Text="Add" Clicked="AddWalk_Clicked" />
    </ContentPage.ToolbarItems>
    <StackLayout>
        <ListView x:Name="WalkEntriesListView" HasUnevenRows="true"
                  SeparatorColor="#ddd"
ItemTapped="myWalkEntries_ItemTapped">
            <ListView.ItemTemplate>
                <DataTemplate>
                    <ViewCell>
                        <ViewCell.ContextActions>
                            <MenuItem Clicked="OnEditItem"
                              CommandParameter="{Binding .}" Text="Edit"
                              IsDestructive="False" />
                            <MenuItem Clicked="OnDeleteItem"
                              CommandParameter="{Binding .}"
Text="Delete"
```

```
                                    IsDestructive="True" />
                            </ViewCell.ContextActions>
                                        ...
                                        ...
                                        ...
                            <StackLayout x:Name="DetailsLayout"
HorizontalOptions="FillAndExpand">
                                        ...
                                        ...
                                        ...
                            <Label Text="{Binding Title}"
FontAttributes="Bold"
                                        TextColor="Black"
Style="{DynamicResource TitleStyle}">
                                        <Label.FontSize>
                                            <OnPlatform
x:TypeArguments="x:Double">
                                                <On Platform="Android,
WinPhone"
                                                    Value="14" />
                                                <On Platform="iOS"
                                                    Value="16" />
                                        </OnPlatform>
                                        </Label.FontSize>
                                        <Label.Effects>
                                            <customEffect:LabelShadowEffect
/>
                                        </Label.Effects>
                            </Label>
                                        ...
                                        ...
                                        ...
                            </StackLayout>
                        </ViewCell>
                    </DataTemplate>
                </ListView.ItemTemplate>
            </ListView>
        </StackLayout>
    </ContentPage>
```

Let's now take a look at what we covered in the preceding code snippet:

1. We started by creating a `xmlns:customEffect` a reference to our `CustomEffects` namespace so that we can access `PlatformEffect` in our XAML that we have defined in our namespace

2. We added the `Label.Effects` attribute to our `Label` attribute for `{Binding Title}`, and then referenced the `customEffect` assembly namespace so that we can access the platform-specific `LabelShadowEffect` to use

Updating the WalkTrailInfoPage to use the LabelShadowEffect

In this section, we will take a look at how to update the user interface for our `WalkTrailInfoPage` to apply `PlatformEffects` and utilize our `LabelShadowEffect` in our XAML, so that our control elements will take on our custom effect based on the platform that is being run.

Let's start by updating the user interface for our `WalkTrailInfoPage` by performing the following steps:

1. Locate and open the `WalkTrailInfoPage.xaml` file, which is located in the `Views` folder, ensure that it is displayed in the code editor, and enter the following highlighted code sections:

```xml
<?xml version="1.0" encoding="UTF-8"?>
<ContentPage xmlns="http://xamarin.com/schemas/2014/forms"
             xmlns:x="http://schemas.microsoft.com/winfx/2009/xaml"
             xmlns:customEffect="clr-
namespace:TrackMyWalks.CustomEffects"
             x:Class="TrackMyWalks.Views.WalkTrailInfoPage">
    <ScrollView>
        <StackLayout.Padding>
            <OnPlatform x:TypeArguments="Thickness">
                <On Platform="Android, WinPhone"
                    Value="2,0" />
                <On Platform="iOS"
                    Value="2,0" />
            </OnPlatform>
        </StackLayout.Padding>
        <StackLayout Orientation="Vertical"
HorizontalOptions="FillAndExpand">
            <Image x:Name="TrailImage" Aspect="AspectFill"
                   Source="{Binding ImageUrl}"
```

```
            HorizontalOptions="FillAndExpand"
                            VerticalOptions="FillAndExpand" />
                    <Label x:Name="TrailName" Text="{Binding Title}"
                            Style="{DynamicResource labelTrailName}">
                        <Label.Effects>
                          <customEffect:LabelShadowEffect />
                        </Label.Effects>
                    </Label>
                    ...
                    ...
                    ...
                    <Button x:Name="BeginTrailWalk" Text="Begin this Trail"
                            Clicked="BeginTrailWalk_Clicked" Margin="20"
                            Style="{StaticResource buttonStyle}">
                    </Button>
                </StackLayout>
            </ScrollView>
        </ContentPage>
```

Let's now take a look at what we covered in the preceding code snippet:

1. We started by creating a xmlns:customEffect, a reference to our CustomEffects namespace, so that we can access the PlatformEffect in our XAML that we have defined in our namespace

2. We added the Label.Effects attribute to our Label attribute for our TrailName, and then referenced the customEffect assembly namespace so that we can access the platform-specific LabelShadowEffect to use

Updating the WalkTrailInfoPage to use the ButtonShadowEffect

In this section, we will take a look at how to update the user interface for our WalkTrailInfoPage to apply PlatformEffects and utilize our ButtonShadowEffect in your XAML, so that our control elements will take on our custom effect based on the platform that is being run.

Let's start by updating the user interface for our `WalkTrailInfoPage` by performing the following steps:

1. Locate and open the `WalkTrailInfoPage.xaml` file, which is located in the `Views` folder, ensure that it is displayed in the code editor, and enter the following highlighted code sections:

```
<?xml version="1.0" encoding="UTF-8"?>
<ContentPage xmlns="http://xamarin.com/schemas/2014/forms"
             xmlns:x="http://schemas.microsoft.com/winfx/2009/xaml"
             xmlns:customEffect="clr-
namespace:TrackMyWalks.CustomEffects"
             x:Class="TrackMyWalks.Views.WalkTrailInfoPage">
    <ScrollView>
        <StackLayout.Padding>
            <OnPlatform x:TypeArguments="Thickness">
                <On Platform="Android, WinPhone" Value="2,0" />
                <On Platform="iOS" Value="2,0" />
            </OnPlatform>
        </StackLayout.Padding>
        <StackLayout Orientation="Vertical"
HorizontalOptions="FillAndExpand">
            <Image x:Name="TrailImage" Aspect="AspectFill"
                   Source="{Binding ImageUrl}"
HorizontalOptions="FillAndExpand"
                   VerticalOptions="FillAndExpand" />
            <Label x:Name="TrailName" Text="{Binding Title}"
                   Style="{DynamicResource labelTrailName}">
                <Label.Effects>
                    <customEffect:LabelShadowEffect />
                </Label.Effects>
            </Label>
                ...
                ...
                ...
            <Button x:Name="BeginTrailWalk" Text="Begin this Trail"
                    Clicked="BeginTrailWalk_Clicked" Margin="20"
                    Style="{StaticResource buttonStyle}">
                <Button.Effects>
                    <customEffect:ButtonShadowEffect />
                </Button.Effects>
            </Button>
        </StackLayout>
    </ScrollView>
</ContentPage>
```

Let's now take a look at what we covered in the preceding code snippet:

1. We started by creating a `xmlns:customEffect`, a reference to our `CustomEffects` namespace, so that we can access `PlatformEffect` in our XAML that we have defined in our namespace.
2. We added the `Button.Effects` attribute to our `Button` attribute for `BeginTrailWalk`, and then referenced the `customEffect` assembly namespace, so that we can access the platform-specific `ButtonShadowEffect` to use.

Whenever you work with the `PlatformEffect` class to create platform-specific classes for each of your mobile platforms, this class exposes a number of properties that you can use and these are explained in the following table:

PlatformEffect	Description
Container	The `Container` type is responsible for referencing the platform-specific control that is being used to implement the layout.
Control	The `Control` type is responsible for referencing the platform-specific control that is being used to implement the `Xamarin.Forms` control.
Element	The `Element` type is responsible for referencing the `Xamarin.Forms` control that is currently being rendered.

Whenever you create your own `PlatformEffects`, they will always inherit from the `PlatformEffect` class, which is dependent on the platform that your app is run on. However, the API for an effect is pretty much identical across each of the platforms, as they derive from `PlatformEffect<T, T>` and will contain different generic parameters.

There are also two very important attributes that you need to ensure that you set for each class that subclasses from the `PlatformEffect` class, and these are explained in the following table:

AttributeType	Description
ResolutionGroupName	This attribute is responsible for setting up a company-wide namespace that prevents name collisions with other effects of the same name. It is worth mentioning that you can create multiple `PlatformEffect` classes, but you can only apply the `ResolutionGroupName` attribute once per project.

ExportEffect	This attribute is responsible for registering the effect with a unique ID that is used by the Xamarin.Forms platform, along with the group name. The ExportEffect attribute takes two parameters, which are the name of the effect and a unique string that will be used to locate the effect prior to applying it to the control.

 For more information on the PlatformEffect class, please refer to the Microsoft Developer Documentation at https://docs.microsoft.com/en-au/xamarin/xamarin-forms/app-fundamentals/effects/.

Now that you have created the necessary PlatformEffects and RoutingEffects class implementations for both the iOS and Android platforms, our next step is to begin creating a ValueConverter class that will be used to display images in our XAML pages based on a String value.

Creating and implementing ValueConverters in your app

In this section, we will begin creating the ImageConverter class for our TrackMyWalks solution. ValueConverters are an important concept in data binding, as they allow you to customize the appearance of a data property at the time it is bound. This process is quite similar to **Windows Presentation Foundation (WPF)** on the Windows application development platform.

The Xamarin.Forms platform provides you with a number of ValueConverter interfaces as part of its API. These are extremely helpful as they allow you to toggle the visibility of elements based on a Boolean property, or display an image based on a String property.

Let's start creating the ImageConverter class for our TrackMyWalks app by performing the following the steps:

1. Ensure that the TrackMyWalks solution is open in the **Visual Studio for Mac IDE**.
2. Right-click on the TrackMyWalks shared project, choose **Add | New Folder** from the pop-up menu, and enter ValueConverters for the name of the new folder to be created.

3. Right-click on the `ValueConverters` folder and choose **Add | New File...** from the pop-up menu, as shown in the following screenshot:

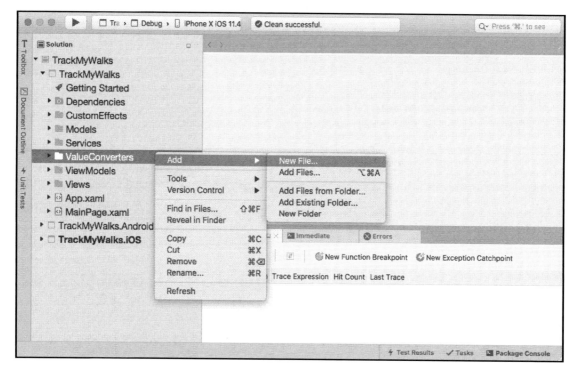

Creating the ImageConverter Class within the ValueConverters folder

4. Create a new **Empty Class** called `ImageConverter` in the `ValueConverters` folder, as you did in the section entitled *Implementing the ButtonShadowEffect RoutingEffect Class* in this chapter.

5. Ensure that the `ImageConverter.cs` file, which is located as part of the `TrackMyWalks` shared project group, is displayed in the code editor and enter the following code snippet:

```
//
//  ImageConverter.cs
//  ValueConverter class for converting difficulty property
//  Values to an image
//
//  Created by Steven F. Daniel on 16/07/2018
//  Copyright © 2018 GENIESOFT STUDIOS. All rights reserved.
//
using System;
```

```
using System.Globalization;
using Xamarin.Forms;

namespace TrackMyWalks.ValueConverters
{
    public class ImageConverter : IValueConverter
    {
        public object Convert(object value, Type targetType,
                              object parameter, CultureInfo culture)
        {
            // Declare our Difficulty Level based on the value
            // parameter
            var DiffLevel = (String)value;

            // Determine the type of URL to return based on the
            // difficulty level
            switch (DiffLevel)
              {
                case "Easy":
                    return "http://www.trailhiking.com.au/wp-content/
                           uploads/2013/08/g1.jpeg";
                case "Medium":
                    return "http://www.trailhiking.com.au/wp-content/
                           uploads/2013/08/g2.jpeg";
                case "Hard":
                    return "http://www.trailhiking.com.au/wp-content/
                           uploads/2013/08/g3.jpeg";
                case "Extreme":
                    return "http://www.trailhiking.com.au/wp-content/
                           uploads/2013/08/g5.jpeg";
                default:
                    return "http://www.trailhiking.com.au/wp-content/
                           uploads/2013/08/g1.jpeg";
              }
        }

        public object ConvertBack(object value, Type targetType,
                                  object parameter, CultureInfo
culture)
        {
            throw new NotImplementedException();
        }
    }
}
```

Let's now take a look at what we covered in the preceding code snippet:

1. We started by including references to the `System`, `System.Globalization`, and `Xamarin.Forms` namespaces, so that we can access the classes that are defined in these namespaces

2. We ensured that our `ImageConverter` class inherits from the `IValueConverter` class, so that we can access the method implementations of the `IValueConverter` class

3. We created the `Convert` method and declared a `DiffLevel` variable, which will contain the data-bound difficulty level from our XAML page, and then we return back the `URL` based on the level of difficulty determined

4. We created the `ConvertBack` method, which will be used to perform any conversions from the `URL` to the difficulty level; we don't need to do anything here in this instance

Updating the BaseViewModel class to include additional properties

Now that we have created our `ImageConverter` class, which will be used to convert a level of difficulty and return the associated `URL` for the image to be displayed in our XAML pages, our next step is to update the underlying C# code in our `BaseViewModel` class. Since our `BaseViewModel` class is used by each of our `ViewModels`, it makes sense to add these additional properties and instance methods in the `BaseViewModel` class.

Let's take a look at how we can achieve this by performing the following steps:

1. Locate and open the `WalkBaseViewModel.cs` class, ensure that it is displayed in the code editor, and enter the following highlighted code sections:

```
//
//   BaseViewModel.cs
//   BaseView Model Class that each of our ViewModels will inherit from
//
//   Created by Steven F. Daniel on 5/06/2018
//   Copyright © 2018 GENIESOFT STUDIOS. All rights reserved.
//
using System.ComponentModel;
using System.Runtime.CompilerServices;
using System.Threading.Tasks;
using TrackMyWalks.Services;
```

```
namespace TrackMyWalks.ViewModels
{
    public abstract class BaseViewModel : INotifyPropertyChanged
    {
        public INavigationService Navigation { get; set; }
        public const string PageTitlePropertyName = "PageTitle";

        string pageTitle;
        public string PageTitle
        {
            get => pageTitle;
            set { pageTitle = value; OnPropertyChanged(); }
        }

        protected BaseViewModel(INavigationService navService)
        {
            Navigation = navService;
        }
        public abstract Task Init();
        public event PropertyChangedEventHandler PropertyChanged;

        protected virtual void OnPropertyChanged([CallerMemberName]
string propertyName = null)
        {
            PropertyChanged?.Invoke(this, new
PropertyChangedEventArgs(propertyName));
        }

        bool isProcessBusy;
        public bool IsProcessBusy
        {
            get => isProcessBusy;
            set { isProcessBusy = value; OnPropertyChanged(); }
        }
    }

    public abstract class BaseViewModel<TParam> : BaseViewModel
    {
        protected BaseViewModel(INavigationService navService) :
base(navService)
        {
        }
    }
}
```

In the preceding code snippet, we begin by creating a Boolean property called IsProcessBusy, which will only be set to True when we are in the process of actually loading data in our ListView or following some process that takes a long time. The IsProcessBusy property defines the getter and setter implementations. Whenever the value of the isProcessBusy variable changes, we make a call to the OnPropertyChanged event to tell the ViewModel that a change has been made.

Updating the WalksMainPageViewModel to use our property

Now that we have updated our BaseViewModel class, which includes our IsProcessBusy property, which will in turn be used and inherited by each of the ViewModels that we create, we can start updating the WalksMainPageViewModel class, so that it can use our IsProcessBusy property whenever we populate data in our ListView.

Let's take a look at how we can achieve this by performing the following steps:

1. Locate and open the WalksMainPageViewModel.cs class, ensure that it is displayed in the code editor, and enter the following highlighted code sections:

```
//
//   WalksMainPageViewModel.cs
//   The ViewModel for our WalksMainPage ContentPage
//
//   Created by Steven F. Daniel on 5/06/2018.
//   Copyright © 2018 GENIESOFT STUDIOS. All rights reserved.
//
using System.Collections.ObjectModel;
using System.Threading.Tasks;
using TrackMyWalks.Models;
using TrackMyWalks.Services;

namespace TrackMyWalks.ViewModels
{
    public class WalksMainPageViewModel : BaseViewModel
    {
        // Create our WalksListModel Observable Collection
        public ObservableCollection<WalkDataModel> WalksListModel;

        public WalksMainPageViewModel(INavigationService navService) :
base(navService)
        {
        }
```

```
            // Instance method to add and retrieve our  Walk Trail items
            public async Task GetWalkTrailItems()
            {
                    // Check our IsProcessBusy property to see if we are
already processing
                    if (IsProcessBusy)
                        return;

                    // If we aren't processing, we need to set our
IsProcessBusy property to true
                    IsProcessBusy = true;

                    // Specify our List Collection to store the items being
read
                    WalksListModel = new ObservableCollection<WalkDataModel> {

                    // Populate our collection with some dummy data that will
be used to populate our ListView
                    new WalkDataModel
                    {
                        Id = 1,
                        Title = "10 Mile Brook Trail, Margaret River",
                        Description = "The 10 Mile Brook Trail starts in the
Rotary Park
                        near Old Kate, a  preserved steam engine at the
northern edge
                        of Margaret River. ",
                        Latitude = -33.9727604,
                        Longitude = 115.0861599,
                        Distance = 7.5,
                        Difficulty = "Medium",
                        ImageUrl =
"http://trailswa.com.au/media/cache/media/images/trails/_mid/
                                FullSizeRender1_600_480_c1.jpg"
                    },
                    new WalkDataModel
                    {
                        Id = 2,
                        Title = "Ancient Empire Walk, Valley of the Giants",
                        Description = "The Ancient Empire is a 450 metre walk
trail that
                        takes you around and through some of the giant tingle
trees including
                        the most popular of the gnarled veterans, known as
Grandma Tingle.",
                        Latitude = -34.9749188,
                        Longitude = 117.3560796,
                        Distance = 450,
```

```
                Difficulty = "Hard",
                ImageUrl =
"http://trailswa.com.au/media/cache/media/images/trails/_mid/
                Ancient_Empire_534_480_c1.jpg"
            }};

            // Add a temporary timer, so that we can see our progress
indicator working
            await Task.Delay(3000);

            // Set our IsProcessBusy property value back to false when
finished
            IsProcessBusy = false;
        }

        // Instance method to initialise the WalksMainPageViewModel
        public override async Task Init()
        {
            await Task.Factory.StartNew(async () =>
            {
                // Call our GetWalkTrailItems method to populate our
collection
                await GetWalkTrailItems();
            });
        }
    }
}
```

Let's take a look at what we covered in the preceding code snippet:

1. We started by modifying the method signature for our `GetWalkTrailItems` instance method, by making it return a `Task` object and also handle asynchronous calls.
2. We checked our `IsProcessBusy` property to see whether we are already processing items, and if we aren't, we initialize our `IsProcessBusy` property to `True`.
3. We added a temporary timer using the `Delay` method of the `Task` object, so that we can see our progress indicator working, but we will be removing this in Chapter 11, *Incorporating Microsoft Azure App Services*, when we load the Walk Trail information from an API. Finally, we set the `IsProcessBusy` property value back to `False` when we have finished to tell `BaseViewModel` that we have completed processing our Walk Trail Items.

Updating the WalksMainPage to use our ImageConverter class

In this section, we will take a look at how to update the user interface for our `WalksMainPage`, to apply `ValueConverters` and utilize `ImageConverter` in our XAML, so that we can display an image for the data-bind property of our Difficulty level.

Let's start by updating the user interface for our `WalksMainPage` by performing the following steps:

1. Locate and open the `WalksMainPage.xaml` file, which is located in the `Views` folder, ensure that it is displayed in the code editor, and enter the following highlighted code sections:

```xml
<?xml version="1.0" encoding="UTF-8"?>
<ContentPage xmlns="http://xamarin.com/schemas/2014/forms"
             xmlns:x="http://schemas.microsoft.com/winfx/2009/xaml"
             xmlns:customEffect="clr-
namespace:TrackMyWalks.CustomEffects"
             xmlns:valueConverters="clr-
namespace:TrackMyWalks.ValueConverters"
             x:Class="TrackMyWalks.Views.WalksMainPage">

    <ContentPage.Resources>
        <ResourceDictionary>
            <valueConverters:ImageConverter x:Key="imageConverter" />
        </ResourceDictionary>
    </ContentPage.Resources>
    <ContentPage.ToolbarItems>
        <ToolbarItem Text="Add" Clicked="AddWalk_Clicked" />
    </ContentPage.ToolbarItems>
    <StackLayout>
        <ListView x:Name="WalkEntriesListView" HasUnevenRows="true"
                  SeparatorColor="#ddd"
ItemTapped="myWalkEntries_ItemTapped">
            <ListView.ItemTemplate>
                <DataTemplate>
                    <ViewCell>
                        <ViewCell.ContextActions>
                            <MenuItem Clicked="OnEditItem"
                             CommandParameter="{Binding .}" Text="Edit"
                             IsDestructive="False" />
                            <MenuItem Clicked="OnDeleteItem"
                             CommandParameter="{Binding .}"
Text="Delete"
                             IsDestructive="True" />
```

```
                                </ViewCell.ContextActions>
                                <StackLayout x:Name="cellLayout"
Orientation="Horizontal"
                                        HorizontalOptions="FillAndExpand">
                            <StackLayout.Padding>
                                <OnPlatform
x:TypeArguments="Thickness">
                                    <On Platform="Android, WinPhone"
                                        Value="0,0" />
                                    <On Platform="iOS"
                                        Value="2,2" />
                                </OnPlatform>
                            </StackLayout.Padding>
                            <Image Aspect="AspectFill" Source="{Binding
ImageUrl}"
                                    WidthRequest="140"
HeightRequest="140"
                                    VerticalOptions="FillAndExpand"
                                    HorizontalOptions="FillAndExpand" />
                            <StackLayout x:Name="DetailsLayout"
HorizontalOptions="FillAndExpand">
                                <StackLayout.Padding>
                                    <OnPlatform
x:TypeArguments="Thickness">
                                        <On Platform="Android,
WinPhone"
                                            Value="5,0" />
                                        <On Platform="iOS"
                                            Value="5,0" />
                                    </OnPlatform>
                                </StackLayout.Padding>
                                <Label Text="{Binding Title}"
FontAttributes="Bold"
                                        TextColor="Black"
Style="{DynamicResource TitleStyle}">
                                    <Label.FontSize>
                                        <OnPlatform
x:TypeArguments="x:Double">
                                            <On Platform="Android,
WinPhone" Value="14" />
                                            <On Platform="iOS" Value="16"
/>
                                        </OnPlatform>
                                    </Label.FontSize>
                                    <Label.Effects>
                                        <customEffect:LabelShadowEffect />
                                    </Label.Effects>
                                </Label>
```

```xml
                        <Label Text="{Binding Distance,
                                StringFormat='Kilometers: {0} km'}"
                                FontAttributes="Bold"
TextColor="#666"
                                Style="{DynamicResource
CaptionStyle}" />
                        <Label Text="{Binding Difficulty,
                                StringFormat='Difficulty: {0}'}"
                                FontAttributes="Bold"
TextColor="Black"
                                Style="{DynamicResource
ListItemTextStyle}" />
                        <Image Aspect="AspectFit"
HeightRequest="50"
                                WidthRequest="50"
HorizontalOptions="Start"
                                Source="{Binding Difficulty,
                                Converter={StaticResource
imageConverter}}" />
                        <StackLayout Spacing="3"
Orientation="Vertical">
                            <Label Text="{Binding Description}"
FontAttributes="None"
                                    TextColor="Blue"
VerticalOptions="FillAndExpand"
                                    Style="{DynamicResource
BodyStyle}" />
                        </StackLayout>
                        </StackLayout>
                    </StackLayout>
                  </ViewCell>
                </DataTemplate>
              </ListView.ItemTemplate>
            </ListView>
        </StackLayout>
    </ContentPage>
```

Let's now take a look at what we cover in the preceding code snippet:

1. We started by creating a `xmlns:valueConverters` reference to our `ValueConverters` namespace, so that we can access the `ImageConverter` in our XAML that we have defined in our namespace

2. We created a `ResourceDictionary` attribute, added the `ImageConverter` class in our `valueConverters` namespace, and defined a value for the `Key` property so that we can reference the `imageConverter` name in our XAML page.

3. We created an `Image` attribute and set the `Aspect` ratio to use, as well as the `Height`, `Width`, and `HorizontalOptions`, and the `Source` property for the image

4. You'll notice that for our `Source` property, we provided the `Converter` property in our binding for our difficulty level, in order to use the `imageConverter` `ValueConverter`, which will take a `String` value for our Difficulty and return the `URL` to use

Updating the WalkEntryPage to use our ImageConverter class

In this section, we will take a look at how to update the user interface for our `WalkEntryPage` to apply `ValueConverters` and utilize `ImageConverter` in your XAML, so that we can display an image for the data-bind property for our difficulty level.

Let's start by updating the user interface for our `WalkEntryPage` by performing the following steps:

1. Locate and open the `WalkEntryPage.xaml` file, which is located in the `Views` folder, ensure that it is displayed in the code editor, and enter the following highlighted code sections:

```xml
<?xml version="1.0" encoding="UTF-8"?>
<ContentPage xmlns="http://xamarin.com/schemas/2014/forms"
             xmlns:x="http://schemas.microsoft.com/winfx/2009/xaml"
             xmlns:valueConverters="clr-
namespace:TrackMyWalks.ValueConverters"
             x:Class="TrackMyWalks.Views.WalkEntryPage">
    <ContentPage.ToolbarItems>
        <ToolbarItem Text="Save" Clicked="SaveWalkItem_Clicked" />
    </ContentPage.ToolbarItems>
    <ContentPage.Resources>
        <ResourceDictionary>
            <valueConverters:ImageConverter x:Key="imageConverter" />
        </ResourceDictionary>
        <ResourceDictionary>
            <!-- Creating an Implicit Style in XAML -->
            <Style TargetType="Picker">
                <Setter Property="VerticalOptions" Value="Center"/>
                <Setter Property="HorizontalOptions"
Value="FillAndExpand"/>
                <Setter Property="TextColor" Value="Red"/>
                <Setter Property="FontSize" Value="{DynamicResource
```

```
CaptionStyle}"/>
                        <Setter Property="BackgroundColor"
Value="LightGoldenrodYellow"/>
                    </Style>
                </ResourceDictionary>
            </ContentPage.Resources>
            <ContentPage.Content>
                <TableView Intent="Form">
                    <TableView.Root>
                        <TableSection Title="Enter Walk Trail Information">
                            <EntryCell Label="Title:" Text="{Binding Title,
Mode=TwoWay}"
                                Placeholder="Provide a Title for this trail" />
                            <EntryCell Label="Description:" Text="{Binding
Description, Mode=TwoWay}"
                                Placeholder="Provide trail description" />
                            <EntryCell Label="Latitude:" Text="{Binding
Latitude, Mode=TwoWay}"
                                Placeholder="Provide latitude coordinates"
Keyboard="Numeric" />
                            <EntryCell Label="Longitude:" Text="{Binding
Longitude, Mode=TwoWay}"
                                Placeholder="Provide longitude coordinates"
Keyboard="Numeric" />
                            <EntryCell Label="Distance:" Text="{Binding
Distance, Mode=TwoWay}"
                                Placeholder="Provide trail distance"
Keyboard="Numeric" />
                            <ViewCell>
                              <StackLayout Orientation="Horizontal">
                                 <StackLayout.Margin>
                                    <OnPlatform x:TypeArguments="Thickness">
                                        <On Platform="Android, WinPhone"
Value="15,0" />
                                        <On Platform="iOS" Value="15,0" />
                                    </OnPlatform>
                                 </StackLayout.Margin>
                                 <Label Text="Difficulty:"
VerticalOptions="Center" />
                                 <Image Aspect="AspectFill" HeightRequest="50"
                                        WidthRequest="50"
HorizontalOptions="Start"
                                        Source="{Binding Difficulty,
                                        Converter={StaticResource
imageConverter}}" />
                                 <Picker Title="Choose Difficulty"
                                        SelectedItem="{Binding
Difficulty, Mode=TwoWay}">
```

```
                                        <Picker.ItemsSource>
                                            <x:Array Type="{x:Type
x:String}">

                                            <x:String>Easy</x:String>
                                            <x:String>Medium</x:String>
                                            <x:String>Hard</x:String>
                                            <x:String>Extreme</x:String>
                                            </x:Array>
                                        </Picker.ItemsSource>
                                    </Picker>
                            </StackLayout>
                        </ViewCell>
                        <EntryCell Label="Image URL:" Text="{Binding
ImageUrl, Mode=TwoWay}"
                            Placeholder="Provide an Image URL" />
                    </TableSection>
                </TableView.Root>
            </TableView>
        </ContentPage.Content>
    </ContentPage>
```

Let's now take a look at what we cover in the preceding code snippet:

1. We started by creating a `xmlns:valueConverters` reference to our
   `ValueConverters` namespace, so that we can access the `ImageConverter` in
   our XAML that we have defined in our namespace.
2. We create a `ResourceDictionary` attribute, added the `ImageConverter` class
   in our `valueConverters` namespace, and defined a value for the `Key` property
   so that we can reference the `imageConverter` name in our XAML page.
3. We created an `Image` attribute and set the `Aspect` ratio to use, as well as `Height`,
   `Width`, and `HorizontalOptions` and the `Source` property for the image.
4. You'll notice that for our `Source` property, we provided the `Converter` property
   in our binding for our difficulty level, in order to use the `imageConverter`
   `ValueConverter`, which will take a `String` value for our Difficulty and return
   the URL to use. Whenever you change the `Picker` value, the image will update to
   represent the chosen difficulty level.

Updating the WalkTrailInfoPage to use our ImageConverter class

In this section, we will take a look at how to update the user interface for our `WalkTrailInfoPage` to apply `ValueConverters` and utilize `ImageConverter` in your XAML, so that we can display an image for the data binding property for our Difficulty level.

Let's start updating the user interface for our `WalkTrailInfoPage` by performing the following steps:

1. Locate and open the `WalkTrailInfoPage.xaml` file, which is located in the Views folder, ensure that it is displayed in the code editor, and enter the following highlighted code sections:

```
<?xml version="1.0" encoding="UTF-8"?>
<ContentPage xmlns="http://xamarin.com/schemas/2014/forms"
             xmlns:x="http://schemas.microsoft.com/winfx/2009/xaml"
             xmlns:valueConverters="clr-
namespace:TrackMyWalks.ValueConverters"
             xmlns:customEffect="clr-
namespace:TrackMyWalks.CustomEffects"
             x:Class="TrackMyWalks.Views.WalkTrailInfoPage">
    <ContentPage.Resources>
        <ResourceDictionary>
            <valueConverters:ImageConverter x:Key="imageConverter" />
        </ResourceDictionary>
        <ResourceDictionary>
            <Style x:Key="labelTrailName" TargetType="Label">
                <Setter Property="HorizontalOptions" Value="Start" />
                <Setter Property="FontAttributes" Value="Bold" />
                <Setter Property="Style" Value="{DynamicResource
TitleStyle}" />
                <Setter Property="TextColor" Value="Black" />
            </Style>
            <Style x:Key="labelTrailKilometers" TargetType="Label">
                <Setter Property="HorizontalOptions" Value="Start" />
                <Setter Property="FontAttributes" Value="Bold" />
                <Setter Property="Style" Value="{DynamicResource
CaptionStyle}" />
                <Setter Property="TextColor" Value="Black" />
            </Style>
            <Style x:Key="labelTrailDifficulty" TargetType="Label">
                <Setter Property="HorizontalOptions" Value="Start" />
                <Setter Property="FontAttributes" Value="Bold" />
                <Setter Property="Style" Value="{DynamicResource
```

```
ListItemTextStyle}" />
                    <Setter Property="TextColor" Value="Black" />
                </Style>
                <Style x:Key="labelTrailDescription" TargetType="Label">
                    <Setter Property="HorizontalOptions" Value="Start" />
                    <Setter Property="Style" Value="{DynamicResource
BodyStyle}" />
                    <Setter Property="TextColor" Value="MidnightBlue" />
                </Style>
            </ResourceDictionary>
        </ContentPage.Resources>
        <ScrollView>
            <StackLayout.Padding>
                <OnPlatform x:TypeArguments="Thickness">
                    <On Platform="Android, WinPhone" Value="2,0" />
                    <On Platform="iOS" Value="2,0" />
                </OnPlatform>
            </StackLayout.Padding>
            <StackLayout Orientation="Vertical"
HorizontalOptions="FillAndExpand">
                <Image x:Name="TrailImage" Aspect="AspectFill"
Source="{Binding ImageUrl}"
                    HorizontalOptions="FillAndExpand"
VerticalOptions="FillAndExpand" />
                <Label x:Name="TrailName" Text="{Binding Title}"
                    Style="{DynamicResource labelTrailName}">
                    <Label.Effects>
                        <customEffect:LabelShadowEffect />
                    </Label.Effects>
                </Label>
                <Label x:Name="TrailKilometers" Text="{Binding Distance,
                    StringFormat='Kilometers: {0} km'}"
                    Style="{StaticResource labelTrailKilometers}"/>
                <Label x:Name="TrailDifficulty" Text="{Binding Difficulty,
                        StringFormat='Difficulty: {0}'}"
                        Style="{StaticResource labelTrailDifficulty}"/>
                <Image Aspect="AspectFill" HeightRequest="50"
WidthRequest="50"
                    HorizontalOptions="Start"
                    Source="{Binding Difficulty, Converter={StaticResource
imageConverter}}"/>
                <Label x:Name="TrailFullDescription" Text="{Binding
Description}"
                        HorizontalOptions="FillAndExpand"
                        Style="{StaticResource labelTrailDescription}"/>
                <Button x:Name="BeginTrailWalk" Text="Begin this Trail"
                        Clicked="BeginTrailWalk_Clicked"
                        Margin="20" Style="{StaticResource buttonStyle}">
```

```
                    <Button.Effects>
                        <customEffect:ButtonShadowEffect />
                    </Button.Effects>
                </Button>
            </StackLayout>
        </ScrollView>
    </ContentPage>
```

Let's now take a look at what we covered in the preceding code snippet:

1. We started by creating a `xmlns:valueConverters` reference to our `ValueConverters` namespace, so that we can access the `ImageConverter` class in our XAML that we have defined in our namespace

2. We created a `ResourceDictionary` attribute, added the `ImageConverter` class in our `valueConverters` namespace, and defined a value for the `Key` property so that we can reference the `imageConverter` name in our XAML page

3. We created an `Image` attribute and set the `Aspect` ratio to use, as well as `Height`, `Width`, and `HorizontalOptions` and the `Source` property for the image

4. You'll notice that, for our `Source` property, we provided the `Converter` property in our binding for our difficulty level, in order to use the `imageConverter ValueConverter`, which will take a `String` value for our Difficulty and return the `URL` to use

Now that you have created the underlying C# code to incorporate `PlatformEffects` and `ValueConverters`, implemented the necessary properties for our `BaseViewModel` and `WalksMainPageViewModel` classes, and then implemented the various `Styles` and applied `Padding` and `Margins` to your XAML pages to change the appearance of control elements for our app, our next step is to compile, build, and run the `TrackMyWalks` application in the **iOS Simulator**.

Launching the TrackMyWalks app using the iOS simulator

In this section, we will compile and run the `TrackMyWalks` application to see how our application looks, since we have made changes to our XAML pages to implement the various styles, such as Device, Implicit, Explicit, and Global Styles, as well as the underlying C# code to work with the `PlatformEffects` API to create `LabelShadowEffect` and `ButtonShadowEffect`, as well as our `ImageConverter`.

Let's see how we can achieve this by performing the following steps:

1. Ensure that you have chosen the `TrackMyWalks.iOS` platform from the drop-down menu.
2. Ensure that you have chosen the **Debug** option from the drop-down menu.
3. Choose your preferred device from the list of available **iOS Simulators**.
4. Select the **Run|Start Debugging** menu option shown in the following screenshot:

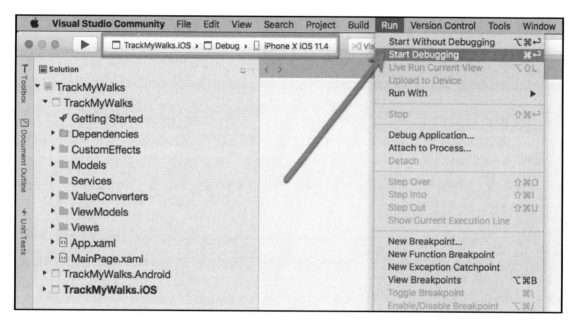

Launching the TrackMyWalks app within the iOS Simulator

5. Alternatively, you can also build and run the `TrackMyWalks` application by pressing the *Command + Return* keys.

When the compilation is complete, the **iOS Simulator** will appear automatically and the `TrackMyWalks` application will be displayed, as shown in the following screenshot:

Navigation flow between each screen for the chosen Walk Trail

The preceding screenshot shows each walk displayed in the `ListView` control; an associated image to represent the level of difficulty, which is pulled from the `ImageValueConverter` class; and the `LabelShadowEffect` `PlatformEffect`. When the **Add** button on the **Track My Walks Listing** page is clicked, this will display the **Adding Trail Details** page, which displays the `ImageConverter` for the chosen level of difficulty when the value changes in the `Picker` control. You'll notice that our `Picker` contains the Implicit Style that we assigned.

Lastly, you can see the navigation flow between each of the pages whenever a trail is selected from `ListView`, which will display the **Trail Walk Information** ContentPage, our `ImageConverter`, and `PlatformEffects` for both `LabelShadowEffect` and `ButtonShadowEffect`, as well as the Global Style that we defined in our `App.xaml`.

Summary

In this chapter, you learned how to customize `DataTemplates` to lay out your `Views` beautifully and neatly in your application's user interface by modifying your ContentPages (Views). You learned how to create and implement the various styles in your XAML pages, prior to getting accustomed to working with the `PlatformEffects` API to customize the appearance by creating a `ButtonShadowEffect` and `LabelShadowEffect` class for both the iOS and Android platforms, so you can style native control elements that can be rendered and used with the XAML pages for each platform. Next, you learned how to set up your margins and padding for each platform using the `OnPlatform` XAML attribute, before moving on to learning how to manipulate the visual appearance of data-bound fields using `ValueConverters` and `ImageConverters`.

In the next chapter, you'll work with the various animation classes that come as part of the `Xamarin.Forms` platform, so that you can customize the appearance of your user interface and control elements. You'll get accustomed to working with basic animations and how to set the duration of an animation, before moving on to learning how to work with easing functions and creating your very own custom easing functions to apply scaling to control elements. Finally, you'll learn how to work with Entrance animations to apply fading, prior to creating your own custom animations and implementing these in your ContentPages (Views).

9
Working with Animations in Xamarin.Forms

In the previous chapter, we learned how to customize `DataTemplates` to lay out your `Views` beautifully and neatly in your application's user interface by modifying your `ContentPages` (Views).

You also learned how to create, implement, and use the various styles in your XAML pages, prior to getting accustomed to working with the `PlatformEffects` API to customize the appearance and styling of native control elements for each platform by creating `ButtonShadow` and `LabelShadow` classes that inherit from the `PlatformEffect` class for each platform.

You then learned how to set up your margins and padding for each platform using the `OnPlatform` XAML tag, before moving on to learning how to manipulate the visual appearance of data-bound fields using `ValueConverters` and `ImageConverters`.

In this chapter, you will learn how to work with the various `Animation` classes that come as part of the `Xamarin.Forms` platform, so that you can apply really cool animations and transition effects to your user interfaces and control elements. You will get accustomed to working with and using **Simple Animations** in your XAML to create the necessary C# code in your `ContentPages` to interact with your XAML control elements, to apply various animation techniques to those controls that `Rotate`, `Scale`, `Translate`, and `Fade`.

You will learn how to implement and use Easing Functions in your ContentPages, using C# code and the `Easing` class, which will allow you to specify a transfer function that controls how animations speed up or slow down as they're running, by creating Custom Easing Functions that interact with your XAML control Visual Elements.

Finally, you'll learn how to work with the different types of transition effects called Entrance Animations, which you can use to apply Fading to your Views using ViewExtensions extension methods, which will allow you to create FadingEntrance, SlidingEntrance, and SwingingEntrance animations for your ContentPage (View) or XAML control elements whenever the ContentPage is displayed on the screen.

This chapter will cover the following points:

- Implementing Simple Animations with Xamarin.Forms in your XAML pages using C#
- Implementing Easing Functions for XAML elements using C#
- Implementing Custom Animations using the Xamarin.Forms and Animation classes and C#
- Implementing Entrance Animations for your XAML elements using C#

Creating and using Simple Animations in Xamarin.Forms

In this section, we will take a look at how to work with Simple Animations in your Xamarin.Forms XAML and ContentPages using C#. The Xamarin.Forms platform includes its own animation classes that are straightforward to use to create simple animations, as well as being versatile enough to provide you with the ability of creating more complex animations.

Simple Animations make use of the ViewExtensions class, which provides you with extension methods that can be used to construct simple animations. The ViewExtensions class provides you with a LayoutTo extension method, which is only intended for use with layouts to animate transitions between layout states that contain size and property changes, and should only be used by classes that use the Layout subclass.

Before we start working with Simple Animations in our XAML and ContentPages (Views), let's take a moment to look at the various extension methods provided to us by the `ViewExtensions` class, which are explained in the following table:

Extension method	Description
TranslateTo	This is responsible for animating the `TranslationX` and `TranslationY` properties of a given visual element that has been defined in your XAML page.
ScaleTo	This is responsible for animating the `Scale` property of a given visual element that has been defined in your XAML page.
RelScaleTo	This is responsible for applying an incremental animated increase or decrease to the `Scale` property of a given visual element that has been defined in your XAML page.
RotateTo	This is responsible for animating the `Rotation` property of a given visual element that has been defined in your XAML page.
RelRotateTo	This applies an incremental animated increase or decrease to the `Rotation` property of a given visual element that has been defined in your XAML page.
RotateXTo	This is responsible for animating around the `RotationX` property of a given visual element that has been defined in your XAML page.
RotateYTo	This is responsible for animating around the `RotationY` property of a given visual element that has been defined in your XAML page.
FadeTo	This is responsible for animating the `Opacity` property of a given visual element that has been defined in your XAML page.

As you can see in the preceding table, the `ViewExtensions` class contains a variety of extension methods, as well as including a `CancelAnimations` method that can be used to cancel animations at any point in time.

Whenever you use these extension methods, they will contain an animation property, which by default has been set to 250 milliseconds. However, you can change the duration of each animation whenever you create the animation, using any of the extension methods. When working with the `animation` property, the extension methods in the `ViewExtensions` class are all `asynchronous` method calls, and these return a `Task<bool>` object. Whenever the animation completes, it will return a value of `false` and if the animation is cancelled, it will return a value of `true`.

Therefore, whenever you define your animation class methods, you should always specify the `await` operator, which will help make it possible to determine whenever your animation completes, and then you can handle it accordingly. Now that you have an understanding of what Simple Animations are, as well as the various extension methods available to you through the `ViewExtensions` class, our next step is to begin implementing some Simple Animations.

Updating the WalkEntryPage to use Simple Animations

In this section, we will take a look at how to update the user interface for our `WalkEntryPage` to include naming to our control elements in our XAML, so that we can access these controls in our code-behind and apply Simple Animations and other animations using C# code.

Let's start updating the user interface for our `WalkEntryPage` by performing the following steps:

1. Locate and open the `WalEntryPage.xaml` file, which is located in the `Views` folder, ensure that it is displayed in the code editor, and enter the following highlighted code sections:

```
<?xml version="1.0" encoding="UTF-8"?>
<ContentPage xmlns="http://xamarin.com/schemas/2014/forms"
             xmlns:x="http://schemas.microsoft.com/winfx/2009/xaml"
             xmlns:valueConverters="clr-
namespace:TrackMyWalks.ValueConverters"
             x:Class="TrackMyWalks.Views.WalkEntryPage">
    <ContentPage.ToolbarItems>
        <ToolbarItem Text="Save" Clicked="SaveWalkItem_Clicked" />
    </ContentPage.ToolbarItems>
    <ContentPage.Resources>
        <ResourceDictionary>
            <valueConverters:ImageConverter x:Key="imageConverter" />
        </ResourceDictionary>
        <ResourceDictionary>
            <Style TargetType="Picker">
                <Setter Property="VerticalOptions"
Value="Center"/>
                <Setter Property="HorizontalOptions"
Value="FillAndExpand"/>
                <Setter Property="TextColor" Value="Red"/>
                <Setter Property="FontSize"
Value="{DynamicResource CaptionStyle}"/>
                <Setter Property="BackgroundColor"
Value="LightGoldenrodYellow"/>
            </Style>
        </ResourceDictionary>
    </ContentPage.Resources>
    <ContentPage.Content>
        <TableView Intent="Form" x:Name="WalkDetails">
            <TableView.Root>
                ...
```

```
        ...
        <Image Aspect="AspectFill" x:Name="DifficultyLevel"
               HeightRequest="50" WidthRequest="50"
               HorizontalOptions="Start"
               Source="{Binding Difficulty,
               Converter={StaticResource imageConverter}}"
/>

                    ...
                    ...
            </TableView.Root>
        </TableView>
      </ContentPage.Content>
  </ContentPage>
```

2. Locate and open the `WalkEntryPage.xaml.cs` code-behind file, which is located in the `Views` folder, ensure that it is displayed in the code editor, and enter the following highlighted code sections:

```
//
//  WalkEntryPage.xaml.cs
//  Data Entry screen that allows new walk information to be
//  added
//
//  Created by Steven F. Daniel on 14/05/2018
//  Copyright © 2018 GENIESOFT STUDIOS. All rights reserved.
//
using System;
using TrackMyWalks.Services;
using TrackMyWalks.ViewModels;
using Xamarin.Forms;

namespace TrackMyWalks.Views
{
    public partial class WalkEntryPage : ContentPage
    {
        // Return the Binding Context for the ViewModel
        WalkEntryPageViewModel _viewModel => BindingContext as
WalkEntryPageViewModel;

        public WalkEntryPage()
        {
            InitializeComponent();
            ...
            ...
        }
        ...
        ...
        // Method to initialise our View Model when the ContentPage
```

appears

```
protected override async void OnAppearing()
{
    base.OnAppearing();

    // Create a Simple Animation to rotate our Difficulty
    // Level Image
    DifficultyLevel.AnchorY = (Math.Min(DifficultyLevel.Width,
                              DifficultyLevel.Height) / 2) /
                              DifficultyLevel.Height;

    await DifficultyLevel.RotateTo(360, 2000,
Easing.BounceOut);
    }
  }
}
```

Let's take a look at what we defined in our XAML and code snippet:

1. We started by adding the `x:Name="WalkDetails"` property to our `TableView` property, so that we can access `TableView` in our code-behind file, in order to apply various animation techniques as we progress through this chapter
2. We added `x:Name="DifficultyLevel"` to our `Image` property, just like we did when we defined our `TableView` property, so that we can access our image in our code-behind file in order to apply various animations
3. We modified our `OnAppearing` method and defined a simple animation to rotate our `DifficultyLevel` Image by setting the `AnchorY` property on our image, which is calculated to center the image from the top of the image to the center point of the layout
4. We used the `await` keyword on our `RotateTo` extension method, and passed in `360`, which will ensure that the image makes a full 360-degree rotation around the center point of the layout, and specify a duration of 2 seconds over which to animate the transition
5. We used the `BounceOut` property of the `Easing` class to bounce our image when the animation completes

We will discuss more about the `Easing` class as we progress through this chapter, particularly in the *Creating and using Easing Functions in Xamarin.Forms* section.

Updating the WalkTrailInfoPage to use Simple Animations

In this section, we will take a look at how to update the user interface for our `WalkTrailInfoPage` to include naming to our control elements in our XAML, so that we can access these controls in our code-behind and apply Simple Animations and other animations using C# code.

Let's start updating the user interface for our `WalkTrailInfoPage` by performing the following steps:

1. Locate and open the `WalkTrailInfoPage.xaml` file, which is located in the `Views` folder, ensure that it is displayed in the code editor, and enter the following highlighted code sections:

```xml
<?xml version="1.0" encoding="UTF-8"?>
<ContentPage xmlns="http://xamarin.com/schemas/2014/forms"
             xmlns:x="http://schemas.microsoft.com/winfx/2009/xaml"
             xmlns:valueConverters="clr-
namespace:TrackMyWalks.ValueConverters"
             xmlns:customEffect="clr-
namespace:TrackMyWalks.CustomEffects"
             x:Class="TrackMyWalks.Views.WalkTrailInfoPage">
    <ContentPage.Resources>
        <ResourceDictionary>
            <valueConverters:ImageConverter x:Key="imageConverter" />
        </ResourceDictionary>
        ...
        ...
    </ContentPage.Resources>
    <ScrollView x:Name="TrailInfoScrollView">
        <StackLayout.Padding>
            <OnPlatform x:TypeArguments="Thickness">
                <On Platform="Android, WinPhone" Value="2,0" />
                <On Platform="iOS" Value="2,0" />
            </OnPlatform>
        </StackLayout.Padding>
        <StackLayout Orientation="Vertical"
HorizontalOptions="FillAndExpand">
            <Image x:Name="TrailImage" Aspect="AspectFill"
                   Source="{Binding ImageUrl}"
                   HorizontalOptions="FillAndExpand"
                   VerticalOptions="FillAndExpand" />
            <Label x:Name="TrailName" Text="{Binding Title}"
                   Style="{StaticResource labelTrailName}">
```

```
                        <Label.Effects>
                          <customEffect:LabelShadowEffect />
                        </Label.Effects>
                      </Label>
                       . . .
                       . . .
                      <Button x:Name="BeginTrailWalk" Text="Begin this
Trail"
                            Clicked="BeginTrailWalk_Clicked"
                            Margin="20" Style="{StaticResource
buttonStyle}">
                        <Button.Effects>
                          <customEffect:ButtonShadowEffect />
                        </Button.Effects>
                      </Button>
                  </StackLayout>
              </ScrollView>
          </ContentPage>
```

2. Locate and open the WalkTrailInfoPage.xaml.cs code-behind file, which is located in the Views folder, ensure that it is displayed in the code editor, and enter the following highlighted code sections:

```
//
// WalkTrailInfoPage.xaml.cs
// Displays related trail information chosen from the WalksMainPage
//
// Created by Steven F. Daniel on 14/05/2018
// Copyright © 2018 GENIESOFT STUDIOS. All rights reserved.
//
using System;
using Xamarin.Forms;
using TrackMyWalks.ViewModels;
using TrackMyWalks.Services;

namespace TrackMyWalks.Views
{
    public partial class WalkTrailInfoPage : ContentPage
    {
        // Return the Binding Context for the ViewModel
        WalkTrailInfoPageViewModel _viewModel =>
                        BindingContext as
WalkTrailInfoPageViewModel;

        public WalkTrailInfoPage()
        {
            InitializeComponent();
            . . .
```

```
        . . .
    }
    // Instance method that proceeds to begin a new walk trail
    public async void BeginTrailWalk_Clicked(object sender,
                                                EventArgs e)
    {
        if (App.SelectedItem == null)
            return;

        // Create a Simple Animation to rotate our Begin Trail
        // Walk Button
        await BeginTrailWalk.RotateTo(360, 1000);
        BeginTrailWalk.Rotation = 0;
        await
_viewModel.Navigation.NavigateTo<WalkDistancePageViewModel>();
    }
  }
}
```

Let's take a look at what we defined in our XAML and code snippet:

1. We started by adding the x:Name="TrailInfoScrollView" property to our
   ScrollView property so that we can access ScrollView in our code-behind file,
   in order to apply various animation techniques as we progress through this
   chapter.
2. We added the x:Name="BeginTrailWalk" property to our Button property,
   just like we did when we defined our ScrollView property, so that we can
   access our button in our code-behind file in order to apply various animations.
3. We modified our OnAppearing method and defined a simple animation to rotate
   our BeginTrailWalk button by using the await keyword on our RotateTo
   extension method. We passed in 360, which will ensure that the image makes a
   full 360-degree rotation around the center point of the layout, and specify a
   duration of 1 second over which to animate the transition.
4. Once the animation completes, we reset the BeginTrailWalk
   button's Rotation property to 0, which ensures that the Rotation property
   doesn't remain at 360 after the animation has concluded.

Creating and using Easing Functions in Xamarin.Forms

In this section, we will take a look at how to work with Easing Functions in your Xamarin.Forms XAML and ContentPages using C#. We are extremely fortunate that the Xamarin.Forms platform includes an Easing class that allows you to specify what is called a *transfer function*, which is able to control how animations speed up or slow down while they are running.

Before we start working with Easing Functions in our XAML and ContentPages (Views), let's take a moment to look at the various predefined Easing Function methods provided to us by the Easing class, which are explained in the following table:

Easing function	Description
BounceIn	This is responsible for bouncing the animation at the beginning.
BounceOut	This is responsible for bouncing the animation at the end.
CubicIn	This is responsible for slowly accelerating the animation.
CubicOut	This is responsible for decelerating the animation quickly.
Linear	This is the default easing function and uses a constant velocity.
SinIn	This is responsible for performing an animation with smooth acceleration.
SinOut	This is responsible for performing an animation with smooth deceleration.
SpringIn	This is responsible for causing the animation to very quickly accelerate towards the end, when the animation completes.
SpringOut	This is responsible for causing the animation to very quickly decelerate towards the end, when the animation completes.

As you can see in the preceding table, the Easing class contains a variety of easing function methods that you can utilize in your Xamarin.Forms and native applications. Now that you have an understanding of what Easing Functions are, as well as starting to become accustomed to the various easing function methods available to you through the Easing class, our next step is to begin implementing some of these Easing Functions.

Updating the WalkTrailInfoPage to use Easing Functions

In this section, we will take a look at how to update our code-behind file for our `WalkTrailInfoPage` to create and implement an Easing Function that will be called whenever the `BeginTrailWalk` button is clicked using C# code.

Let's start updating the code-behind for our `WalkTrailInfoPage` by performing the following steps:

1. Locate and open the `WalkTrailInfoPage.xaml.cs` code-behind file, which is located in the `Views` folder, ensure that it is displayed in the code editor, and enter the following highlighted code sections:

```
//
//  WalkTrailInfoPage.xaml.cs
//  Displays related trail information chosen from the
//  WalksMainPage
//
//  Created by Steven F. Daniel on 14/05/2018
//  Copyright © 2018 GENIESOFT STUDIOS. All rights reserved.
//
using System;
using Xamarin.Forms;
using TrackMyWalks.ViewModels;
using TrackMyWalks.Services;

namespace TrackMyWalks.Views
{
    public partial class WalkTrailInfoPage : ContentPage
    {
        // Return the Binding Context for the ViewModel
        WalkTrailInfoPageViewModel _viewModel =>
                        BindingContext as
WalkTrailInfoPageViewModel;

        public WalkTrailInfoPage()
        {
            InitializeComponent();
            ...
            ...
        }
        // Instance method that proceeds to begin a new walk trail
        public async void BeginTrailWalk_Clicked(object sender,
                                                EventArgs e)
        {
```

```
        if (App.SelectedItem == null)
            return;

        // Create a Simple Animation to rotate our Begin Trail
        // Walk Button
        await BeginTrailWalk.RotateTo(360, 1000);
        BeginTrailWalk.Rotation = 0;

        // Create and Apply an Easing Function to our Button
        await BeginTrailWalk.RotateTo(15, 1000, new Easing(t =>
                            Math.Sin(Math.PI * t) *
                            Math.Sin(Math.PI * 20 * t)));

            await
_viewModel.Navigation.NavigateTo<WalkDistancePageViewModel>();
        }
    }
}
```

Let's take a look at what we defined in the preceding code snippet:

1. We started by modifying our `OnAppearing` method to define an Easing
   Function that will essentially be used to rotate our `BeginTrailWalk` button,
   using the `await` keyword on our `RotateTo` extension method, and passed in 15,
   which will ensure that the button performs a 15-degree rotation. We specified a
   duration length of 1 second over which to animate the transition.

2. You will notice that our `RotateTo` extension method looks quite similar to
   the Simple Animation that we declared previously, with the exception that we
   are using the `Easing` constructor to create a custom easing function by
   specifying a lambda expression, and using the `Math.Sin` method to create a fast
   wobble effect.

For more information on the `ViewExtensions` class, please refer to the
Xamarin.Forms documentation at `https://docs.microsoft.com/en-us/`
`dotnet/api/xamarin.forms.viewextensions?view=xamarin-forms`.

Creating and implementing your own Custom Animations

In this section, we will take a look at how to we can work with Custom Animations, and implement these in your `Xamarin.Forms` XAML and `ContentPages` using C#. Custom Animations make use of the `Animation` class, which essentially is the parent class for all `Xamarin.Forms` animations, as well as making use of the extension methods contained in the `ViewExtensions` class, to create one or a series of Animation objects.

Whenever you create an `Animation` object, you'll need to specify a number of parameter objects, as well as include the starting and ending values for the property that is being animated. You will also need to ensure you declare a `Callback` method that changes the value of the property.

You can also use the `Animation` object to specify any number of child animations, which can be run in parallel, by calling the `Commit` method and specifying the duration of the animation. Now that you have an understanding of what Custom Animations are, our next step is to begin implementing them and see how we can use them in our code-behind through C# code.

Updating our WalkTrailInfoPage to use Custom Animations

In this section, we will take a look at how to update our code-behind file for our `WalkTrailInfoPage` to create and implement a Custom Animation using the `Animation` class, which will be called whenever the `BeginTrailWalk` button is clicked using C# code.

Let's start updating the code-behind for our `WalkTrailInfoPage` by performing the following steps:

1. Locate and open the `WalkTrailInfoPage.xaml.cs` code-behind file, which is located in the `Views` folder, ensure that it is displayed in the code editor, and enter the following highlighted code sections:

```
//
// WalkTrailInfoPage.xaml.cs
// Displays related trail information chosen from the
// WalksMainPage
//
// Created by Steven F. Daniel on 14/05/2018
```

```
//  Copyright © 2018 GENIESOFT STUDIOS. All rights reserved.
//
using System;
using Xamarin.Forms;
using TrackMyWalks.ViewModels;
using TrackMyWalks.Services;

namespace TrackMyWalks.Views
{
    public partial class WalkTrailInfoPage : ContentPage
    {
        // Return the Binding Context for the ViewModel
        WalkTrailInfoPageViewModel _viewModel =>
                            BindingContext as
WalkTrailInfoPageViewModel;

        public WalkTrailInfoPage()
        {
            InitializeComponent();
            ...
            ...
        }
        // Method to initialise our View Model when the ContentPage
appears
        protected override async void OnAppearing()
        {
            base.OnAppearing();

            // Create a Custom Animation for our BeginTrailWalk button
            var animation = new Animation(v =>
                        BeginTrailWalk.BackgroundColor =
Color.FromHsla(
                                                        v, 1, 0.5), start:
0, end: 1);

            animation.Commit(this, "BeginWalkCustomAnimation",
                            16,
                            5000,
                            Easing.Linear, (v, c) =>
                            BackgroundColor = Color.Default, () =>
true);
        }
        // Instance method that proceeds to begin a new walk trail
        public async void BeginTrailWalk_Clicked(object sender,
EventArgs e)
        {
            if (App.SelectedItem == null)
                return;
```

```
                    . . .
                    . . .
              }
          }
      }
```

Let's take a look at what we defined in the preceding code snippet:

1. We started by creating and implementing our `OnAppearing` method to create a Custom Animation for our `BeginTrailWalk` button.

2. We declared an `animation` variable, which creates an instance of our `Animation` class and uses a callback lambda expression method, which, when executed when the animated value changes, animates the `BackgroundColor` of the `BeginTrailWalk` button created by the `Color.FromHsla` method using hue values ranging from 0 to 1.

3. We used the `Commit` method on the `animation` variable and specified a name for our Custom Animation that will be used to access and track the animation, as well as its current state. Then, we specified a time in milliseconds that will be used to run between frames, as well as a duration of 5 seconds.

4. We specified the `Easing.Linear` to use for the transition, and then create an `Action` to set `BackgroundColor` to `Color.Default` when the animation has completed, prior to creating and specifying a function that will be called to return the value of `true`.

Updating our WalksMainPage to use Custom Animations

In this section, we will take a look at how to update the user interface for our `WalksMainPage` to include naming to our control elements in our XAML, so that we can access these controls in our code-behind and apply **Custom Animations** and other animations using C# code.

Let's start updating the user interface for our `WalksMainPage` by performing the following steps:

1. Locate and open the `WalksMainPage.xaml` file, which is located in the `Views` folder, ensure that it is displayed in the code editor, and enter the following highlighted code sections:

```
<?xml version="1.0" encoding="UTF-8"?>
```

```xml
<ContentPage xmlns="http://xamarin.com/schemas/2014/forms"
             xmlns:x="http://schemas.microsoft.com/winfx/2009/xaml"
             xmlns:customEffect="clr-
namespace:TrackMyWalks.CustomEffects"
             xmlns:valueConverters="clr-
namespace:TrackMyWalks.ValueConverters"
             x:Class="TrackMyWalks.Views.WalksMainPage">
    <ContentPage.Resources>
        <ResourceDictionary>
            <valueConverters:ImageConverter x:Key="imageConverter" />
        </ResourceDictionary>
    </ContentPage.Resources>
    <ContentPage.ToolbarItems>
        <ToolbarItem Text="Add" Clicked="AddWalk_Clicked" />
    </ContentPage.ToolbarItems>
    <StackLayout>
        <ActivityIndicator IsRunning="true" x:Name="progressIndicator"
                           HorizontalOptions="CenterAndExpand"
                           VerticalOptions="CenterAndExpand"
                           IsVisible="{Binding IsProcessBusy}" />
        <Label Text="Loading Walk Information..."
FontAttributes="Bold"
               TextColor="Black" HorizontalTextAlignment="Center"
               IsVisible="{Binding IsProcessBusy}"
x:Name="LoadingWalkInfo">
            <Label.FontSize>
            <OnPlatform x:TypeArguments="x:Double">
                <On Platform="Android, WinPhone" Value="12" />
                <On Platform="iOS" Value="14" />
            </OnPlatform>
            </Label.FontSize>
        </Label>
        ...
        ...
        <ListView x:Name="WalkEntriesListView" HasUnevenRows="true"
                  SeparatorColor="#ddd"
ItemTapped="myWalkEntries_ItemTapped">
            <ListView.ItemTemplate>
                <DataTemplate>
                    <ViewCell>
                        ...
                        ...
                    </ViewCell>
                </DataTemplate>
            </ListView.ItemTemplate>
        </ListView>
    </StackLayout>
</ContentPage>
```

2. Locate and open the `WalksMainPage.xaml.cs` code-behind file, which is located in the `Views` folder, ensure that it is displayed in the code editor, and enter the following highlighted code sections:

```
//
//  WalksMainPage.xaml.cs
//  Displays Walk Information in a ListView control from an array
//
//  Created by Steven F. Daniel on 14/05/2018
//  Copyright © 2018 GENIESOFT STUDIOS. All rights reserved.
//
using System;
using TrackMyWalks.Models;
using TrackMyWalks.Services;
using TrackMyWalks.ViewModels;
using Xamarin.Forms;

namespace TrackMyWalks.Views
{
    public partial class WalksMainPage : ContentPage
    {
        // Return the Binding Context for the ViewModel
        WalksMainPageViewModel _viewModel =>
                            BindingContext as
WalksMainPageViewModel;

        public WalksMainPage()
        {
            InitializeComponent();
            ...
            ...
        }
        ...
        ...
        // Method to initialise our View Model when the ContentPage
appears
        protected override async void OnAppearing()
        {
            base.OnAppearing();

            if (_viewModel != null)
            {
                // Call the Init method to initialise the ViewModel
                await _viewModel.Init();
            }

            // Create a Custom Animation for our LoadingWalkInfo Label
```

```
            // Create parent animation object
            var parentAnimation = new Animation();

            // Create "ZoomIn" animation and add to parent.
            var ZoomInAnimation = new Animation(v =>
LoadingWalkInfo.Scale = v,
                                    1, 2,
                                    Easing.BounceIn,
null);
            parentAnimation.Add(0, 0.5, ZoomInAnimation);

            // Create "ZoomOut" animation and add to parent.
            var ZoomOutAnimation = new Animation(v =>
LoadingWalkInfo.Scale = v,
                                    2, 1,
                                    Easing.BounceOut,
null);
            parentAnimation.Insert(0.5, 1, ZoomOutAnimation);
            // Commit parent animation
            parentAnimation.Commit(this, "CustomAnimation", 16, 5000,
null, null);
            ...
            ...
        }
    }
}
```

Let's take a look at what we defined in our XAML and code snippet:

1. We started by adding the `x:Name="LoadingWalkInfo"` property to our `Label` property for our `ActivityIndicator`, which will be used by our **Loading Walk Information...** so that we can access our `LabelWalkInfo` in our code-behind file, in order to apply various animation techniques as we progress through this chapter.

2. We defined a `Label.FontSize` attribute and set the `FontSize` based on the platform that our app is running using the `OnPlatform` attribute, and then specifying the `x:TypeArguments` of `Double`.

3. We modified our `OnAppearing` method to define a Custom Animation that will be used to animate our `LabelWalkInfo` label, and we created a `parentAnimation` object variable that will be used to add child animations to it so that they can be run in parallel.

4. We declares a `ZoomInAnimation` object variable, which creates an instance of the `Animation` class that uses a callback lambda expression method, which will adjust the `Scale` property, as well as specifying the starting and ending values and the transition effect to use for `Easing.BounceIn` and the method to call when the animation completes.

5. We used the `Add` property of our `parentAnimation` object to add our `ZoomInAnimation` object. We also specified at which points the animation should begin and finish, as well as the name of the animation object that we would like to add.

6. We declared a `ZoomInAnimation` object variable, which creates an instance of the `Animation` class that uses a callback lambda expression method that will adjust the `Scale` property, as well as specifying the starting and ending values and the transition effect to use of `Easing.BounceOut` and the method to call when the animation completes.

7. We used the `Add` property of our `parentAnimation` object to add our `ZoomOutAnimation` object. We also specified at which points the animation should begin and finish, as well as the name of the animation object that we would like to add.

8. We used the `Commit` method on the `parentAnimation` variable, and specified a name for our Custom Animation that will be used to access and track the animation, as well as its current state and specify a time in milliseconds that will be used to run between frames as well as the duration of 5 seconds, and specifying a value of null when the animation has completed, and specifying null that will be called to return the value.

For more information on the `Animation` class, please refer to the `Xamarin.Forms` documentation at `https://docs.microsoft.com/en-us/dotnet/api/xamarin.forms.animation?view=xamarin-forms`.

Creating and implementing Entrance Animations

In this section, we will take a look at how to we can work with Entrance Animations and implement these in your `Xamarin.Forms` XAML and `ContentPages` using C#. When you create Entrance Animations, these make use of the `Animation` class, which is the parent class for all `Xamarin.Forms` animations, as well as making use of the extension methods contained in the `ViewExtensions` class to create one or a series of `Animation` objects.

Before we start working with Entrance Animations in our XAML and ContentPages (Views), let's take a moment to look at the various predefined Entrance Animation methods provided to us by the `ViewExtensions` and `Animation` classes, which are explained in the following table:

Entrance animation	Description
`FadingEntrance`	This animation type uses the `FadeTo` extension method to allow you to fade in the contents of your XAML page.
`SlidingEntrance`	This animation type uses the `TranslateTo` extension method to allow you to slide in the contents of your XAML page from the side.
`SwingingEntrance`	This animation type uses the `RotateYTo` extension method to allow you to animate around the `RotationY` axis. You can also use the `RotateXTo` extension method, which will allow you to animate around the `RotationX` axis.

Now that you have an understanding of what Easing Functions are, as well as starting to get accustomed to the various easing functions methods available to you through the `ViewExtensions` class, our next step is to begin implementing some of these Entrance Animations.

Updating the WalkTrailInfoPage to use Entrance Animations

In this section, we will take a look at how to update our code-behind file for our `WalkTrailInfoPage` to create and implement a `SlidingEntrance` animation through the `TranslateTo` extension method in the `OnAppearing` method, using C# code that will be called whenever our `ContentPage` is displayed.

Let's start updating the code-behind for our `WalkTrailInfoPage` by performing the following steps:

1. Locate and open the `WalkTrailInfoPage.xaml.cs` code-behind file, which is located in the `Views` folder, ensure that it is displayed in the code editor, and enter the following highlighted code sections:

```
//
//  WalkTrailInfoPage.xaml.cs
//  Displays related trail information chosen from the WalksMainPage
//
//  Created by Steven F. Daniel on 14/05/2018
//  Copyright © 2018 GENIESOFT STUDIOS. All rights reserved.
//
using System;
using Xamarin.Forms;
using TrackMyWalks.ViewModels;
using TrackMyWalks.Services;
using System.Threading.Tasks;

namespace TrackMyWalks.Views
{
    public partial class WalkTrailInfoPage : ContentPage
    {
        // Return the Binding Context for the ViewModel
        WalkTrailInfoPageViewModel _viewModel =>
                                BindingContext as
WalkTrailInfoPageViewModel;

        public WalkTrailInfoPage()
        {
            InitializeComponent();
            ...
            ...
        }

        // Method to initialise our View Model when the ContentPage
appears
        protected override async void OnAppearing()
        {
            base.OnAppearing();

            // Create a SlidingEntrance Animation for
WalkTrailInfoPage
            double offset = 1000;
            foreach (View view in TrailInfoScrollView.Children)
            {
```

```
                    view.TranslationX = offset;
                    offset *= -1;
                    await Task.WhenAny(view.TranslateTo(0, 0, 1000,
                                            Easing.SpringOut),
Task.Delay(100));
            }
            . . .
            . . .
        }

        // Instance method that proceeds to begin a new walk trail
        public async void BeginTrailWalk_Clicked(object sender,
                                            EventArgs e)
        {
            if (App.SelectedItem == null)
                return;
            . . .
            . . .
        }
    }
}
```

Let's take a look at what we covered in the preceding code snippet:

1. We started by including a reference to our `System.Threading.Tasks` namespace so that we can access the classes that are defined in this namespace.
2. We modified our `OnAppearing` method to create a `SlidingEntrance` animation, declare an offset variable, and then iterate through every child view contained in the `TrailInfoScrollView` section of our XAML ContentPage.
3. We set the `TranslationX` property to our `offset` variable, and then updated the `offset` variable from the values between `1000` and `-1000`. We used the `Task.WhenAny` method that creates a task that will complete when any of the supplied tasks have completed in the method.
4. We used the `TranslateTo` extension method, which will animate each child view's `TranslationX` and `TranslationY` properties, as well as updating their current values to their new values.
5. We specified the transition effect to use for `Easing.SpringOut`, as well as specifying a delay, in milliseconds, of `0.1` seconds using the `Task.Delay` method.

For more information on the `TranslateTo` extension method, please refer to the `Xamarin.Forms` documentation at `https://docs.microsoft.com/` `en-us/dotnet/api/xamarin.forms.viewextensions.translateto?view=` `xamarin-forms#Xamarin_Forms_ViewExtensions_TranslateTo_Xamarin_` `Forms_VisualElement_System_Double_System_Double_System_UInt32_` `Xamarin_Forms_Easing_.`

Updating our WalksMainPage to use Entrance Animations

In this section, we will take a look at how to update our code-behind file for our `WalksMainPage` to create and implement a `FadingEntrance` animation with the `FadeTo` extension method in the `OnAppearing` method, using C# code that will be called whenever our `ContentPage` is displayed.

Let's start updating the code-behind for our `WalksMainPage` by performing the following steps:

1. Locate and open the `WalksMainPage.xaml.cs` code-behind file, which is located in the `Views` folder, ensure that it is displayed in the code editor, and enter the following highlighted code sections:

```
//
//  WalksMainPage.xaml.cs
//  Displays Walk Information in a ListView control from an array
//
//  Created by Steven F. Daniel on 14/05/2018
//  Copyright © 2018 GENIESOFT STUDIOS. All rights reserved.
//
using System;
using TrackMyWalks.Models;
using TrackMyWalks.Services;
using TrackMyWalks.ViewModels;
using Xamarin.Forms;

namespace TrackMyWalks.Views
{
    public partial class WalksMainPage : ContentPage
    {
        // Return the Binding Context for the ViewModel
        WalksMainPageViewModel _viewModel =>
                            BindingContext as
```

```
WalksMainPageViewModel;

            public WalksMainPage()
            {
                InitializeComponent();
                ...
                ...
            }
            ...
            ...
            // Method to initialise our View Model when the ContentPage
appears
            protected override async void OnAppearing()
            {
                base.OnAppearing();

                if (_viewModel != null)
                {
                    // Call the Init method to initialise the ViewModel
                    await _viewModel.Init();
                }

                // Create a FadingEntrance Animation to fade our
WalkEntriesListView
                WalkEntriesListView.Opacity = 0;
                await WalkEntriesListView.FadeTo(1, 4000);
                ...
                ...
            }
        }
    }
```

Let's take a look at what we covered in the preceding code snippet:

1. We started by modifying our `OnAppearing` method to create a `FadingEntrance` animation, and set the `Opacity` property for our `WalkEntriesListView` to fade our `ListView`.

2. We used the `FadeTo` extension method, which will animate our `WalkEntriesListView`, and we specified the `Opacity` value to fade to, as well as specifying a duration in milliseconds of 4 seconds over which to animate the transition.

 For more information on the `FadeTo` extension method, please refer to the Xamarin.Forms documentation at https://docs.microsoft.com/en-us/ dotnet/api/xamarin.forms.viewextensions.fadeto?view=xamarin- forms

Updating our WalkEntryPage to use Entrance Animations

In this section, we will take a look at how to update our code-behind file for our WalkEntryPage, to create and implement a SwingingEntrance animation with the RotateYTo extension method in the OnAppearing method, using C# code that will be called whenever our ContentPage is displayed.

Let's start updating the code-behind for our WalkEntryPage by performing the following steps:

1. Locate and open the WalkEntryPage.xaml.cs code-behind file, which is located in the Views folder, ensure that it is displayed in the code editor, and enter the following highlighted code sections:

```
//
//  WalkEntryPage.xaml.cs
//  Data Entry screen that allows new walk information to be added
//
//  Created by Steven F. Daniel on 14/05/2018
//  Copyright © 2018 GENIESOFT STUDIOS. All rights reserved.
//
using System;
using TrackMyWalks.Services;
using TrackMyWalks.ViewModels;
using Xamarin.Forms;

namespace TrackMyWalks.Views
{
    public partial class WalkEntryPage : ContentPage
    {
        // Return the Binding Context for the ViewModel
        WalkEntryPageViewModel _viewModel =>
                                BindingContext as
WalkEntryPageViewModel;

        public WalkEntryPage()
        {
            InitializeComponent();
            ...
            ...
        }

        // Method to initialise our View Model when the ContentPage
appears
```

```
protected override async void OnAppearing()
{
    base.OnAppearing();

    // Create a SwingingEntrance Animation for our WalkDetails
TableView
    WalkDetails.RotationY = 180;
    await WalkDetails.RotateYTo(0, 1000, Easing.BounceOut);
    WalkDetails.AnchorX = 0.5;
    ...
    ...
}
}
}
```

Let's take a look at what we covered in the preceding code snippet:

1. We started by modifying our OnAppearing method to create a
   SwingingEntrance animation, and then we set the RotationY property for our
   WalkDetails, which will be the final rotation value that will be set to our
   TableView.

2. We used the RotateYTo extension method, which will animate around the
   RotationY property for our WalkDetails XAML visual element. We specified a
   rotation value of 0 to use, as well as specifying a length in milliseconds of 10
   seconds over which to animate the transition using the Easing.BounceOut
   transition effect, prior to setting and initializing the AnchorX property to 0.5,
   which will anchor the view to the top-left position.

   For more information on the RotateYTo extension method, please refer to
   the Xamarin.Forms documentation at https://docs.microsoft.com/en-
   us/dotnet/api/xamarin.forms.viewextensions.rotateyto?view=
   xamarin-forms.

Now, you have applied the necessary changes to our XAML ContentPages, as well as the
underlying C# code to incorporate SimpleAnimations, EasingFunctions,
CustomAnimations, and finally EntranceAnimations, which we can use to apply
beautiful animation and transition effects to each of your XAML of a given visual element
that has been defined in your XAML page. Our next step is to compile, build, and run
the TrackMyWalks application in the iOS simulator.

Launching the TrackMyWalks app using the iOS simulator

In this section, we will compile and run the `TrackMyWalks` application to see how our application looks, since we have made changes to our XAML pages while creating the underlying C# code to implement the various animation and transition effects.

Let's see how we can achieve this by performing the following steps:

1. Ensure that you have chosen the `TrackMyWalks.iOS` platform from the drop-down menu.
2. Ensure that you have chosen the **Debug** option from the drop-down menu.
3. Choose your preferred device from the list of available iOS Simulators.
4. Select the **Run | Start Debugging** menu option, as shown in the following screenshot:

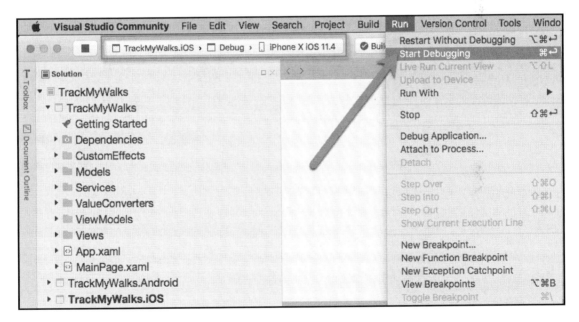

Launching the TrackMyWalks app within the iOS Simulator

5. Alternatively, you can also build and run the `TrackMyWalks` application by pressing the *Command + Return* keys.

When the compilation is complete, the iOS Simulator will appear automatically and the `TrackMyWalks` application will be displayed, as shown in the following screenshot:

Displays the various animation techniques applied to each of the screens

The preceding screenshot shows the `ActivityIndicator` spinner control, along with the associated **Loading Walk information...** text, which is displayed while the trail walks are loaded in the `ListView`, which contains the Custom Animation that we applied to `ZoomIn` and `ZoomOut` out `Label`. You'll also notice that our `ListView` control also contains our `FadingEntrance` animation, which nicely fades our `ListView` control in.

When the **Add** button on the **Track My Walks Listing** page is clicked, this will display the **Adding Trail Details** page, which creates a Simple Animation that will rotate our Difficulty Level image and use our `SwingingEntrance` animation, which performs a swinging animation effect on our `TableView` object:

Displays the Trail Walk Information screen using the SlidingEntrance animation

The preceding screenshot displays the **Trail Walk Information** ContentPage whenever a trail has been selected from ListView. You will also notice that we are using our SlidingEntrance animation effect, which slides our View in from the right-hand side, as well as using our Custom Animation, which performs a color cycle effect on our **Begin this Trail** button.

Summary

In this chapter, you learned how to work with the various `Animation` classes that come as part of the `Xamarin.Forms` platform so that you can apply really cool animations and transition effects to your user interfaces and control elements. You learned how to use and implement Simple Animations in your XAML, as well as create the necessary C# code in your `ContentPages` to interact with your XAML control elements so that you can apply various animation techniques to those controls that `Rotate`, `Scale`, `Translate`, and `Fade`.

You learned how to implement Easing Functions by creating the necessary C# code in your ContentPages, as well as using the Easing class, which allows you to specify a transfer function that controls how animations speed up or slow down as they're running, by creating Custom Easing Functions that interact with your XAML visual control elements.

Lastly, you worked with the different types of transition effects which are called Entrance Animations, which you can use to apply Fading to your Views using the `FadingEntrance` class, as well as the `SlidingEntrance` and `SwingingEntrance` classes, to provide animations to your ContentPage (View) or XAML control elements whenever `ContentPage` is displayed to the screen.

In the next chapter, you'll learn about the Razor HTML Templating Engine, and how you can use it to create a hybrid mobile solution. You'll learn how to build a mobile book library solution using the power of Razor templates, as well as how to use and define models in your application.

Finally, you will learn how to work with SQLite and connect our book library solution up to a database to store, retrieve, update, and delete book details.

10
Working with the Razor Templating Engine

In the previous chapter, we learned how to work with the various Animation classes that come as part of the Xamarin.Forms platform, so that you can apply really cool animations and transition effects to your user interfaces and control elements. We learned how to work with and use simple animations within your XAML, as well as how to create the necessary C# code within your ContentPages to interact with your XAML control elements in order to apply various animation techniques to the controls that Rotate, Scale, Translate, and Fade.

We also learned about easing functions, and how you can implement these within your ContentPages using C# code by making use of the Easing class, which allows you to specify a transfer function that is able to control the speed of running animations by creating custom easing functions that are able to interact with your XAML control visual elements.

Lastly, you learned how to work with the different types of transition effects, which you can use to apply Fading to your views using the FadingEntrance class, as well as the SlidingEntrance and SwingingEntrance classes, which you can use to provide animations to your ContentPage (view) or XAML control elements whenever the ContentPage is displayed on the screen.

In this chapter, you will learn about the **Razor templating engine**, and how you can use it to create a hybrid mobile solution. You'll learn how to build a book library mobile solution using the power of Razor templates, as well as how to use and define BookItem database models within your application.

You'll learn how to incorporate the `SQLite-net` NuGet package that you will use in order to create a `BookDatabase` interface and class, which will include a number of class instance methods that will be used to communicate with our SQLite database so that you can create, update, retrieve, and delete book items. Finally, you will learn how to create the necessary Razor template pages that will integrate with our `BookItem` data model, as well as how to implement the necessary class instance methods within the `WebViewController` class.

This chapter will cover the following topics:

- Understanding what exactly the Razor templating engine is
- Building a Book Library app using the Razor templating engine
- Incorporating the `SQLite-net` NuGet package to our solution
- Creating and implementing a `BookDatabase` class using C#
- Creating the `BookLibrary` database model for our Book Library app
- Creating and implementing the `BookLibaryListing` Razor template page
- Creating and implementing the `BookLibaryAddEdit` Razor template page
- Updating the `BookLibrary` Cascading Style Sheet (CSS)
- Implementing the necessary class instance methods within the `WebViewController` class

Understanding the Razor templating engine

The Razor templating engine was first introduced as part of the ASP.NET MVC architecture, and was originally designed to run on a web server to generate HTML files to be served to a variety of web browsers. Since Razor made its first appearance on the development scene, the Razor engine has definitely come a long way, and now extends the standard HTML syntax so that you can use C# to express the layout of your HTML files, as well as incorporate CSS stylesheets and JavaScript very easily.

Razor is a markup syntax for embedding server-based code into web pages, and is generally identified as having a `.cshtml` file extension. When working with the static model class within Razor templates, each Razor template has the ability to reference a `Model` class, which can be of any custom type, and properties can be accessed directly from within the template by having the ability to mix HTML and C# syntax easily, as you can see in the following screenshot:

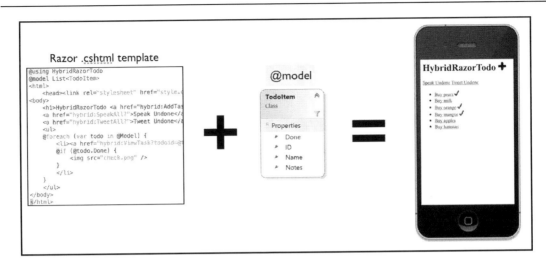

Razor Templating Engine using the Static Model

When working with Razor templates using the SQLite database model, you can use a Razor template to reference a `Model` class using the `@model` directive to communicate with an SQLite database, and then write to those properties contained within the `Model`, and display information within those properties in your template, as you can see in the following screenshot:

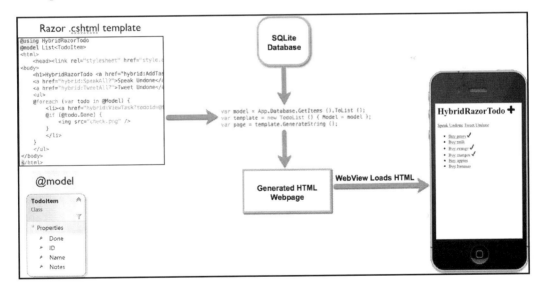

Razor Templating Engine using the SQLite database model

As you work through this chapter, you will see how you can utilize the Razor templating engine and equip yourself with the flexibility of building cross-platform, templated, HTML views that make use of both JavaScript and CSS, as well as how to gain access to the underlying platform APIs using the power of C#.

For more information on ASP.NET web programming using the Razor syntax (C#), please refer to the Microsoft developer documentation at `https://docs.microsoft.com/en-us/aspnet/web-pages/overview/ getting-started/introducing-razor-syntax-c`.

Building a BookLibrary app using the Razor templating engine

In this section, we will take a look at how to create a Razor templating solution. We will begin by developing the basic structure for our application, as well as creating a `BookItem` data model and a `BookDatabase` class, designing the Razor template pages user interface files using HTML5, and implementing the necessary class instance methods within the `WebViewController` class.

Before we can proceed, we need to create our **BookLibrary** project for the iOS platform. It is very simple to create this using Visual Studio for Mac. Simply go through the following steps:

1. Launch the **Visual Studio for Mac** application.
2. Next, choose the **New Solution...** option, or, alternatively, choose **File | New | Solution...** or simply press *Shift + Command + N*.
3. Then, choose the **WebView App** option, which is located under the **iOS | App** section, as shown in the following screenshot. Ensure that you have selected C# as the programming language to use:

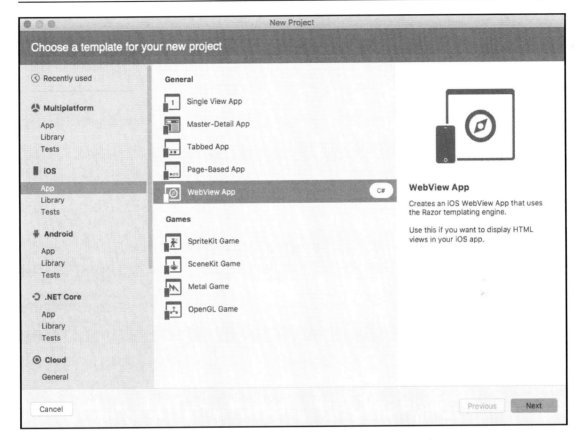

New Project

Choose a template for your new project

Recently used	General			WebView App

Multiplatform
App
Library
Tests

iOS
App
Library
Tests

Android
App
Library
Tests

.NET Core
App
Library
Tests

Cloud
General

General
Single View App
Master-Detail App
Tabbed App
Page-Based App
WebView App   C#

Games
SpriteKit Game
SceneKit Game
Metal Game
OpenGL Game

WebView App
Creates an iOS WebView App that uses the Razor templating engine.

Use this if you want to display HTML views in your iOS app.

Cancel   Previous   Next

Creating a new WebView App iOS Project

4. Next, enter BookLibrary as the name for your app in the **App Name** field and then specify a name for the **Organization Identifier** field.

5. Then, ensure that both **iPad** and **iPhone** have been selected for the **Devices** field, and also ensure that you have chosen the minimum version of iOS that we would like our app to support in the **Target** field, as shown in the following screenshot:

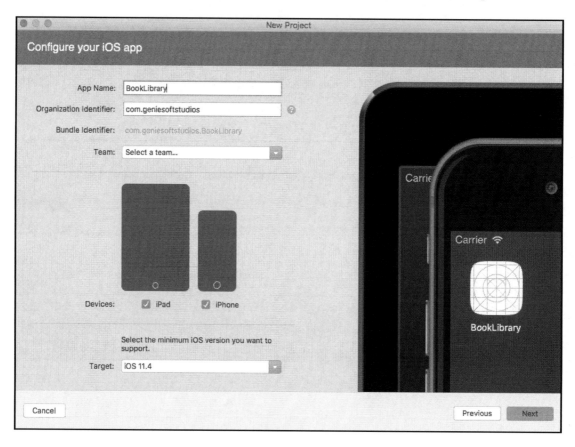

Configuring your iOS app details

 The **Organization Identifier** option for your app needs to be unique. Xamarin recommends that you use the reverse domain style to write the name (for example, `com.domainName.appName`).

6. Then, click on the **Next** button to proceed to the next step in the wizard, as shown in the following screenshot:

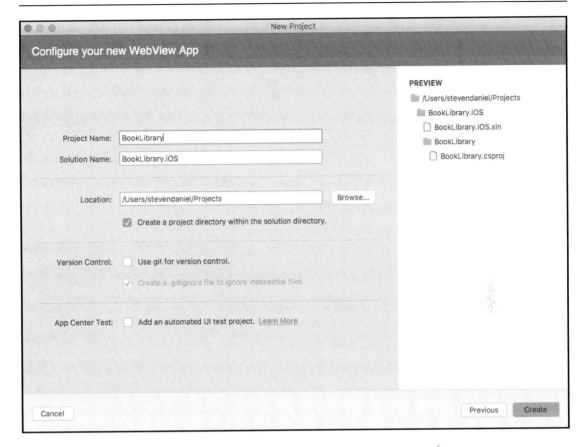

Configuring your new WebView App

7. Next, ensure that you update the **Solution Name** field to **BookLibrary.iOS**, and ensure that the **Create a project directory within the solution directory**. checkbox has been selected.

8. Finally, click on the **Create** button to save your project at the specified location.

Once your project has been created, you will be presented with the **Visual Studio for Mac Community** development environment, containing several project files that the template wizard created for you, as shown in the following screenshot:

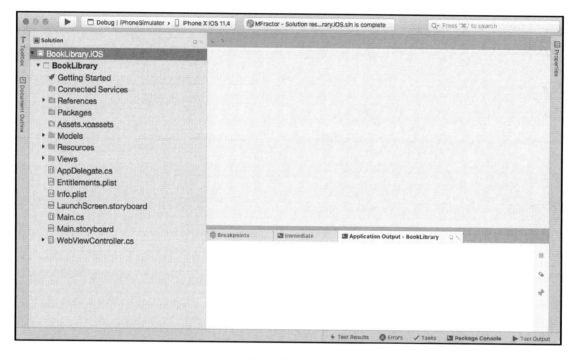

The BookLibrary iOS app Project Structure

As you can see from the preceding screenshot, the BookLibrary project has been divided into three separate folders. The following table provides brief descriptions of what each section is used for:

Folder Name	Description
Models	This section is responsible for representing the model that our views will use, and contains a structure of the fields that will be displayed or written to by our Razor template pages.
Resources	This section contains a place for you to add any images and **Cascading style sheets (CSS)** or JavaScript files that will be used by your application.
Views	This section contains all of the HTML5 Razor template pages that will be used and referenced by your application in order to function correctly. These files need to contain the .cshtml extension.

To find out what each of the additional project files are used for and the roles that each play within the solution, refer to the *Creating a Xamarin project for both iOS and Android* section in `Chapter 1`, *Setting Up Visual Studio for Mac*.

Adding the SQLite-net NuGet package to our solution

In this section, we will begin by adding the SQLite-net NuGet package to our `BookLibrary` project—which is essentially a cross-platform library that you can use to create, retrieve, update, or permanently delete (CRUD) information within the SQLite database—by writing a few lines of code to access the various properties and methods available within this class.

Let's start by adding the SQLite-net NuGet package to our `BookLibrary` project by going through the following steps:

1. Right-click on the `Packages` folder and choose the **Add Packages...** menu option, as shown in the following screenshot:

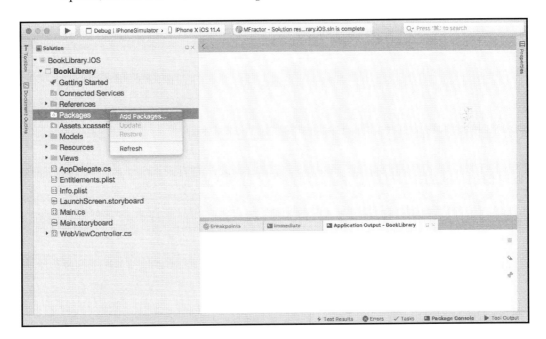

Adding new NuGet Packages to the BookLibrary project

2. Next, within the **Search** field located within the **Add Packages** dialog, enter SQLite-net and then select the **sqlite-net** option within the list, as shown in the following screenshot:

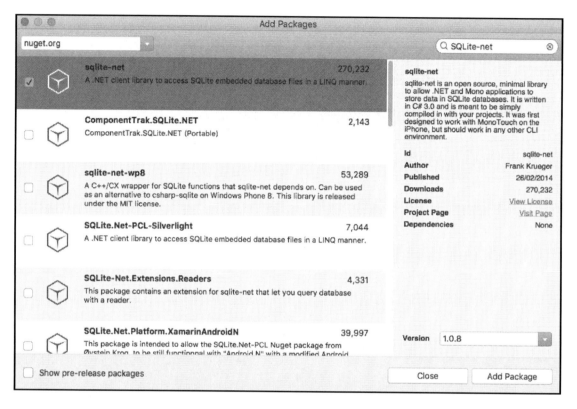

Adding the sqlite-net NuGet Package to the BookLibrary Project

3. Then, ensure that you have chosen the latest version to install for the **Version** field (this will be displayed by default).

4. Finally, click on the **Add Package** button to add the `sqlite-net` NuGet package to your solution.

Now that you have added the `sqlite-net` NuGet package to your `BookLibrary` project, our next step is to start creating our `BookItem` data model that will represent each of our book items, as well as creating each of the Razor template pages that will be used to represent our user interface for our `BookLibrary` app using HTML5.

Creating and implementing the BookLibrary data model

In this section, we will take a look at how to create our BookLibrary data model class, which will define information relating to our book item entries, as well as define database-specific attributes and attach them to properties defined within our model. It will also implement the remaining required properties within our data model.

The advantage of creating a data model is that it is much easier to add additional properties to this model and then implement these in the relevant class files, or Razor template pages. Another advantage of using a data model is that you can bind this model to a database or bind this to data stored within a Microsoft Azure database. As we progress throughout this chapter, you'll see how you can use this model to communicate with our SQLite database to create, retrieve, update, and delete information, by performing CRUD operations.

Let's start by creating the `BookItem` class for our `BookLibrary` app by going through the following steps:

1. Ensure that the `BookLibrary.iOS` solution is open within the Visual Studio for Mac IDE.

2. Next, right-click on the Models folder contained within the BookLibrary project, and choose **Add | New File...** from the pop-up menu, as shown in the following screenshot:

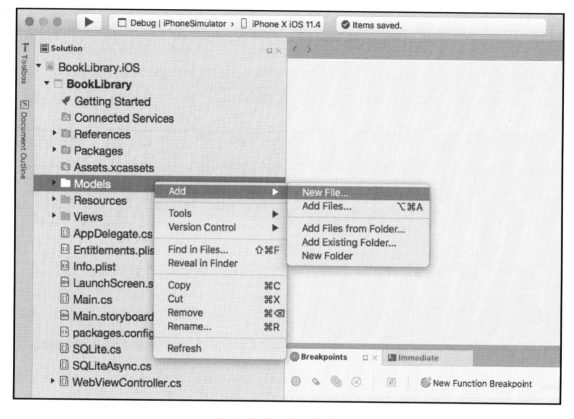

Creating a New File within the Models folder

3. Next, choose the **Empty Class** option under the **General** section and enter BookItem for the name of the class to be created, as shown in the following screenshot:

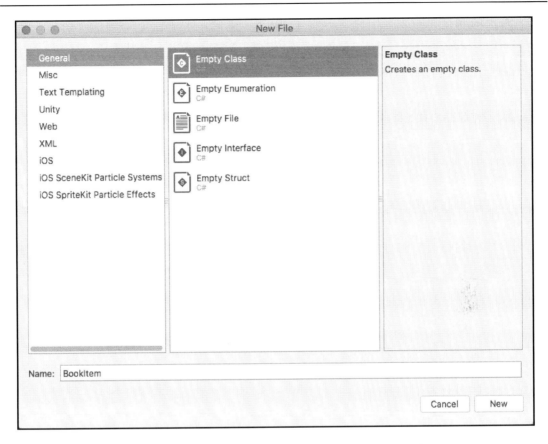

Creating the BookItem Class

4. Next, click on the **New** button to allow the wizard to proceed and create the new file, as shown in the preceding screenshot. Now that we have created our `BookItem` class file, we can proceed with implementing the required code for our class.

5. Locate and open the `BookItem.cs` file, which is located within the `Models` folder as part of the `BookLibrary` project, and ensure that it is displayed within the code editor. Enter the following code snippet:

```
//
//  BookItem.cs
//  BookLibrary Database Model
//
//  Created by Steven F. Daniel on 02/08/2018.
//  Copyright © 2018 GENIESOFT STUDIOS. All rights reserved.
//
using SQLite;

namespace BookLibrary.Models
{
    public class BookItem
    {
        [PrimaryKey, AutoIncrement]
        public int Id { get; set; }
        public string Title { get; set; }
        public string Author { get; set; }
        public string Category { get; set; }
        public string PublishedYear { get; set; }
        public string Publisher { get; set; }
        public string NoPages { get; set; }
        public string Isbn { get; set; }
        public string Summary { get; set; }
        public string ImageUrl { get; set; }
    }
}
```

Let's now start by taking a look at what we entered in the preceding code snippet:

1. We started by including a reference to the `SQLite` namespace so that we can access the classes and instance method implementations that are defined within the namespace.

2. Next, we defined a `[PrimaryKey, AutoIncrement]` database attribute for our `Id` field, which will tell our `BookLibrary` database to set the `Id` property to automatically increment whenever a new item is added to our database.

3. Finally, we declare additional property attributes that will make up our database model.

If you've used relational databases in the past, such as Microsoft SQL Server, Oracle, or Microsoft Access, this should be quite familiar to you.

Now that you have added the NuGet package for the `SQLite-net`, we can begin utilizing this control by creating a `BookDatabase` interface and class that will be used by our Razor template pages and handling all of the connections to our database, as well as handling all of the (CRUD) operations of each of our book entries.

The Android version of the `BookItem` class database model is available in the companion source code for this book.

Creating and implementing the BookDatabase interface

In this section, we'll take a look at how to create the `IBookDatabase` class that will essentially contain various instance methods that will be used by our `BookDatabase` class. The advantage of creating an `IBookDatabase` class is that it's much easier to add additional class instance methods that will be used by any classes that utilize this interface.

Let's start by creating the `IBookDatabase` interface for our `BookLibrary` app by going through the following steps:

1. Ensure that the `BookLibrary.iOS` solution is open within the Visual Studio for Mac IDE.

2. Next, right-click on the `BookLibrary` project and choose **Add | New Folder** from the pop-up menu, as shown in the following screenshot:

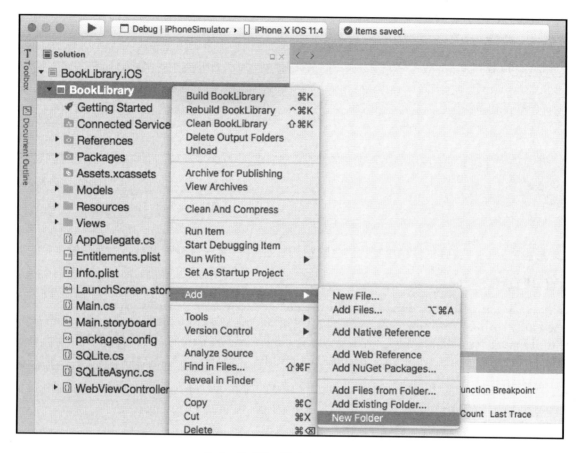

Creating a New Folder within the BookLibrary Project

3. Then, enter the name of the new folder to be created in `Database` for, right-click on the `Database` folder, and choose **Add | New File...** from the pop-up menu, as shown in the following screenshot:

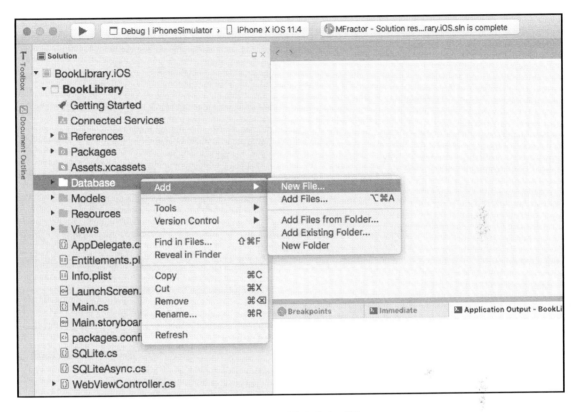

Creating a New File within the Database Folder

4. Next, choose the **Empty Interface** option under the **General** section and enter IBookDatabase for the name of the interface that is to be created, as shown in the following screenshot:

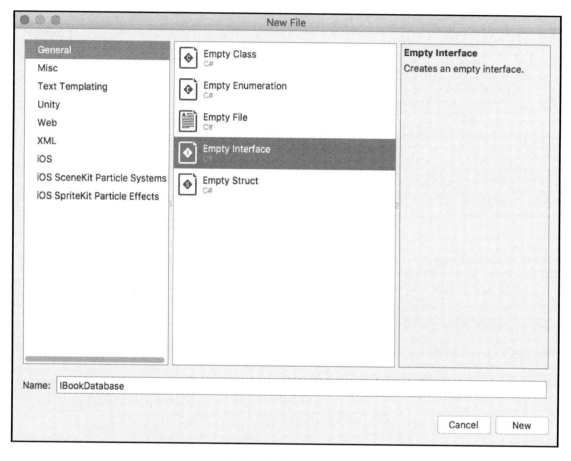

Creating the IBookDatabase Interface

5. Next, click on the **New** button to allow the wizard to proceed and create the new file, as shown in the preceding screenshot. Now that we have created our IBookDatabase interface, we can proceed with implementing the required code for our class.

6. Locate and open the `IBookDatabase.cs` file, which is located within the `Database` folder, as part of the `BookLibrary` project, and ensure that it is displayed within the code editor. Enter the following code snippet:

```
//
//  IBookDatabase.cs
//  Book Database Interface used by our Book Database Class
//
//  Created by Steven F. Daniel on 02/08/2018.
//  Copyright © 2018 GENIESOFT STUDIOS. All rights reserved.
//
using System.Collections.Generic;
using BookLibrary.Models;

namespace BookLibrary.Database
{
    public interface IBookDatabase
    {
        // Gets all of the book library items from our database.
        IEnumerable<BookItem> GetItems();

        // Gets a specific book item from the database.
        BookItem GetItem(int id);

        // Saves the book item currently being edited.
        int SaveItem(BookItem item);

        // Deletes a specific book item from the database.
        int DeleteItem(int id);
    }
}
```

Let's take a look at what we entered in the preceding code snippet:

1. We started by including references to the `System.Collections.Generic` namespace so that we can access the classes that are defined within these namespaces. We also included a reference to the `BookLibrary.Models` namespace so that we can access our `BookItem` database model.

2. Next, we created an interface class that will contain various class instance methods that will be utilized by our `BookDatabase` class, as well as our `WebViewController` class.

3. Then, we declared a `GetItems` instance method that will be responsible for retrieving all of the existing book items from the SQLite database.

4. Next, we declared a GetItem instance method that will essentially retrieve a specific book item from the SQLite database using the Id within the database.

5. Then, we declared a SaveItem instance method that will be responsible for saving the book item that is currently being added or edited.

6. Finally, we declared a DeleteItem instance method that will essentially permanently delete a specific book item from the SQLite database using the Id within the database.

Creating and implementing the BookDatabase class

In this section, we will take a look at how to create the BookDatabase class that will inherit from our IBookDatabase interface and implement the underlying instance methods that we declared within our interface class so that we can communicate with SQLite.net in order to perform all database actions for our BookLibrary application.

Let's start by creating the BookDatabase class for our BookLibrary app by going through the following steps:

1. Ensure that the BookLibrary.iOS solution is open within the Visual Studio for Mac IDE.

2. Next, right-click on the Database folder and choose **Add | New File...** from the pop-up menu.

3. Then, choose the **Empty Class** option under the **General** section and enter BookDatabase as the name of the class to be created, as shown in the following screenshot:

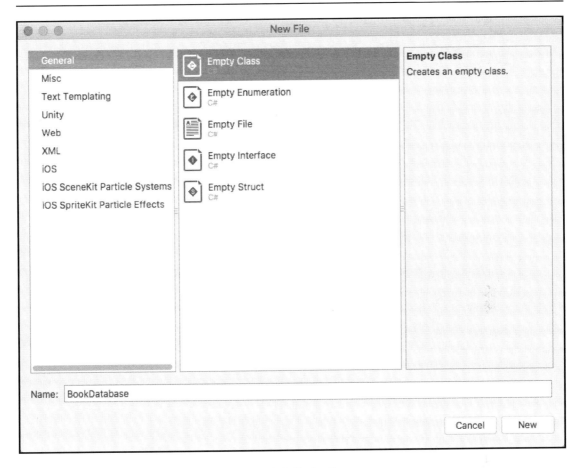

Creating the BookDatabase Class

4. Next, click on the **New** button to allow the wizard to proceed and create the new file, as shown in the preceding screenshot. Now that we have created our `BookDatabase` class, we can proceed with implementing the required code for our class.

5. Locate and open the `BookDatabase.cs` file, which is located within the `Database` folder as part of the `BookLibrary` project, and ensure that it is displayed within the code editor. Enter the following code snippet:

```
//
//  BookDatabase.cs
//  Book Database Class that will be used to handle performing of CRUD
operations
//
//  Created by Steven F. Daniel on 02/08/2018.
//  Copyright © 2018 GENIESOFT STUDIOS. All rights reserved.
//
using System.Collections.Generic;
using System.Linq;
using BookLibrary.Models;
using SQLite;

namespace BookLibrary.Database
{
    public class BookDatabase : IBookDatabase
    {
        static object locker = new object();
        static SQLiteConnection conn;
        static BookDatabase database;

        /// <summary>
        /// Returns an instance of our BookDatabase class
        /// </summary>
        /// <value>The current BookDatabase class instance.</value>
        public static BookDatabase Database => database;

        /// <summary>
        /// Create our Book Library Database tables.
        /// </summary>
        /// <param name="connection">Connection.</param>
        public static void CreateDatabase(SQLiteConnection connection)
        {
            conn = connection;

            // Create the tables within our Book Library Database
            conn.CreateTable<BookItem>();
            database = new BookDatabase();
        }
        /// <summary>
        /// Gets all of the book library items from our database.
        /// </summary>
        /// <returns>The items.</returns>
        public IEnumerable<BookItem> GetItems()
```

```
        {
            // Set a mutual-exclusive lock on our database, while
            // retrieving items.
            lock (locker)
            {
                return conn.Table<BookItem>().ToList();
            }
        }
        /// <summary>
        /// Gets a specific book item from the database.
        /// </summary>
        /// <returns>The item.</returns>
        /// <param name="id">Identifier.</param>
        public BookItem GetItem(int id)
        {
            // Set a mutual-exclusive lock on our database, while
            // retrieving the book item.
            lock (locker)
            {
                return conn.Table<BookItem>().FirstOrDefault(x => x.Id
== id);

            }
        }
        /// <summary>
        /// Saves the book item currently being edited.
        /// </summary>
        /// <returns>The item.</returns>
        /// <param name="item">Item.</param>
        public int SaveItem(BookItem item)
        {
            // Set a mutual-exclusive lock on our database, while
            // saving/updating our book item.
            lock (locker)
            {
                if (item.Id != 0)
                {
                    conn.Update(item);
                    return item.Id;
                }
                else
                {
                    return conn.Insert(item);
                }
            }
        }
        /// <summary>
        /// Deletes a specific book item from the database.
        /// </summary>
```

```
/// <returns>The item.</returns>
/// <param name="id">Identifier.</param>
public int DeleteItem(int id)
{
    // Set a mutual-exclusive lock on our database, while
    // deleting our book item.
    lock (locker)
    {
        return conn.Delete<BookItem>(id);
    }
}
    }
}
```

Let's take a look at what we entered in the preceding code snippet:

1. We started by including references to the `System.Collections.Generic`, `System.Linq`, and `SQLite` namespaces so that we can access the classes that are defined within these namespaces. We included a reference to the `BookLibrary.Models` namespace so that we can access our `BookItem` database model.

2. Next, we created a `locker` variable that will be used to create a mutually-exclusive lock on the database while we are either creating, retrieving, updating, or deleting book items.

3. Then, we declared a `conn` variable that will point to an `instance` of our `SQLiteConnection` object, which is located within the `SQLite.cs` class, as well as declaring a `Database` variable that will point to an instance of our `BookDatabase` so that we can perform database operations.

4. Next, we create the `CreateDatabase` instance method that accepts a `conn` object, which is an instance of our `SQLiteConnection` class, and this instance method will be used to create the necessary database table structure, based on our `BookItem` data model.

5. Then, we create the `GetItems` instance method that will be used to extract all of the existing book entries that have been saved to the database. We use the LINQ language query syntax to iterate and retrieve all items from our `BookItem` table and convert this collection to a `List` instance, as determined by the `ToList()` method.

6. Next, we create the `SaveItem` instance method that will save the book item to the `BookItem` database table. In this instance method, you will notice that we are handling two different case scenarios. The first scenario stipulates that, if the item we are saving is an existing item, then we need to check the `id` for the book item, and if it is a non-zero value, then we proceed to update the book item using the `Update` method on the database object and return the book item `id`. However, if the item is a new book record—all new books that get created will have an `id` of 0—then this will be directly inserted into the `BookItem` table using the `Insert` method on the `database` object.

7. Finally, we create the `DeleteItem` instance method that will, as you might have guessed, delete an existing book item from the `BookItem` database table using the book item's `id`, and then call the `Delete` method on the database object.

Now that you have created the `BookDatabase` interface and class that will be used to handle all of the operations for creating, retrieving, updating, and deleting book items from our `BookLibary` database, this will be used by our `WebViewController.cs` class to interact with each of our Razor template pages.

 The Android version of the `BookDatabase` class is available in the companion source code for this book.

Creating and implementing the BookLibraryListing page

In this section, we will begin by building the user interface for our `BookLibraryListing` using HTML by defining HTML tags. This Razor template page will use our `BookItem` data model to visually display all items that have been added to the `BookItem` database table, as well as allow the user to create new book items.

Let's start by creating the user interface for our `BookLibraryListing` by going through the following steps:

1. Right-click on the `Views` folder and choose **Add | New File...** from the pop-up menu.

2. Then, choose the **Preprocessed Razor Template** option under the **Text Templating** section and enter `BookLibraryListing` for the name of the Razor template to be created, as shown in the following screenshot:

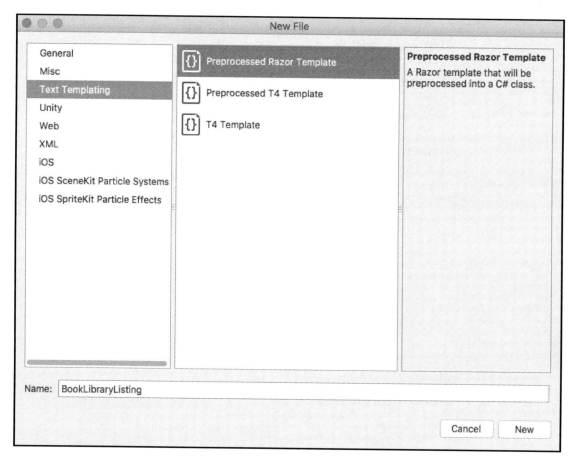

Creating the Book Library Listing Razor Template

3. Then, click on the **New** button to allow the wizard to proceed and create the new file, as shown in the preceding screenshot. Now that we have created our `BookLibraryListing` Razor template page, we can proceed with defining the user interface and implementing the underlying code for our class.

4. Locate and open the `BookLibraryListing.cshtml` file, which is located in the `Views` folder, and ensure that it is displayed within the code editor. Enter the following code snippet:

```
@using BookLibrary.Models
@model List<BookItem>
<html>
<head>
    <link rel="stylesheet" href="style.css" />
</head>
<body>
<p></p>
<h1>Book Library Listing</h1>
<table>
    <thead>
        <tr>
            <th></th>
            <th>Image</th>
            <th>Title</th>
            <th>Author</th>
            <th>ISBN</th>
        </tr>
    </thead>
    <tr>
      <a href="hybrid:CreateNewBook?">Add New Book</a>
    </tr>
    @foreach (var book in @Model)
    {
        <tbody>
            <tr>
            <td>
                <a href="hybrid:EditBookDetails?id=@book.Id">Edit</a>
            </td>
            <td><img src="@book.ImageUrl" /></td>
            <td>@book.Title</td>
            <td>@book.Author</td>
            <td>@book.Isbn</td>
            </tr>
        </tbody>
    }
</table>
</body>
</html>
```

Let's take a look at what we defined in the preceding Razor template page:

1. We started by defining the HTML layout information that will be used by our `BookLibraryListing` Razor template page, and then we import the `BookLibrary` namespace so that we can have access to our `BookItem` data model, as specified by the `@model` directive, and this must be the very first line preceding the `<html>` tag within each Razor template page. You will notice that we specify a `List` type for our `@model` directive. This is because we are iterating through each of our book items within our `Model`, and display the `ImageUrl`, `Title`, `Author`, and `Isbn` details for each book that we read from our `BookItem` database table.

2. Next, we set up an `href` tag that points to our `WebViewController.cs` class, and we specify a `hybrid:CreateNewBook` tag to call the `BookLibraryAddEdit.cshtml` Razor template page to allow the user to create a new book entry. We don't need to pass in an `id` for the book, as this will be automatically assigned once the book has successfully been written to the `BookItem` database table.

3. Finally, we set up an `href` tag that points to our `WebViewController.cs` class, and we specify a `hybrid:EditBookDetails` tag to call the `BookLibraryAddEdit.cshtml` Razor template page to allow the user to retrieve and display the book entry details for the chosen book item using the associated `id`.

Creating and implementing the BookLibraryAddEdit page

In the previous section, we created and implemented the `BookLibraryListing` Razor template page that will be used to display a list of all book items that have been previously added to the `BookItem` database table. Our next step is to begin creating the `BookLibraryAddEdit` Razor template page—which will be used to allow the user to create a new book item or edit an existing book item—and save this to our `BookItem` database table.

Let's start by creating the user interface for our `BookLibraryAddEdit` by going through the following steps:

1. Right-click on the `Views` folder and choose **Add | New File...** from the pop-up menu, as you did when creating the `BookLibraryListing`, in the *Creating and implementing the BookLibraryListing page* section in this chapter.

2. Next, choose the **Preprocessed Razor Template** option under the **Text Templating** section and enter `BookLibraryAddEdit` as the name of the Razor template to be created.

3. Finally, click on the **New** button to allow the wizard to proceed and create the new file. Now that we have created our `BookLibraryAddEdit` Razor template, we can proceed with defining the user interface and implementing the underlying code for our class.

4. Locate and open the `BookLibraryAddEdit.cshtml` file, which is located in the `Views` folder, and ensure that it is displayed within the code editor. Enter the following code snippet:

```
@using BookLibrary.Models
@model BookItem
<html>
<head>
<link rel="stylesheet" href="style.css" />
</head>
<body>
    @if (Model.Id > 0)
    {
        <h1>Editing Book Details</h1>
    }
    else
    {
        <h1>Adding Book Details</h1>
    }
    <table>
        <form action="hybrid:SaveBookDetails" method="GET">
            <input name="Id" type="hidden" value="@Model.Id" />
            <tr>
                <td>
                  <label for="Title">Book Title:</label>
                  <input id="Title" name="Title" type="text"
                         placeholder="Book Title" value="@Model.Title"
/>
                </td>
            <tr>
            <td>
                <label for="ImageUrl">Book Image URL:</label>
```

```html
                    <input id="ImageUrl" name="ImageUrl" type="text"
                            placeholder="Book Image URL"
value=@Model.ImageUrl />
                </td>
                <tr>
                <td>
                    <label for="Author">Author Name:</label>
                    <input id="Author" name="Author" type="text"
                            placeholder="Author name" value="@Model.Author"
/>
                </td>
                <tr>
                <td>
                    <label for="Category">Category:</label>
                    <input id="Category" name="Category" type="text"
                     placeholder="Book Category" value="@Model.Category"
/>
                </td>
                <tr>
                <td>
                    <label for="PublishedYear">Published Year:</label>
                    <input id="PublishedYear" name="PublishedYear"
                            placeholder="Published Year"
value="@Model.PublishedYear" />
                </td>
                <tr>
                <td>
                    <label for="Publisher">Publisher:</label>
                    <input id="Publisher" name="Publisher"
                            placeholder="Publisher"
value="@Model.Publisher" />
                </td>
                <tr>
                <td>
                    <label for="Pages">No. Pages:</label>
                    <input id="Pages" name="NoPages" type="number"
                            placeholder="Total Pages" maxlength="4"
value="@Model.NoPages" />
                </td>
                <tr>
                <td>
                    <label for="ISBN">Book ISBN:</label>
                    <input id="ISBN" name="Isbn" type="text"
                            placeholder="Book ISBN" value="@Model.Isbn" />
                </td>
                <tr>
                <td>
                    <label for="Summary">Book Summary:</label>
```

```
                        <textarea id="Summary" name="Summary"
placeholder="Book Summary"
                                rows="10"
cols="45">@Model.Summary</textarea>
                </td>
                <tr>
                <td colspan="8">
                    <input type="submit" name="Button" value="Save" />
                    <input type="submit" name="Button" value="Cancel" />
                    @if (Model.Id > 0)
                    {
                        <input type="submit" name="Button" value="Delete"
/>
                    }
                </td>
                </tr>
            </form>
        </table>
    </body>
    </html>
```

Let's take a look at what we defined within the preceding Razor template page:

1. As we did for our `BookLibraryListing` Razor template page, we started by defining the HTML layout information that will be used by our `BookLibraryAddEdit` Razor Template page, and then we imported the `BookLibrary` namespace so that we can have access to our `BookItem` data model, as specified by the `@model` directive. We've already explained that this must be the very first line preceding the `<html>` tag within each Razor template page.

2. Next, we used some JavaScript code that will check whether we are creating or editing an existing book within our `BookLibrary` database, and then we displayed the relevant heading to the `BookLibraryAddEdit` Razor template page.

3. Then, we set up a `form action` tag that will be used when the form gets submitted whenever the `Save`, `Cancel`, or `Delete` button is pressed, and we make a call to the `WebViewController.cs` class to call the appropriate action.

4. Finally, we specified a `hybrid:SaveBookDetails` tag that will pass the form parameters to our `WebViewController.cs` class in order to save the book details to the `BookItem` database table for the associated `id`. You will notice that we have some JavaScript code that checks to see whether we are currently editing an existing book. Once it has done this, it will display the `Delete` button so that the user can choose to delete the book entry.

The **Android** versions for each of the Razor template pages are available in the companion source code for this book.

Updating the Book Library cascading style sheet (CSS)

In this section, we will need to make some additional changes to the `Styles.css` file. This file is essentially a cascading style sheet (CSS) that can be used by each of our Razor template pages. As a result, the Razor template pages will inherit everything that it contains.

We will basically be adding some additional tags that will apply changes to the table and body component of each of our Razor template pages, as well as setting padding to margins, font sizes, font styles, font colors, and URL link colors.

Let's start by updating the `Style.css` file by going through the following steps:

1. Locate and open the `Style.css` file, which is located in the `Resources` folder or the `Assets` folder (in Android) and ensure that it is displayed within the code editor. Enter the following highlighted code sections:

```
/* This is a minimal style sheet intended to demonstrate how to include
static content
        in your hybrid app.  Other static content, such as javascript files
and images, can
        be included in this same folder(Resources on iOS or Assets on
Android), with the same
        Build Action (BundleResource on iOS or AndroidAsset on Android), to
be accessible from
        a path starting at the root of your hybrid application.  */

    #page {
```

```
        margin-top: 10px;
}
input {
    width: 100%;
}
img {
    width: 100%;
    height: auto;
}
html, body {
    margin: 7px;
    padding: 0px;
    border: 0px;
    color: #000;
    background: #ffffe0;
}
html, body, p, th, td, li, dd, dt {
    font: 1em Arial, Helvetica, sans-serif;
}
h1 {
    font-family: Arial, Helvetica, sans-serif;
    font-size: 28;
}
thead {
    color: green;
}
tbody {
    color: blue;
}
table, th, td {
    border: 1px solid black;
}
a:link {
    color: #00f;
}
```

In the preceding snippet, we started by specifying and defining a number of HTML tags that each of our Razor template pages will inherit. Let's take a look at what we defined within the preceding Razor template:

1. We started by specifying and defining a number of HTML tags that each of our Razor template pages will inherit. We specified an `input` tag that will adjust the width to `100%` for all `input` tags that have been defined within the Razor template pages.

2. Next, we specify an `img` tag that defines the `width` and `height` to use for all images that have been declared within an `img` tag within each of your Razor template pages. We also specify tags for both our `html` and `body`, and provide values for our `margin`, `padding`, `border`, `color`, and `background color`.

3. Then, we specify and define the `font` style that will be used for each of our `html`, `body`, `p`, `th`, `td`, `li`, `dd`, and `dt` tags. We also specify the `font-family` and `font-size` for all `h1` tags that have been defined within each of the Razor template pages.

4. Finally, we declare colors for our `thead` and `tbody` tags, as well as define border colors and border width, for each of our `table`, `th`, and `td` tags. We also specify the color to use for all website URL links.

> The Android version of the `Style.css` file is available in the companion source code for this book.

Updating the WebViewController class using C#

In this section, we will begin implementing the code for our `BookLibrary` application that will be responsible for communicating and interacting with our Razor template pages, as well as handling the actions associated with each Razor template page. The `WebViewController` class will communicate with and use our `BookDatabase` class in order to handle the addition, retrieval, and deletion of book items.

Let's start by updating the `WebViewController.cs` by going through the following steps:

1. Locate and open the `WebViewController.cs` file, which is located in the `BookLibrary` project, and ensure that it is displayed within the code editor. Enter the following highlighted code sections:

```
//
//   WebViewController.cs
//   Web Container for representing Razor Templates within a Web View
//
//   Created by Steven F. Daniel on 02/08/2018.
//   Copyright © 2018 GENIESOFT STUDIOS. All rights reserved.
//
```

```
using System;
using Foundation;
using UIKit;
using System.IO;
using SQLite;
using BookLibrary.Views;
using System.Collections.Specialized;
using BookLibrary.Database;
using BookLibrary.Models;
using System.Linq;

namespace BookLibrary
{
    public partial class WebViewController : UIViewController
    {
        static bool UserInterfaceIdiomIsPhone
        {
            get { return UIDevice.CurrentDevice.UserInterfaceIdiom ==
                    UIUserInterfaceIdiom.Phone; }
        }
        protected WebViewController(IntPtr handle) : base(handle)
        {
            // Note: this .ctor should not contain any initialization
logic.
        }
        public override void ViewDidLoad()
        {
            base.ViewDidLoad();
            // Intercept URL loading to handle native calls from
browser
            WebView.ShouldStartLoad += HandleShouldStartLoad;

            // Declare the name to use for our database name
            var sqliteFilename = "BookLibrary.db";
            string documentsPath =
Environment.GetFolderPath(Environment.SpecialFolder.Personal);
            string libraryPath = Path.Combine(documentsPath, "..",
"Library");
            var databasePath = Path.Combine(libraryPath,
sqliteFilename);

            // Set a connection to our database
            var databaseConn = new SQLiteConnection(databasePath);
            BookDatabase.CreateDatabase(databaseConn);

            // Render the view to use our BookLibraryListing.cshtml
file
            var model = BookDatabase.Database.GetItems().ToList();
```

```
        var template = new BookLibraryListing() { Model = model };
        var page = template.GenerateString();

        // Load the rendered HTML into the view with a base URL that points
        // to the root of the bundled Resources folder
        WebView.LoadHtmlString(page, NSBundle.MainBundle.BundleUrl);
    }

    public override void DidReceiveMemoryWarning()
    {
        base.DidReceiveMemoryWarning();
        // Release any cached data, images, etc that aren't in use.
    }

    bool HandleShouldStartLoad(UIWebView webView, NSUrlRequest request,
                               UIWebViewNavigationType navigationType)
    {
        // If the URL is not our own custom scheme, just let the webView
        // load the URL as usual
        const string scheme = "hybrid:";
        if (request.Url.Scheme != scheme.Replace(":", ""))
            return true;
        // This handler will treat everything between the protocol and
        // "?" as the method name. The querystring has all of the parameters.
        var resources = request.Url.ResourceSpecifier.Split('?');
        var method = resources[0];
        var parameters = System.Web.HttpUtility.ParseQueryString(resources[1]);

        switch (method)
        {
            case "CreateNewBook":
                CreateNewBook(webView);
                break;
            case "EditBookDetails":
                EditBookDetails(webView, parameters);
                break;
            case "SaveBookDetails":
                SaveBookDetails(webView, parameters);
                break;
            default:
```

```
                    // Cases not covered are handled here.
                    break;
            }
            return false;
        }
        /// <summary>
        /// Handles the creation of our new book entry.
        /// </summary>
        /// <param name="webView">Web view.</param>
        void CreateNewBook(UIWebView webView)
        {
            var template = new BookLibraryAddEdit() { Model = new
BookItem() };
            var page = template.GenerateString();
            webView.LoadHtmlString(page,
NSBundle.MainBundle.BundleUrl);
        }
        /// <summary>
        /// Handles the editing of our book details.
        /// </summary>
        /// <param name="webView">Web view.</param>
        /// <param name="parameters">Parameters.</param>
        void EditBookDetails(UIWebView webView, NameValueCollection
parameters)
        {
            var model =
BookDatabase.Database.GetItem(Convert.ToInt32(parameters["Id"]));
            var template = new BookLibraryAddEdit() { Model = model };
            var page = template.GenerateString();
            webView.LoadHtmlString(page,
NSBundle.MainBundle.BundleUrl);
        }
        /// <summary>
        /// Saves the book details to the SQLite BookDetails Database.
        /// </summary>
        /// <param name="webView">Web view.</param>
        /// <param name="parameters">Parameters.</param>
        void SaveBookDetails(UIWebView webView, NameValueCollection
parameters)
        {
            // Points to our Edit Book Details HTML page.
            var button = parameters["Button"];
            switch (button)
            {
                case "Save":
                    SaveDetailsToDatabase(parameters);
                    break;
                case "Delete":
```

```
                    DeleteBookDetails(parameters);
                    break;
                case "Cancel":
                    break;
                default:
                    // Cases not covered are handled here.
                    break;
            }
            var model = BookDatabase.Database.GetItems().ToList();
            var template = new BookLibraryListing() { Model = model };
            webView.LoadHtmlString(template.GenerateString(),
NSBundle.MainBundle.BundleUrl);
        }
        /// <summary>
        /// Saves the book details to our SQLite database.
        /// </summary>
        /// <returns>The details to database.</returns>
        /// <param name="parameters">Parameters.</param>
        void SaveDetailsToDatabase(NameValueCollection parameters)
        {
            var book = new BookItem
            {
                Id = Convert.ToInt32(parameters["Id"]),
                Title = parameters["Title"],
                Author = parameters["Author"],
                Category = parameters["Category"],
                PublishedYear = parameters["PublishedYear"],
                Publisher = parameters["Publisher"],
                NoPages = parameters["NoPages"],
                Isbn = parameters["Isbn"],
                Summary = parameters["Summary"],
                ImageUrl = parameters["ImageUrl"]
            };
            BookDatabase.Database.SaveItem(book);
        }
        /// <summary>
        /// Handle when the Delete button has been pressed
        /// </summary>
        /// <returns>The book details.</returns>
        /// <param name="parameters">Parameters.</param>
        void DeleteBookDetails(NameValueCollection parameters)
        {
BookDatabase.Database.DeleteItem(Convert.ToInt32(parameters["Id"]));
        }
    }
}
```

Let's take a look at what we entered in the preceding code snippet:

1. First, we started by including references to the `System.IO`, `SQLite`, `System.Collections.Generic`, and `System.Linq` namespaces so that we can access the classes that are defined within these namespaces. We include references to our `BookLibrary.Views`, `BookLibrary.Database`, and `BookLibrary.Models` namespaces so that we can access each of our Razor pages, as well as the instance methods defined within our `BookDatabase` class and our `BookItem` database model.

2. Next, we modified the `ViewDidLoad` method and declared the name to use for our database name. Then we specified the location to save the `BookLibrary.db` database to, which is determined by the `databasePath` string, and then proceeded to set up a connection to our database.

3. Then, we called the `GetItems` instance method on our `BookDatabase.Database` namespace to return all existing book entries within the database and assign this to our model.

4. Next, we specified the `BookLibraryListing` Razor page and passed in the model that will be used to populate the `Model` within our Razor page. Then we proceeded to call the `GenerateString` method on our template so that we can execute the template within the main application bundle and return the output as a string, prior to loading this within our `WebView` using the `LoadHtmlString` method.

5. Then, within the `HandleShouldStartLoad` method, we created a `switch` statement to handle the type of method operation that we obtained from our Razor page directly, using the `hybrid:` tag.

6. Next, we created and implemented the `CreateNewBook` instance method that will be responsible for handling the creation of our new book entry. This method accepts the name of the `webView` so that it knows where to display its content. We specified the `BookLibraryAddEdit` Razor page and set the `Model` to our `BookItem` data model to populate the content. We called the `GenerateString` method on our template to execute the Razor page within the main application bundle and return the output as a string, prior to loading this within our `webView` using the `LoadHtmlString` method.

7. Then, we created and implemented the `EditBookDetails` instance method that will be responsible for handling the editing of our existing book entry. This method accepts the name of the `webView` so that it knows where to display its content. We specified the `BookLibraryAddEdit` Razor page and set the `Model` to our `BookItem` data model to populate the content. We called the `GenerateString` method on our template to execute the Razor page within the main application bundle and return the output as a string, prior to loading this within our `webView` using the `LoadHtmlString` method.

8. Next, we created and implemented the `SaveBookDetails` instance method that will be responsible for handling the saving of the book entry. This method accepts the name of the `webView` so that it knows where to display its content, as well as the parameters used and the button that was pressed within the `BookLibraryAddEdit` Razor page. We used a `switch` statement to handle the type of button operation and handle it accordingly.

9. Then, we created and implemented the `SaveDetailsToDatabase` instance method that will be responsible for handling the saving of our book entry to the `BookLibrary` SQLite database. This method accepts a list of parameters that have been entered within the `BookLibraryAddEdit` Razor page, and constructs a `BookItem` database model that gets passed to the `SaveItem` instance method within our `BookDatabase` class.

10. Finally, we created the `DeleteBookDetails` instance method that will be responsible for deleting our book entry within the `BookLibrary` SQLite database. This method accepts a list of parameters that have been entered within the `BookLibraryAddEdit` Razor page and passes the `id` of the book entry to the `DeleteItem` instance method within our `BookDatabase` class.

The Android version of the `MainActivity.cs` class is available in the companion source code for this book.

Now that we have finished creating all of the necessary Razor template pages, as well as our `BookItem` database model and `BookDatabase` interface and class, as well as implementing the required instance methods within our `WebViewController` class, our next step is to compile, build, and run our application within the iOS simulator.

Launching the BookLibrary app using the iOS simulator

In this section, we will compile, build, and run the `BookLibrary` application to see how our application looks, since we have created each of our Razor template pages, and have made some modifications to our updated `style.css` **cascading style sheet (CSS)**.

Let's see how we can achieve this by going through the following steps:

1. Ensure that you have chosen the **Debug | iPhoneSimulator** option from the drop-down menu.
2. Next, choose your preferred device from the list of available iOS simulators.
3. Then, select the **Run | Start Debugging** menu option, as shown in the following screenshot:

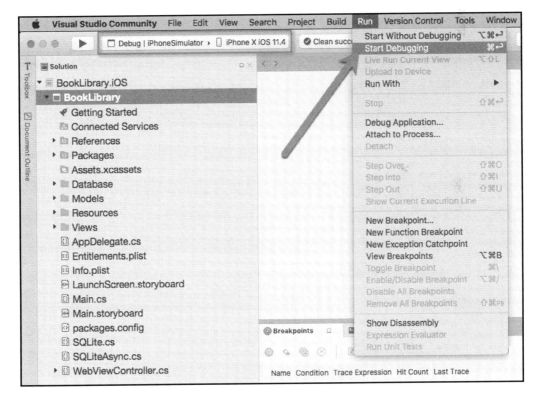

Launching the BookLibrary app within the iOS Simulator

4. Alternatively, you can also build and run the `BookLibrary` application by pressing *Command + Return* on the keyboard.

When the compilation is complete, the iOS simulator will appear automatically and the **BookLibrary** application will be displayed, as shown in the following screenshot:

Adding new Book Details to the Book Library Listing

The preceding screenshot displays our **Book Library Listing** Razor page, which shows a blank listing the first time the application is run. The `BookLibrary` database has been created. When the **Add New Book** link is clicked on, this will display the **Adding Book Details** Razor page, along with some information that has been populated, as shown in the following screenshot:

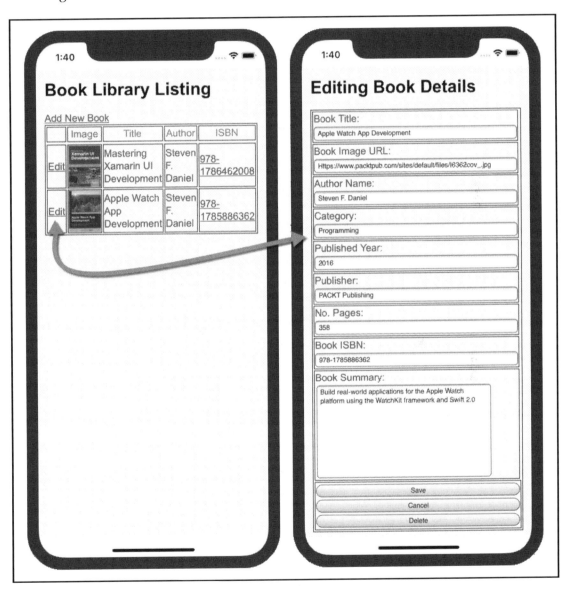

Editing an existing Book within the Book Library Listing screen

The preceding screenshot displays our **Book Library Listing** Razor page, which is populated with book entries that have been entered within our `BookLibrary` database. Clicking on the **Edit** link beside the book item will display the **Editing Book Details** Razor page with the information retrieved from the `BookLibrary` SQLite database. You will notice that since we are editing an existing book entry, our **BookListingAddEdit** Razor page will display the **Delete** button, which wasn't displayed when we were creating a new book entry.

Summary

In this chapter, you learned about the Razor templating engine, the components of a Razor template solution, and the differences between using a static model class and the SQLite database model within our Razor templates.

You then learned how to build a `BookLibrary` application and incorporate the `SQLite-net` NuGet package, as well as how to define a `BookItem` database model and create a `BookDatabase` interface and class, which will include a number of class instance methods that will be used to communicate with our SQLite database so that you can create, update, retrieve, and delete book items. Lastly, you learned how to create the necessary Razor template pages that will integrate with our `BookItem` data model, as well as how to implement additional HTML tags within our `style.css` file. You also learned how to implement the necessary class instance methods within the `WebViewController` class.

In the next chapter, you'll learn about Microsoft Azure App Services and how you can use this to create your very first live, cloud-based backend HTTP web service to handle all communications between the cloud and the app. You will do this by creating a `RestWebService` interface and class that will allow the app to consume RESTful web services so that it can store, retrieve, and delete walk trail information from a Microsoft Azure database that we will be creating for a `TrackMyWalks` app.

11
Incorporating Microsoft Azure App Services

In the previous chapter, you learned about the Razor templating engine, the components of a Razor template solution, and the differences between using a static model class and the SQLite database model, before moving on to learning how to build a `BookLibrary` mobile solution using the power of Razor templates and how to use and define `BookItem` database models within your application.

You then learned how to incorporate the `SQLite-net` NuGet package that you will use in order to create a `BookDatabase` interface and class. As part of learning this, you also learned about a number of class instance methods that will communicate with our SQLite database so that you can create, update, retrieve, and delete book items. Lastly, you learned how to create the necessary Razor template pages that will integrate with our `BookItem` data model and how to implement additional HTML tags within our `style.css` file, as well as how to implement the necessary class instance methods within the `WebViewController` class.

In this chapter, you'll learn about the Microsoft Azure App Services platform, and how you can leverage this platform to create your cloud-based databases using RESTful web service APIs that will be used to handle all communication between the `TrackMyWalks` mobile application. You will then set up and configure a Microsoft Azure app service in order to create a mobile app service, data connection, SQL Server database, and `WalkEntries` table. You will also learn how to incorporate the `Newtonsoft.Json` NuGet package, as well as modify the `WalkDataModel` data model.

Next, you will create a `RestWebservice` interface and class, which will include a number of class instance methods that will be used to communicate with our `TrackMyWalks` SQL Server database so you can perform CRUD operations to create, update, retrieve, and delete walk entries.

You will then modify the `BaseViewModel` class to include an `AzureDatabase` property to our `RestWebService` class, as well as make some changes to the underlying code-behind files that will communicate with our SQL Server database.

Finally, you will update the user interface for the `WalkEntryPage` to include an `ActivityIndicator`, which will display information to the user whenever a walk item is being saved to the database. You will also make changes to the `WalkEntryPageViewModel` to initialize properties for communicating with the `ActivityIndicator`.

This chapter will cover the following topics:

- Setting up our `TrackMyWalks` app to use Microsoft Azure App Services
- Incorporating the `Json.Net` NuGet package to our `TrackMyWalks` solution
- Updating the `WalkDataModel` database model for our `TrackMyWalks` app
- Creating and implementing a `RestWebService` interface and class using C#
- Updating the `BaseViewModel` class to use our `RestWebService` class
- Updating the `WalkEntryPageViewModel` to use our `RestWebService` class
- Updating the `WalksMainPageViewModel` to use our `RestWebService` class
- Updating the `WalksMainPage` to use the updated `ViewModel`
- Launching the `TrackMyWalks` app using the iOS simulator

Understanding the Microsoft Azure App services platform

In this section, we will look at the steps required to set up the `TrackMyWalks` application within Microsoft Azure. Nearly all mobile applications that you will develop will require the ability to communicate with an API in order to store, retrieve, update, and delete information. This API can be an existing one that someone within your organisation has already created, but sometimes you will need to create your own API for your application.

Microsoft Azure (or *Azure* as it's commonly known) is essentially a cloud-based platform that was created by Microsoft back in February 2010. Azure was designed for building, deploying, and managing several applications and their associated services, such as SaaS, PaaS, and IaaS.

The following table provides a brief description of each of the Microsoft Azure-specific associated services and what each one is used for:

Service	Description
Saas	The software-as-a-service component basically provides a software licensing and delivery model, where software is licensed on a subscription basis and is hosted centrally.
Paas	The platform-as-a-service component essentially provides customers with a platform to develop, run, and manage applications without the complexities of maintaining the infrastructure when developing and launching an app.
Iaas	The infrastructure-as-a-service component provides virtualized computing resources over the internet.

Now that you have a reasonably good understanding of each of the components that are contained within the Microsoft Azure platform, our next step is to begin setting up and configuring our application, as well as creating the SQL Server database and data connections, including the database tables that will be used by our TrackMyWalks application to store walk trail information.

One of the main benefits of using Microsoft Azure mobile apps is that it provides you with a very quick and easy way to get a fully functional backend service up and running within a matter of minutes.

Setting up and configuring Microsoft Azure App services

In this section, we will begin by setting up and configuring our TrackMyWalks app within the Microsoft Azure platform. We will look at the steps involved in creating our TrackMyWalks Azure App service—as well as those involved in creating the SQL Server database and the data connections—prior to creating the WalkEntries table so that we can store our walk trail information using the TrackMyWalks app.

Let's take a look at how we can achieve this by going through the following steps:

1. First, open your browser, type in `https://portal.azure.com/`, and log in to the **Microsoft Azure Portal** using your credentials.

     If you don't already have a Microsoft Azure account, you can create one for free at `https://azure.microsoft.com/en-us/pricing/free-trial/`.

2. Next, from the **Microsoft Azure** page, click on the **Create a resource** button and select the **Mobile** option under the **Azure Marketplace** section, and then choose the **Mobile App** option under the **Featured** section, as shown in the following screenshot:

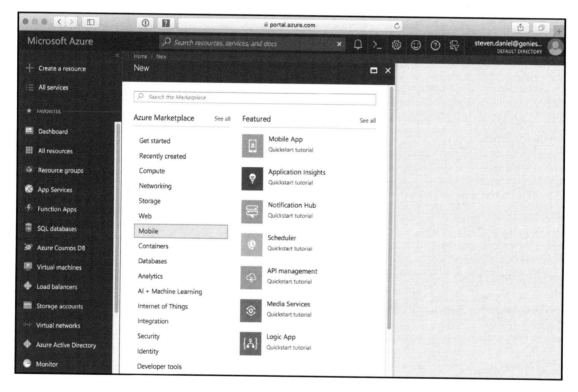

Microsoft Azure Marketplace Dashboard

3. Next, enter `TrackMyWalks` as the name for our app in the **App name** field, and choose your **Subscription** type from the drop-down list. Then, ensure that the **Create new** option has been selected, or you can use an existing one.

4. Then, enter `TrackMyWalks` for the **Resource Group** and click on the **Create** button to create our **Mobile App**, as shown in the following screenshot:

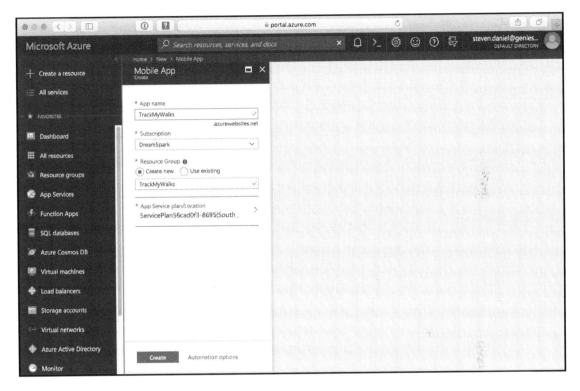

Creating a new Mobile App within the Microsoft Azure Portal

Now that you have successfully created your **Mobile App** within the Microsoft Azure platform, our next step is to begin setting up the database that will allow our **TrackMyWalks** app to store walk trail information.

Let's start setting up the database by going through the following steps:

1. Click on the **Dashboard** button under the **Microsoft Azure** section, and click on the **trackmywalk App Service** from the **Dashboard** section, as shown in the following screenshot:

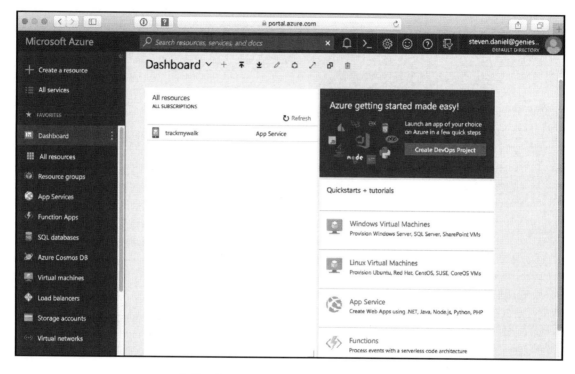

The Microsoft Azure Dashboard showing the trackmywalk App Service

2. Next, within the search field, enter `Data` and then click on the **Data connections** option under the **MOBILE** section, as shown in the following screenshot:

The Microsoft Azure Data Connections section

3. Then, within the **trackmywalk – Data connections** screen, click on the **Add** button, as shown in the following screenshot:

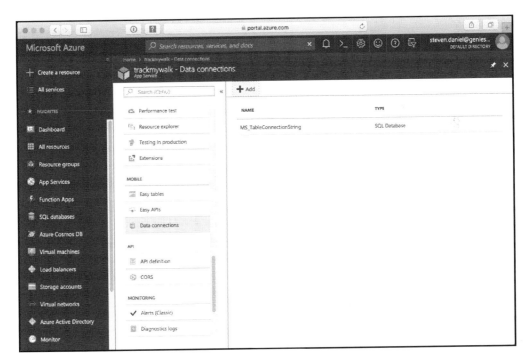

The TrackMyWalk - Data Connections Screen

4. Next, within the **Add Data connection** screen, ensure that you have selected **SQL Database** from the **Type** drop-down, and click on the **OK** button to save your changes in order to create a new data connection for our TrackMyWalks SQL Server database, as shown in the following screenshot:

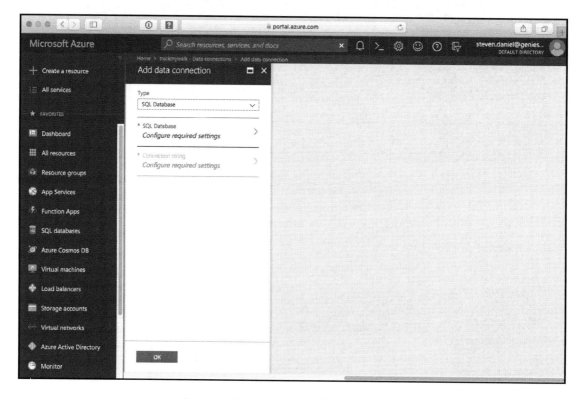

Creating a new data connection for our TrackMyWalks SQL Database

Once you have created the **TrackMyWalks Mobile App** and SQL Server database within the Microsoft Azure platform, by default, your database won't contain any database tables or table data. Before we can start communicating and consuming the RestWebService API within our TrackMyWalks app, we will need to create a new table that will be used to store our walk trail entries.

Let's create a new table within our database by going through the following steps:

1. First, from the **Dashboard**, click on the **trackmywalk App Service** and choose the **Easy tables** option, located under the **MOBILE** section on the **trackmywalk – Easy tables** page, as shown in the following screenshot:

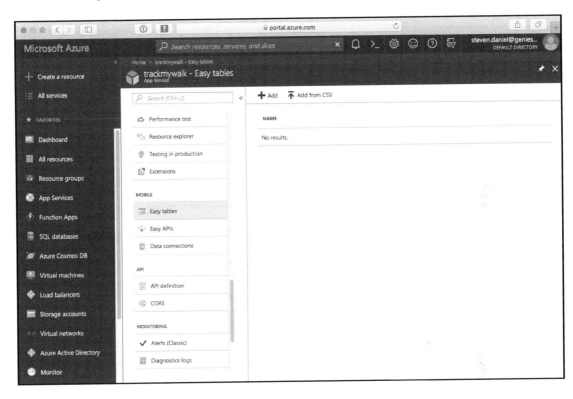

The TrackMyWalk - Easy Tables screen

2. Next, click on the **Add** button to display the **Add a table** screen, and enter WalkEntries in the **Name** field.

3. Then, leave the default permissions that have been set for our **Insert permission**, **Update permission**, **Delete permission**, **Read permission**, and **Undelete permission** drop-down entries, as shown in the following screenshot:

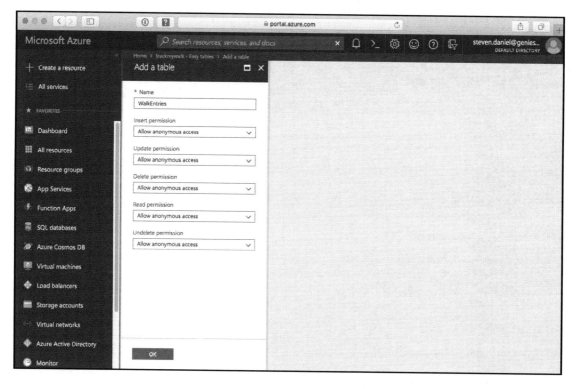

Creating the WalkEntries table for the TrackMyWalks app

4. Finally, click on the **OK** button to save your changes, and your `WalkEntries` table will be created and displayed under the **trackmywalks – Easy tables** section.

Whenever you choose the **Allow anonymous access** permission during the creation of your tables, you are essentially making the API available without providing any specific authentication headers as part of the HTTP request.

Before we can start making any calls to our `RestWebService` API and consuming this within our `TrackMyWalks` app, we will run a quick check to see whether our API endpoint is working correctly. This is achieved by issuing a `GET HTTPMethod` request, using the `curl https://trackmywalk.azurewebsites.net/tables/WalkEntries --header "ZUMO-API-VERSION:2.0.0"` command.

If you have set everything up correctly within the **Microsoft Azure Portal**, you should receive a `200` (success) status code back, along with an empty collection in the response body, as follows:

```
curl https://trackmywalk.azurewebsites.net/tables/WalkEntries --header
"ZUMO-API-VERSION:2.0.0" []
```

If you prefer not to use the command, there are several REST console clients that exist out there for you to choose from. I tend to use Postman for handling REST APIs, which can be downloaded from `http://www.getpostman.com/`.

Now, you have successfully created the `TrackMyWalks` SQL Server database, as well as the **Data Connections**, and `WalkEntries` table. Our next step is to add the `Newtonsoft.Json` NuGet package to our `TrackMyWalks` solution.

Adding the Newtonsoft.Json NuGet package to our solution

In this section, we will begin by adding the `Newtonsoft.Json` NuGet package to our `TrackMyWalks` shared-core solution, which is essentially a high-performance JSON framework for the .NET platform, which allows you to serialize and deserialize any type of .NET object with help from the JSON serializer class.

We will also have the ability to translate LINQ capabilities into JSON to enable us to create, parse, query, and modify the JSON structure that we receive back from our `WalkEntries` table, located on the Microsoft Azure platform.

Let's start by adding the `Newtonsoft.Json` NuGet package to our `TrackMyWalks` app by going through the following steps:

1. Right-click on the **Dependencies | NuGet** folder, located within the `TrackMyWalks` solution, and choose the **Add Packages...** menu option, as you did in `Chapter 4`, *Creating the TrackMyWalks Native App*.

2. Next, within the **Search** field located within the **Add Packages** dialog, you need to enter `json.net` and select the **Newtonsoft.Json** option within the list, as shown in the following screenshot:

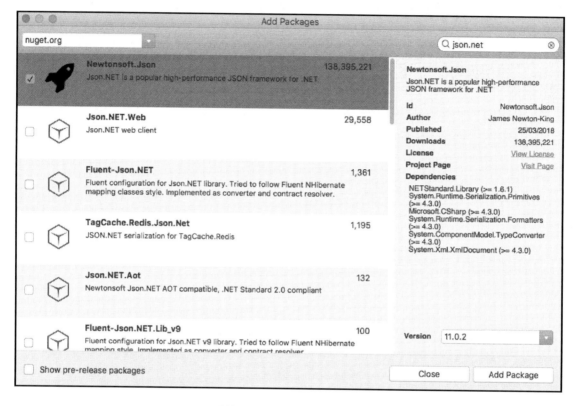

Adding the Newtonsoft.Json NuGet Package

3. Then, make sure that you choose the latest version to install from the drop-down list for the **Version** field (this will be displayed by default).

4. Finally, click on the **Add Package** button to add the **Newtonsoft.Json** NuGet package to the `TrackMyWalks` shared-core solution.

Now that you have added the NuGet package for the **Newtonsoft.Json**, we can begin utilizing this control by updating our `WalkDataModel` class to include additional `JsonProperty` attributes that will be used by our instances of `ViewModel` and `ContentPage` (views), which we will cover in the next section.

Updating the WalkDataModel for our TrackMyWalks app

In this section, we will begin updating our `WalkDataModel` so that it can communicate and interact with our `RestWebService` class, which will call methods to perform CRUD operations to create, retrieve, update, and delete walk trail information within our SQL Server database.

Let's take a look at how we can achieve this by going through the following steps:

1. Locate and open the `WalkDataModel.cs` file, which is located in the `Models` folder, and ensure that it is displayed within the code editor. Enter the following highlighted code sections:

```
//
//  WalkDataModel.cs
//  Data Model that will store Walk Trail Information
//
//  Created by Steven F. Daniel on 14/05/2018
//  Copyright © 2018 GENIESOFT STUDIOS. All rights reserved.
//
using System;
using Newtonsoft.Json;

namespace TrackMyWalks.Models
{
    public class WalkDataModel
    {
        [JsonProperty("id")]
        public string Id { get; set; }
        public string Title { get; set; }
        public string Description { get; set; }
        public double Latitude { get; set; }
        public double Longitude { get; set; }
        public double Distance { get; set; }
        public string Difficulty { get; set; }
        public string ImageUrl { get; set; }
    }
}
```

Let's now start by taking a look at what we covered in the preceding code snippet:

1. First, we included a reference to the `Newtonsoft.Json` namespace so that we have access to the classes that are defined within this namespace.

2. Lastly, we defined a `[JsonProperty("id")]` attribute for our `Id` string property that will serve as a unique primary key for each record that we will store within the database. The `id` property will create a database table field for the corresponding `Id` string property name.

 For more information on the `JsonProperty` properties, refer to the json.NET documentation at `https://www.newtonsoft.com/json/help/html/Properties_T_Newtonsoft_Json_Serialization_JsonProperty.htm`.

Creating and implementing the RestWebService interface

In this section, we'll take a look at how to create the `IRestWebService` class, which will essentially contain various instance methods that will be used by our `RestWebService` class. The advantage of creating an `IRestWebService` class is that it's much easier to add additional class instance methods that will be used by those instances of `ViewModel` and `ContentPage` (views) that utilize this interface.

Let's start by creating the `IRestWebService` interface for our `TrackMyWalks` app by going through the following steps:

1. Ensure that the `TrackMyWalks` solution is open within the Visual Studio for Mac IDE.

2. Next, right-click on the `Services` folder and choose **Add | New File...** from the pop-up menu, as you did in the *Creating and implementing the LocationService interface* section in `Chapter 7`, *Adding Location-based Features Within Your App*.

3. Then, choose the **Empty Interface** option under the **General** section and enter `IRestWebService` for the name of the interface to be created, as shown in the following screenshot:

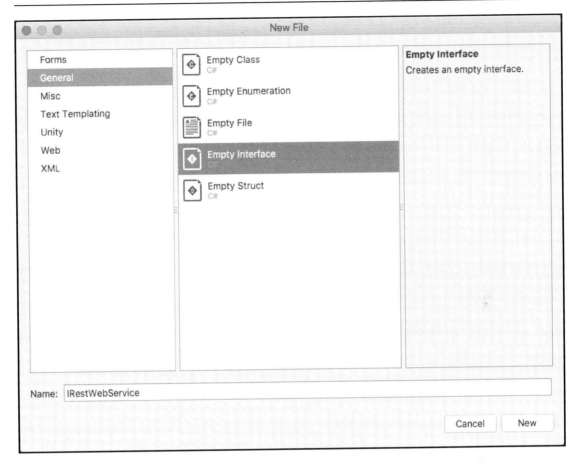

Creating the IRestWebService Interface

4. Next, click on the **New** button to allow the wizard to proceed and create the new file, as shown in the preceding screenshot. Now that we have created our IRestWebService interface, we can proceed with implementing the required code for our class.

5. Then, locate and open the IRestWebService.cs file, which is located within the Services folder, and ensure that it is displayed within the code editor. Enter the following code snippet:

```
//
//   IRestWebService.cs
//   REST WebService Interface used by our Rest WebService Class
//
//   Created by Steven F. Daniel on 06/08/2018.
```

```
//  Copyright © 2018 GENIESOFT STUDIOS. All rights reserved.
//
using System.Collections.Generic;
using System.Threading.Tasks;
using TrackMyWalks.Models;

namespace TrackMyWalks.Services
{
    public interface IRestWebService
    {
        // Gets all of the Walk Entries from our database.
        Task<List<WalkDataModel>> GetWalkEntries();

        // Saves our Walk Entry to the database.
        Task SaveWalkEntry(WalkDataModel item, bool isAdding);

        // Deletes a specific Walk Entry from the database.
        Task DeleteWalkEntry(string id);
    }
}
```

Let's now take a look at what we covered in the preceding code snippet:

1. We started by including references to the `System.Collections.Generic` and the `System.Threading.Tasks` namespaces so that we can access the classes that are defined within these namespaces. We also included a reference to the `TrackMyWalks.Models` namespace so that we can access our `WalkDataModel` database model.

2. Next, we declared a `GetWalkEntries` instance method that will be responsible for asynchronously retrieving all of the existing walk entries from our SQL Server database contained on our Microsoft Azure platform and returning a `List WalkDataModel` object.

3. Then, we declared a `SaveWalkEntry` instance method that will be responsible for asynchronously saving the book item that is currently being added or edited to the `WalkEntries` table within the SQL Server database.

4. Finally, we declared a `DeleteWalkEntry` instance method that will essentially permanently delete a specific walk entry from the SQL Server database, using the id within the `WalkEntries` table.

The `Task` class is essentially used to handle asynchronous operations, which is done by ensuring that the method you initiated will eventually finish, thus completing the task and returning a `Task` object almost instantaneously, although the underlying work within the method could likely finish later.

> Whenever you use the `Task` object, you can use the `await` keyword to wait for the task to complete, which will essentially block the current thread and wait until the asynchronous method has completed.

Creating and implementing the RestWebService class

In this section, we will take a look at how to create the `RestWebService` class that will inherit from our `IRestWebService` interface and implement the underlying instance methods that we declared within our interface class to help us communicate with our SQL Server database, so that we can perform CRUD operations that will be used by our instances of `ViewModel` and `ContentPage` (views).

Let's start by creating the `RestWebService` class for our `TrackMyWalks` app by going through the following steps:

1. Right-click on the `Services` folder and choose **Add** | **New File...** from the pop-up menu.

2. Then, choose the **Empty Class** option under the **General** section and enter `RestWebService` as the name of the class to be created, as shown in the following screenshot:

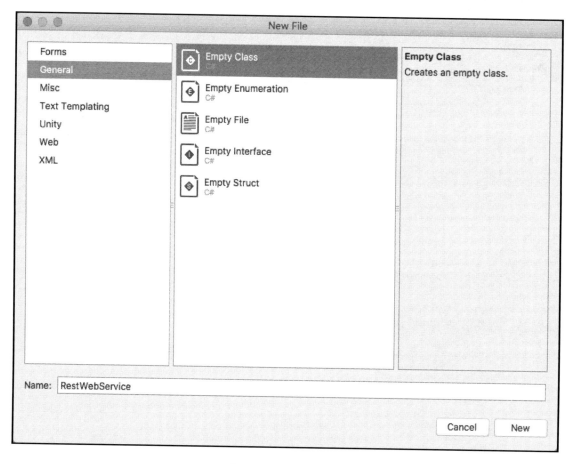

Creating the RestWebService Class

3. Next, click on the **New** button to allow the wizard to proceed and create the new file, as shown in the preceding screenshot. Now that we have created our `RestWebService` class, we can proceed with implementing the required code for our class.

4. Then, locate and open the `RestWebService.cs` file, which is located within the `Services` folder, and ensure that it is displayed within the code editor. Enter the following code snippet:

```
//
//   RestWebService.cs
//   REST WebService Class that will be used to handle performing of
CRUD operations
//
//   Created by Steven F. Daniel on 06/08/2018.
//   Copyright © 2018 GENIESOFT STUDIOS. All rights reserved.
//
using System;
using System.Collections.Generic;
using System.Diagnostics;
using System.Net.Http;
using System.Text;
using System.Threading.Tasks;
using Newtonsoft.Json;
using TrackMyWalks.Models;

namespace TrackMyWalks.Services
{
    public class RestWebService : IRestWebService
    {
        // Declare our HttpClient manager object
        HttpClient client;

        // Declare our RestWebService Constructor
        public RestWebService()
        {
            client = new HttpClient();
            client.BaseAddress = new
Uri("https://trackmywalk.azurewebsites.net");
            client.MaxResponseContentBufferSize = 256000;
            client.DefaultRequestHeaders.Add("ZUMO-API-VERSION",
"2.0.0");
        }

        // Retrieves all of the Walk Entries from our database.
        public async Task<List<WalkDataModel>> GetWalkEntries()
        {
            // Declare our WalkEntries Items List Collection to
populate resultset
            var Items = new List<WalkDataModel>();
            try
            {
                var response = await
```

```
client.GetAsync("tables/WalkEntries");
                    if (response.IsSuccessStatusCode)
                    {
                        var content = await
response.Content.ReadAsStringAsync();
                        Items =
JsonConvert.DeserializeObject<List<WalkDataModel>>(content);
                    }
                }
                catch (Exception ex)
                {
                    // Catch and output any error messages that have
occurred
                    Debug.WriteLine("An error occurred {0}", ex.Message);
                }
                return Items;
            }


        // Saves the Walk Entry item that is currently being
added/edited.
            public async Task SaveWalkEntry(WalkDataModel item, bool
isAdding)
            {
                try
                {
                    HttpResponseMessage responseMessage;
                    var json = JsonConvert.SerializeObject(item);
                    var content = new StringContent(json, Encoding.UTF8,
"application/json");

                    // Check to see if we are adding or editing, handle
accordingly.
                    if (isAdding)
                    {
                        responseMessage = await
client.PostAsync("tables/WalkEntries", content);
                    }
                    else
                    {
                        responseMessage = await
client.PutAsync("tables/WalkEntries", content);
                    }
                    // Check to see if we have successfully written the
item to the database
                    if (responseMessage.IsSuccessStatusCode)
                    {
                        Debug.WriteLine("WalkEntry Item successfully
saved.");
```

```
                    }
            }
            catch (Exception ex)
            {
                // Catch and output any error messages that have
occurred
                Debug.WriteLine("An error occurred {0}", ex.Message);
            }
        }

            // Deletes a specific Walk Entry from the database using the
id.
            public async Task DeleteWalkEntry(string id)
            {
                try
                {
                    var response = await
client.DeleteAsync("/tables/WalkEntries/" + id);
                    if (response.IsSuccessStatusCode)
                    {
                        Debug.WriteLine("WalkEntry Item was successfully
deleted.");
                    }
                }
                catch (Exception ex)
                {
                    // Catch and output any error messages that have
occurred
                    Debug.WriteLine("An error occurred {0}", ex.Message);
                }
            }
        }
    }
```

Let's take a look at what we covered in the preceding code snippet:

1. We started by including references to the various System namespaces, as well as the Newtonsoft.Json namespace, so that we can access the classes that are defined within these namespaces. We also included a reference to the TrackMyWalks.Models namespace so that we can access our WalkDataModel database model.

2. Next, we need to ensure that our RestWebService class inherits from the IRestWebService interface so that it can access the instance methods, as well as any getters and setters.

3. Then, we created a `client` variable that will be used to create an `HttpClient` manager object that we can use to perform REST HTTP requests.

4. Next, we modified the `RestWebService` class constructor to set up and initialize our `client` object to a new instance of the `HttpClient` class and set the `BaseAddress` property to a new `Uri` object that will point to our Microsoft Azure endpoint Url of `TrackMyWalks`.

5. Then, we set the `MaxResponseContentBufferSize` property on the `client` object, which is responsible for getting or setting the maximum number of bytes to buffer when reading the response content.

6. Next, we set the `DefaultRequestHeaders` property on the `client` object, which is responsible for getting the headers. This property should be sent with each request that is sent. We used the `Add` method and specify the key–value pair of `ZUMO-API-VERSION` and `2.0.0`, which is essentially a special header that is used by the HTTP client when communicating with Microsoft Azure databases.

7. Then, we declared a `GetWalkEntries` instance method that will be responsible for asynchronously retrieving all of the existing walk entries from our SQL Server database contained on our Microsoft Azure platform. We declared an `Items List` object variable, and we called the `client.GetAsync` method to send the `GET` request to the web service by specifying our `tables/WalkEntries` URI. Then we received the response from the web service.

8. Next, we checked the `IsSuccessStatusCode` property of the `response` object to indicate whether the HTTP request succeeded or failed. If the REST service sends back an HTTP status code of 200 (OK) in the response, then we read the content of the response asynchronouslyusing the `ReadAsStringAsync` method and convert the content from JSON to a `List` of `WalkDataModel` objects.

9. Then, we declared a `SaveWalkEntry` instance method that will be responsible for asynchronously saving the walk entry that is currently being added or edited to our SQL Server database contained on our Microsoft Azure platform. We then declared a `responseMessage` variable that will contain the response returned from the REST service, and convert the `WalkDataModel` item object to a JSON payload that will be embedded within the body of the HTTP content that will be sent to the web service.

10. Next, we checked to see whether we are adding, and then called either the `client.PostAsync` or `client.PutAsync` method to send the `POST` or `PUT` request to the web service by specifying our `tables/WalkEntries` URI, and then received the `response` from the web service. We checked the status code of the `IsSuccessStatusCode` property of the response object to see whether the HTTP request succeeded or failed.

11. Finally, we declared a `DeleteWalkEntry` instance method that will essentially permanently delete a specific walk entry from the SQL Server database using the `id` within the `WalkEntries` table. We called the `client.DeleteAsync` method to send the DELETE request to the web service by specifying our `tables/WalkEntries` URI, passing in the `id` as the parameter of the item to delete, and then receiving the `response` from the web service. We checked the status code of the `IsSuccessStatusCode` property of the `response` object to indicate whether the HTTP request succeeded or failed.

The HTTP class exposes several different types of HTTP methods that are used by the `HttpMethod` class. These are explained in the following table, which also contains a brief description of what each `HttpMethod` is used for:

HTTP Method	Description
GET	GET tells the `HttpMethod` class protocol that we are ready to request message content over HTTP to retrieve information from our REST API and then return this information, based on the representation format specified within the REST API.
POST	POST tells the `HttpMethod` class protocol that we want to create a new entry within our table, as specified by the REST API.
PUT	PUT tells the `HttpMethod` class protocol that we want to update an existing entry within our table, as specified by the REST API.
DELETE	DELETE tells the `HttpMethod` class protocol that we want to delete an existing entry within our table, as specified by the REST API.

For more information on the `HttpClient` class, refer to the Microsoft developer documentation at `https://msdn.microsoft.com/en-us/library/system.net.http.httpclient(v=vs.118).aspx`. If you are interested in learning more about client and server versioning in mobile apps and mobile services, refer to the Microsoft Azure documentation at `https://docs.microsoft.com/en-us/azure/app-service-mobile/app-service-mobile-client-and-server-versioning`.

Updating the BaseViewModel class to include our RestWebService

Now we have created both our `RestWebService` interface and class, which will allow us to communicate with the Microsoft Azure platform, as well as our SQL Server database to perform CRUD operations, that will enable us to create, retrieve, update, and delete walk entries.

Our next step is to update the underlying C# code within our `BaseViewModel` class. Since our `BaseViewModel` class is used by each of our instances of `ViewModel`, it makes sense to add these additional properties and instance methods within the `BaseViewModel` class.

Let's start by updating the `BaseViewModel` class for our `TrackMyWalks` app by going through the following steps:

1. Locate and open the `BaseViewModel.cs` file, which is located within the `ViewModels` folder, and ensure that it is displayed within the code editor. Enter the following highlighted code sections:

```
//
//   BaseViewModel.cs
//   BaseView Model Class that each of our ViewModels will inherit from
//
//   Created by Steven F. Daniel on 5/06/2018
//   Copyright © 2018 GENIESOFT STUDIOS. All rights reserved.
//
using System.ComponentModel;
using System.Runtime.CompilerServices;
using System.Threading.Tasks;
using TrackMyWalks.Services;

namespace TrackMyWalks.ViewModels
{
    public abstract class BaseViewModel : INotifyPropertyChanged
    {
        public INavigationService Navigation { get; set; }
        Public IRestWebService AzureDatabase { get; set; }

        public const string PageTitlePropertyName = "PageTitle";

        string pageTitle;
        public string PageTitle
        {
            get => pageTitle;
            set { pageTitle = value; OnPropertyChanged(); }
```

```
        }

        protected BaseViewModel(INavigationService navService)
        {
            Navigation = navService;
            AzureDatabase = new RestWebService();
        }

        public abstract Task Init();
        public event PropertyChangedEventHandler PropertyChanged;

        protected virtual void OnPropertyChanged([CallerMemberName]
string propertyName = null)
        {
            PropertyChanged?.Invoke(this, new
PropertyChangedEventArgs(propertyName));
        }
        bool isProcessBusy;
        public bool IsProcessBusy
        {
            get => isProcessBusy;
            set { isProcessBusy = value; OnPropertyChanged(); }
        }
    }

    public abstract class BaseViewModel<TParam> : BaseViewModel
    {
        protected BaseViewModel(INavigationService navService) :
base(navService)
        {
        }
    }
}
```

Let's take a look at what we covered in the preceding code snippet:

1. First, we created an AzureDatabase property that points to our
   IRestWebService class, and we defined the getter and setter properties.
2. Lastly, we modified the BaseViewModel class constructor to initialize our
   AzureDatabase property to a new instance of our RestWebService class.

Updating the WalksMainPage code-behind using C#

Now, we have updated our `BaseViewModel` class to include a property that references our `RestWebService` class. Our next step is to begin updating the underlying C# code within our `WalksMainPage` code-behind file so that it can communicate with our `RestWebService` class and the associated `ViewModel` to populate our `ListView` with information from our `WalkDataModel`, which we will populate from our SQL Server database within the Microsoft Azure platform.

Let's take a look at how we can achieve this by going through the following steps:

1. Locate and open the `WalksMainPage.xaml.cs` file, which is located within the `Views` folder, and ensure that it is displayed within the code editor. Enter the following highlighted code sections:

```
//
//  WalksMainPage.xaml.cs
//  Displays Walk Information within a ListView control from an array
//
//  Created by Steven F. Daniel on 14/05/2018
//  Copyright © 2018 GENIESOFT STUDIOS. All rights reserved.
//
using System;
using TrackMyWalks.Models;
using TrackMyWalks.Services;
using TrackMyWalks.ViewModels;
using Xamarin.Forms;

namespace TrackMyWalks.Views
{
    public partial class WalksMainPage : ContentPage
    {
        // Return the Binding Context for the ViewModel
        WalksMainPageViewModel _viewModel =>
                              BindingContext as
WalksMainPageViewModel;

        public WalksMainPage()
        {
            InitializeComponent();
            ...
            ...
        }
        ...
```

```
            ...
            // Instance method to remove the trail item from our collection
            public async void OnDeleteItem(object sender, EventArgs e)
            {
                // Get the selected item to be deleted from our ListView
                var selectedItem =
(WalkDataModel)((MenuItem)sender).CommandParameter;

                // Prompt the user with a confirmation dialog to confirm
                if (await DisplayAlert("Delete Walk Entry Item",
                    "Are you sure you want to delete this Walk Entry
Item?",
                    "OK", "Cancel"))
                {
                    // Remove Walk Item from our WalkListModel collection
                    // and SQL Server database
                    _viewModel.WalksListModel.Remove(selectedItem);

                    await
_viewModel.AzureDatabase.DeleteWalkEntry(selectedItem.Id);
                    await DisplayAlert("Delete Walk Entry Item",
                        selectedItem.Title +
                        " has been deleted from the database.", "OK");
                }
                else
                    return;
            }

            // Method to initialise our View Model when the ContentPage
appears
            protected override async void OnAppearing()
            {
                base.OnAppearing();

                if (_viewModel != null)
                {
                    // Call the Init method to initialise the ViewModel
                    await _viewModel.Init();
                }
                    ...
                    ...
            }
        }
    }
```

Let's take a look at what we covered in the preceding code snippet:

1. We modified the `OnDeleteItem` instance method that will be called whenever the **Delete** context menu item is tapped within the `ListView`. We then got the selected item that was to be deleted using the `CommandParameter` of the `sender` object from the `MenuItem` class and displayed a confirmation dialog that will prompt the user to confirm the deletion.

2. Next, assuming that the user clicked the **OK** button, we proceeded to delete the `selectedItem` from our SQL Server database, by calling the `DeleteWalkEntry` method on our `AzureDatabase` property using the `Id` of the `selectedItem`.

3. Finally, we removed the selected walk item from our `WalkListModel` object collection using the `Remove` method and passing in the `selectedItem` object. Alternatively, we just return from the `OnDeleteItem` instance method.

Updating the WalksMainPageViewModel using C#

Now, we have updated our `WalksMainPage` code-behind file to handle deletions from the SQL Server database. Our next step is to start implementing the necessary code within the `WalksMainPageViewModel` class, which will be used by our `WalksMainPage`.

The `WalksMainPageViewModel` ViewModel class will be used to populate our data model from our SQL Server database by calling the `GetWalkEntries` on our `AzureDatabase` property and displaying the information within our `ListView` by setting the `BindingContext` within the `ContentPage`.

Let's take a look at how we can achieve this by going through the following steps:

1. Locate and open the `WalksMainPageViewModel.cs` file, which is located within the `ViewModels` folder, and ensure that it is displayed within the code editor. Enter the following highlighted code sections:

```
//
//  WalksMainPageViewModel.cs
//  The ViewModel for our WalksMainPage ContentPage
//
//  Created by Steven F. Daniel on 5/06/2018.
//  Copyright © 2018 GENIESOFT STUDIOS. All rights reserved.
//
using System.Collections.ObjectModel;
using System.Threading.Tasks;
using TrackMyWalks.Models;
using TrackMyWalks.Services;
```

```
namespace TrackMyWalks.ViewModels
{
    public class WalksMainPageViewModel : BaseViewModel
    {
        // Create our WalksListModel Observable Collection
        public ObservableCollection<WalkDataModel> WalksListModel;

        public WalksMainPageViewModel(INavigationService navService) :
                                    base(navService)
        {
        }

        // Instance method to add and retrieve our  Walk Trail items
        public async Task GetWalkTrailItems()
        {
            // Check our IsProcessBusy property to see if we are
            // already processing
            if (IsProcessBusy)
                return;

            // If we aren't processing, we need to set our IsProcessBusy
            // property to true
            IsProcessBusy = true;

            // Populate our WalkListModel List Collection with items
from our
            // Microsoft Azure Web Service
            WalksListModel = new ObservableCollection<WalkDataModel>
await
                                AzureDatabase.GetWalkEntries());

            // Set our IsProcessBusy property value back to false when
finished
            IsProcessBusy = false;
        }

        // Instance method to initialise the WalksMainPageViewModel
        public override async Task Init()
        {
            await Task.Factory.StartNew(async () =>
            {
                // Call our GetWalkTrailItems method to populate our
collection
                await GetWalkTrailItems();
            });
        }
    }
}
```

Let's take a look at what we covered in the preceding code snippet:

1. We started by modifying our `GetWalkTrailItems` instance method to include the `async` keyword so that our method can handle asynchronous calls.
2. Next, we created a `WalksListModel ObservableCollection` collection object that will raise an event whenever an object is added to or removed from our `WalksListModel` collection.
3. Finally, we used the `await` keyword and called the `GetWalkEntries` instance method on our `AzureDatabase` property that we defined within our `BaseViewModel` to populate our `WalksListModel` collection.

Updating the WalkEntryPage user interface using XAML

In this section, we will take a look at how to update the user interface for our `WalkEntryPage` so that it includes an `ActivityIndicator` as well as a `Label` control element within our XAML, so that we can access these controls within our code-behind file, and provide information feedback to the user whenever walk entry information is being saved to our SQL Server database.

Let's start by updating the user interface for our `WalkEntryPage` by going through the following steps:

1. Locate and open the `WalkEntryPage.xaml` file, which is located within the `Views` folder, and ensure that it is displayed within the code editor. Enter the following highlighted code sections:

```
<?xml version="1.0" encoding="UTF-8"?>
<ContentPage xmlns="http://xamarin.com/schemas/2014/forms"
             xmlns:x="http://schemas.microsoft.com/winfx/2009/xaml"
             xmlns:valueConverters="clr-
namespace:TrackMyWalks.ValueConverters"
             x:Class="TrackMyWalks.Views.WalkEntryPage">
    <ContentPage.ToolbarItems>
        <ToolbarItem Text="Save" Clicked="SaveWalkItem_Clicked" />
    </ContentPage.ToolbarItems>
    <ContentPage.Resources>
        . . .
        . . .
    </ContentPage.Resources>
    <ContentPage.Content>
```

```
<StackLayout>
 <ActivityIndicator IsRunning="true" x:Name="progressIndicator"
        HorizontalOptions="CenterAndExpand"
        VerticalOptions="CenterAndExpand"
        IsVisible="{Binding IsProcessBusy}" />
        <Label Text="Saving walk information..."
FontAttributes="Bold"
                TextColor="MediumVioletRed"
HorizontalTextAlignment="Center"
                IsVisible="{Binding IsProcessBusy}"
x:Name="SavingWalkInfo">
            <Label.FontSize>
                <OnPlatform x:TypeArguments="x:Double">
                    <On Platform="Android, WinPhone" Value="12" />
                    <On Platform="iOS" Value="14" />
                </OnPlatform>
            </Label.FontSize>
        </Label>
        <TableView Intent="Form" x:Name="WalkDetails">
            <TableView.Root>
                . . .
                . . .
            </TableView.Root>
        </TableView>
    </StackLayout>
    </ContentPage.Content>
</ContentPage>
```

2. Next, locate and open the `WalkEntryPage.xaml.cs` file, which is located in the `Views` folder, and ensure that it is displayed within the code editor. Enter the following highlighted code sections:

```
//
//  WalkEntryPage.xaml.cs
//  Data Entry screen that allows new walk information to be added
//
//  Created by Steven F. Daniel on 14/05/2018
//  Copyright © 2018 GENIESOFT STUDIOS. All rights reserved.
//
using System;
using TrackMyWalks.Services;
using TrackMyWalks.ViewModels;
using Xamarin.Forms;

namespace TrackMyWalks.Views
{
    public partial class WalkEntryPage : ContentPage
    {
```

```
                    // Return the Binding Context for the ViewModel
                    WalkEntryPageViewModel _viewModel =>
                                            BindingContext as
WalkEntryPageViewModel;

            public WalkEntryPage()
            {
                    InitializeComponent();

                    // Update the Title and Initialise our BindingContext
                    // for the Page
                    Title = "New Walk Entry Page";
                    BindingContext = new
WalkEntryPageViewModel(DependencyService.
                                    Get<INavigationService>());
                    SetBinding(TitleProperty, new
Binding(BaseViewModel.PageTitlePropertyName));
            }

            // Instance method that saves the new walk entry
            public async void SaveWalkItem_Clicked(object sender, EventArgs
e)
            {
                    // Prompt the user with a confirmation dialog to confirm
                    if (await DisplayAlert("Save Walk Entry Item", "Proceed and
save changes?",
                                    "OK", "Cancel"))
                    {
                            // Attempt to save and validate our Walk Entry Item
                            if (!await _viewModel.ValidateFormDetailsAndSave())
                                    // Error Saving - Must have Title, Description and
Image URL
                                    await DisplayAlert("Validation Error",
                                            "Title, Description, and Image URL are
required.", "OK");
                            else
                                    // Navigate back to the Track My Walks Listing page
                                    await _viewModel.Navigation.RemoveViewFromStack();
                    }
                    else
                    {
                            // Navigate back to the Track My Walks Listing page
                            await _viewModel.Navigation.RemoveViewFromStack();
                    }
            }

            // Method to initialise our View Model when the ContentPage
appears
```

```
protected override async void OnAppearing()
{
        base.OnAppearing();
            . . .
            . . .
    }
  }
}
```

Let's take a look at what we defined within our XAML and code snippet:

1. First, we started by adding the `ActivityIndicator` within a `StackLayout` attribute, and provided values for the name property `x:Name="progressIndicator"`, as well as specifying an `IsRunning` property that will be used to determine the running status.

2. Next, we specified the `IsVisible` property that will be bound to our `IsProcessBusy` property that we declared within our `BaseViewModel` class, which we will set accordingly within our `ViewModel`.

3. Then, we added the `x:Name="SavingWalkInfo"` property to our `Label` property for our `ActivityIndicator` that will be used to display informative feedback information to the user whenever they click on the `Save Toolbar` button in order to save a walk item to the SQL Server database.

4. Next, we defined a `Label.FontSize` attribute and set the `FontSize` based on the platform that our app is running on using the `OnPlatform` attribute and specifying the `x:TypeArguments` of `Double`.

5. Then, we updated the `SaveWalkItem_Clicked` instance method to update our `ValidateFormDetailsAndSave` method declared within our `WalkEntryPageViewModel`, so that it included the `await` keyword, since our instance method calls our `SaveWalkEntry` instance method on our `AzureDatabase` property within the `WalkEntryPageViewModel`.

6. Finally, we called the `RemoveViewFromStack` instance method on the `_viewModel.Navigation` property to remove the `WalkEntryPage` from the navigation stack.

Updating the WalkEntryPageViewModel using C#

Now that we have updated our `WalkEntryPage` user interface to include our `ActivityIndicator`, as well as made some changes to the code-behind file for the `SaveWalkItem_Click` method, we can now proceed to update the `WalksEntryPageViewModel` class so it can use our `AzureDatabase` property to save walk entries to our SQL Server database.

Let's take a look at how we can achieve this by going through the following steps:

1. Locate and open the `WalkEntryPageViewModel.cs` file, which is located in the `ViewModels` folder, and ensure that it is displayed within the code editor. Enter the following highlighted code sections:

```
//
//  WalkEntryPageViewModel.cs
//  The ViewModel for our WalkEntryPage ContentPage
//
//  Created by Steven F. Daniel on 5/06/2018.
//  Copyright © 2018 GENIESOFT STUDIOS. All rights reserved.
//
using System;
using System.Threading.Tasks;
using TrackMyWalks.Models;
using TrackMyWalks.Services;

namespace TrackMyWalks.ViewModels
{
    public class WalkEntryPageViewModel : BaseViewModel
    {
        // Handle Adding/Editing of Walk Entry Items
        bool isAdding;

        public WalkEntryPageViewModel(INavigationService navService) :
            base(navService)
        {
            // Update the title if we are creating a new Walk Entry
            if (App.SelectedItem == null)
            {
                PageTitle = "Adding Trail Details";
                App.SelectedItem = new WalkDataModel();

                // We are adding a new Walk Entry to our Azure Database
                isAdding = true;

                // Set the default values when creating a new Trail
```

```
                        Title = "New Trail Entry";
                        Difficulty = "Easy";
                        Distance = 1.0;
                }
                else
                {
                        // Otherwise, we must be editing an existing entry
                        PageTitle = "Editing Trail Details";
                        isAdding = false;
                }
        }

        // Checks to see if we have provided a Title and Description
        public async Task<bool> ValidateFormDetailsAndSave()
        {
                if (App.SelectedItem != null &&
                    !string.IsNullOrEmpty(App.SelectedItem.Title) &&
                    !string.IsNullOrEmpty(App.SelectedItem.Description) &&
                    !string.IsNullOrEmpty(App.SelectedItem.ImageUrl))
                {
                        // Check our IsProcessBusy property to see if we are
                        // already processing
                        if (IsProcessBusy)
                            return false;

                        // If we aren't processing, we need to set our
IsProcessBusy
                        // property to true
                        IsProcessBusy = true;

                        // Save our Walk Entry details to our Microsoft Azure
Database
                        await AzureDatabase.SaveWalkEntry(App.SelectedItem,
isAdding);
                        IsProcessBusy = false;
                }
                else
                {
                        // Initialise our IsProcessBusy property to false
                        IsProcessBusy = false;
                        return false;
                }
                // Initialise our IsProcessBusy property to false
                IsProcessBusy = false;
                return true;
        }
                ...
                ...
```

```
             // Instance method to initialise the WalkEntryPageViewModel
             public override async Task Init()
             {
                 await Task.Factory.StartNew(async () =>
                 {
                     // Initialise our IsProcessBusy property to false
                     IsProcessBusy = false;

                     // Call our GetMyLocation method to obtain our
                     // GPS Coordinates
                     await GetMyLocation();
                 });
             }
         }
     }
```

Let's take a look at what we covered in the preceding code snippet:

1. We started by creating an isAdding that is responsible for determining whether we are adding or editing a new or existing walk item. Then we modified the WalkEntryPageViewModel constructor to initialize our isAdding property.

2. Next, we updated the ValidateFormDetailsAndSave instance method and checked to see whether we had a value for our App.SelectedItem. We also checked whether the user had provided values for our Title, Description, and ImageUrl properties, prior to saving the details.

3. Then, we checked our IsProcessBusy property to see whether we are currently processing, and initialized our IsProcessBusy property to true, prior to calling the SaveWalkEntry instance method on our AzureDatabase property to save the walk entry to the SQL Server database.

4. Next, we initialized the IsProcessBusy property to false to stop hiding the SavingWalkInfo Label, located on our WalkEntryPage XAML, and returned true to the calling method that called our ValidateFormDetailsAndSave instance method.

5. Finally, within the Init method, we initialized our IsProcessBusy property to false when the WalkEntryPageViewModel was initialized.

Now that you have finished making the necessary changes to the WalkDataModel model, as well as creating the RestWebService interface and class, and have updated all of the required XAML pages, including making the necessary changes to the instances of ViewModel to take advantage of our AzureDatabase property and the RestWebService class, our next step is to compile, build, and run our application within the iOS simulator.

Launching the TrackMyWalks app using the iOS simulator

In this section, we will compile, build, and run the `TrackMyWalks` application to see how our application looks, since we have made additional changes to our `WalkEntryPage`, and have implemented RESTful API calls to our SQL Server database, which is located on the Microsoft Azure platform.

Let's see how we can achieve this by going through the following steps:

1. Ensure that you have chosen the `TrackMyWalks.iOS` platform from the drop-down menu.
2. Next, ensure that you have chosen the **Debug** option from the drop-down menu.
3. Then, choose your preferred device from the list of available iOS simulators.
4. Next, select the **Run | Start Debugging** menu option, as shown in the following screenshot:

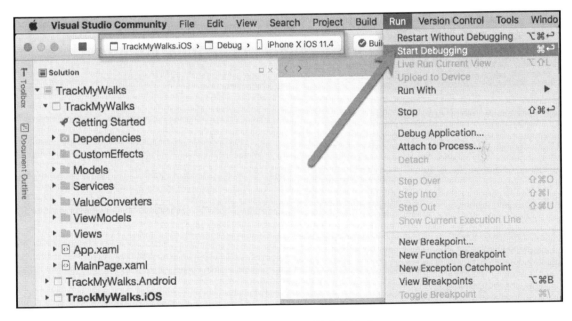

Launching the TrackMyWalks app within the iOS Simulator

5. Alternatively, you can also build and run the `TrackMyWalks` application by pressing *Command + Return* on the keyboard.

When the compilation is complete, the iOS simulator will appear automatically and the `TrackMyWalks` application will be displayed, as shown in the following screenshot:

Adding and Saving of new Trail Details within the Track My Walks application

The preceding screenshot displays our `TrackMyWalks` application with an empty **Track My Walks Listing**, since our `TrackMyWalks` SQL Server database doesn't contain any walk entries at the moment. Clicking on the **Add** button will display the **Adding Trail Details**, where you can begin entering information relating to the trail. Clicking on the **Save** button will display a dialog asking the user whether they would like to proceed and save the changes made.

Upon clicking the **OK** button, it will display an `ActivitySpinner` control, along with the associated **Saving Walk Information...** text, which is displayed while the trail is written to our SQL Server database, after which you will be taken back to the **Track My Walks Listing**, where your walk information will be displayed as it is. Alternatively, clicking on the **Cancel** button will not save the walk information to the database, and will take you back to the **Track My Walks Listing** page.

The following screenshot displays the **Track My Walks Listing** page, along with the trail walk information that you just saved to the SQL Server database. Sliding the walk entry from the left will display the `ContextMenu`, which will give you the option to either **Edit** or **Delete** the walk entry information from the database:

Deleting an existing Walk Entry Item from the Track My Walks Listing Screen

Clicking on the **Delete** button will display a dialog asking the user whether they would like to proceed with the deletion of the walk entry, and if the user clicks the **OK** button, then the walk entry will be deleted from the database and a dialog will be displayed letting the user know that this has happened. Alternatively, clicking on the **Cancel** button will dismiss the dialog.

Summary

In this chapter, you learned about the Microsoft Azure App services platform and how you can use this platform to create your cloud-based databases using RESTful web service APIs to handle all communication between the `TrackMyWalks` mobile application. You then set up and configured a Microsoft Azure App service to create a mobile app service, data connection, SQL Server database, and a `WalkEntries` table, and learned how to incorporate the `Newtonsoft.Json` NuGet package, as well as modify the `WalkDataModel` data model.

Next, you created a `RestWebservice` interface and class—which included a number of class instance methods that will be used to communicate with our database—so that you can perform CRUD operations to create, update, retrieve, and delete walk entries. You then made changes to the `BaseViewModel` class so that it included an `AzureDatabase` property in our `RestWebService` class, and then you made several changes to the underlying code-behind files to communicate with our SQL Server database in order to perform operations for the saving and deletion of walk entry items.

Lastly, you made changes to the user interface for the `WalkEntryPage` so that it included an `ActivityIndicator`, which will display information to the user whenever a walk item is saved to the database. You also made some underlying changes to the `WalkEntryPageViewModel` to initialize properties for communicating with the `ActivityIndicator`.

In the next chapter, you'll learn how to apply for a Twitter developer account so that you can incorporate social networking features by creating and registering our `TrackMyWalks` app within the Twitter Developer Portal. You'll incorporate the `Xamarin.Auth` NuGet package within our solution and create a `TwitterService` interface and class so that we can communicate with the Twitter APIs using RESTful web service calls. You will then create a `TwitterSignInPage`, as well as the associated `TwitterSignInPageViewModel` and `TwitterSignInPageRenderer` classes, so that users can sign into your app using their Twitter credentials. Finally, you'll update the `WalksMainPage` code-behind to call our `TwitterSignInPage` to check to see whether the user has signed in. You will also make changes to our `WalkDistancePage` XAML and code-behind so that we can utilize our `TwitterService` class to display profile information, as well as to post information about the trail to the user's Twitter feed.

12
Making Our App Social Using the Twitter API

In the previous chapter, you learned about the Microsoft Azure App Services Platform, and how you can leverage this platform to create your cloud-based databases, using RESTful Webservice APIs that will be used to handle all communication between the `TrackMyWalks` mobile app. You learned how to set up and configure a Microsoft Azure App Service to create a Mobile AppService, Data connection, SQL Server database, and the `WalkEntries` table, prior to incorporating the `Newtonsoft.Json` NuGet package and modifying the `WalkDataModel` data model.

Next, you created a `RestWebservice` Interface and Class that included a number of class instance methods used to communicate with our `TrackMyWalks` SQL Server database, so that you could perform **CRUD** operations to Create, Update, Retrieve, and Delete walk entries, and modified the `BaseViewModel` class to include an `AzureDatabase` property with our `RestWebService` class. You also made some changes to the underlying code-behind files that will communicate with our SQL Server database. Finally, you updated the user interface for the `WalkEntryPage` to include an `ActivityIndicator`, which will display information to the user whenever a walk item is being saved to the database, as well as made changes to the `WalkEntryPageViewModel` to initialize properties for communicating with the `ActivityIndicator`.

In this chapter, you'll learn how to apply for a Twitter developer account so that you can incorporate social networking features by creating and registering our TrackMyWalks app within the Twitter Developer Portal. You'll incorporate the Xamarin.Auth NuGet package within our solution and create a TwitterService Interface and Class that we can use to communicate with the Twitter APIs using RESTful webservice calls. You will then create a TwitterSignInPage as well as the associated TwitterSignInPageViewModel and TwitterSignInPageRenderer classes so that users can sign into your app using their Twitter credentials.

Finally, you'll update the WalksMainPage code-behind to call our TwitterSignInPage to check to see whether the user has signed in, as well as make changes to our WalkDistancePage XAML and code-behind so that we can utilize our TwitterService class to display profile information, as well as post information about the trail to the user's Twitter feed.

This chapter will cover the following topics:

- Creating and registering the TrackMyWalks app with the Twitter Developer Portal
- Incorporating the Xamarin.Auth NuGet package into our TrackMyWalks solution
- Creating and implementing the TwitterAuthDetails class using C#
- Creating and implementing a TwitterService Interface and Class using C#
- Creating and implementing the user interface for the TwitterSignInPage
- Creating and implementing the TwitterSignInPageViewModel using C#
- Creating and implementing the TwitterSignInPageRenderer (iOS)
- Updating the WalksMainPage code-behind to call our TwitterSignInPage
- Updating the WalkDistancePage user interface using XAML and code-behind using C#
- Updating the App.xaml to add the TwitterSignInPage to our MVVM navigation
- Launching the TrackMyWalks app using the iOS Simulator

Creating and registering the TrackMyWalks app with the Twitter Developer Portal

In this section, we will begin by applying for a Twitter Developer account, and then move on to creating and registering the `TrackMyWalks` application by creating an AppID within the Twitter Developer Portal that we can associate our app with. Doing this, we can then communicate with Twitter using the Twitter APIs.

Let's take a look at how we can achieve this by performing the following steps:

1. First, open your browser, type in `https://developer.twitter.com/en/apply-for-access`, and click on the **Apply for a developer account** button:

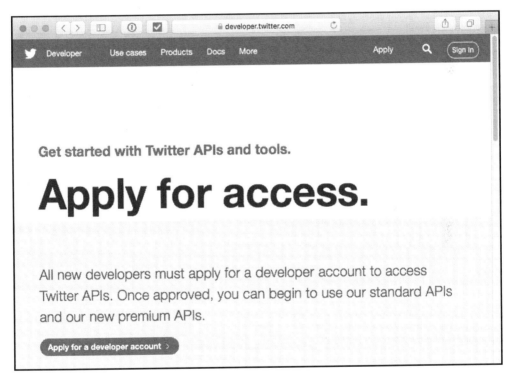

Applying for a Twitter Developer Account

2. Next, you will be prompted to log into Twitter using your Twitter credentials. Once you have done that, you will be presented with the **Account / Getting Started** screen.

3. Then, click on the **Create an app** button that is located under the **Getting Started** heading, as shown in the following screenshot:

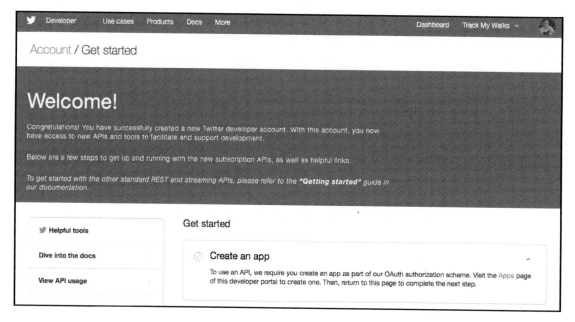

Creating/Registering a new app within the Twitter Portal

4. Next, click on the **Create an app** button located under the **Create your first app** heading within the **Apps** section, as shown in the following screenshot:

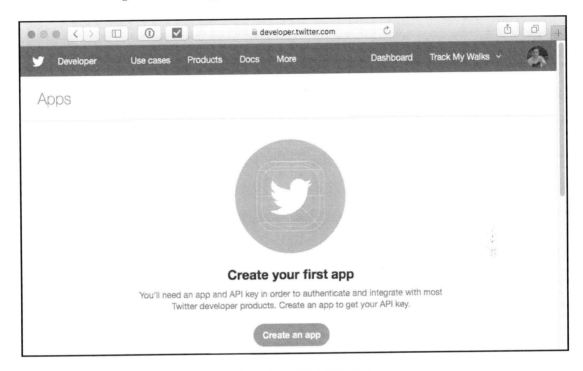

Creating your first app within the Twitter Portal

5. Then, enter **Track My Walks** as the name for our app in the **App name (required)** field, which will be displayed within the Twitter sign in page for our app.

6. Next, enter **Track My Walks app** to describe our app in the **Application description (required)** field. Also, provide a website **URL** to use for our app for the **Website URL (required)** field, as shown in the following screenshot:

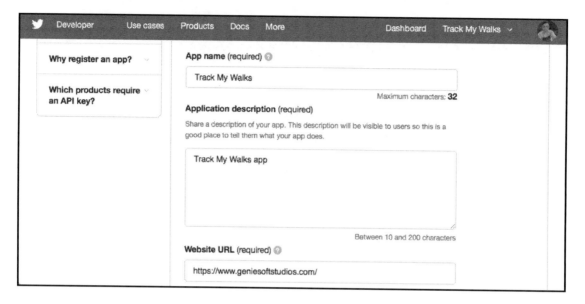

Specifying application details for your app

7. Then, enter `https://mobile.twitter.com/home` in the **Callback URLs** field, which will be used to redirect the user to the page upon successfully signing into Twitter and your app.

8. Next, enter the name for your organization in the **Organization name** field (this field is completely optional). This is displayed within the Twitter sign-in page for your app, as shown in the following screenshot:

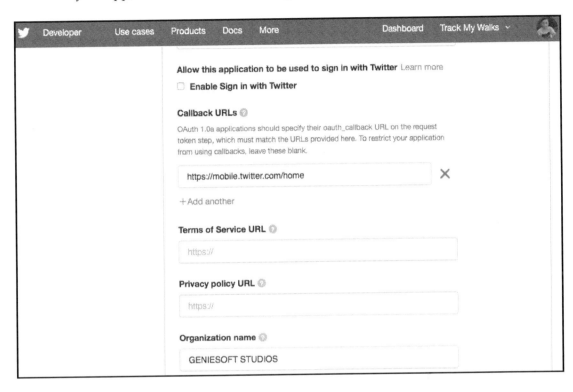

Specifying application details for your app

9. Then, you will need to provide a description to describe your application for the **Tell us how this app will be used (required)** field, as shown in the following screenshot:

 The **Tell us how this app will be used (required)** field is a mandatory requirement, and is only visible to Twitter employees. This is to help them better understand how your app will be used, as well as what your app will enable your customers to achieve.

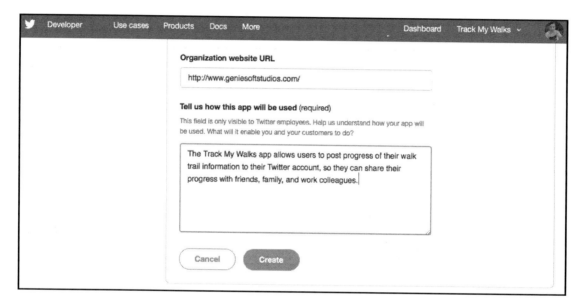

Specifying application details for your app

10. Next, click on the **Create** button to display the **Review our Developer Terms** dialog, which you will need to adhere to, prior to your app being created, as shown in the following screenshot:

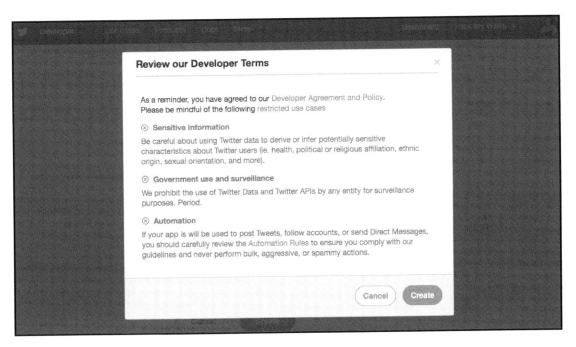

Reviewing the Developer Agreement and Policy Terms

11. Finally, click on the **Create** button to proceed with the creation of your app. You will then be presented with the **App Details** section with details about the app you just created within the Twitter Developer Portal, as shown in the following screenshot:

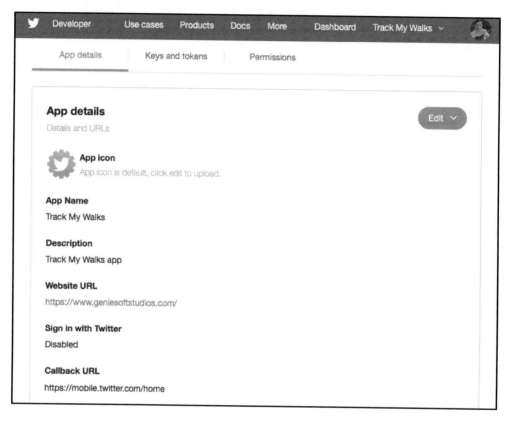

Your newly created App Details within the Twitter Developer Portal

Now that we have successfully applied for a Twitter developer account, as well as successfully created the **Track My Walks App details** within the Twitter Developer Portal, our next step is to take a look at what each of the relevant tabs contains and is used for, as shown in the following screenshot:

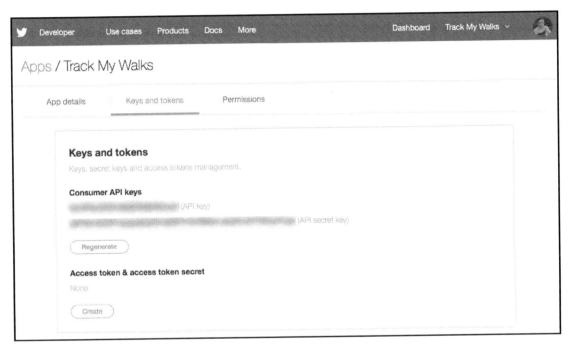

Track My Walks Application Keys and tokens section

The **Keys and tokens** section contains important information that will allow our TrackMyWalks app to successfully communicate with our **Track My Walks App ID**, using the **Consumer API keys** for both our **API Key** and **API secret Key**. We will need to provide these for our RESTful Webservice when calling the Twitter API to allow our app to sign in, as can be seen in the preceding screenshot.

You have the option of regenerating new **Consumer API Keys**, if you don't like the ones that were generated for you initially, by clicking on the **Regenerate** button.

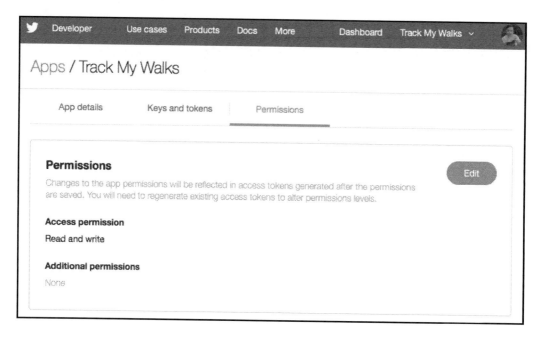

Track My Walks Application Access Permissions section

The **Permissions** section, contains important information pertaining to how the TrackMyWalks app will function. Within this screen, you can set different levels of access permissions that will affect how your application will function and communicate with Twitter through the use of the Twitter APIs.

Any changes that you make to the **Permissions** section for your app on this screen will be reflected in the access tokens that are generated once the permissions are updated.

Now that you have successfully created the **TrackMyWalks** application ID within the Twitter **Developer Portal**, our next step is to add the Xamarin.Auth NuGet package to our TrackMyWalks solution.

Adding the Xamarin.Auth NuGet Package to our solution

In this section, we will begin by adding the `Xamarin.Auth` NuGet package to our **TrackMyWalks** shared-core solution. The `Xamarin.Auth` package is essentially a cross-platform API that is used for authenticating users by using API calls.

Let's start by adding the `Xamarin.Auth` NuGet package to our `TrackMyWalks` app by performing the following steps:

1. Right-click on **Dependencies | NuGet** folder, located within the `TrackMyWalks` solution, and choose the **Add Packages...** menu option, as you did in `Chapter 4`, *Creating the TrackMyWalks Native App*.

2. Next, within the **Search** field located within the **Add Packages** dialog, you need to enter `xamarin.auth` and select the **Xamarin.Auth** option within the list, as shown in the following screenshot:

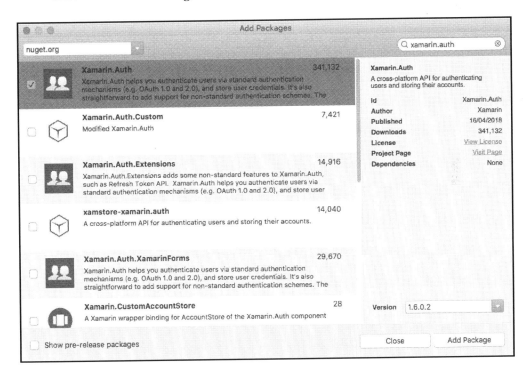

Adding the Xamarin.Auth NuGet Package

3. Then, make sure that you choose the latest version to install from the drop-down list for the **Version** field (*this will be displayed by default*).

4. Finally, click on the **Add Package** button to add the `Xamarin.Auth` NuGet package to the `TrackMyWalks` shared core solution.

Now that you have added the `Xamarin.Auth` NuGet package, we can begin utilizing this control by creating a `TwitterAuthDetails` class that will be used by our `ViewModels` and ContentPages (Views), which we will cover in the next section.

Creating and implementing the TwitterAuthDetails class

In this section, we will create the `TwitterAuthDetails` class, which will essentially contain various properties and instance methods that will be used by our `TwitterWebService` class.

Let's start by creating the `TwitterAuthDetails` class for our `TrackMyWalks` app by performing the following steps:

1. Ensure that the `TrackMyWalks` solution is open within the Visual Studio for Mac IDE.

2. Next, right-click on the `Services` folder, and choose **Add | New File...** from the pop-up menu, as you did in the section entitled *Creating and implementing the LocationService class* within `Chapter 7`, *Adding Location-based Features Within Your App*.

3. Then, choose the **Empty Class** option under the **General** section and enter `TwitterAuthDetails` for the name of the class to be created, as shown in the following screenshot:

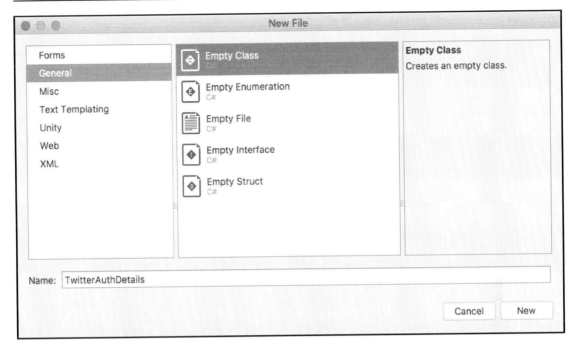

Creating the TwitterAuthDetails Class

4. Next, click on the **New** button to allow the wizard to proceed and create the new file, as shown in the preceding screenshot. Now that we have created our `TwitterAuthDetails` class, we can proceed with implementing the required code for our class.

5. Then, locate and open the `TwitterAuthDetails.cs` file, which is located within the `Services` folder, and ensure that it is displayed within the code editor. Then, enter the following code snippet:

```
//
//  TwitterAuthDetails.cs
//  TwitterAuthDetails class that will store Twitter related
information
//
//  Created by Steven F. Daniel on 10/08/2018
//  Copyright © 2018 GENIESOFT STUDIOS. All rights reserved.
//
using Newtonsoft.Json.Linq;
using Xamarin.Auth;

namespace TrackMyWalks.Services
{
```

```
public class TwitterAuthDetails
{
    // Property to store the currently logged in user
    public static bool isLoggedIn =>
!string.IsNullOrWhiteSpace(AuthToken);

    // Declare and define your Twitter Consumer Key
    public static string ConsumerKey => "YOUR_CONSUMER_API_KEY";
    public static string ConsumerSecret =>
"YOUR_CONSUMER_API_SECRET";

    // Declare a property to get our Twitter User Details
    static JObject _userDetails;
    public static JObject UserDetails => _userDetails;

    // Instance method to store our Twitter User Details
    public static void StoreUserDetails(JObject userDetails)
    {
        _userDetails = userDetails;
    }

    // Property to get our Twitter Authentication Token
    static string _authToken;
    public static string AuthToken => _authToken;

    // Instance method to store our Twitter Auth Token
    public static void StoreAuthToken(string authToken)
    {
        _authToken = authToken;
    }

    // Property to get our Twitter Authentication Token Secret
    static string _authTokenSecret;
    public static string AuthTokenSecret => _authTokenSecret;

    // Instance method to store our Twitter Auth Token Secret
    public static void StoreTokenSecret(string authTokenSecret)
    {
        _authTokenSecret = authTokenSecret;
    }

    // Property to get our Twitter Authentication Account Details
    static Account _authAccount;
    public static Account AuthAccount => _authAccount;

    // Instance method to store our Twitter Authentication Account
Details
    public static void StoreAccountDetails(Account authAccount)
```

```
        {
            _authAccount = authAccount;
        }
    }
}
```

Now, let's start by taking a look at what we covered in the preceding code snippet:

1. First, we included a reference to the `Newtonsoft.Json.Linq` and `Xamarin.Auth` namespaces so that we have access to the classes that are defined within this namespace.

2. Next, we defined an `isLoggedIn` property method, which will be used to determine whether the user has been signed into Twitter and our app by checking the `AuthToken` property.

3. Then, we declare and define our **Twitter Consumer Keys**, which can be obtained from the **Consumer API Keys** section within the **Keys and tokens** tab within the **App Details** section in the Twitter Developer Portal.

4. Finally, we declared various properties to get and store our Twitter user details and obtained our authentication tokens for the logged-in `AuthToken` and `AuthTokenSecret` token keys.

Creating and implementing the TwitterWebService interface

In this section, we will create the `ITwitterWebService` class, which will essentially contain various instance methods that will be used by our `TwitterWebService` class. The advantage of creating an `ITwitterWebService` class is that it's much easier to add additional class instance methods that will be used by other classes that utilize this interface.

Let's start by creating the `ITwitterWebService` interface for our `TrackMyWalks` app by performing the following steps:

1. Right-click on the **Services** folder, and choose **Add | New File...** from the pop-up menu, as you did in the section entitled *Creating and implementing the LocationService interface* within `Chapter 7`, *Adding Location-based Features Within Your App*.

2. Then, choose the **Empty Interface** option under the **General** section and enter `ITwitterWebService` for the name of the interface to be created, as shown in the following screenshot:

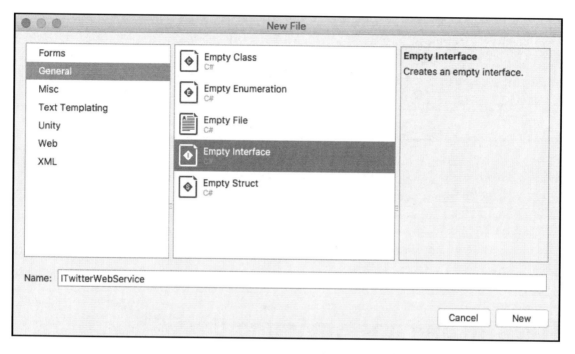

Creating the ITwitterWebService Interface

3. Next, click on the **New** button to allow the wizard to proceed and create the new file, as shown in the preceding screenshot. Now that we have created our `ITwitterWebService` interface, we can proceed with implementing the required code for our class.

4. Then, locate and open the `ITwitterWebService.cs` file, which is located within the `Services` folder, and ensure that it is displayed within the code editor. Then, enter the following code snippet:

```
//
//   ITwitterWebService.cs
//   TwitterWebService Interface used by our TwitterWebService Class
//
//   Created by Steven F. Daniel on 10/08/2018.
//   Copyright © 2018 GENIESOFT STUDIOS. All rights reserved.
//
using System.Threading.Tasks;
```

```
using Newtonsoft.Json.Linq;
using Xamarin.Auth;

namespace TrackMyWalks.Services
{
    public interface ITwitterService
    {
        // Instance method to get the user's Twitter Profile Details
        Task<JObject> GetTwitterProfile(Account e);

        // Instance method to post a Tweet message to the users Twitter
Feed
        Task<string> TweetMessage(string message, Account e);
    }
}
```

Now, let's start by taking a look at what we covered in the preceding code snippet:

1. We started by including references to the `System.Threading.Tasks`, `Newtonsoft.Json.Linq`, and `Xamarin.Auth` namespaces so that we can access the classes that are defined within these namespaces.

2. Next, we declared a `GetTwitterProfile` instance method, which will be responsible for asynchronously retrieving the Twitter profile details for the logged-in user.

3. Finally, we declared a `TweetMessage` instance method that will be responsible for asynchronously posting walk trail information to the logged-in Twitter user's feed.

Creating and implementing the TwitterWebService class

In this section, we will create the `TwitterWebService` class that will inherit from our `ITwitterWebService` interface and implement the underlying instance methods that we declared within our interface class. They will help us to communicate with our app that we created within the Twitter Developer Portal.

Let's start by creating the `TwitterWebService` class for our `TrackMyWalks` app by performing the following steps:

1. Firstly, right-click on the **Services** folder and choose **Add | New File...** from the pop-up menu.
2. Next, create a new **Empty Class** called `TwitterWebService` within the `Services` folder, as you did in the section entitled *Creating and implementing the TwitterAuthDetails class*, located within this chapter.
3. Then, ensure that the `TwitterWebService.cs` file, which is located within the `Services` folder, is displayed within the code editor, and enter the following code snippet:

```
//
//  TwitterWebService.cs
//  TwitterWebService Class that will communicate with the Twitter API
//
//  Created by Steven F. Daniel on 10/08/2018.
//  Copyright © 2018 GENIESOFT STUDIOS. All rights reserved.
//
using System;
using System.Collections.Generic;
using System.Net.Http;
using System.Threading.Tasks;
using Newtonsoft.Json.Linq;
using Xamarin.Auth;

namespace TrackMyWalks.Services
{
    public class TwitterWebService : ITwitterWebService
    {
        // Declare our HttpClient Manager objects
        HttpClient client;

        // Declare our Twitter Web Service Class Constructor
        public TwitterWebService()
        {
            client = new HttpClient();
            client.BaseAddress = new
Uri("https://api.twitter.com/1.1");
            client.MaxResponseContentBufferSize = 256000;
        }

        // Gets the users Twitter Profile Information using the
supplied
        // Account information
        public async Task<JObject> GetTwitterProfile(Account account)
```

```
        {
                // Construct our RequestUrl using our BaseAddress and the
Twitter API
                var RequestUrl = new
Uri(String.Format($"{client.BaseAddress}/account/
                                verify_credentials.json"));

                // Get our profile information using the RequestUrl and the
account
                // information of the user
                var oRequest = new OAuth1Request("GET", RequestUrl, null,
account);

                var response = await oRequest.GetResponseAsync();

                // Return the response object back to the caller
                return JObject.Parse(response?.GetResponseText());
        }

        // Sends a twitter message using the supplied Account
information
        public async Task<string> TweetMessage(string message, Account
account)
        {
                // Construct our RequestUrl using our BaseAddress and the
Twitter API
                var RequestUrl = new
Uri(String.Format($"{client.BaseAddress}/statuses/update.json"));

                // Add the Authentication headers that are required for the
request
                var oAuthData = new Dictionary<string, string>();
                oAuthData.Add("status", message);
                oAuthData.Add("trim_user", "1");

                // Post the Tweet, using the RequestUrl and oAuthData
header information
                var oRequest = new OAuth1Request("POST", RequestUrl,
oAuthData, account);
                var response = await oRequest.GetResponseAsync();

                // Return the response string back to the caller
                return response?.GetResponseText();
        }
    }
  }
```

Now, let's start by taking a look at what we covered in the preceding code snippet:

1. First, we started by including references to the `System.` namespaces, `Newtonsoft.Json.Linq` and `Xamarin.Auth`, so that we can access the classes that are defined within these namespaces.

2. Next, we needed to ensure that our `TwitterWebService` class inherits from the `ITwitterWebService` interface so that it can access the instance methods as well as any getters and setters.

3. Next, we declared a `client` variable, which will be used to create an `HttpClient` manager object. We can use this to perform HTTP requests. We also modified the `TwitterWebService` class constructor to set up and initialize our client object to a new instance of the `HttpClient` class and set the `BaseAddress` property to a new `Uri` object that will point to the Twitter endpoint.

4. Then, we set the `MaxResponseContentBufferSize` property on the `client` object, which is responsible for getting or setting the maximum number of bytes to buffer when reading the response content.

5. Next, we declared a `GetTwitterProfile` instance method that will be responsible for asynchronously retrieving the user's Twitter profile information using their `Account` details. We then created a `RequestUrl` variable that constructs our Twitter API endpoint using the `BaseAddress` of the `client` object and declared a `oRequest` object variable and called the `GET` method on our `OAuth1Request` class.

6. Next, we sent the `RequestUrl` to our `oRequest.GetResponseAsync` method to receive the response from the web service, and then parsed the `Result.GetResponseText` using the `JObject.Parse` method and returned the value.

7. Then, we declared a `TweetMessage` instance method that will be responsible for asynchronously retrieving the user's Twitter profile information using their `Account` details and creating a `RequestUrl` variable that constructs our Twitter API endpoint using the `BaseAddress` of the `client` object. We then declared a `oRequest` object variable and called the `POST` method on our `OAuth1Request` class.

8. Finally, we sent the `RequestUrl` to our `oRequest.GetResponseAsync` method to receive the response from the web service, and parsed the `response?.GetResponseText`, which will return the string value that was posted to Twitter.

Creating and implementing the TwitterSignInPageViewModel using C#

In this section, we'll take a look at how to create the `TwitterSignInPageViewModel` class so that it can communicate with our `TwitterSignInPage`, as well as any data bindings associated with the `ContentPage` that will be used by the `ViewModel`. We will create and implement the underlying C# code for our ViewModel, which will be used by our `TwitterSignInPage` code-behind file so that it can navigate within our `NavigationStack`.

Let's start by creating the `TwitterSignInPageViewModel` for our `TrackMyWalks` app by performing the following steps:

1. Ensure that the **TrackMyWalks** solution is open within the **Visual Studio for Mac** IDE.
2. Next, right-click on the `ViewModels` folder, and choose **Add | New File...** from the pop-up menu, as you did in the section entitled *Creating the WalksMainPageViewModel using C#* within Chapter 5, *MVVM and Data Binding*.
3. Then, ensure that the `TwitterSignInPageViewModel.cs` file, which is located within the `ViewModels` folder, is displayed within the code editor, and enter the following code snippet:

```
//
//   TwitterSignInPageViewModel.cs
//   The ViewModel for our TwitterSignInPage ContentPage
//
//   Created by Steven F. Daniel on 10/08/2018.
//   Copyright © 2018 GENIESOFT STUDIOS. All rights reserved.
//
using System.Threading.Tasks;
using TrackMyWalks.Services;

namespace TrackMyWalks.ViewModels
{
    public class TwitterSignInPageViewModel : BaseViewModel
    {
        public TwitterSignInPageViewModel(INavigationService
navService) :
                                           base(navService)
        {
        }
        // Instance method to initialise the TwitterSignInPageViewModel
        public override async Task Init()
```

```
            {
                await Task.Factory.StartNew(() =>
                {
                });
            }
        }
    }
```

Now, let's start by taking a look at what we covered in the preceding code snippet:

1. We started by including references to the `System.Threading.Tasks` namespace so that we can access the classes that are defined within this namespace. We have also included a reference to the `TrackMyWalks.Services` namespace so that we can access our `Navigation` object, which will enable us to navigate within the `NavigationStack`.

2. Next, we made sure that our `TwitterSignInPageViewModel` inherits from our `BaseViewModel` class and created the `Init` instance method that we defined within our `BaseViewModel` so that it can initialize our `TwitterSignInPageViewModel`.

Creating and implementing the user interface for the TwitterSignInPage

In this section, we will update the underlying C# code within our `TwitterSignInPage` code-behind file so that it can communicate with our `TwitterSignInPageViewModel`. This will be used as a container to display our Twitter sign in dialog that will use our `TwitterSignInPageRenderer PageRenderer`, which we will create as we progress throughout this chapter.

Let's start by creating the `TwitterSignInPage` interface for our `TrackMyWalks` app by performing the following steps:

1. Right-click on the `Services` folder and choose **Add | New File...** from the pop-up menu.

2. Next, create a new **Forms ContentPage XAML** class called `TwitterSignIn` within the `Views` folder, as you did in the section entitled *Creating the WalksMainPage interface using XAML*, located within `Chapter 4`, *Creating the TrackMyWalks Native App*.

3. Then, ensure that the `TwitterSignInPage.xaml.cs` file, which is located within the `Views` folder, is displayed within the code editor, and enter the following code snippet:

```
//
//  TwitterSignInPage.xaml.cs
//  Displays the Twitter Sign In Page using the Twitter API
//
//  Created by Steven F. Daniel on 10/08/2018
//  Copyright © 2018 GENIESOFT STUDIOS. All rights reserved.
//
using TrackMyWalks.Services;
using TrackMyWalks.ViewModels;
using Xamarin.Forms;

namespace TrackMyWalks.Views
{
    public partial class TwitterSignInPage : ContentPage
    {
        // Return the Binding Context for the ViewModel
        TwitterSignInPageViewModel _viewModel =>
                                BindingContext as
TwitterSignInPageViewModel;

        public TwitterSignInPage()
        {
            InitializeComponent();

            // Update the Title and Initialise our BindingContext for
the Page
            this.Title = "Track My Walks Twitter Sign In";
            this.BindingContext = new
TwitterSignInPageViewModel(DependencyService.
                                Get<INavigationService>());
        }

        // Method to initialise our View Model when the ContentPage
appears
        protected override async void OnAppearing()
        {
            base.OnAppearing();

            // Check to see if we have logged in and remove our Twitter
            // Sign In Page
            if (_viewModel != null && TwitterAuthDetails.isLoggedIn)
            {
                // Pops our Twitter Sign In Page from our Navigation
Stack
```

```
                      await Navigation.PopAsync();
                }
            }
        }
    }
```

Now, let's start by taking a look at what we covered in the preceding code snippet:

1. We started by including references to the `Xamarin.Forms` namespace so that we can access the classes that are defined within this namespace. We have included a reference to the `TrackMyWalks` namespaces so that we can access our `Navigation` methods and properties defined within our `BaseViewModel` class.

2. Next, we returned the `BindingContext` that will be used by our `TwitterSignInPage` `ContentPage` by returning the `TwitterSignInPageViewModel`. We also set the `Title` property of our `ContentPage` and set the `BindingContext` to a new instance of our `TwitterSignInPageViewModel` to use our `DependencyService` class, which will include our `INavigationService` interface.

3. Then, we created the `OnAppearing` method, which will be used to initialize our `ViewModel` whenever the `ContentPage` appears on screen. We checked to see whether our `_viewModel` contains a value, and we checked the `isLoggedIn` property that we declared within our `TwitterAuthDetails` class to see whether the user had logged into Twitter using our `TrackMyWalks` app.

4. Finally, if our `isLoggedIn` property contains a valid `AuthToken`, which we objected from Twitter, we proceed to remove our Twitter sign in page from our Navigation Stack.

Creating and implementing the TwitterSignInPageRenderer (iOS)

In this section, we'll take a look at how to create the `TwitterSignInPageRender` class for the iOS section of our `TrackMyWalks` solution, which will essentially contain platform-specific methods relating to the iOS platform. These will communicate with our Twitter API in order to display the Twitter sign in dialog within our `TwitterSignInPage` XAML `ContentPage`.

Let's start by creating the `TwitterSignInPageRenderer` class for our `TrackMyWalks` app by performing the following steps:

1. Ensure that the `TrackMyWalks` solution is open within the Visual Studio for Mac IDE.
2. Next, within the `TrackMyWalks.iOS` project, right-click on the **CustomRenderers** folder, and choose **Add | New File...** from the pop-up menu.
3. Then, create a new **Empty Class** called `TwitterSignInPageRenderer` within the `CustomRenderers` folder, as you did in the section entitled *Creating and implementing the CustomMapRenderer (iOS)* within `Chapter 7`, *Adding Location-Based Features Within Your App.*
4. Next, ensure that the `TwitterSignInPageRenderer.cs` file, which is located as part of the `TrackMyWalks.iOS` group, is displayed within the code editor, and enter the following code snippet:

```
//
//  TwitterSignInPageRenderer.cs
//  TrackMyWalks Twitter SignIn Page (iOS)
//
//  Created by Steven F. Daniel on 10/08/2018.
//  Copyright © 2018 GENIESOFT STUDIOS. All rights reserved.
//
using System;
using Xamarin.Forms;
using Xamarin.Forms.Platform.iOS;
using Xamarin.Auth;
using TrackMyWalks.iOS;
using TrackMyWalks.Views;
using TrackMyWalks.Services;

[assembly: ExportRenderer(typeof(TwitterSignInPage),
typeof(TwitterSignInPageRenderer))]
namespace TrackMyWalks.iOS
{
    public class TwitterSignInPageRenderer : PageRenderer
    {
        string oAuth_Token = String.Empty;
        string oAuth_Token_Secret = String.Empty;

        public override void ViewDidAppear(bool animated)
        {
            base.ViewDidAppear(animated);

            // Instance method that will display a Twitter Sign In Page
            var auth = new OAuth1Authenticator(
```

```
                    consumerKey: TwitterAuthDetails.ConsumerKey,
                    consumerSecret: TwitterAuthDetails.ConsumerSecret,
                    requestTokenUrl: new
Uri("https://api.twitter.com/oauth/request_token"),
                    authorizeUrl: new
Uri("https://api.twitter.com/oauth/authorize"),
                    accessTokenUrl: new
Uri("https://api.twitter.com/oauth/access_token"),
                    callbackUrl: new
Uri("https://mobile.twitter.com/home"));


                // Prevent displaying the Cancel button on the Twitter sign
on page
                auth.AllowCancel = false;


                // Define our completion handler once the user has
successfully signed in
                auth.Completed += (object sender,
AuthenticatorCompletedEventArgs e) =>
                {
                    if (e.IsAuthenticated)
                    {
                        e.Account.Properties.TryGetValue("oauth_token", out
oAuth_Token);
e.Account.Properties.TryGetValue("oauth_token_secret", out
oAuth_Token_Secret);

                        // Instantiate our class to Store our Twitter
Authentication Token
                        TwitterAuthDetails.StoreAuthToken(oAuth_Token);
TwitterAuthDetails.StoreTokenSecret(oAuth_Token_Secret);
                        TwitterAuthDetails.StoreAccountDetails(e.Account);
                    }
                    // Dismiss our Twitter Authentication UI Dialog
                    DismissViewController(true, () =>
                    {
                    });
                };
                PresentViewController(auth.GetUI(), true, null);
            }
        }
    }
```

Now, let's start by taking a look at what we covered in the preceding code snippet:

1. We started by including references to the `System`, `Xamarin.Forms`, and `TrackMyWalks` namespaces so that we can access the classes that are defined within these namespaces. You'll notice that we have also included a reference to the `Xamarin.Auth` namespace so that we can communicate with our Twitter platform by sending web service requests. We included a reference to the `ExportRenderer` assembly attribute to our class so that it can register the `PageRenderer` with `Xamarin.Forms`, and so that we can reference this within our `TwitterSignInPage`.

2. Next, we needed to ensure that our `TwitterSignInPageRenderer` class inherits from the `PageRenderer` class so that we can access each of the platform-specific method implementations of the `ViewRenderer` class. We also initialized the values for our `oAuth_Token` and `oAuth_Token_Secret` variables. We then proceeded to create and implement the `ViewDidAppear` method that will be called when the `ViewController` appears on screen, and we declared an `auth` variable that calls the `OAuth1Authenticator` class, which is responsible for managing the user interface and handling communication with Twitter authentication services.

3. Then, we passed in the API key values for our `consumerKey` and `consumerSecret`, which we can obtain for our app within the Twitter Developer Portal. We also provided values for `authorizeUrl`, `accessTokenUrl`, and `callbackUrl`, which will be called when we have successfully signed into Twitter. We set the `AllowCancel` property of our `auth` object to `false` to prevent our form from being dismissed by the user and started listening to the `Completed` event of the `OAuth1Authenticator` instance. Finally, we checked the `IsAuthenticated` property of the `AuthenticatorCompletedEventArgs` to determine whether the authentication succeeded.

4. Next, we obtained values for `oauth_token` and `oauth_token_secret` and stored them in the `StoreAuthToken` and `StoreTokenSecret` methods, along with the `Account` property of our `AuthenticatorCompletedEventArgs`, and stored these within the `StoreAccountDetails` method.

5. Finally, if we have determined that a successful login has happened, we make a call to the `DismissViewController` method to dismiss the currently presented Twitter UI. If we haven't determined that the user has signed in, we display the `PresentViewController` dialog, which is passing in the `auth.GetUI` method.

The Android version of the `TwitterSignInPageRenderer` is available in the companion source code for this book.

Updating the WalksMainPage code-behind using C#

Now that we have created the `TwitterSignInPageRenderer` class that will be responsible for displaying the Twitter UI dialog, our next step is to begin updating the underlying C# code within our `WalksMainPage` code-behind file. This will give it the ability to display our `TwitterSignInPage` ViewModel if we haven't determined that the user has signed in.

Let's take a look at how we can achieve this by following these steps:

1. Locate and open the `WalksMainPage.xaml.cs` file, which is located within the `Views` folder, ensuring that it is displayed within the code editor, and enter the following highlighted code sections:

```
//
//  WalksMainPage.xaml.cs
//  Displays Walk Information within a ListView control from an array
//
//  Created by Steven F. Daniel on 14/05/2018
//  Copyright © 2018 GENIESOFT STUDIOS. All rights reserved.
//
using System;
using TrackMyWalks.Models;
using TrackMyWalks.Services;
using TrackMyWalks.ViewModels;
using Xamarin.Forms;

namespace TrackMyWalks.Views
{
    public partial class WalksMainPage : ContentPage
    {
        // Return the Binding Context for the ViewModel
        WalksMainPageViewModel _viewModel =>
                            BindingContext as
WalksMainPageViewModel;

        public WalksMainPage()
```

```
        {
            InitializeComponent();
            ...
            ...
        }
        ...
        ...
        // Method to initialise our View Model when the ContentPage
appears
        protected override async void OnAppearing()
        {
            base.OnAppearing();

            // Perform a check to see if we have logged into Twitter
already
            if (_viewModel != null)
            {
                // Call the Init method to initialise the ViewModel
                await _viewModel.Init();

                if (!TwitterAuthDetails.isLoggedIn)
                {
                    // We need to Navigate and display our Twitter Sign
In Page
                    await
_viewModel.Navigation.NavigateTo<TwitterSignInPageViewModel>();
                }
            }
            ...
            ...
```

In the preceding code snippet, we started by modifying the OnAppearing method that will check the isLoggedIn property within our TwitterAuthDetails class to determine whether the user has already signed into our app, and then navigated to our TwitterSignInPageViewModel using the Navigation property of our _viewModel and the NavigateTo instance method.

Updating the WalkDistancePage user unterface using XAML

In this section, we will update the user interface for our `WalkDistancePage` in order to modify our `ToolbarItem`, since we will need to display additional items when retrieving Twitter profile information and posting Tweets to the users Twitter feed. Within our code-behind file, we will use the `DisplayActionSheet` method to display a list of choices that the user can choose from so that they can retrieve profile information, post tweets, and end the current trail in progress.

Let's start by updating the user interface for our `WalkDistancePage` by performing the following steps:

1. Locate and open the `WalkDistancePage.xaml` file, which is located within the **Views** folder, ensuring that it is displayed within the code editor, and enter the following highlighted code sections:

```xml
<?xml version="1.0" encoding="UTF-8"?>
<ContentPage xmlns="http://xamarin.com/schemas/2014/forms"
             xmlns:x="http://schemas.microsoft.com/winfx/2009/xaml"
             xmlns:local="clr-
namespace:TrackMyWalks.Views.MapOverlay;assembly=TrackMyWalks"
             x:Class="TrackMyWalks.Views.WalkDistancePage">
    <ContentPage.ToolbarItems>
        <ToolbarItem Text="Options" Clicked="OptionsButton_Clicked"/>
    </ContentPage.ToolbarItems>
    <ContentPage.Content>
         . . .
         . . .
    </ContentPage.Content>
</ContentPage>
```

2. Next, locate and open the `WalkDistancePage.xaml.cs` file, which is located in the `Views` folder, ensuring that it is displayed within the code editor, and enter the following highlighted code sections:

```
//
//  WalkDistancePage.xaml.cs
//  Displays related trail information within a map using a pin
placeholder
//
//  Created by Steven F. Daniel on 14/05/2018
//  Copyright © 2018 GENIESOFT STUDIOS. All rights reserved.
//
```

```
using System;
using Plugin.Geolocator.Abstractions;
using TrackMyWalks.Services;
using TrackMyWalks.ViewModels;
using Xamarin.Forms;
using Xamarin.Forms.Maps;
using System.Threading.Tasks;
using TrackMyWalks.Views.MapOverlay;
using System.Text;

namespace TrackMyWalks.Views
{
    public partial class WalkDistancePage : ContentPage
    {
        // Return the Binding Context for the ViewModel
        WalkDistancePageViewModel _viewModel =>
                                BindingContext as
WalkDistancePageViewModel;

        // Create a variable that will store our original saved
Position
        Task<Plugin.Geolocator.Abstractions.Position> origPosition;

        // Create a TwitterObject variable that will contain an
instance to
        // our TwitterWebService class
        TwitterWebService TwitterObject;

        public WalkDistancePage()
        {
            InitializeComponent();

            // Create an instance to our TwitterWebService class
            TwitterObject = new TwitterWebService();
            ...
            ...
        }
            ...
            ...
        // Instance method that presents the user with additional
options
        public async void OptionsButton_Clicked(object sender,
EventArgs e)
        {
            // Display our Action Sheet with a list of choices for the
user to choose
            var action = await DisplayActionSheet("What would you like
to do?",
```

```
                                              "Cancel", null,
                                              "Show Twitter
Profile",

                                              "Post Twitter
Message",

                                              "End Current Trail");
                switch (action)
                {
                    case "Show Twitter Profile":
                        ShowTwitterProfile();
                        break;
                    case "Post Twitter Message":
                        PostTwitterMessage();
                        break;
                    case "End Current Trail":
                        EndTrailButton_Clicked(sender, e);
                        break;
                }
            }
            // Instance method to get our Twitter Profile Details
            public async void ShowTwitterProfile()
            {
                // Call our Instance method to get the user's Twitter
Profile Details
                var ProfileInfo = await TwitterObject.GetTwitterProfile(
                                    TwitterAuthDetails.AuthAccount);

                // Construct our message to display within an alert dialog
                var profileDetails = new StringBuilder();
                profileDetails.AppendFormat("\nId: {0}",
                            ProfileInfo.GetValue("id"));
                profileDetails.AppendFormat("\nName: {0}",
                            ProfileInfo.GetValue("name"));
                profileDetails.AppendFormat("\nScreen Name: {0}",
                            ProfileInfo.GetValue("screen_name"));
                profileDetails.AppendFormat("\nLocation: {0}",
                            ProfileInfo.GetValue("location"));
                profileDetails.AppendFormat("\nDescription: {0}",
                            ProfileInfo.GetValue("description"));
                profileDetails.AppendFormat("\nFriends: {0}",
                            ProfileInfo.GetValue("friends_count"));
                profileDetails.AppendFormat("\nFollowers: {0}",
                            ProfileInfo.GetValue("followers_count"));
                profileDetails.AppendFormat("\nFavourites: {0}",
                            ProfileInfo.GetValue("favourites_count"));
                profileDetails.AppendFormat("\nurl: {0}",
                            ProfileInfo.GetValue("url"));
```

```
            // Display an alert dialog with the user's profile details
            await DisplayAlert("Twitter Profile Details",
                               profileDetails.ToString(), "OK");
        }

        // Instance method to allow the user to post a message to their
Twitter Feed
        public async void PostTwitterMessage()
        {
            // Construct our message to post to the users Twitter Feed
            var sbMessage = new StringBuilder();
            sbMessage.AppendLine("Track My Walks - Trail Details");
            sbMessage.AppendFormat("\nTitle: {0}",
App.SelectedItem.Title);
            sbMessage.AppendFormat("\nDistance: {0}",
App.SelectedItem.Distance);
            sbMessage.AppendFormat("\nDifficulty: {0}",
App.SelectedItem.Difficulty);
            sbMessage.AppendFormat("\nImageURL: {0}",
App.SelectedItem.ImageUrl);

            // Call our Instance method to Tweet the message to the
            // users twitter page. We need to truncate our string so
that it
            // is within the Twitter allowable message constraints
            var tweet = sbMessage.ToString().Substring(0, 128);
            var response = TwitterObject.TweetMessage(tweet,
TwitterAuthDetails.AuthAccount);

            // Display an alert dialog to let the user know their
message
            // has been posted.
            await DisplayAlert("Posted to Twitter",
                               "Trail Information has been posted.",
"OK");
        }
        // Instance method to terminate the current Trail
        public async void EndTrailButton_Clicked(object sender,
EventArgs e)
        {
            // Initialise our Selected Item property
            App.SelectedItem = null;

            // Stop listening for location updates prior to navigating
            _viewModel.OnStopUpdate();

            // Navigate back to the Track My Walks Listing Page
            await _viewModel.Navigation.BackToMainPage();
```

}

Now, let's start by taking a look at what we defined within our XAML and code snippet:

1. First, we started by modifying the `ToolbarItem` within the `ContentPage.ToolbarItems` section, and provided values for the `Text` property. We also updated the `Clicked` property to call our `OptionsButton_Clicked` instance method declared within our `WalkDistancePage` code-behind so as to display a list of choices for the user to choose from.

2. Then, we included a reference to our `System.Text` namespace so that we can access the classes that are defined within these namespaces, which we will use for our `StringBuilder` class.

3. Next, within our `WalkDistancePage` class constructor, we created a `TwitterObject` variable, which will be used to create an instance to our `TwitterWebService` class, and create a `OptionsButton_Clicked` instance method that will display an `ActionSheet` with a list of choices for the user to choose from when the `Options` button is clicked within our `WalkDistancePage` XAML `ContentPage`.

4. Then, we created the `ShowTwitterProfile` instance method, which will be used to get the Twitter profile details for the logged-in user, and call our `GetTwitterProfile` method within our `TwitterWebService` class and pass in the `AuthAcount` details for the user. We used the `StringBuilder` class to construct the information that we would like to display about the user and displayed this within an alert dialog using the `DisplayAlert` class.

5. Next, we created the `PostTwitterMessage` instance method that will be used to post a message to the user's Twitter feed for the logged-in user. We used the `StringBuilder` class to construct information about the current walk that we would like to post, and created a `tweet` variable to truncate the string so that it is within Twitter's allowable message length of 128 characters.

6. Finally, we called our `TweetMessage` method within our `TwitterWebService` class and passed in our tweet message variable as well as the `AuthAcount` details for the user, and displayed an alert dialog using the `DisplayAlert` class to let the user know that their message has been posted.

Registering the TwitterSignInPage within the App.xaml class

Now that we have successfully updated each of our `ViewModels` and `ContentPages` to take advantage of our `TwitterSignInPage` and our `TwitterWebService`, our next step is to make additional changes within our `OnStart` method in order to register our `TwitterSignInPage` and `TwitterSignInPageViewModel` within our `NavigationService`. We are doing this so that we can navigate between each of our `ViewModels`.

Let's take a look at how we can achieve this by following these steps:

1. Locate and open the `App.xaml.cs` file, which is located in the `TrackMyWalks` project folder, ensuring that it is displayed within the code editor, and enter the following highlighted code sections:

```
//
//  App.xaml.cs
//  Main class that gets called whenever our TrackMyWalks app is
started
//
//  Created by Steven F. Daniel on 14/05/2018
//  Copyright © 2018 GENIESOFT STUDIOS. All rights reserved.
//
using System;
using System.Threading.Tasks;
using TrackMyWalks.Models;
using TrackMyWalks.Services;
using TrackMyWalks.ViewModels;
using TrackMyWalks.Views;
using Xamarin.Forms;
using Xamarin.Forms.Xaml;

[assembly: XamlCompilation(XamlCompilationOptions.Compile)]
namespace TrackMyWalks
{
    public partial class App : Application
    {
        public App()
        {
            InitializeComponent();
            ...
            ...
        }
        protected override void OnStart()
```

```
            {
                ...
                ...
                // Register each of our View Models on our Navigation Stack
NavService.RegisterViewMapping(typeof(WalksMainPageViewModel),
                                        typeof(WalksMainPage));
NavService.RegisterViewMapping(typeof(WalkEntryPageViewModel),
                                        typeof(WalkEntryPage));
NavService.RegisterViewMapping(typeof(WalkTrailInfoPageViewModel),
                                        typeof(WalkTrailInfoPage));
NavService.RegisterViewMapping(typeof(WalkDistancePageViewModel),
                                        typeof(WalkDistancePage));
NavService.RegisterViewMapping(typeof(TwitterSignInPageViewModel),
                                        typeof(TwitterSignInPage));
            }
            // Declare our SelectedItem property that will store our Walk
Trail details
            public static WalkDataModel SelectedItem { get; set; }
            // Declare our NavService property that will be used to
navigate between ViewModels
            public static NavigationService NavService { get; set; }

            #region Twitter Sign In Page Property and Instance methods to
remove
                    and Navigate (Android Only)
            // Action property method to remove our TwitterSignInPage from
            // the NavigationStack
            public static Action RemoveTwitterSignInPage =>
                            new Action(() =>
NavService.XFNavigation.PopAsync());

            // Navigate to our WalksMainPage, once we have successfully
signed in
            public async static Task NavigateToWalksMainPage()
            {
                await NavService.XFNavigation.PushAsync(new
WalksMainPage());
            }
            #endregion
            ...
            ...
        }
    }
```

Now, let's start by taking a look at what we covered in the preceding code snippet:

1. We started by calling the `RegisterViewMapping` instance method on the `NavService` property to register our `TwitterSignInPage` and `TwitterSignInPageViewModel` on our navigation stack.

2. Next, we declared a `RemoveTwitterSignInPage` property to call the `PopAsync` method on our `XFNavigation` property that is contained within our `NavService` class in order to remove our `TwitterSignInPageViewModel` from the navigation stack.

3. Finally, we created the `NavigateToWalksMainPage` instance method, which will call the `PushAsync` method on our `XFNavigation` property that is contained within our `NavService` class, in order to push our `WalksMainPage` `ContentPage` onto our navigation stack.

Now that you have finished creating the `TwitterWebService`, and have updated all of the required XAML pages, including making the necessary changes to the `ViewModels` and `ContentPages` to take advantage of our `TwitterWebService` class, our next step is to compile, build, and run our application within the iOS Simulator.

Launching the TrackMyWalks app using the iOS simulator

In this section, we will compile, build, and run the `TrackMyWalks` application to see how our application looks. We have made considerable changes to our `TrackMyWalks` application to include social networking features that will communicate with the Twitter APIs using our `TwitterWebService` class.

Let's see how we can achieve this by performing the following steps:

1. Ensure you have chosen the **Debug | iPhoneSimulator** option from the drop-down menu.
2. Next, choose your preferred device from the list of available iOS Simulators.

3. Then, select the **Run | Start Debugging** menu option, as shown in the following screenshot:

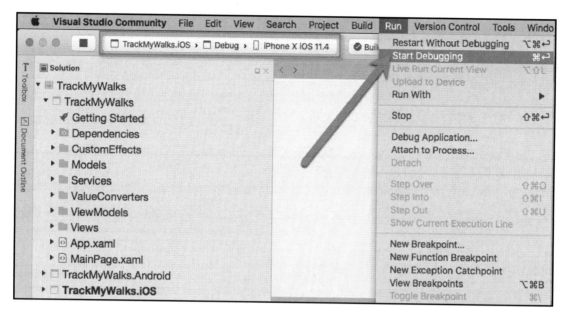

Launching the TrackMyWalks app within the iOS Simulator

4. Alternatively, you can also build and run the `TrackMyWalks` application by pressing the *Command + Return* key combinations. When the compilation is complete, the iOS Simulator will appear automatically and the `TrackMyWalks` application will be displayed, as shown in the following screenshot:

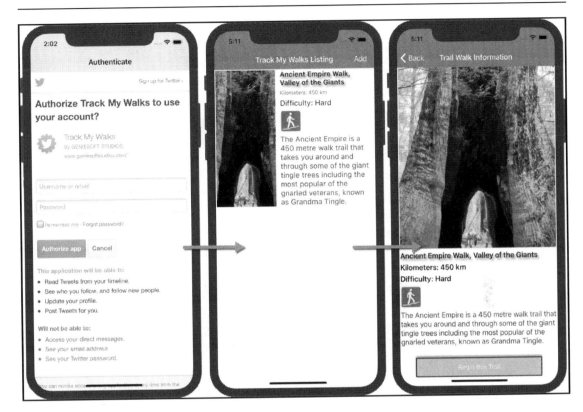

Displays the Twitter Authentication SignIn Screen

The preceding screenshot displays our `TrackMyWalks` application along with our **Twitter Sign In Page**, which asks the user if they would like to **Authorize Track My Walks to use your account?**

In order to proceed, you will need to provide your login credentials and click on the **Authorize app** button. Upon successfully determining that your login credentials have been validated by Twitter, you will then see the **Track My Walks Listing** page displayed, along with the **Trail Walk Information** page whenever an item has been selected within the **Track My Walks Listing** screen:

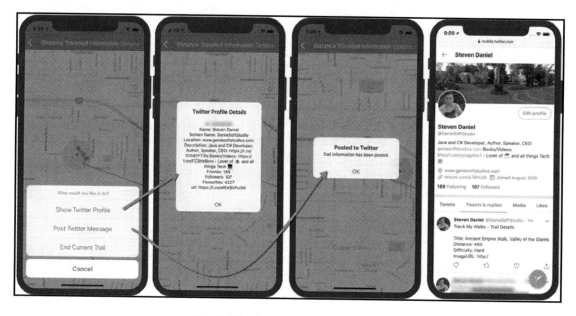

Twitter Profile Details and Posting to the users Twitter Feed

The preceding screenshot displays the **Distance Travelled Information** page, with the trail walk that you chose on the previous screen. Clicking on the **Options** button will display a pop-up dialog, asking the user to choose from a list of options. If the user clicks on the **Show Twitter Profile** button, it will display the **Twitter Profile Details** within a dialog. If you click on the **Post Twitter Message** button, it will post the current walk trail information to the user's Twitter feed, as can be seen in the final screen. Alternatively, clicking on the **End Current Trail** button will end the trail and take the user back to the **Track My Walks Listing** page, as can be seen in the previous screenshot.

Summary

In this chapter, you learned how to apply for a Twitter developer account so that you can incorporate social networking features by creating and registering our `TrackMyWalks` app within the Twitter Developer Portal. You then incorporated the `Xamarin.Auth` NuGet package within our solution and created a `TwitterService` Interface and Class that we can use to communicate with the Twitter APIs using RESTful web service calls. Next, you created the `TwitterSignInPage`, along with the associated `TwitterSignInPageViewModel` and `TwitterSignInPageRenderer` classes, so that users can sign into your app using their Twitter credentials. You updated the `WalksMainPage` code-behind to call our `TwitterSignInPage` to check whether the user has signed in.

Finally, you made changes to our `WalkDistancePage` XAML and code-behind so that we can utilize our `TwitterService` class to display profile information, as well as post information about the trail to the user's Twitter feed.

In the final chapter, you'll learn how to create and run unit tests using the `NUnit` and `UITest` frameworks. You will also learn how to write unit tests for our `ViewModels`, which will essentially test the business logic to validate that everything is working correctly. After this, we will move on to learning how to use the `UITest` framework to perform testing on the `TrackMyWalks` user interfaces by using Automated Testing.

13
Unit Testing Your Xamarin.Forms Apps

In the previous chapter, you learned how to apply for a Twitter developer account so that you could incorporate social networking features by creating and registering our `TrackMyWalks` app within the Twitter Developer Portal. You then incorporated the `Xamarin.Auth` NuGet package within our solution and created a `TwitterService` Interface and Class that we can use to communicate with the Twitter APIs using RESTful web service calls. You created a `TwitterSignInPage`, as well as the associated `TwitterSignInPageViewModel` and `TwitterSignInPageRenderer` classes, so that users can sign into your app using their Twitter credentials.

Finally, you updated the `WalksMainPage` code-behind to call our `TwitterSignInPage` to check to see whether the user has signed in, as well as made changes to our `WalkDistancePage` XAML and code-behind so that we can utilize our `TwitterService` class to display profile information and post information about the trail to the user's Twitter feed.

In this final chapter, you will learn how to create and run each of your unit tests using the `Xunit` and `Xamarin.UITest` frameworks. You will also learn how to write unit tests for our `ViewModels`, which will essentially test the business logic to validate that everything is working correctly. After this, we will move on to learning how to use the `Xamarin.UITest` framework to perform testing on the `TrackMyWalks` user interfaces by using automated UI testing.

This chapter will cover the following topics:

- Creating a new Unit Testing project within the `TrackMyWalks` solution
- Incorporating the `Moq` NuGet package into our `TrackMyWalks.UnitTests` project
- Creating and implementing the `WalksMainPageViewModelTest` class using C#

- Creating and implementing the `WalkEntryPageViewModelTest` class using C#
- Creating a new `Xamarin.UITest` project within our `TrackMyWalks` solution
- Understanding the most commonly used `UITest testing` methods
- Creating and implementing the `CreateNewTrailDetails` class using C#
- Updating the `WalksMainPage` code-behind using C#
- Adding the `Xamarin.TestCloud.Agent` NuGet package to our `TrackMyWalks.iOS` project
- Updating the `AppDelegate` class within the `TrackMyWalks.iOS` project
- Running your unit tests and UI tests using the Visual Studio for Mac IDE

Creating the Unit Testing project within the TrackMyWalks solution

During the development of our `TrackMyWalks` application, we have designed the user interfaces using the XAML markup language, as well as created each of our `ViewModels` and `ContentPages`, as well as the required class files for handling the navigation between each of our `ViewModels`. We also obtained the user's GPS coordinates and handling communication with Microsoft Azure App Services and Twitter using their APIs.

In this section, we will begin by creating a unit testing project for our `TrackMyWalks` application so that we can run these independently from our `TrackMyWalks` iOS and Android projects. One of the great benefits of using Visual Studio or Visual Studio for Mac to handle your Unit Tests is that they leverage the popular `NUnit` testing framework for performing unit tests.

Let's take a look at how we can achieve this by performing the following steps:

1. First, ensure that the `TrackMyWalks` solution is open within the Visual Studio for Mac IDE.
2. Next, right-click on the `TrackMyWalks` solution and choose **Add | Add New Project...** from the pop-up menu, as shown in the following screenshot:

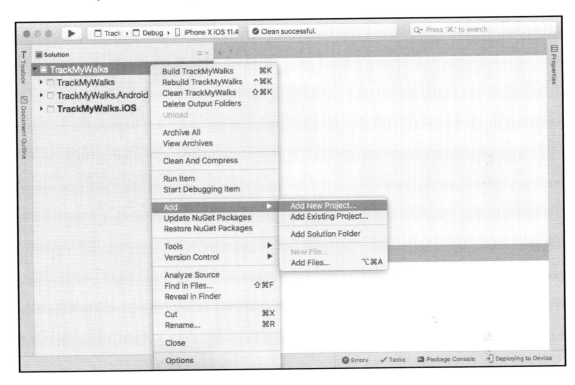

Adding a New Project to the TrackMyWalks Solution

3. Then, choose the **xUnit Test Project** option located under the **Multiplatform |
Tests** section, ensuring that you have selected **C#** as the programming language
to use:

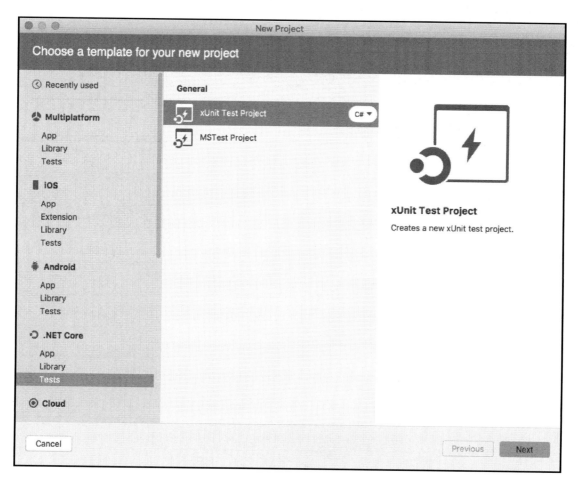

Creating a new xUnit Test Project

4. Then, click on the **Next** button to proceed to the next step in the wizard and accept the default **Target Framework** to use (this will be displayed by default), as shown in the following screenshot:

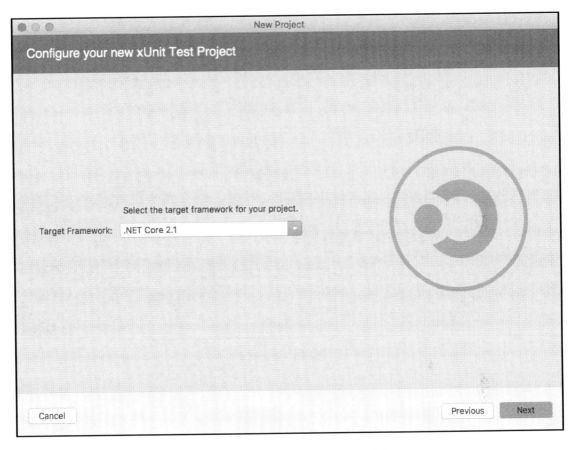

Configuring the Target Framework to use for the xUnit Test Project

5. Then, enter `TrackMyWalks.UnitTests` to use as the name for your new project in the **Project Name** field, as shown in the following screenshot:

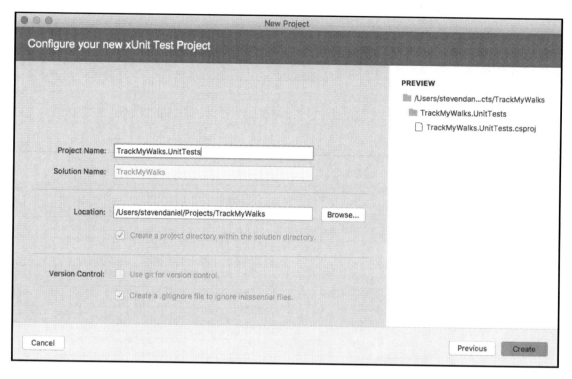

Configuring the xUnit Test Project

6. Finally, click on the **Create** button to proceed with the creation of your project at the specified location.

Now that we have successfully created the `TrackMyWalks.UnitTests` project within our `TrackMyWalks` solution, our next step is to begin adding the `Moq` NuGet package to our `TrackMyWalks.UnitTests` project.

Adding the Moq NuGet package to the TrackMyWalks.UnitTests project

In this section, we will begin by adding the Moq (pronounced as Mock) NuGet package to our `TrackMyWalks.UnitTests` project. The Moq library is essentially one of the most popular mocking frameworks that is available for the .NET platform, and we will be using it to help us test our `ViewModels` for our `TrackMyWalks` application.

Let's take a look at how we can achieve this by performing the following steps:

1. Right-click on the **Dependencies|NuGet** folder, which is located within the `TrackMyWalks.UnitTests` project, and choose the **Add Packages...** menu option, as you did in the section entitled *Adding the Newtonsoft.Json NuGet package to our solution* within `Chapter 11`, *Incorporating Microsoft Azure App Services:*

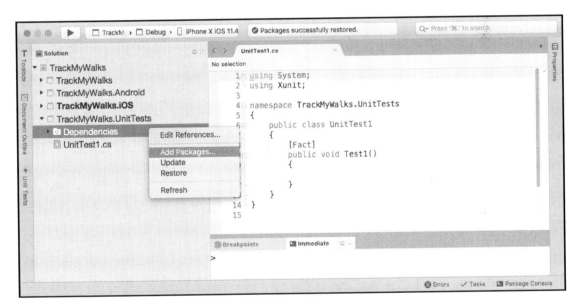

Adding a new Dependency to the TrackMyWalks.UnitTests Project

2. Next, within the **Search** field located within the **Add Packages** dialog, you need to enter Moq and select the **Moq** option within the list, as shown in the following screenshot:

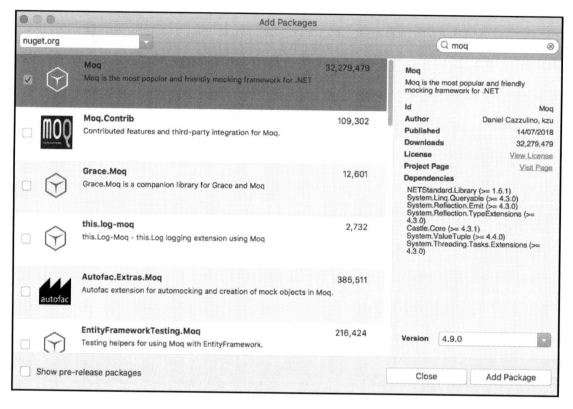

Adding the Moq NuGet Package to the TrackMyWalks.UnitTests Project

3. Then, make sure that you choose the latest version to install from the drop-down list for the **Version** field (*this will be displayed by default*).

4. Finally, click on the **Add Package** button to add the Moq NuGet package to the TrackMyWalks.UnitTests project.

Now that you have added the Moq NuGet package, we can begin utilizing this control when we start creating and writing the test case scenarios for our each of our unit tests, which we will cover as we progress through this chapter.

Adding the TrackMyWalks project to the TrackMyWalks.UnitTests project

In this section, since we will be creating unit tests that will be used to perform testing on our `ViewModels`, we will need to ensure that we have added a reference to our **TrackMyWalks** project within the `TrackMyWalks.UnitTests` project.

Let's take a look at how we can achieve this by performing the following steps:

1. Right-click on the `Dependencies` folder and choose **Edit References...** from the pop-up menu, as shown in the following screenshot:

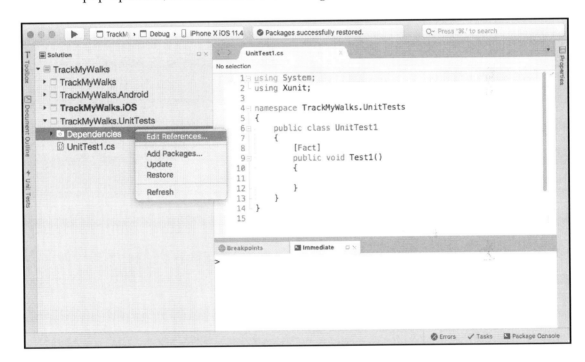

Adding the TrackMyWalks Project to the TrackMyWalks.UnitTests Project

2. Next, select the `TrackMyWalks` project by clicking on the checkbox, which will essentially include both our iOS and Android platform projects, as shown in the following screenshot:

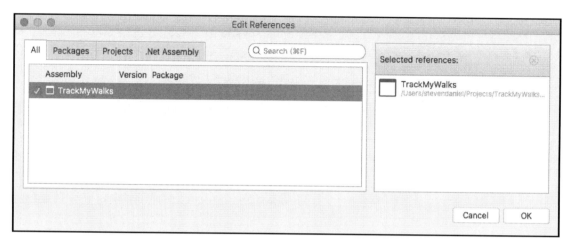

Including the TrackMyWalks Project for both the iOS and Android Platforms

3. Finally, click on the **OK** button so that it will add the `TrackMyWalks` project to our `TrackMyWalks.UnitTests` project.

Creating and implementing the WalksMainPageViewModelTest class

In this section, we'll take a look at how to create the `WalksMainPageViewModelTest` class, which will essentially check to see when our `ViewModel` passes or fails under different test scenarios.

Let's see how we can achieve this by performing the following steps:

1. Right-click on the `TrackMyWalks.UnitTests` project, choose **Add | New File...** from the pop-up menu, and choose the **Empty Class** option under the **General** section.

2. Next, enter `WalksMainPageViewModelTest` for the name of the class to be created, as shown in the following screenshot:

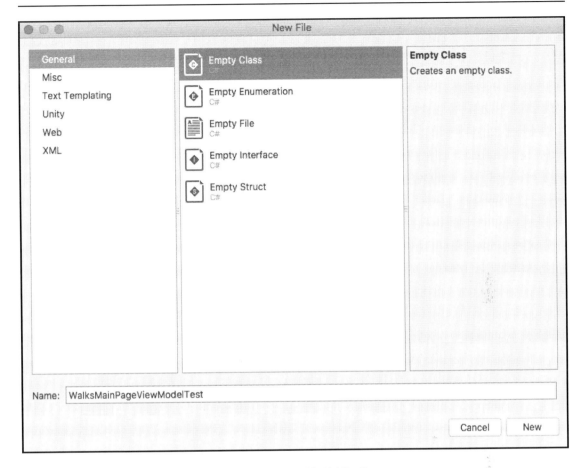

Creating the WalksMainPageViewModelTest Class

3. Then, click on the **New** button to proceed and create the new class. Then, with the `WalksMainPageViewModelTest.cs` file open, enter the following code snippet:

```
//
//   WalksMainPageViewModelTest.cs
//   Unit Test of the WalksMainPageViewModel
//
//   Created by Steven F. Daniel on 14/08/2018
//   Copyright © 2018 GENIESOFT STUDIOS. All rights reserved.
//
using System.Threading.Tasks;
using Moq;
using TrackMyWalks.Services;
using TrackMyWalks.ViewModels;
```

```
using Xunit;

namespace TrackMyWalks.UnitTest
{
    public class WalksMainPageViewModelTest
    {
        [Fact]
        public async Task CheckIfWalkEntryIsNotNull()
        {
            var navMock = new Mock<INavigationService>().Object;
            var viewModel = new WalksMainPageViewModel(navMock);
            // Arrange
            viewModel.WalksListModel = null;
            // Act
            await viewModel.GetWalkTrailItems();
            // Assert
            Assert.NotNull(viewModel.WalksListModel);
        }
    }
}
```

Now, let's start by taking a look at what we covered in the preceding code snippet:

1. First, we included references to the `System.Threading.Tasks`, `Moq`, and `Xunit` namespaces so that we have access to the class method implementations that are defined within these namespaces. You'll notice that we have also included references to both our `TrackMyWalks.Services` and `TrackMyWalks.ViewModels` namespaces so that we can access our `ViewModels` and `NavigationService` class.

2. Next, within the `WalksMainPageViewModelTest` class, we defined the `[Fact]` attribute, which is part of the `Xunit` namespace, to indicate that our method should be run by the `Xunit` Test Runner component. Then, we created our `CheckIfWalkEntryIsNotNull` instance method that will handle asynchronous calls and be responsible for performing a test to see if our `WalksListModel` contains valid items.

3. Then, we declared a `navMock` variable instance of the `Mock` class that is contained within our `Moq` library to create a new instance of our `INavigationService` interface, and then we initialized our `WalksListModel` to `null`.

4. Next, we called the `GetWalkTrailItems` instance method that is contained within our `ViewModel` to communicate with our Microsoft Azure App Services using RESTful webservice API calls in order to return a list of all walk items that are contained within the `WalkEntries` table.

5. Finally, we used the `NotNull` method on the `Assert` class to determine if the `WalksListModel` contains items which will render the test as passing or failing.

 The `[Fact]` attribute indicates that our method should be run by the Xunit Test Runner component. To find out more information about the `Assert` class, refer to the Microsoft Developer documentation at `https://msdn.microsoft.com/en-us/library/microsoft.visualstudio.testtools.unittesting.assert.aspx`.

Creating and implementing the WalksEntryPageViewModelTest class

In this section, we'll take a look at how to create the `WalkEntryPageViewModelTest` class that will be used for our second unit test to ensure that our `ViewModel` is properly initialized after the `Init` instance method is called to determine if our unit test passes or fails under each of the different test conditions.

Let's see how we can achieve this by performing the following steps:

1. Right-click on the `TrackMyWalks.UnitTests` project and choose **Add | New File...** from the pop-up menu. Then, choose the **Empty Class** option under the **General** section, as you did in the section entitled *Creating and implementing the WalksMainPageViewModelTest* located within this chapter.

2. Next, enter `WalkEntryPageViewModelTest` for the name of the class to be created and click on the **New** button to proceed. Then, with the `WalkEntryPageViewModelTest.cs` file open, enter the following code snippet:

```
//
//  WalkEntryPageViewModelTest.cs
//  Unit Test of the WalkEntryPageViewModel
//
//  Created by Steven F. Daniel on 14/08/2018
//  Copyright © 2018 GENIESOFT STUDIOS. All rights reserved.
//
using System.Threading.Tasks;
using Moq;
using TrackMyWalks.Services;
using TrackMyWalks.ViewModels;
using Xunit;

namespace TrackMyWalks.UnitTest
```

```
    {
        public class WalkEntryPageViewModelTest
        {
            [Fact]
            public async Task CheckIfEntryTitleIsEqual()
            {
                var navMock = new Mock<INavigationService>().Object;
                var viewModel = new WalkEntryPageViewModel(navMock);
                // Arrange
                viewModel.Title = "New Walk Entry";
                // Act
                await viewModel.Init();
                // Assert
                Assert.Equal("New Walk Entry", viewModel.Title);
            }
            [Fact]
            public async Task CheckIfDifficultyIsEqual()
            {
                var navMock = new Mock<INavigationService>().Object;
                var viewModel = new WalkEntryPageViewModel(navMock);
                // Arrange
                viewModel.Difficulty = "Easy";
                // Act
                await viewModel.Init();
                // Assert
                Assert.Equal("Hard", viewModel.Difficulty);
            }
            [Fact]
            public async Task CheckIfDistanceIsNotEqual()
            {
                var navMock = new Mock<INavigationService>().Object;
                var viewModel = new WalkEntryPageViewModel(navMock);
                // Arrange
                viewModel.Distance = 256;
                // Act
                await viewModel.Init();
                // Assert
                Assert.NotEqual("0", viewModel.Difficulty);
            }
        }
    }
```

Now, let's start by taking a look at what we covered in the preceding code snippet:

1. First, we included references to the `System.Threading.Tasks`, `Moq`, and `Xunit` namespaces, so we have access to the class method implementations that are defined within these namespaces. You'll notice that we have also included references to our `TrackMyWalks.Services` and `TrackMyWalks.ViewModels` namespaces, so that we can access our `ViewModels` and `NavigationService` class.

2. Next, within the `WalkEntryPageViewModelTest` class, we defined the `[Fact]` attribute to indicate that our method should be run by the `Xunit` Test Runner component. Then, we created our `CheckIfEntryTitleIsEqual` instance method that will handle asynchronous calls as well as perform a test to see if the `Title` property contained within our `WalkEntryPageViewModel` is equal. We then declared a `navMock` variable instance of the `Mock` class that is contained within our `Moq` library in order to create a new instance of our `INavigationService` interface.

3. Then, we initialized the `Title` property within our `ViewModel` to the value that we want to check and called the `Init` instance method. We then used the `Equal` method on the `Assert` class to determine after our `ViewModel` was initialized whether the `Title` property matches the value we want to check to determine if our test passes or fails.

4. Next, we created our `CheckIfDifficultyIsEqual` instance method that will handle asynchronous calls as well as perform a test to see if the `Difficulty` property is equal. We declared a `navMock` variable instance of the `Mock` class that is contained within our `Moq` library, to create a new instance of our `INavigationService` interface.

5. Then, we initialized the `Title` property within our ViewModel to the value that we want to check, prior to calling the `Init` instance method, and used the `Equal` method on the `Assert` class to determine if the `Difficulty` property matches the value we want to check. We do this to determine if our test passes or fails.

6. Next, we created our `CheckIfDistanceIsNotEqual` instance method that will handle asynchronous calls as well as perform a test to see if the `Distance` property is equal. We declared a `navMock` variable instance of the `Mock` class that is contained within our `Moq` library to create a new instance of our `INavigationService` interface.

7. Finally, we initialized the `Distance` property within our `ViewModel` to the value that we want to check, prior to calling the `Init` instance method, and used the `NotEqual` method on the `Assert` class to determine if the `Distance` property matches the value we want to check. We do this to determine if our test passes or fails.

You will notice that for each of the unit tests that we created in the preceding code snippets, they were presented with the `[Fact]` attribute, as well as the Arrange-Act-Assert pattern. The following table provides a brief description of what each of the Arrange-Act-Assert patterns are used for:

Pattern	Description
Arrange	The Arrange test pattern will essentially perform all of the setting up and initialization conditions for your test.
Act	The Act test pattern will ensure that your test will successfully interact with the application.
Assert	The Assert test pattern will examine the results of the actions that were initially performed within the Act step to verify the results.

 For more information on the Arrange-Act-Assert pattern, refer to the Unit Testing Enterprise Apps documentation at `https://docs.microsoft.com/en-us/xamarin/xamarin-forms/enterprise-application-patterns/unit-testing`.

Now that you have created your unit tests and have a reasonably good understanding of what each of the Arrange-Act-Assert patterns are, our next step is to begin running our unit tests within the Visual Studio for Mac IDE.

Running unit tests within the Visual Studio for Mac IDE

In this section, we will take a look at how we can use the Visual Studio for Mac IDE to run each of our unit tests, containing the various test conditions that we created in the previous sections. The advantage of running these tests within Visual Studio for Mac is that you can see if your unit tests pass or fail, as well as the reasons behind it.

Let's take a look at how we can achieve this by performing the following steps:

1. First, ensure that you have chosen the **Debug** option from the drop-down menu.
2. Next, select the **Run | Run Unit Tests** menu option, as shown in the following screenshot:

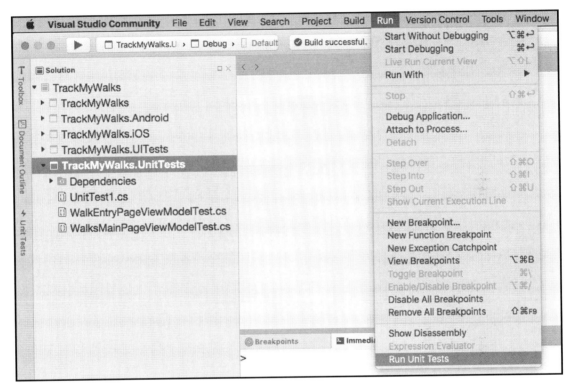

Running the Unit Tests using the Visual Studio for Mac IDE

When the compilation of the unit tests is complete, you will be presented with the outcome of each of the test results, which can be filtered by which were **Successful Tests**, **Failed Tests**, or **Ignored Tests** within the **Test Results** pane, as shown in the following screenshot:

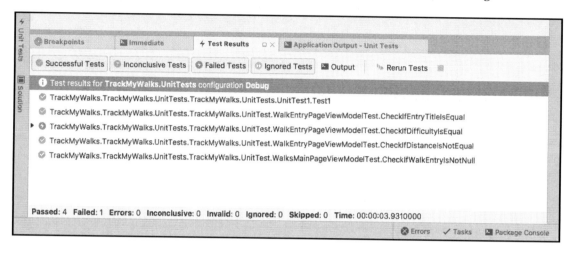

Test Results for each of the Unit Tests that have been run

Should any of your tests fail, these will be displayed within the **Test Results** pane under the **Failed Tests** tab, along with their associated **Stack Trace**, which shows the source code file where the exception occurred. You will also notice that the message that we provided within the `Assert.Equal` method will also be displayed as part of the **Failure** result, as shown in the following screenshot:

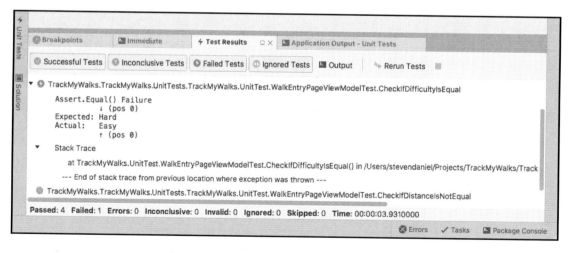

Test Results Pane showing the Stack Trace and Errors of each Failed Test

Within the **Test Results** pane, you have the option of filtering each of your test results or even rerunning your unit tests again by clicking on the **Rerun Tests** button.

The following table provides a brief description of what each test result relates to within the **Test Results** pane:

Test Result	Description
Successful Tests	The **Successful Tests** section displays all successfully executed tests that passed all of the test case conditions.
Inconclusive Tests	The **Inconclusive Tests** section displays each of the test results that were found to be inconclusive, meaning that a firm result could not be determined.
Failed Tests	The **Failed Tests** section displays each test that did not meet the test case conditions that were specified.
Ignored Tests	The **Ignored Tests** section displays each test that was ignored as specified by the `[Ignore]` attribute within the test case conditions.
Output	The **Output** section displays a console output for each of the tests that were executed and will contain any unit tests that successfully passed, failed, or ignored, or were found to be inconclusive.
Rerun Tests	The **Rerun Tests** section enables you to rerun your unit tests again, without the need for recompiling your test case conditions.

Now that you have a good understanding of how to create your own unit tests using the `Xunit` testing framework, we can now look at how to create another form of unit testing, which is called automated UI testing, using the `Xamarin.UITest` framework that we will be covering in the next section.

Creating a UITest project within the TrackMyWalks solution

In the previous section, we saw how easy it is to create various unit tests that enable us to create different test case scenarios to test each of our `ViewModels` within the `TrackMyWalks` project. That said, while unit testing generally ensures that a significant amount of code is tested, it is primarily focused on testing the actual business logic contained within the app, which unfortunately leaves the user interface portion of your application untested.

In this section, we will look at how we can use automated UI testing to automate specific actions within your application's user interface to ensure that it is working as expected. Fortunately, Visual Studio for Mac provides you with a rich set of tools for creating automated UI test scenarios that can be written using either C# or F# and makes use of the `UITest` framework.

Let's take a look at how we can achieve this by performing the following steps:

1. First, right-click on the `TrackMyWalks` solution and choose **Add | Add New Project...** from the pop-up menu, as you did in the section entitled *Creating the unit testing project solution using Xunit* located within this chapter.

2. Next, choose the **UI Test App** option which is located under the **Multiplatform | Tests** section, ensuring that you have selected **C#** as the programming language to use:

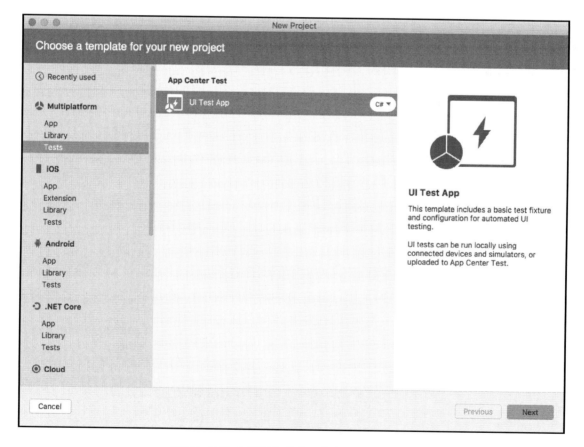

Creating and Adding the UI Test App Project to the TrackMyWalks Solution

3. Then, click on the **Next** button to proceed to the next step in the wizard and enter `TrackMyWalks.UITests` as the name for your new project in the **Project Name** field, as shown in the following screenshot:

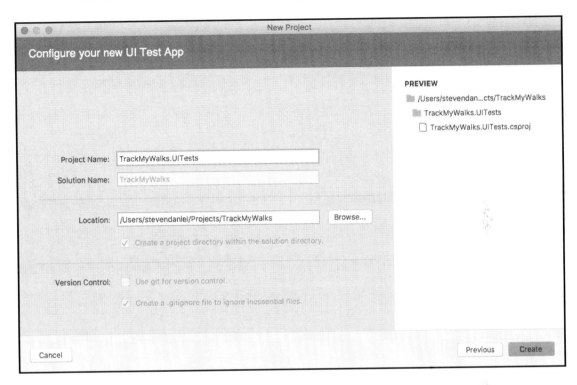

Configuring your new UI Test App Project

4. Finally, click on the **Create** button to proceed with the creation of your project at the specified location, as shown in the following screenshot:

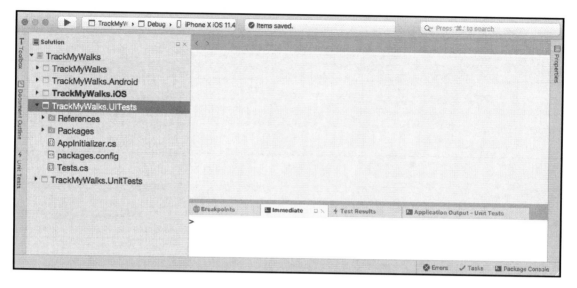

The TrackMyWalks.UITests Project displayed within the TrackMyWalks Solution

You will notice that when we created our `TrackMyWalks.UITests` project, the wizard created two class files, `Tests.cs` and `AppInitializer.cs`. `Tests.cs` is used as a starting point to write automated UI tests and the `AppInitializer.cs` class is used by `Tests.cs` and any other UI tests that you create on your own.

Understanding the most commonly used Xamarin.UITest testing methods

In this section, we will learn about some of the commonly used methods that we can use with the `Xamarin.UITest` framework, which provides you with a way in which you can automate the interactions between your Android or iOS apps, using either C# or F#, as well as the `NUnit` testing framework.

The following table describes some of the more commonly used methods and the ones that we will be using to test the `TrackMyWalks` app:

UITest methods	Description
Screenshot()	The Screenshot method is used to take a screenshot of the current state of the app.
Tap()	The Tap method is used to send a tap to interact with a specific element that is contained on the app's current screen.
EnterText()	The EnterText method is used to populate text within a specific element that is contained on the app's current screen.
ClearText()	The ClearText method is used to remove text within a specific element that is contained on the app's current screen.
Query()	The Query method is used to find a specific element or all elements that are contained within the app's current screen.
Repl()	The Repl method is commonly used to interact in real-time with the app through the terminal command line using the UITest APIs.
WaitForElement()	The WaitForElement method is used to pause the execution of the current running test, until a specific element appears on the app's current screen, within a specific timeout period.

Using methods such as `Query` and `WaitForElement` returns an `AppResult[]` array object that you can use to determine the results of a call. An example would be that, if you use the `Query` method call that returns an empty result, you can be sure that the element doesn't exist within the app's current screen.

 The Xamarin `UITest` framework only provides support for both the iOS and Android platforms and doesn't provide support for the UWP platform.

The following table describes the methods relating to the `AppQuery` class that are used by the `Query` and `WaitForElement` methods of the `IApp` interface:

AppQuery Methods	Description
Class()	The Class method is used to find elements that are contained within the app's current screen based on their class type.

Marked()	The `Marked` method is used to find elements that are contained within the app's current screen, by referring to them by their text values or identifier.
Css()	The `Css` method is used to perform CSS selector operations on the contents of a `WebView` that are contained on the app's current screen.

 For more information on the `Xamarin.UITest` class methods, refer to the Xamarin developer documentation at `https://developer.xamarin.com/api/namespace/Xamarin.UITest/`.

Now that you have some insight into some of the most commonly used `UITest` methods, we can start to create and implement our UI tests using some of the methods of the `Xamarin.UITest` framework that we will be covering over the next couple of sections.

Creating and implementing the CreateNewTrailDetails class for iOS

In this section, we'll take a look at how to create and implement the `CreateNewTrailDetails` class, which will be used to perform automated UI testing for the iOS platform so that we can handle signing into Twitter and create a brand new walk trail entry using the `Xamarin.UITest` framework.

Let's see how we can achieve this by performing the following steps:

1. Right-click on the `TrackMyWalks.UITests` project and choose **Add | New File...** from the pop-up menu. Then, choose the **Test Fixture** option under the **NUnit** section.

2. Next, enter `CreateNewTrailDetails` for the name of the class to be created, as shown in the following screenshot:

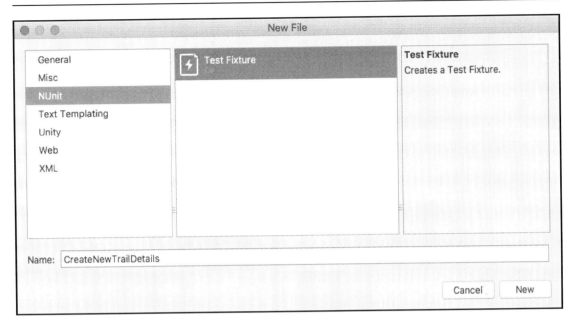

Creating the CreateNewTrailDetails Test Fixture Class

3. Then, click on the **New** button to proceed and create the new class. With the `CreateNewTrailDetails.cs` file open, enter the following code snippet:

```
//
//   CreateNewTrailDetails.cs
//   Automated UI Testing to validate signing into Twitter and create
//   a new Walk Trail Entry
//
//   Created by Steven F. Daniel on 14/08/2018
//   Copyright © 2018 GENIESOFT STUDIOS. All rights reserved.
//
using System;
using System.Linq;
using NUnit.Framework;
using Xamarin.UITest;

namespace TrackMyWalks.UITests
{
    // Set this attribute to indicate which platforms you would like to
test
    // i.e., iOS and Android
    [TestFixture(Platform.iOS)]
    public class CreateNewTrailDetails
    {
```

```
            // IApp interface is responsible for handling the communication
with the app
            IApp app;

            // Platform parameter is responsible for indicating on which
            // platform Xamarin should launch
            Platform platform;
            string entryCellPlatformClassName;

            // This is the class constructor for the CreateNewTrailDetails
with
            // setting for the platform
            public CreateNewTrailDetails(Platform platform)
            {
                this.platform = platform;
                entryCellPlatformClassName = (this.platform == Platform.iOS
? "UITextField" :
"EntryCellEditText");
            }

            // The BeforeEachTest instance method is setup before each test
is
            // launched and the app object is initialised
            [SetUp]
            public void BeforeEachTest()
            {
                app = AppInitializer.StartApp(platform);
            }

            // The AppLaunches instance method REPL console is invoked
(with REPL
            // we are able to test our app manually and all actions will be
displayed
            // within the app screen
            [Test]
            public void AppLaunches()
            {
                app.Repl();
            }

            // Create the CreateBrandNewTrailEntry Test to create a new
Trail Entry
            [Test]
            public void CreateBrandNewTrailEntry()
            {
                // Sign in to Twitter (If using Two-Factor Authentication,
you'll
                // need to comment this out)
```

```
                    HandleTwitterSignIn();

                    // Wait for the Track My Walks Listing to appear by
checking the
                    // navigation bar title
                    var navigationBarTitle = "Track My Walks Listing";
                    var mainScreen = app.WaitForElement(x =>
x.Marked(navigationBarTitle)
.Class("UINavigationBar"));

                    // Validate to ensure that our Track My Walks Listing
screen was displayed
                    Assert.IsTrue(mainScreen.Any(), navigationBarTitle +
"screen wasn't
                                    shown after signing in.");

                    // Click on the Add button from our Track My Walks Listing
screen
                    app.Tap(x => x.Marked("Add"));
                    var WalkEntryPageScreenTitle = "Adding Trail Details";
                    var WalkEntryPageScreen = app.WaitForElement(x =>
x.Marked(WalkEntryPageScreenTitle)
.Class("UINavigationBar"));
                    // Validate to ensure that our Adding Trail Details screen
was displayed
                    Assert.IsTrue(WalkEntryPageScreen.Any(),
WalkEntryPageScreenTitle + "
                                    screen wasn't shown after tapping the Add
button.");

                    // Populate our Adding Trail Details EntryCell Fields
                    PopulateWalkEntryDetailsForm();

                    // Tap on the Save button to save the details and exit
                    app.Tap(x => x.Marked("Save"));
                    var SaveWalkEntryDialogTitle = "Save Walk Entry Item";
                    var SaveWalkEntryDialogScreen = app.WaitForElement(x =>
x.Marked(SaveWalkEntryDialogTitle));
                    app.Tap(x => x.Marked("OK"));

                    // Validate to ensure that our Save Walk Entry Item Details
screen
                    // was displayed
                    Assert.IsTrue(SaveWalkEntryDialogScreen.Any(),
navigationBarTitle + "
                                    screen wasn't shown after tapping the Save
button.");
            }
```

```
            // Instance method to handle populating the Walk Entry Details
Form
            public void PopulateWalkEntryDetailsForm()
            {
                // Clear the default text entry for our Title EntryCell
                app.ClearText(x =>
x.Class(entryCellPlatformClassName).Index(0));
                app.EnterText(x =>
x.Class(entryCellPlatformClassName).Index(0),
                             "New UITest Walk Entry");
                app.DismissKeyboard();

                // Enter in some default text for our Description EntryCell
                app.ClearText(x =>
x.Class(entryCellPlatformClassName).Index(1));
                app.EnterText(x =>
x.Class(entryCellPlatformClassName).Index(1), "This is a
                             new description entry, using the UITest
automation features");
                app.DismissKeyboard();

                // Enter in some default text for our Distance EntryCell
                app.ClearText(x =>
x.Class(entryCellPlatformClassName).Index(4));
                app.EnterText(x =>
x.Class(entryCellPlatformClassName).Index(4), "256");
                app.DismissKeyboard();

                // Enter in some default text for our Image URL
                app.ClearText(x =>
x.Class(entryCellPlatformClassName).Index(6));
                app.EnterText(x =>
x.Class(entryCellPlatformClassName).Index(6),"https://heuft.com/
                upload/image/400x267/no_image_placeholder.png");
                app.DismissKeyboard();
            }

            // Instance methods that will handle signing into Twitter
            public  void HandleTwitterSignIn()
            {
                // Set up and initialise our Twitter Credentials
                var TwitterUsername = "YOUR_TWITTER_USERNAME";
                var TwitterPassword = "YOUR_TWITTER_PASSWORD";

                // Enter values for our username and password within the
WebView
                app.Tap(x => x.WebView().Css("[id=username_or_email]"));
                app.EnterText(x =>
```

```
x.WebView().Css("[id=username_or_email]"), TwitterUsername);
            app.DismissKeyboard();
            app.Tap(x => x.WebView().Css("[id=password]"));
            app.EnterText(x => x.WebView().Css("[id=password]"),
TwitterPassword);
            app.DismissKeyboard();

            // Tap the Authorize app button in the WebView use
            // id=cancel for Cancel button
            app.ScrollDownTo(x => x.WebView().Css("[id=allow]"));
            app.Tap(x => x.WebView().Css("[id=allow]"));
        }
    }
}
```

Now, let's start by taking a look at what we covered in the preceding code snippet:

1. First, we included references to the `System`, `System.Linq` and `Xamarin.UITest` namespaces so that we have access to the class method implementations that are defined within these namespaces.

2. Next, we updated and set the `TestFixture` attribute to indicate which platforms we would like to test. For example, iOS and Android declare an `IApp app` interface that is responsible for handling all of the communication within the app, as well as declare a platform variable that is responsible for indicating which platform `Xamarin.UITest` should launch. It also declares a string variable called `entryCellPlatformClassName` that will be responsible for returning the `TextField` property depending on the platform that we are testing on. If we are testing on iOS, we will return the `UITextField` class, whereas under Android, it will use the `EntryCellEditText` class.

3. Then, we updated our `CreateNewTrailDetails` class constructor method and added the `Platform platform` parameter. We then updated the parameter variable that we declared at the beginning of our class, as well as updated our `entryCellPlatformClassName` variable, to use the correct `TextField` based on the platform we are testing on, prior to creating the `BeforeEachTest` instance method and specifying the `[SetUp]` attribute that will be called before each test is launched to initialize the `app` object using the `platform` parameter that we are testing on.

4. Next, we created the `AppLaunches` instance method that will invoke the REPL console, where you can manually test the app, as well as perform actions that will interact and be displayed within the app screen.

5. Then, we created the `CreateBrandNewTrail` instance method that will perform actions to create a new trail entry when it is executed by the `Xamarin.UITest` framework. Within this method, we called the `HandleTwitterSignIn` instance method, which will perform the steps required to sign in to Twitter.

6. Next, we declared a `navigationBarTitle` variable and a `mainScreen` variable. We used the `app.WaitForElement` method to check and wait for the text contained within the `navigationBarTitle` to appear on-screen and used the `Assert.IsTrue` method to validate that our screen appeared on screen.

7. Then, we performed the steps to click on the `Add` button that is located on the **Track My Walks Listing** page and used the `WaitForElement` method to validate that the associated text for the `Adding Trail Details` appeared on screen. We then used the `Assert.IsTrue` method to validate accordingly.

8. Next, we called the `PopulateWalkEntryDetailsForm` instance method to perform the steps to populate the `EntryCell` fields within the `WalkEntryPage`, and clicked on the `Save` button to display the `Save Walk Entry Item` dialog. Then, we used the `WaitForElement` method to wait for the dialog to appear and then used the `Tap` method to click on the `OK` button, at which point we saved the details to the SQL Server database that is stored within Microsoft Azure App Services. We used the `Assert.IsTrue` method to validate that our `Save Walk Entry Item` dialog did actually appear on screen.

9. Then, we declared the `PopulateWalkEntryDetailsForm` instance method that will be responsible for handling the steps specifically for the creation of a new walk entry. We used the `ClearText` and `EnterText` methods of the `Xamarin.UITest` framework that will locate each `EntryCell` within the `Adding Trail Details` form and populated it with the necessary information. The `DismissKeyboard` method is responsible for dismissing the keyboard from the view and continued to the next step.

10. Finally, we created the `HandleTwitterSignIn` instance method that will be responsible for handling the steps specifically related to the Twitter sign-in process. This process uses the user's login credentials to automate the login process, prior to carrying out other steps within the Twitter user interface.

Updating the WalksMainPage code-behind using C#

Now that we have created the `CreateNewTrailDetails` class that will be responsible for handling the automated UI testing using the `UITest` framework, our next step is to begin updating the underlying C# code within our `WalksMainPage` code-behind file in order to disable displaying our `TwitterSignInPage` ViewModel.

Let's take a look at how we can achieve this by following these steps:

1. Locate and open the `WalksMainPage.xaml.cs` file which is located within the `Views` folder, ensuring that it is displayed within the code editor, and enter the following highlighted code sections:

```
//
//  WalksMainPage.xaml.cs
//  Displays Walk Information within a ListView control from an array//
//  Created by Steven F. Daniel on 14/05/2018
//  Copyright © 2018 GENIESOFT STUDIOS. All rights reserved.
//
using System;
using TrackMyWalks.Models;
using TrackMyWalks.Services;
using TrackMyWalks.ViewModels;
using Xamarin.Forms;

namespace TrackMyWalks.Views
{
    public partial class WalksMainPage : ContentPage
    {
        // Return the Binding Context for the ViewModel
        WalksMainPageViewModel _viewModel => BindingContext as
WalksMainPageViewModel;

        public WalksMainPage()
        {
            InitializeComponent();
            ...
            ...
        }
            ...
            ...
        // Method to initialise our View Model when the ContentPage
appears
        protected override async void OnAppearing()
```

```
        {
            base.OnAppearing();

            // Perform a check to see if we have logged into Twitter
already
            if (_viewModel != null)
            {
                // Call the Init method to initialise the ViewModel
                await _viewModel.Init();
                /*
                if (!TwitterAuthDetails.isLoggedIn)
                {
                    // We need to Navigate and display our Twitter Sign
In Page
                    await
_viewModel.Navigation.NavigateTo<TwitterSignInPageViewModel>();
                }
                */
            }
            ...
            ...
```

2. In the preceding code snippet, we started by modifying the `OnAppearing` method by commenting out the code that checks the `isLoggedIn` property within our `TwitterAuthDetails` class in order to determine if the user has already signed into our app. Then, we navigated to our `TwitterSignInPageViewModel` using the `Navigation` property of our `_viewModel` and the `NavigateTo` instance method.

If you have configured your Twitter account to use Two-Factor Authentication, you will need to comment out the preceding code within the code snippet, as this will cause problems when running the `UITests`, as you'll need to manually enter in the code that is generated and provided by Twitter. Alternatively, if you are not using Two-Factor Authentication, you can skip this section altogether.

Adding the Xamarin.Test Cloud.Agent NuGet package

In this section, we will begin by adding the `Xamarin.TestCloud.Agent` NuGet package to our `TrackMyWalks.iOS` project. The `Xamarin.TestCloud.Agent` library allows you to execute your `Xamarin.UITest` using the C# programming language as well as the `NUnit` framework to validate the functionality of your iOS and Android apps within the Visual Studio for Mac environment.

Let's take a look at how we can achieve this by performing the following steps:

1. Right-click on the **Dependencies | NuGet** folder that is located within the `TrackMyWalks.iOS` project and choose the **Add Packages...** menu option, as you did in the section entitled *Adding the Moq NuGet package to our TrackMyWalks.UnitTests project*, located within this chapter.

2. Next, within the **Search** field located within the **Add Packages** dialog, you need to enter `testcloud` and select the **Xamarin.TestCloud.Agent** option within the list, as shown in the following screenshot:

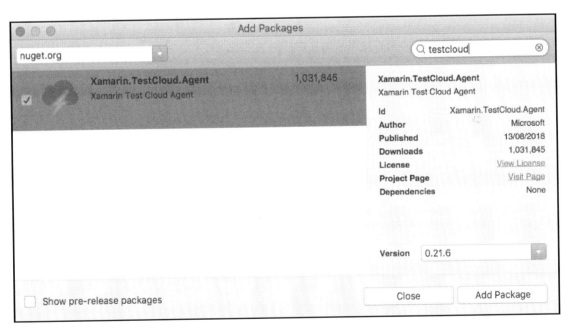

Adding the Xamarin.TestCloud.Agent NuGet Package

3. Then, make sure that you choose the latest version to install from the drop-down list for the **Version** field (*this will be displayed by default*).

4. Next, click on the **Add Package** button to add the `Xamarin.TestCloud.Agent` NuGet package to the `TrackMyWalks.iOS` project.

5. Then, locate and open the `AppDelegate.cs` file which is located in the `TrackMyWalks.iOS` project folder, ensuring that it is displayed within the code editor, and enter the following highlighted code sections:

```
//
//  AppDelegate.cs
//  Application Delegate class for the TrackMyWalks.iOS Project
//
//  Created by Steven F. Daniel on 14/05/2018
//  Copyright © 2018 GENIESOFT STUDIOS. All rights reserved.
//
using Foundation;
using UIKit;

namespace TrackMyWalks.iOS
{
        ...
        ...
        public override bool FinishedLaunching(UIApplication app,
NSDictionary options)
        {
            global::Xamarin.Forms.Forms.Init();

            // Initialise our Xamarin.FormsMaps library
            Xamarin.FormsMaps.Init();
            #if ENABLE_TEST_CLOUD
            Xamarin.Calabash.Start();
            #endif
            LoadApplication(new App());
            return base.FinishedLaunching(app, options);
        }
}
```

In the preceding code snippet, we started by defining the ENABLE_TEST_CLOUD compiler variable that is wrapped within the #if and #endif directive that includes a call to the Xamarin.Calabash.Start method. The Xamarin.Calabash.Start method will only be started when it has been defined under specific configurations, as defined within the compiler configurations settings for the TrackMyWalks.iOS project.

> Calabash is essentially an Automated UI Acceptance Testing framework that allows you to write and execute tests that validate the functionality of your iOS and Android applications.

We have just added the code that will essentially start our Xamarin Test Cloud functionality, however, for this to work, we will need to perform an additional step, which is to make some modifications to the compiler configurations of our TrackMyWalks.iOS project.

1. Right-click on the TrackMyWalks.iOS project, and choose the **Options** menu option.
2. Next, within the **Project Options – TrackMyWalks.iOS** dialog, choose the **Compiler** option which is located under the **Build** section.
3. Then, ensure that you have chosen **Debug(Active)** from the **Configuration** drop-down.
4. Next, ensure that you have chosen the **iPhoneSimulator** from the **Platform** drop-down.

5. Then, add the **ENABLE_TEST_CLOUD** to the end of the existing list within the **Define Symbols** section, as shown in the following screenshot:

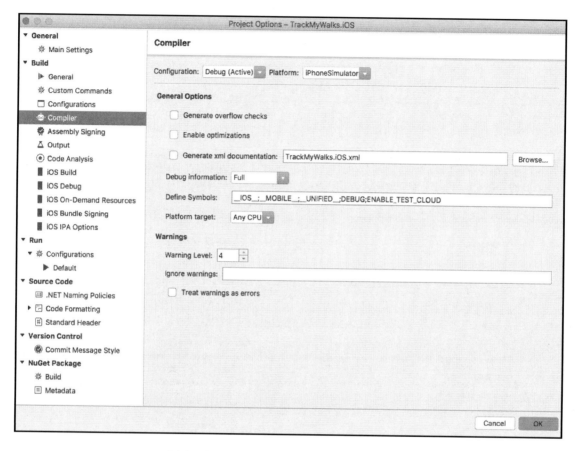

Defining additional Compiler Configurations for Enabling Test Cloud Support

6. Finally, click on the **OK** button to save your changes and close the dialog.

Now that you have modified the compiler configurations for your `TrackMyWalks.iOS` project, we can finally build and run our `Xamarin.UITests` right within the Visual Studio for Mac IDE, similarly to how we did when executing our `Xunit` tests. However, this needs to be handled very differently, which we will be covering in the next section.

Running UITests within the Visual Studio for Mac IDE

In this section, we will take a look at how to run our `Xamarin.UITests` using the Visual Studio for Mac IDE. Prior to running your `TrackMyWalks.UnitTests` project, you will need to add your iOS and Android projects to the **Test Apps** node of the **Unit Tests** pane. If you don't do this, your `Xamarin.UITests` will continually fail until you add these projects to your `TrackMyWalks.UITests` project.

Let's take a look at how we can achieve this by performing the following steps:

1. First, ensure that you have chosen the **Debug** option from the drop-down menu.
2. Next, select the **View|Unit Tests** menu option, as shown in the following screenshot:

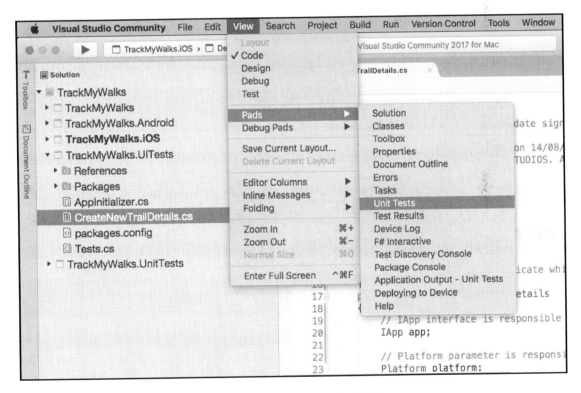

Running UITests within the Visual Studio for Mac IDE

3. Then, right-click on the **Test Apps** node within the **Unit Tests** pane, and click on the **Add App Project** menu option, as shown in the following screenshot:

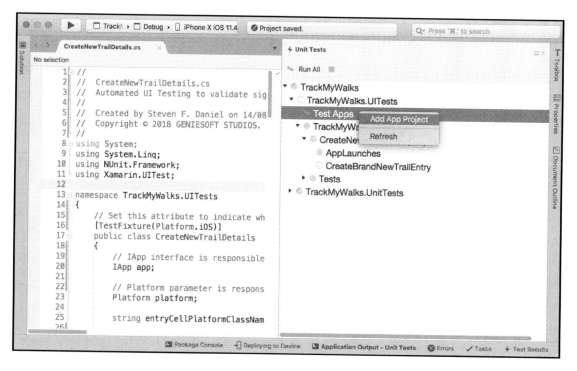

Adding a new App Project to run the UI Tests against

4. Next, from the **Select a project or solution** dialog, select each of your projects for the various platforms, as shown in the following screenshot:

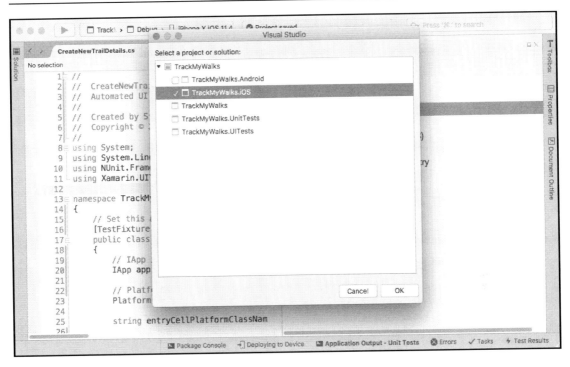

Selecting the TrackMyWalks.iOS Project to add to the list of UI Tests

5. Then, click on the **OK** button to save your changes and close the dialog.

If you don't see your TrackMyWalks.iOS app project listed within the **Select a project or solution** dialog, you have have forgotten to add the Xamarin Test Cloud Agent NuGet package to your TrackMyWalks.iOS project.

6. Finally, right-click on the `TrackMyWalks.UITests` node, located within the **Unit Tests** pane, and click on the **Run Test** menu option, as shown in the following screenshot:

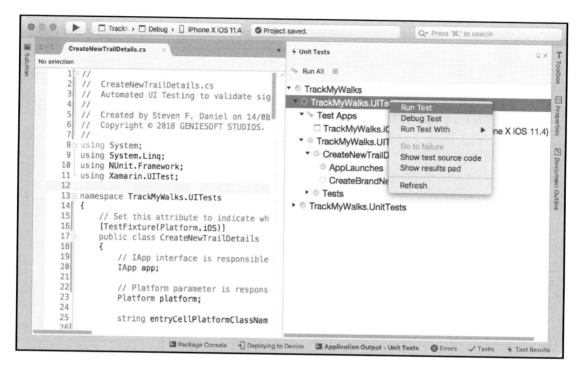

Running the TrackMyWalks UITests within the Visual Studio for Mac IDE

When the `TrackMyWalks` application starts to run, the `Xamarin.UITest` framework will automatically deploy your app to the iOS Simulator and run through each of the steps that you have specified within your test methods which have the `[Test]` attribute. Once each of the tests have been completed, they will appear within the **Unit Tests** pane.

Summary

In this chapter, you learned how to create and run unit tests and UITests for the TrackMyWalks application, using the Xunit and Xamarin.UITest frameworks. You learned how to add the Moq NuGet package to the TrackMyWalks.UnitTests project within the TrackMyWalks solution so that you can test the business logic within your ViewModels in order to validate that everything is working correctly, and returning the results you are looking for.

Next, we moved on and created the TrackMyWalks.UITests project using the Xamarin.UITest framework so that we could perform testing on the user interface using Automated UI Testing. You then learned how to create, test, and execute each of your tests locally using the Xamarin Test Cloud Agent and the Calabash framework by adding the iOS projects to the TrackMyWalks.UITests project.

This was the final chapter. I sincerely hope that you had lots of fun developing apps throughout our journey working through this book. You are now equipped with enough knowledge and expertise to understand what it takes to build rich and engaging apps for both the Xamarin and Xamarin.Forms platforms by using a host of exciting concepts and techniques that are unique to each platform. I can't wait to see what you build and I wish you the very best of luck with your Xamarin and Xamarin.Forms adventures.

Other Books You May Enjoy

If you enjoyed this book, you may be interested in these other books by Packt:

Mastering Xamarin.Forms - Second Edition
Ed Snider

ISBN: 9781788290265

- Implement the Model-View-View-Model (MVVM) pattern and data-binding in Xamarin.Forms mobile apps
- Extend the Xamarin.Forms navigation API with a custom ViewModel-centric navigation service
- Leverage the inversion of control and dependency injection patterns in Xamarin.Forms mobile apps
- Work with online and offline data in Xamarin.Forms mobile apps
- Test business logic in Xamarin.Forms mobile apps
- Use platform-specific APIs to build rich custom user interfaces in Xamarin.Forms mobile apps
- Explore how to improve mobile app quality using Visual Studio AppCenter

Xamarin Blueprints
Michael Williams

ISBN: 9781785887444

- Discover eight different ways to create your own Xamarin applications
- Improve app performance by using SQLite for data-intensive applications
- Set up a simple web service to feed JSON data into mobile applications
- Store files locally with Xamarin.Forms using dependency services
- Use Xamarin extension libraries to create effective applications with less coding

Leave a review - let other readers know what you think

Please share your thoughts on this book with others by leaving a review on the site that you bought it from. If you purchased the book from Amazon, please leave us an honest review on this book's Amazon page. This is vital so that other potential readers can see and use your unbiased opinion to make purchasing decisions, we can understand what our customers think about our products, and our authors can see your feedback on the title that they have worked with Packt to create. It will only take a few minutes of your time, but is valuable to other potential customers, our authors, and Packt. Thank you!

Index

A

Android 51
App.xaml class
    updating, navigation service used 251
asynchronous operations 262

B

background location permissions
    enabling 286, 288, 291
background location updates
    enabling 286, 288, 291
BaseViewModel
    class, updating to RestWebService 456
    creating 182, 183, 184, 186
    implementing 182, 183, 184, 186
    updated, for using navigation service 232, 234
Book Library cascading style sheet (CSS)
    updating 420, 421
BookLibrary app
    building, Razor templating engine used 392, 396
    launching, iOS simulator used 429, 431
BookLibraryAddEdit page
    creating 416
    implementing 417
BookLibraryListing page
    creating 413, 416
    implementing 413, 416
Breakpoints
    conditional Breakpoints, creating to perform
        action 41, 42
    displaying, Breakpoints Pad used 39, 40
    setting, in code 38
    setting, in Planetary App solution 38
    used, in code 38

C

C# code
    about 51
    used, for creating CustomMapOverlay class 273
    used, for creating TwitterSignInPageViewModel
        495
    used, for creating WalkDistancePageViewModel
        208
    used, for creating WalkEntryPageViewModel
        195
    used, for creating WalksMainPageViewModel
        186, 187, 198
    used, for creating WalkTrailInfoPageViewModel
        203, 205
    used, for implementing
        TwitterSignInPageViewModel 495
    used, for implementing WalkDistancePage code
        164, 166
    used, for implementing WalkEntryPage code
        155
    used, for implementing WalksMainPage code
        150, 153
    used, for implementing WalkTrailInfoPage code
        158
    used, for updating SplashPage code-behind 249
    used, for updating WalkDistancePage code-
        behind 247, 249, 275, 279
    used, for updating WalkDistancePageViewModel
        245, 247, 270
    used, for updating WalkEntryPage code-behind
        240, 242
    used, for updating WalkEntryPageViewModel
        239, 267, 466
    used, for updating WalksMainPage code-behind
        236, 239, 458, 502, 547
    used, for updating WalksMainPageViewModel
        234

used, for updating WalkTrailInfoPage code-
behind 244
used, for updating WalkTrailInfoPageViewModel
242, 243
used, for updating WebViewController class 422,
427
camera
permissions, setting up 77
Cascading style sheets (CSS) 396
CoreAnimation
about 88, 132
animations, applying 132
animations, creating for SlidingTiles game 132,
134
animations, implementing for SlidingTiles game
132, 134
reference link 134
working with 132
Create, Update, Retrieve, and Delete (CRUD) 473
Custom Animations
about 373
creating 371
implementing 371
used, for updating WalksMainPage 373, 376
used, for updating WalkTrailInfoPage 371
CustomMapOverlay class
creating, C# code used 272
CustomMapRenderer (Android)
creating 284
implementing 284
CustomMapRenderer (iOS)
creating 280, 283
implementing 280, 283

D

data model
creating 143, 144, 146
implementing 143, 144, 146
DataTemplate
customizing, in WalksMainPage 298
device camera
interacting 78, 80, 82

E

Easing Functions
creating, in Xamarin.Forms 368
used, for updating WalkTrailInfoPage 369
used, in Xamarin.Forms 368
Entrance Animations
creating 378
implementing 378
used, for updating WalkEntryPage 383
used, for updating WalksMainPage 381
used, for updating WalkTrailInfoPage 378
Explicit Styles 307

I

ILocationService interface
creating 259, 261
implementing 259, 261
Implicit Styles 307
iOS 51
iOS section 280
iOS simulator
about 88, 134
used, for launching BookLibrary app 429, 431
used, for launching SlidingTiles game 134, 136,
215, 216
used, for launching TrackMyWalks app 214,
217, 292, 356, 385, 469, 511

L

LocationService class
creating 262, 266
implementing 262, 266

M

Material Design Themes 72
Material Design
about 72
implementing, in PhotoLibrary app 72
Microsoft Azure App services
configuring 435, 438, 440, 443
platform 434
setting up 435, 438, 440, 443
Model-View-ViewModel (MVVM)
about 179, 219, 255

architectural pattern 180, 181

N

native Android app
  creating, Visual Studio used for Mac 52, 54, 55
  Strings XML file, updating to UI control values
    62, 64
  Styles XML file, creating for PhotoLibrary app
    64, 66
  user interface, creating for PhotoLibrary app
    using XML 59, 62
  Xamarin Media Plugin NuGet package, adding
    56, 57, 58
native iOS app
  creating, Visual Studio used for Mac 88, 91, 92
navigation approach
  versus ViewModel approach 222, 223
navigation service
  used, for updating App.xaml class 251
  used, for updating BaseViewModel 232, 234
NavigationService class
  creating 228, 232
  implementing 228, 232
NavigationService interface
  creating 223, 225, 226, 227, 228
  implementing 223, 225, 226, 227, 228
Newtonsoft.Json NuGet package
  adding, to solution 443

P

photo album
  interacting 78, 80, 82
  permissions, setting up 77
PhotoLibrary Activity class
  creating 67, 70
  implementing 67, 70
  updating 70
PhotoLibrary app
  about 51, 59
  custom styles, creating for UI controls 73
  custom themes, applying 75, 76
  custom themes, creating 72
  launching, Android emulator used 83, 84
  used, for implementing Material Design 72
Platform Effects

ButtonShadowEffect (Android), creating 323
ButtonShadowEffect (Android), implementing
  323
ButtonShadowEffect (iOS), creating 317, 320
ButtonShadowEffect (iOS), implementing 317,
  320
ButtonShadowEffect RoutingEffect class,
  implementing 328
creating, in app 317
LabelShadowEffect (Android), creating 326
LabelShadowEffect (Android), implementing 326
LabelShadowEffect (iOS), creating 321
LabelShadowEffect (iOS), implementing 321
LabelShadowEffect RoutingEffect class,
  implementing 331
used, in app 317
WalksMainPage, updating LabelShadowEffect
  used 333
WalkTrailInfoPage, updating ButtonShadowEffect
  used 336
WalkTrailInfoPage, updating LabelShadowEffect
  used 335
platform-specific services
  creating, within app 256
  plugin geolocator NuGet package, adding to
    solution 257
  used, within app 256

R

Razor templating engine 389, 390
  used, for building BookLibrary app 392, 396
RestWebService class
  creating 449, 453
  implementing 449, 453
RestWebService interface
  creating 446, 448
  implementing 446, 448

S

Simple Animations
  about 359
  creating, in Xamarin.Forms 360
  used, for updating WalkEntryPage 362
  used, for updating WalkTrailInfoPage 365
  used, in Xamarin.Forms 360

SlidingTiles Game
  about 137
  CreateGameBoard method, creating 123, 125, 126
  CreateGameBoard method, implementing 123, 125, 126
  game logic, implementing 111
  Game Tiles, shuffling on Game Board 128, 129
  GameTile class, creating 115, 118, 120
  GameTile class, implementing 115, 118, 120
  GameTile interface class, creating 111, 113, 115
  GameTile interface class, implementing 111, 113, 115
  launching, iOS simulator used 134, 136
  ResetGame_Clicked method, creating 126
  ResetGame_Clicked method, implementing 126
  StartNewGame Instance method, implementing 129
  touch events, handling in Game Board user interface 130, 131, 132
  ViewController class, updating to implement class methods 121
SlidingTiles
  about 87
  GameTile image, adding 110
  label, adding to ViewController in Storyboard 95, 96, 98
  reset button, adding to ViewController in Storyboard 102, 103, 105, 106
  shuffle button, adding to ViewController in Storyboard 106, 109
  user interface, creating Storyboards used 93, 94
  view, adding to ViewController in Storyboard 99, 101
SplashPage code-behind
  updating, C# code used 249
SplashPage code
  implementing, C# code used 171
SplashPage interface
  creating, XAML used 169, 170
SQLite-net NuGet package
  adding, to solution 397
  BookDatabase class, creating 408, 412
  BookDatabase class, implementing 408, 412
  BookDatabase interface, creating 403

BookDatabase interface, implementing 403, 406
  BookLibrary data model, creating 399, 401
  BookLibrary data model, implementing 399, 401
Strings XML file
  updating, to UI control values 62, 64
Styles XML file
  creating, for PhotoLibrary app 64, 66
Styles
  creating, in app 307
  Device Style, used, for updating WalksMainPage 309
  Explicit Styles, used for updating WalkTrailInfoPage 312
  Global Styles, creating XAML used 307
  Global Styles, implementing XAML used 307
  Global Styles, used for updating WalkTrailInfoPage 312
  implementing, in app 307
  Implicit Styles, used for updating WalksEntryPage 314

T

TrackMyWalks app
  creating, with Twitter Developer Portal 475, 478, 482, 483
  launching, iOS simulator used 214, 215, 216, 217, 291, 355, 385, 469, 471, 511
  Moq NuGet package, adding to TrackMyWalks.UnitTests project 523
  project, adding to TrackMyWalks.UnitTests project 525
  registering, with Twitter Developer Portal 475, 479, 482, 483
  WalksEntryPageViewModelTest class, creating 529, 532
  WalksEntryPageViewModelTest class, implementing 529, 532
  WalksMainPageViewModelTest class, creating 526
  WalksMainPageViewModelTest class, implementing 526
TrackMyWalks project solution
  creating 138, 140, 141
  NuGet packages, updating 142
TrackMyWalks.Android MainActivity

updating 168
TrackMyWalks.iOS AppDelegate
  updating 166, 168
Twitter Developer Portal 484
TwitterAuthDetails class
  creating 486, 489
  implementing 486, 489
TwitterSignInPage
  registering, with App.xaml class 509
  used, for creating user interface 496
  used, for implementing user interface 496
TwitterSignInPageRenderer (iOS)
  creating 498, 501
  implementing 498, 501
TwitterSignInPageViewModel
  creating, C# code used 495
  implementing, C# code used 495
TwitterWebService class
  creating 491, 494
  implementing 491, 494
TwitterWebService interface
  creating 489
  implementing 489

U

UITest project
  CreateNewTrailDetails class, creating for iOS 540, 545
  CreateNewTrailDetails class, implementing for iOS 540, 545
  creating, within TrackMyWalks solution 535, 538
  Xamarin.UITest testing methods 538
UITests
  executing, within Visual Studio for Mac IDE 553, 555
Unit Testing project
  creating, within TrackMyWalks solution 518, 522
unit tests
  executing, within Visual Studio for Mac IDE 532, 535
user interface
  creating, for PhotoLibrary app using XML 59, 62
  creating, for user interface 496
  implementing, for TwitterSignInPage 496

V

ValueConverters
  BaseViewModel class, updating to additional properties 342
  creating, in app 339
  implementing, in app 339
  WalkEntryPage, updating to ImageConverter class 350
  WalksMainPage, updating to ImageConverter class 347
  WalksMainPageViewModel, updating to property 344
  WalkTrailInfoPage, updating to ImageConverter class 353
View Transitions 88, 132
ViewModel approach
  versus navigation approach 222, 223
Visual Studio for Mac IDE 318
Visual Studio
  .NET Runtimes, configuring 19
  .NET Runtimes, including 19
  Android SDK locations, defining 20, 22
  debugger, used through code 45, 46, 47
  downloading, for Mac 12
  exploring, for Mac IDE 17, 18
  immediate window, used to print code variable contents 48, 49
  installing, for Mac 12, 15, 16
  installing, for Xamarin 12, 15, 16
  iOS SDK locations, defining 20, 22
  overview, for Mac debugger 44
  used, for Mac built-in debugger 43

W

WalkDataModel
  updating, for TrackMyWalks app 445
WalkDistancePage code-behind
  updating, C# code used 247, 249, 275, 279
WalkDistancePage code
  implementing, C# code used 164, 166
WalkDistancePage interface
  creating, XAML used 162, 164
WalkDistancePage user interface
  updating, XAML used 274, 504, 508

WalkDistancePageViewModel
  code-behind, updating C# code used 211
  creating, C# code used 208
  updating, C# code used 245, 247, 270
  user interface, updating XAML used 210, 211
WalkEntryPage code-behind
  updating, C# code used 240, 242
WalkEntryPage code
  implementing, C# code used 155
WalkEntryPage interface
  creating, XAML used 153, 155
WalkEntryPage user interface
  updating, XAML used 462, 465
WalkEntryPageViewModel
  code-behind, updating C# code used 201
  creating, C# code used 195, 198
  updating, C# code used 239, 267, 466, 468
  user interface, updating XAML used 199, 201
WalksMainPage code-behind
  updating, C# code used 236, 239, 458, 502,
  547
WalksMainPage code
  implementing, C# code used 150, 153
WalksMainPage interface
  creating, XAML used 147, 149, 150
WalksMainPageViewModel
  code-behind, updating C# code used 192, 195
  creating, C# code used 186, 187
  updating, C# code used 234, 460
  user interface, updating XAML used 190
WalkTrailInfoPage code-behind
  updating, C# code used 244
WalkTrailInfoPage code
  implementing, C# used 158
  maps, implementing 160, 161, 162
  maps, integrating 160, 161
  maps, intergrating 162
WalkTrailInfoPage interface
  creating, XAML used 156, 158
WalkTrailInfoPageViewModel
  code-behind, updating C# code used 206, 207,
  208
  creating, C# code used 203, 205
  updating, C# code used 242, 243
  user interface, updating XAML used 205

WebViewController class
  updating, C# code used 422, 427
Windows Presentation Foundation (WPF) 339

X

Xamarin Media Plugin NuGet package
  adding 56, 57, 58
Xamarin mobile platform
  about 22
  apps, developing Xamarin.Forms approach used
  24, 25
  native apps, developing Xamarin approach used
  23, 24
  used, for developing apps 23
Xamarin project
  creating, for Android 25, 26, 27, 28, 29, 32
  creating, for iOS 25, 26, 27, 28, 29, 32
  list of planet names, displaying C# code used 33
  Planetary app, launching iOS simulator used 35,
  36, 37, 38
  user interface, creating for planetary app using
  XAML 32
Xamarin.Auth NuGet Package
  adding 485
Xamarin.Forms 11
Xamarin.Forms Navigation API
  about 220, 222
  Hierarchical 220
  Modal 220
Xamarin.Test Cloud.Agent NuGet package
  adding 549, 551
XAML layouts
  margins, applying 300
  padding, applying 300
  used, for updating WalkEntryPage User Interface
  303
  used, for updating WalksMainPage user
  interface 301
  used, for updating WalkTrailInfoPage user
  interface 305
XAML pages 307
XAML
  used, for creating SplashPage interface 169,
  170
  used, for creating WalkDistancePage interface

162, 164
used, for creating WalkEntryPage interface 153, 155
used, for creating WalksMainPage interface 147, 149, 150
used, for creating WalkTrailInfoPage interface

156, 158
used, for updating WalkDistancePage user interface 274, 504, 508
used, for updating WalkEntryPage user interface 462, 465

24673451R00326

Made in the USA
San Bernardino, CA
06 February 2019